T0305375

Bankruptcy and Debt Collection in Liberal Capitalism

Social History, Popular Culture, and Politics in Germany
Kathleen Canning, Series Editor

Recent Titles

Bankruptcy and Debt Collection in Liberal Capitalism: Switzerland, 1800–1900
    Mischa Suter
*Marking Modern Movement: Dance and Gender in the Visual Imagery of
    the Weimar Republic*
    Susan Funkenstein
Anti-Heimat Cinema: The Jewish Invention of the German Landscape
    Ofer Ashkenazi
Dispossession: Plundering German Jewry, 1933–1953
    Christoph Kreutzmüller and Jonathan R. Zatlin, Editors
*Sex between Body and Mind: Psychoanalysis and Sexology in the
    German-speaking World, 1890s–1930s*
    Katie Sutton
Imperial Fictions: German Literature Before and Beyond the Nation-State
    Todd Kontje
White Rebels in Black: German Appropriation of Black Popular Culture
    Priscilla Layne
*Not Straight from Germany: Sexual Publics and Sexual Citizenship
    since Magnus Hirschfeld*
    Michael Thomas Taylor, Annette F. Timm, and Rainer Herrn, Editors
Passing Illusions: Jewish Visibility in Weimar Germany
    Kerry Wallach
Cosmopolitanisms and the Jews
    Cathy S. Gelbin and Sander L. Gilman
Bodies and Ruins: Imagining the Bombing of Germany, 1945 to the Present
    David Crew
The Jazz Republic: Music, Race, and American Culture in Weimar Germany
    Jonathan Wipplinger
The War in Their Minds: German Soldiers and Their Violent Pasts in West Germany
    Svenja Goltermann
Three-Way Street: Jews, Germans, and the Transnational
    Jay Howard Geller and Leslie Morris, Editors
Beyond the Bauhaus: Cultural Modernity in Breslau, 1918–33
    Deborah Ascher Barnstone
Stop Reading! Look! Modern Vision and the Weimar Photographic Book
    Pepper Stetler
*The Corrigible and the Incorrigible: Science, Medicine, and the
    Convict in Twentieth-Century Germany*
    Greg Eghigian
An Emotional State: The Politics of Emotion in Postwar West German Culture
    Anna M. Parkinson
Germany's Wild East: Constructing Poland as Colonial Space
    Kristin Kopp

For a complete list of titles, please see www.press.umich.edu

Bankruptcy and Debt Collection in Liberal Capitalism

Switzerland, 1800–1900

Mischa Suter

Translated by Adam Bresnahan

University of Michigan Press • *Ann Arbor*

English translation copyright 2021 by Mischa Suter
All rights reserved

For questions or permissions, please contact um.press.perms@umich.edu

Published in the United States of America by
the University of Michigan Press
Printed and bound by CPI Group (UK) Ltd, Croydon, CR0 4YY

First published June 2021

A CIP catalog record for this book is available from the British Library.

ISBN 978-0-472-13252-2 (hardcover : alk. paper)
ISBN 978-0-472-12885-3 (ebook)

Financial support for the translation has been provided by the Freiwillige Akademische
Gesellschaft Basel.

Rechtstrieb: Schulden und Vollstreckung im liberalen Kapitalismus 1800–1900
By Mischa Suter
© 2016 by Konstanz University Press / Wallstein Verlag.

Contents

Acknowledgments to the German Version   vii

Acknowledgments to the English Translation   ix

Introduction   1

1   Enter *Kaufmann*   18

2   Law as Local Knowledge 1800–1870   43

3   Theoretical Interlude: The Anthropology of Debt   71

4   Debt and Subjectification in Narrative   83

5   Bankruptcy and Social Classification   119

6   Collateral: Confusion over Persons and Things   152

Conclusion   192

Notes   201

Bibliography   279

Index   317

Digital materials related to this title can be found on the Fulcrum platform via the following citable URL https://doi.org/10.3998/mpub.11600140

Contents

Acknowledgments to the German Version

This book is the revised and shortened version of a doctoral thesis at the University of Zurich. I would like to thank Jakob Tanner first and foremost: he helped me obtain financial support to write this book and provided a stimulating atmosphere at the Institute for Social and Economic History. His intellectual curiosity kept me motivated while I composed the book, and it continues to fascinate me. Thanks to Monika Dommann for her constant willingness to discuss my project and her untiring engagement with it. I am grateful to both for their openness, particularly when our ideas diverged. Caroline Arni at Basel's Department of History shared her brilliance by giving detailed comments on the entire manuscript.

The Schweizerische Nationalfonds and the Vögelin-Bienz-Stiftung offered monetary aid critical for completing the project. A very special thanks to the archivists and librarians who helped me; without their patience and countless tips the work would not have been possible. Alexander Schmitz at Konstanz University Press provided editing advice without which this could not have become a book.

Thanks to my many colleagues and friends who were always willing to discuss drafts and ideas with me, even when the drafts were in their rudimentary stages: Sara Bernasconi, Brigitta Bernet, Eva Brugger, Barbara Grimpe, Ruben Hackler, Almut Höfert, Niklaus Ingold, Daniela Janser, Anna Joss, Sandra Maß, Ute Tellmann, Magaly Tornay, Koni Weber, Mario Wimmer, and many others. Thanks to Andreas Fasel, Sara Gasteiger, Claudia Graf, Evelyn Thar, and Daniel Weiss for conversations dating back to when this study was just starting to take shape, a time when it seems like the entire world was talking so much about the stock market and trust but not yet about debts and relations of power.

Two research stays were decisive for the project. Thanks to Kathleen Canning for inviting me to the University of Michigan, where the work started to find its form in the spring of 2012. My discussions with her, Jacqueline Larios, and Geoff Eley, who offered astute advice on how to structure the chapters, are fond memories. Thanks to Jan Goldstein for allowing me to spend a good bit of 2013 at the University of Chicago, where she, along with William Sewell and Erika Vause, posed pertinent, generous questions about the project in its later stages. Thanks to Andrew Zimmerman for advice and encouragement.

A large nod to the musicians who accompanied me while writing. After many years immersed in soul and reggae, I found my way back to the heartland of electronic music: from the classics from Chicago and Detroit to younger talents like Laurel Halo, Actress, Daniel Avery, and The Black Madonna.

At a young age, my parents, Regula and Daniel Suter, introduced me and my sister, Anja Suter, to a world of books and intellectual inquisitiveness. I am ever grateful to my family for their enduring support.

This book is about debt, but there are relations that transcend the principle of exchange, no matter what Mauss might have said about it. Angelika Strobel shared with me her sense for stories, both in our everyday conversations and in her critical comments on the manuscript. I thank her for this generosity, and for much, much more. For years, Sylvia Kafehsy has given me the gift of her analytic imagination, which no thanks can ever do justice.

Zurich and Basel, April 2016

Acknowledgments to the English Translation

Although in all cases the argument differs substantially from what has appeared elsewhere in print, bits and pieces of the material of some chapters have been put forward in other publications, which include:

"Das Wissen der Schulden: Recht, Kulturtechnik und Alltagserfahrung im liberalen Kapitalismus." *Berichte zur Wissenschaftsgeschichte* 37, no. 2 (2014): 148–64.

"'Falliment'—the Social Life of a Legal Category: Knowledge and Morals in Bankruptcy Proceedings (Basel, 1840s)." In *Debtors, Creditors, and Their Networks: Social Dimensions of Monetary Dependence from the Seventeenth to the Twentieth Century*, edited by Andreas Gestrich and Martin Stark, 217–51. London: German Historical Institute London, 2015.

"The Boundaries of Debt: Bankruptcy between Local Practices and Liberal Rule in Nineteenth-Century Switzerland." In *The Cultural History of Money and Credit: A Global Perspective*, edited by Chia Yin Hsu, Thomas Luckett, and Erika Vause, 51–66. Lanham, MD: Lexington Books, 2016.

"Debt and Its Attachments: Collateral as an Object of Knowledge in Nineteenth-Century Liberalism." *Comparative Studies in Society and History* 59, no. 3 (2017): 715–42.

"Moral Economy as a Site of Conflict: Debates on Debt, Money, and Usury in the Nineteenth and Early Twentieth Century." *Geschichte und Gesellschaft* special issue 26, "Moral Economies," ed. Ute Frevert (2019): 75–101.

Since the German version of this book entered production in early 2016, critical thinking about debt has surged. While I resisted the urge to address this new stream of exciting scholarship for the purpose of the translation—that would have required another book altogether—I do engage with it in other work begun since then. The process of rereading and new reading, just as much as of rewriting and new thinking, makes translation a vertiginous experience across times and languages. Suffice it to say that translation is fundamentally a collaborative undertaking. Thus I would like to express my gratitude to Adam Bresnahan. Not only has he superbly fulfilled "the task of the translator," he has also made the collaboration a pleasurable one. I alone, however, am responsible for any prevailing errors and shortcomings. The Freiwillige Akademische Gesellschaft Basel provided financial support. I am grateful in particular to Kathleen Canning for her interest in the project. I thank her and the members of the editorial board of "Social History, Popular Culture, and Politics in Germany" for including the book in their interdisciplinary series. Geoff Eley and Andrew Zimmerman kindly offered advice over the years. I would like to thank Christopher Dreyer and everyone involved at the University of Michigan Press and, especially, the two anonymous reviewers who wrote generous reports on the English version.

Zurich, May 2020

Introduction

We don't know exactly when Felix Escher began harboring a grudge against Hans Heinrich Schinz. But when Escher wrote a letter to Schinz on July 1, 1842, it was not the first time the Zurich painter had leveled grievances against the former debt collector. In the letter, Escher protested that Schinz had all too hastily come to collect his outstanding debts, which had brought him into distress:

> Debt enforcement [*Rechtstrieb*] does not consist in being suspicious of the debtor, & of slandering him, of totally & completely sucking him dry, especially when one is convinced that he is doing his best; if you take a look at natural instinct [*Naturtrieb*], if God treated you & the rest of humanity in the same way you treat me, natural life and with it all of mother nature would perish, the whole world would suffer the fate of Sodom.[1]

In both the everyday speech and the legal jargon of nineteenth-century Switzerland, the term *Rechtstrieb* signified the compulsory collection of a delinquent debt by a civil servant. Though roughly translatable as "debt enforcement" or simply "debt collection," the connotations of the German *Rechtstrieb* are difficult to capture in English, as the word is composed of two stems: *Recht*, which is variously translated as "right," "law," and "justice," and *Trieb*, generally translated as "drive" or "instinct." In his letter, Escher juxtaposed it with "natural instinct" (*Naturtrieb*). Apparently, Escher found unnatural the way in which Schinz sought to collect his outstanding debts. He invoked the city of Sodom and claimed that "the Sodomites" were casting out "their nets and arrows" in an effort to catch him, an upstanding man free of all vice.

What's more, Escher reminded Schinz: "You are just a debt collector emeritus [*Altschuldenschreiber*]. But there is someone who keeps a ledger of your debts and who is older than you; it is the Eternal to whom I can pray & and to whom I will pray to 'forgive my debts and save me from sin.'" Escher thus condemned the cold-hearted economic demand by drawing on moral and religious principles, and he followed it all up with a torrent of demeaning insults that climaxed in disparaging Schinz as a sodomite.[2] The letter was adorned with drawings: an angel, a devil, and a cross on the front, and two men having anal sex on the reverse.

The case was more complicated than this one source might suggest. Schinz had to appear in court on multiple occasions: he sued Escher for libel, while his detractor officially accused him of harboring "unnatural desires." The tides turned against him, and the court found the erstwhile debt collector guilty of the crime of "unnatural desires," despite pleas from Schinz's lawyer that in the course of honestly pursuing his work, his client had drawn the ire of a number of his fellow citizens.[3] More generally, the case demonstrates well that when it came to debt collection, people in the nineteenth century quickly alternated among discursive registers, including the economic, the moral, and the political. The following examines more closely the contexts and consequences of these heterogeneous discourses and practices, exploring their meanings in liberal capitalism and the ways in which they shaped social relations in nineteenth-century Switzerland.

This book is about debts. Debts are profoundly relational phenomena, quilts patched together out of legal prescriptions, economic forces, and moral judgments. Debts are fundamentally historical: time passes as the debt persists unpaid, and the relation between debtor, creditor, and other interested parties can shift. Changing circumstances determine how much has been paid and how much is still owed. In this sense, debt reveals the gap between the real-life situations of those involved on the one hand and their needs and demands on the other. Debts are a node of necessity, lack, and desire. That guilt (*Schuld*) and debts (*Schulden*) share a common vocabulary gives the latter a special status in the moral imagination.

The meanings of debts and the forms they take change over history, but they acquire particular significance when the economy of everyday life starts to show cracks; then debts come to bridge an indigent present and an uncertain future. Borrowing, pawning, paying off, counting what's left, these are some of the constituent activities of precarity. In turn, precarious situations make the debt relation ripe for antagonism;

when a debtor of limited means is confronted with unforeseen problems, even otherwise harmless events can be enough to cause a crisis. Mere happenstance can blow up into material conflict. The relation between creditor and debtor takes place in a framework both shared and divided. In debt, attitudes and expectations meet. Sometimes the views of creditor and debtor align, but they can easily clash. In the end, the debt relation is a relation of forces.[4]

When a debt becomes unpayable, tensions grow acute, and when the time to collect on an outstanding debt rolls around, past promises catch up with the present, thereby placing restrictions on the future. This temporal structure is why this book places the moment when debts become unpayable front and center. The book tells a history of relations. It is concerned with pawned furniture, notices of overdue payment, pledged harvests, sureties, and contested bills of exchange. It analyzes relations between people, things, legal procedures, and the written texts that hold them all together: insolvency protocols, pawn ledgers, registries of bankrupt persons.

Because debts gain their social force through the ways in which they tie together legal, economic, and moral relations, the historian might focus on the assessments and judgments made by historical actors. This might start with the connotations of the words themselves. "Credit" opens possibilities for the future, while the pressing obligation of "debt" places constraints on the present.[5] Of course, credit and debt can be viewed as two sides of the same coin, and the basics of accounting say that every credit is balanced by a debit. But this fails to do justice to the historical constellations of debt. After all, the various meanings of debt and credit always have social significance and describe different types of relations: "the burden of debt" and "enjoying credit" are related, but not the same. Inquiring into how such distinctions came to be established is a matter of understanding the operations lying at the origins of the categories that structure everyday legal and economic relations. This book argues that the settlement of unpaid debts—and the conflicts and everyday interactions involved in it—reveals the contradictions at the heart of liberal capitalism's relations of exchange.

Debt Collection and Liberalism

While there are many ways to approach debt as an object of study, the setting of this book is the economy of precarity in the nineteenth century. If it is true that our present era is defined by neoliberalism and our lives are increasingly influenced by a new form of pauperism, then studying the beginnings of liberalism can help us both deepen our analysis of capitalism and expand the horizon of our political imagination. In the nineteenth century, "pauperism" was a social diagnosis and a threatening scenario that went hand-in-hand with the genesis of a liberal model of society. Pauperism and liberal principles were, simply put, co-constitutive. Liberal thought conceived of poverty as a social danger and poverty relief not so much as a guarantee of individual rights, but rather as a tool to moralize society.[6] This was particularly true in Switzerland, an exemplar of economic and political liberalism. Like in other European countries, borrowing and lending played an important role in everyday economic life there, a fact born out of the reality that for most of the century, a majority of the population had to make do with irregular incomes.[7] Insecurity and precarity were not just problems in periods of crisis, only to disappear when things turned back to normal. Rather, in the nineteenth century, debts permeated the everyday lives of people of all classes. Consequently, unpayable debts took on special relevance.

The legal measures for collecting on a delinquent debt—in Swiss German idiom the *Rechtstrieb*—generally took two forms: seizing the debtor's assets as collateral, and bankruptcy proceedings. Countless debts ended up in debt collection. In a few cases, such as with large bankruptcies, debt collection was a spectacle, but usually it was mundane. Debt collection consisted of a series of everyday practices, dull procedures, deadlines, and forms. But it had serious consequences for those involved. In the run of the bankruptcy proceedings known as *Falliment* in Switzerland, men lost their civic rights, while women were placed in special forms of gender guardianship.

Debt collection in Switzerland was heterogeneous until 1889, when it was codified in federal law. The Federal Statute on Debt Enforcement and Bankruptcy (*Bundesgesetz über Schuldbetreibung und Konkurs*) went into effect in 1892 and, for the most part, remains on the books today.[8] The law had the effect of stabilizing the conditions regulating economic exchange. In the period before the federal codification, a whole range of laws and legal procedures existed alongside one another, many of which simply bestowed the form of law onto social conventions of dealing with debt. In Germanophone Switzerland, they had a peculiar, yet highly significant feature: government-administered debt collection proceedings could be initiated without having to obtain a judge's approval, and they thus generally took place without judicial intervention. As long as the debtor did not contest the creditor's claims, the creditor could send notices and set deadlines. If the deadlines passed without payment being received, a government debt collector stepped in. Thus, debt collection was, for the most part, an administrative procedure carried out by local bailiffs alone and without much involvement by the state. It was characterized by a bureaucratic efficiency based on a clearly ordered sequence of events and obligations.

A rudimentary analysis of the etymology of *Rechtstrieb* makes clear its intertwining of autonomous action and external compulsion. The history of the word *Trieb* associates it with coercion, causal succession, and guiding. The word initially signified "path," "way," or "trace," as suggested by the word *Viehtrieb* (the act of leading cows to the pasture).[9] The word *Trieb* first appears in a legal context in laws regulating community-owned pasture land. Martin Luther established the word's meaning of internal stimuli or instinct.[10] But it never lost its connotation of external coercion. The association of *Trieb* ("drive") with bodily pleasure became stronger in the run of the eighteenth century.[11] Still it was in no way the dominant meaning in all contexts, as exemplified by the industry term *Triebfeder* (mainspring), which came about around the same time and was also used in a figurative sense.[12] External and internal compulsion, mechanical impulse, and guided pathway, the expression *Rechtstrieb* combined internalized norms and the external force of sanctions. This sphere of law would have been inconceivable without a series of routine procedures, widely accepted norms, exact forms of notation, and moderating gestures. In debt collection, liberalism coopted habituated customs and conventionalized these practices for its own ends.

The contradictory norms and practices of debt collection had their origins in social problems specific to the nineteenth century. This confronts the historian with a number of questions: How did relations between debtors and creditors change during a time that was increasingly expanding bureaucratic administration and standardizing procedures in all spheres of society? How were debt payments structured in a period often referred to as the "age of acceleration," a time when Switzerland was transitioning from an agricultural society to an industrial society? In which ways did debt collection subject male and female debtors to different, gendered legal conditions, especially considering that while women had limited legal rights, they had always played an integral role in everyday economic relations? How present was the *Fallit*—the male debtor who filed bankruptcy and had thereby lost his civic rights—in a period when the republican state was giving all men the right to vote and nationalism was becoming a powerful mobilizing force? What did people think about the seizure of property as collateral in an age when person-hood was coming to be grounded in property ownership?

This book primarily focuses on the period between 1830 and 1870, a time when Switzerland's government was undergoing intense liberal reforms to such a degree that it was internationally considered to be a "laboratory of liberalism."[13] Liberalism was governance based on mini-mal direct exertion of authority and distanced, more mediated methods of enforcement. Accordingly, liberalism both required and cultivated reflexive subjects who could and would maneuver these procedures of their own free will. Liberal governance brought about new forms of state practice and governmental expertise,[14] and state institutions sought to facilitate what they viewed as the free circulation of money, commodities, people, and information.[15]

At the height of liberalism in the nineteenth century, two historical processes that frame the issues studied here took hold. The first was standardization and homogenization.[16] Throughout Switzerland in the 1830s, cantonal states began developing laws and methods to systemati-cally regulate everyday affairs. At the same time, they came up with new ways of taking accountability for their own actions. They worked to for-malize trade relations with the aim of letting them flow unimpeded. The idea of instituting uniform rules for collecting debts was first brought up in the cantons, and then, with the revision of the Federal Constitution of the Swiss Federation in 1874, on the federal level. The standardiza-tion of debt collection accomplished by the 1889 federal law mentioned above was defined by a key distinction. "Merchants," an abstract status whose sole criterion was a person being listed in a commercial registry, were subject to specific bankruptcy laws. All other claims to payment not arising in a commercial context were to be collected through the seizure of assets as collateral. Chapter 1 outlines the historical background that informed the legislature's decision to draw this distinction. Chapter 2 then takes a step back and traces the longer history of the various pecu-liar modalities of debt collection that had been dominant for most of the century before the passage of the federal law.

These techniques of debt collection were inextricably bound up with the other process that sets the stage of the story told here, namely, the reconception and valorization of the concept of "property" in liberal-ism.[17] The abolition of feudal dues was arguably the most fundamen-tal transformation in property relations in nineteenth-century western Europe.[18] Property came to signify unlimited power of disposal over a thing. The epitome of this conception was the 1804 French *Code Civil*'s definition of "property" as absolute ownership,[19] which bestowed upon property a theretofore unheard-of importance. Debt collection was supposed to secure property relations by guaranteeing the debtor's liability to pay. In the run of debt collection proceedings, officials were permitted to seize a debtor's assets as collateral. In turn, third parties, such as the debtor's wife, could make claims to their own property and contest the act of expropriation. Debt collection was thus an intense process of determining who owned what property under what conditions.

The liberal conception of property clashed with other, more gradated conceptions. This was particularly true for the "economy of makeshifts" of the subaltern classes,[20] which was based on borrowing, renting, swapping, and pawning things and ownership rights.[21] The everyday economics of the nineteenth century were defined by the complex force relations of the debt economy, which was foreign territory for the liberal, nonrelational concept of "property" as absolute ownership. The binding promise associated with debt put the economy of makeshifts in opposition to the liberal notions of personality and autonomy anchored in individual property ownership.

The story of debt in the nineteenth century is a story of how debt collection caused problems for the relationship between individual rights, personal freedom, and structures of authority, such as when men who had lost their civic rights also lost their privileges of gender tutelage over their wives and children. It is a story in which economic categories and legal rights emerged and were disputed and transformed. After all, life wasn't over when bankruptcy began. It was a mode of existence that the insolvent actively lived. Of course, being a bankrupt was associated with the total loss of civic rights and privileges, but there is even stronger evidence that the bankrupt was a veritable player in everyday economic life and an established character in the social imagination. For their part, the transitory state of being insolvent forced women to make surprising appearances on the legal stage. Chapters 2 and 4 of this book analyze the modes of living brought forth by debt collection in Switzerland in the period before it was standardized by the 1889 federal law, modes of living described in sources as different as the fiction of the national poet Gottfried Keller and the political theory of the utopian communist Wilhelm Weitling. In general terms, debt and property relations in the nineteenth century constituted a system of proximity and distance. People balanced their debts to nearby creditors by heading to the greater anonymity of the city to borrow larger sums or by taking out a number of smaller loans with multiple different lenders.[22] The rise of financial institutions in the nineteenth century changed these relations, and new mediating instances and forms of communication intervened between creditor and debtor.[23] Cantonal banks and savings banks centralized credit. Nevertheless, the extent to which personal interactions in credit relations were supplanted by impersonal, face-to-faceless forms is not known.[24] There is much evidence supporting the hypothesis that personal credit relations continued to have considerable significance. The expansion of banking in the nineteenth century thus did not imply the immediate institutionalization of everyday finance.[25] For most people living in the nineteenth century, the cash nexus was "not impersonal or anonymous in most of its manifestations."[26]

A history of debt in the nineteenth century thus necessarily complicates extant analyses of the transition to modernity,[27] and taking a historical perspective on debt and credit reveals divergent, nonsynchronic temporalities.[28]

A fundamental challenge to established narratives of historical transformation is mounted by David Graeber's *Debt: The First 5000 Years*, which proposes a grand narrative of its own. Graeber subsumes questions of continuity and change under a single schema that traverses history, namely, state power's role in guaranteeing that debts get paid. Graeber indeed zooms in on debt as a relation of forces. He defines debt as a hierarchically structured "exchange that has not been brought to completion."[29] But he fails to explain the specific forms taken by this relation of forces, the ambivalences and contradictory interests of those involved in it, and when and how debt relations become open to shifts and changes. Because he only offers a single schema, Graeber's book overlooks the concrete processes that make some too big to fail while others are forced into debt peonage.

A historical account that seeks to leave behind the established binaries of continuity and change, of stages and oscillations in social development, has to take a different approach. This book shifts the perspective by analyzing the legal dimensions of the different modes of evaluating and appraising insolvent persons and their property. Debt collection was a matter of evaluating things and values, people and relations. In turn, the various forms of evaluation were a cause for confusion in the era of liberalism. Banal things like accounting balances and seized objects set central categories of economics like "insolvency" and "property" in motion. As chapter 5 demonstrates, debtors came up with their own versions of events, justifying their inability to pay and thereby placing the repayment of debts within a cacophony of interests, demands, suggestions, and replies. The knowledge necessary for identifying who had to do what when in relations of debt and credit was constantly shifting and affected both the relationship between debtor and creditor and the relationship between people and things. Defining an object as collateral, separating it from its context, seizing it, and thus making it temporarily unusable infringed upon the mutual constitution of the status of persons and things in liberalism. Debt enforcement tended "to animate objects and to objectify persons," as research on gift exchange suggests.[30] Assets became liquid when an official inspected them and "made them silver," as converting collateral into money was called. Even more, debtors themselves could serve as collateral if they were imprisoned, which remained a distinct possibility up until about 1870. Chapter 6 analyzes these manifold difficulties that debt posed for the concept of property and its relation to personhood in the nineteenth century.

The mundane methods of assessment that shaped the debt relationship helped draw a line between what counted as economic and what didn't. In this sense, the conflicts between the various parties wrapped up in debt collection proceedings had an epistemic dimension.[31] Analyzing the connection between systematic power relations and the inconspicuous techniques of assessing the value of things and the trustworthiness of people reveals a plethora of confrontations over where the sphere of economics ended and other fields of action began.[32] Studying the historical particulars of this situation, the book takes the contradictions of capitalism as its guiding analytical framework, a choice informed by practical issues in contemporary research. While the cultural turn undermined the master narratives of the social sciences with local studies that eluded their universalizing sweep, it left the economy as a central sphere of social analysis largely untouched.[33] In the process, it failed to challenge the dominance of analytical premises drawn from the discipline of economics. As Patrick Joyce and Timothy Mitchell have argued, the cultural turn erected an implicit division between the practical, material, and real and the world of meanings, representations, and convictions instead of reflecting on the status these concepts might have in future research.[34] But our goal should be to get to the bottom of both sides and reveal their interconnections, asking how forms of meaning and interpretation lay the foundations for certain material exchanges and, conversely, how material constellations structure symbolic practices. Of interest are contingent situations that gain enough momentum to give rise to their own rules and conditions and take on a life of their own, as well as the structural nexus between exploitation and accumulation, which transcends the relations between individual actors and "their semiotic reach."[35] This book seeks to account for these various dimensions and the way they were cobbled together in the debt relations of nineteenth-century Switzerland.

Capitalism, Subjectification, Knowledge

Karl Marx is the go-to theoretician for those wanting to understand "capital" as a social relation. Marx is an important, yet complicated point of reference for a history of debt, simply because credit and debt do not have a clear-cut place in his writings.[36] Nevertheless, Marx's work sheds some light on the phenomena of personal and commercial debt. In this book, he functions as both a source of theoretical orientation and as a nineteenth-century "voice from the field," as an ethnographer might say. Marx was no doubt qualified to speak on the subject, as he and his wife, Jenny Marx-Westphalen, were constantly battling with debt during their life in exile in London.[37] When their daughter Jenny asked her mother to answer questions about herself in her album, she wrote next to the words "your aversion": "debts."[38] Peter Stallybrass composed an essay on Marx's personal "economy of makeshifts."[39] Under pressure to pay his daily debts to the grocer, he pawned his coat, which he then had to get back right away in order to don the appearance of respectability necessary to be admitted into the British Library. This experience does not find mention in his works, although one might wonder whether it informed the choice of examples in the discussion of the commodity form in the first chapter of *Das Kapital*, where twenty yards of linen and ten pounds of tea are depicted as the equivalent of one coat. Conflict as much as confusion result when labor as concrete human activity is confronted with labor as an abstract measure of exchange value in capitalist society. It is a paradox that makes tables dance and turns people into things.[40]

Marx's individual experience of debt and the way it transported his coat between the pawn shop and the library and back has more than merely anecdotal value. A text Marx wrote in 1844 concretizes how debt accomplishes a sort of contradictory objectification of social relations. In his notes on James Mill's *Elements of Political Economy*, Marx discusses money and debt in relation to alienation, a concept he had started to explore at that time. Marx writes that the money-form makes social relations into things.[41] The money-form is a necessary moment of alienation, but not its end station, because exchange mediated through money takes place within the system of private property. And because private property is defined according to its exchange value, it is already alienated from itself. When instead of money promises are the object of exchange, as in the credit system, "it appears as if the power of the alien, material force were broken, the relationship of self-estrangement abolished and man had once more human relations to man," because human relations themselves are being traded.[42]

For this reason, some socialists of the time demanded that credit be made available to all. Marx, however, thought this "abolition of estrangement" was an illusion, arguing that "the self-estrangement, the dehumanisation, is all the more infamous and extreme because its element is no longer commodity, metal, paper, but man's *moral* existence, man's *social* existence, the inmost depths of his heart."[43] When a "rich man" lends money to a "poor man," "all the social virtues of the poor man, the content of his vital activity, his existence itself, represent for the rich man the reimbursement of his capital."[44] "Within the credit relationship, it is not the case that money is transcended in man, but that man himself is turned into *money*, or money is *incorporated* in him."[45] Marx believed that the social relations that came to bear in credit devolved into a certain form of evaluating people: "One ought to consider how vile it is to *estimate* the value of a man in *money*, as happens in the credit relationship."[46] But credit as "the economic judgment on the morality of a man"[47] did not stop at the evaluation of a person's behavior. The "guarantee" to the creditor represented by the poor man's "existence itself" was enforced with a whole palette of coercive measures.

The way in which money is "incorporated" in the debtor informs the two axes of analysis pursued in this book: subjectification and knowledge. Marx's text quoted here contains the seeds of a theory of subjectification.[48] At stake for Marx are the social and individual existence of humans ("man's social existence, the inmost depths of his heart") as they are rendered through exchange value. Particularly remarkable is the way in which Marx sees a specific vocabulary of morality at work in the credit relation and how he connects social being and inner life. At its very core, subjectification is no less relational than debt. The subject is literally subjected, a being whose actions are informed by its knowledge of itself.[49] And like social relations, power also shapes the subject's relation to itself. In Michel Foucault's pregnant formula, power is "an action upon an action"; it does not affect a passive being, but an active—and in this respect a free—subject.[50] Subjectification takes place in the moment when an action that deploys power elicits—immediately or in a roundabout fashion—an action from the subject.[51] Out of this originate both unpredictability and subordination, because the application of power does not determine the entire run of the process, but can also occasion the "conditions for revolt."[52]

Three key points for the analysis of the relation between subjectification and debt should be outlined here. First, subjectification is dependent upon the placement of subjects in social positions, a process rife with unforeseeable contingencies. A good example is the attribution of legal statuses such as that of being insolvent, which can open a whole spectrum of different forms of subjectification. Second, the low-level administrations charged with collecting debts were characterized by their "guiding the possibility of conduct and putting in order the possible outcome."[53] Debt collection as a branch of justice almost without judges functioned by compelling subjects to adapt techniques of self-conduct and routine patterns of behavior that normalized the debt relation. Moreover, the intertwining of social norms and judicial coercion has a connection to the broader relation between freedom and power, as freedom served as a particularly efficacious means of governance under liberalism. Subjectification was executed through the deadlines and threats of dispossession that both structured and intensified the relation between debtor and creditor. This touches on the third point: the problem of time, a constitutive element of every debt relation. The deferment inherent to debt opens up a field of relations of forces between debtor and creditor.[54] This open-endedness of debt makes "time" into a crucial factor. Debt collection aimed to close the temporal gap of the debt relation and implemented its own temporal regime to this end. For those wrapped up in the process of debt collection, time was not a continuous flow, but was punctuated by a staggered series of deadlines: the receipt of a request for payment, the seizure of home wares as collateral, the public bankruptcy hearing, all were experienced by the parties involved as temporal turning points. What seemed like a logical progression of events from the bird's-eye perspective of the administrator was, for the debtor, a jarring sequence of tasks that each generated a new situation to navigate.[55]

The "estimation of the value of a man in money" that Marx wrote about forms the basis of the other primary focus of this study: problems of knowledge historical actors faced when entangled in the process of debt collection. Economic historians studying credit markets have analyzed the significance of the asymmetrical distribution of information and the ways in which historical actors have coped with it.[56] The formal models of the economics of information assume that creditors always have less information about the future behavior of debtors than the latter do themselves.[57] Some aspects of this insight into the centrality of information in credit relationships can be adopted for a more cultural-analytical perspective that elucidates the media techniques and forms of systematization through which knowledge on debt was processed in nineteenth-century Switzerland.

A widely held assumption has it that while information is "raw," which is to say practical and specific, knowledge is "cooked," processed and thought through, remembered and learned.[58] Certainly, information might be "raw," but it is not a given. Rather, specialized techniques bring *in formation* a dazzling array of impressions, or "data."[59] In short, information is "data organized in a systematic fashion."[60] Memory, categorization, and reflection constitute the conditions of possibility for the generation of "raw" information and data, which is to say that information is always connected to knowledge that precedes it. Or, as a historian of media technology put it: "'Raw data' is an oxymoron."[61] People at the market might be on the search for "raw" information, but they do so by employing capacities and techniques provided by a society's order of knowledge.[62]

In the run of debt collection proceedings, creditors, debtors, and officials tasked with collection fought over information: debtors sought to hide assets, creditors sought to make claim to assets or sniff out assets not yet on the ledger. These conflicts were a matter of gathering evidence and classifying objects; in other words, they played out as processes of knowledge production. The media of debt collection gave these processes a certain form, namely that of paperwork, short for a whole series of bureaucratically authorized techniques of protocolling and recording. As the sources drawn upon in this study show, however, paperwork is prone to glitches; it fractalizes power, sometimes into confounding twists.[63] Paperwork gave debt collection its body and its material volatility.

The approach sketched here does not assume some kind of inner essence of capitalism. Rather, I seek to analyze the relation between epistemic uncertainties and social conflict. This approach is distinct from two influential takes on capitalism that deserve mention. Many scholars view capitalism as an umbrella concept that brings together economic, social, and political phenomena.[64] The theory is that with private property as their fundament, individualized actors cooperate and act with the aim of accruing profits in the future. The keywords of this understanding of capitalism as a macrosocial process are competition, risk, profit motive, "creative destruction," and, above all, "dynamics." This nuanced perspective attributes to capitalism a logic of expansion and an ability to produce heterogeneous outcomes, but in the end, it does not take social conflict as its starting point of analysis.[65] What is more, it tends to set limits on its own ability to gain insights into the historical genealogy of its own categories, regardless of whether it places primacy on cultural or economic factors. Adherents of this approach show how shifting attitudes toward risk, profit, and competition push capitalism forward, or they characterize capitalism as a double movement of expansion and restriction of market forces, but they generally do not inquire into the historical origins of these categories themselves. The consequence is the acceptance of formal economic categories as givens, thus creating the appearance that singular local cases are mere examples of "underlying" large-scale processes.

A different approach is taken by researchers interested in how things, bodies, relationships, and activities are commodified.[66] Treating capitalism as a system of commodification, these scholars inquire into the techniques used to translate qualitative differences into quantitative ones and the practices of organization and discipline that form economic subjects.[67] For example, the topic of this book—debts—confronts us with the question of how social demands and administrations tasked with evaluating debtors' assets and ability to pay came to shape personal identities.[68] Such an approach has much to say about the organization of knowledge and the production of the self under capitalism. But with its stress on normative inscriptions alone, it has difficulty conceiving of capitalism as a contested form of domination. In this perspective, the self is always already molded into a pregiven normative frame. Still, a more concrete understanding of the formation of self and its relation to commodification can be gained by situating actual historical conflicts between different norms and practices at the center of critical analysis. It is in this precise sense that the concept of the "unevenness" of capitalism is used here.

"Unevenness" is a metaphor used by scholars to help explore the relation between the historical forms of capitalism, the conditions of its expansion, and the contradictions at its foundations.[69] The term "unevenness" was coined to capture the unequal developments of the capitalist world system.[70] In a more extended sense, the word can signify the interlacement of received and emergent practices of exploitation and accumulation. Capitalism aligns exchange relations and temporalities, synchronizing differences without homogenizing them. Thus, it is unremarkable, everyday arrangements that keep capitalism running, all the while reproducing its contradictions.

"At *every* bloody level"

According to a much-quoted dictum, anthropologists "don't study vil-lages . . . they study *in* villages."[71] It doesn't quite get at the heart of the matter though, because, of course, anthropologists don't just study in villages. Many conduct multisited ethnographies with the aim of learn-ing more about the capitalist world system.[72] They trace the travels of people, things, metaphors, and conflicts over the expanse of many locations. While anthropologists go into the field, historians go to the archive. Researching *in* the archives and conducting multisited histori-ography means treating the archive as a "centre of interpretation," tak-ing its material less as a mass of data to be plowed through and more as an effect produced by the object of analysis itself.[73] To this end, the book develops an anthropology of procedure[74]: it focuses on how people get entangled in superpersonal systems and logics, how their actions are formed, conditioned, and supported by juridical techniques, and how administrative proceedings are nevertheless again and again inter-rupted by frictions and difficulties that allow something singular to shine through institutionalized repetition. Thus, this book contains what I term a particular history of systemic regulation. That is to say, I seek to show how the formal logics of legal procedures were generated out of the experiences of singular cases, and that abstract economic concepts were born out of concrete interventions. Tracing the genesis of such abstractions through a history of the particular systems of debt collection in nineteenth-century Switzerland and the rules that defined them is the task taken up by the chapters that follow. Accordingly, the book works with the thesis that each procedure has its own texture and that we can only study this texture as it was actualized in concrete situations. This is what is meant by a particular history of systemic regulation.

Thus this book looks at the margins of legal sources and the chal-lenges and confusion expressed in them.[75] Law does not constitute a social level among others or a superstructure. Rather, it manifests itself, to use an expression of E. P. Thompson, "at *every* bloody level."[76] This perspective doesn't chuck out the division between rules on the one hand and practices on the other, but it does make it porous. To say it again, norms were developed out of heterogeneous practices.[77] A partic-ular history of systemic regulation treats law not as a derivative category dependent on other spheres, such as economic development, but rather as a semiautonomous set of practices to be studied in its own right.

At the same time, the semiautonomous field of law forms a piece in the puzzle of other social practices.[78] In order to probe the minute fractures and differences in these patterns that permeated the social world, this book draws on a wide range of sources, from legislative debates, legal texts, and standard operating procedures for officials, debtors, and creditors, to fiction, petitions, police interrogations, and asset seizure protocols. Many of the sources record the development, implementation, observation, or breakdown of the rules and procedures of debt collection. Some texts bear witness to debates on the meaning of law itself. In the discussions in the 1870s and early 1880s on what would ultimately become the Federal Statute on Debt Enforcement and Bankruptcy, legislators on the federal level sought to synchronize the economic rhythms of different regions. Other texts offer a close look at the measures taken to establish certain procedures of debt collection as permanent and uniform, and sources like instructions for officials and judges' decisions make palpable the perspectives of those who observed the whole process. Complaints and petitions pinpoint gaps and fault lines by thematizing things that had until then gone unspoken. Finally, this study draws on literary texts to do justice to narrative accounts of the experience of debt and the various measures taken to make debtors pay.

The inquiry is, in a sense, a patchwork, but this does not mean that it dispenses with methodological rigor. Two points should be emphasized in the conclusion of this introduction. First, my research focuses on moments of encounter, events in which the heterogeneous, contradictory dimensions of debt collection came to bear.[79] To repeat one of the book's overarching claims, it was in these moments that the everyday contradictions of liberal capitalism found expression. From this point of view, the cases studied here are less *examples* of a unified, all-encompassing structure and more *incidents*, singular manifestations of a motley complex of related practices.[80]

Comparing and contrasting the different practices that fell under the heading of debt collection gives the study coherence. But their particularities were shaped by the concrete places in which they occurred, demanding that they be treated in context: the protoindustrial, yet rural canton of Zurich was distinct from the commercial Basel; in the capital Bern, divergent regional interests joined up with experts on federal governance. Forms of writing significant for disparate fields are brought together here: familial conflicts in diaries stand alongside bourgeois national literature and communist tracts. All these elements form part of a broader history of Europe in the nineteenth century.

The second point that makes the instability of the research method into a fruitful resource concerns the form of debt collection as a legal procedure. Coherence can be created by focusing on the operations that generate typicality in the source material, because these operations connect individual cases.[81] The historian can seek to identify the techniques used to create "cases" in the first place and to understand the conditions and problems involved. The systematicity of procedures applicable to a range of cases only ever unfolded in concrete situations. This is why the argument proceeds as a spiral moving its way into the heart of the research problem.

It begins with the end of the period studied, namely with the codification of capitalist exchange relations laid down in the 1889 Federal Statute on Debt Enforcement and Bankruptcy. Tracking backwards from this moment of stabilization, the study winds through the diverse, mostly local practices as they existed before the federal law (chapter 2). After these two chapters in inverted chronological order, chapter 3 engages in theoretical reflection on cultural-anthropological perspectives on debt; it thus provides a bridge of sorts to the more systematic discussion of key aspects of debt collection that follows in the remainder of the book. Chapter 4 draws on various forms of narrative in order to dissect the ways in which debts and debt collection formed subjects. The last two chapters tackle the two dominant procedures, namely bankruptcy and asset seizure. The power of classifying things and evaluating people in bankruptcy proceedings is the main topic of chapter 5, but so too are the problems caused when those forced into bankruptcy refused to play by the rules. The final chapter takes up the constant difficulties involved in determining the status of seized assets and, in the end, the difficulties in maintaining the clear-cut separation between the concept of the person and the concept of things (chapter 6).

ONE | Enter *Kaufmann*

Passed in 1889 and entering into effect in 1892, the Federal Statute on Debt Enforcement and Bankruptcy normalized capitalist relations of exchange in the Swiss Confederation. The federal law supplanted the diverse practices of debt enforcement in the cantons, discarding some while stitching others into the fabric of the nation-state and, by extension, its international trade relations. Some federal jurists argued that the reforms were simply an exigency of modern commerce. The core of the law was the distinction it drew between two different debt collection procedures and the classification of who would be subject to the one or the other. *Kaufmänner*, or merchants, were now subject to bankruptcy proceedings (*Konkurs*). The status of being a merchant was determined exclusively by a person being entered into a special register that had been established shortly before. Everybody else—the "nonmerchants"— had their assets seized bit by bit. In the first case, a special formula was used to divvy up the debtor's assets among their creditors, an event that occurred all at once. In the second, every single creditor's claim was resolved individually through the attachment of a particular quantity of the debtor's assets, a process that took place over a duration of time.

In order to facilitate smooth exchange, the drafts of the law contained special rules sensitive to the temporal, spatial, and economic differences between business and agriculture. The world of commerce revolved around the immediate settling of accounts, itself based on the assumption that merchants were always in possession of assets that could easily be liquidated. Thus the inability to make payments was perceived as the primary consequence of insolvency. Conforming to this temporality, the law resolved the issue through the synchronic cut of bankruptcy proceedings. Agricultural rhythms ran on a different clock marked by periodic cash shortages and the cyclical availability of sellable goods; federal lawmakers thus found a diachronic resolution more appropriate. Debt collection was punctuated by these differing temporalities. In order to define which insolvent persons were subject to which procedure, the law employed the *Handelsregister*, or commercial register, which gave birth to a new category, the *Kaufmann*, or merchant. This category culled together a series of special regulations for businesspeople that had been developing since the early modern era. But by making entry in the commercial register the sole defining criterion, the law transformed the merchant into a purely formal legal entity. Similarly, many of the procedures newly assembled by the federal law had been long-standing custom: bankruptcy and asset seizure had, in varying forms and intensities, featured in the different cantonal laws on debt collection. The project of codifying these distinctions in a federal law encountered resistance. Conservatives tried to defeat the planned law by putting it to a referendum, which took place on November 17, 1889. The law barely passed, with 244,317 for and 217,921 against.[1]

This chapter details the context in which the federal law came into being. In doing so, it seeks to advance a more general argument: the guiding distinction between bankruptcy and asset seizure facilitated by the adoption of the commercial register helped solidify the existence of the modern economy as an objective, autonomous sphere of action.[2] The law was composed at a time when the economy was coming to separate itself off from other parts of society, and it gave shape to debates over new conceptions of what was legitimate in the collection of debt. The legal regulation of debt collection also involved a fight over the form that economic exchange should take and the weight it should hold in social and political life. Thus the latent content of the manifestly legislative issue was a conflict over what exactly the economy was. In order to demonstrate this, the chapter explores the intersections between media history and the history of social conflicts. It first details the development of and debates over the federal bankruptcy law and then explains the differing economic rhythms that the law sought to accommodate. The solution that it ultimately proposed—the commercial register—is then analyzed as a cultural technique that articulated economic knowledge in a particular media format. This instrument, however, was divorced neither from the regional customs that preceded the law nor from the social controversies over its meaning. The chapter thus elucidates how the register came to be the principal medium of the social relation of debt. Against the intentions of legislators, the extensive political debates over the federal law made clear that the two methods of debt collection did not uniformly apply to one economic sphere or the other. Political conservatives opposed the law on the grounds that it prescribed measures inappropriate to the issue it was supposed to address; their objections were fueled in particular by the "honor sanctions" imposed upon insolvent debtors, who were stripped of their civic rights.

The Homogenization of Bankruptcy Law

The stupefying multitude of debt enforcement laws, wrote federal jurist Alfred Brüstlein[3] in 1889, did "great damage to credit and public welfare."[4] In a brochure campaigning for the approval of the federal bankruptcy law, he explained to voters that the current laws had "grown out of routine" and were inadequate to the need for a system in an increasingly complex economy: "The splintered laws might have been able to be tolerated if not for the economic transformation that has taken place with such rapidity as the world has never seen before. Europe has become covered with a network of railways; industry has developed with its steam engines and mass production; the exchange of goods from region to region, country to country, has taken on wholly new proportions."[5] From this perspective, expanding communications, increasing trade, and accelerating monetary exchange called for comprehensive measures. In the waning nineteenth century, Europe witnessed the standardization of countless aspects of economic life, a process that was coordinated and regulated with interstate treaties and new domestic legislative packages. Brüstlein mentioned the law on legal capacity (1882), the copyright law (1884), and, most importantly, the Code of Obligations (*Obligationensrecht*); passed in 1881 and entering into effect in 1883, this unified commercial code came late in comparison to Switzerland's neighbors France, with its Code de Commerce (1807), and Germany, with its Allgemeines Deutsches Handelsgesetzbuch (1861).[6] Those involved in domestic trade in particular were insistent that the confederation adopt uniform rules.[7] The purpose of the commerce law was to make it easier to lend and borrow money, which legislators believed would lead to an increase in domestic and international trade.[8] They wanted to make superfluous the legal advisers, repo men, and all the other "bothersome and expensive agents"[9] who profited on the collection of debts, thereby saving borrowers and lenders money and avoiding lawsuits.[10]

However much the reforms to debt collection laws might have aimed at homogenizing and standardizing bankruptcy procedures, the legislative process took nearly two decades and passed through all kinds of happenstance events.[11] A first version drafted in 1874 by Basel professor Andreas Heusler prescribed the bankruptcy system exclusively, thus adhering to the laws of his hometown.[12] Basel, a center of Switzerland's silk weaving and finance industries, had a well-organized administrative apparatus and strong domestic and foreign trade connections, both of which informed its method of debt collection: a specialized bureaucracy seized the debtor's accounting books and used them to compile an inventory of accounts receivable and assets that could be realized. Basing debt collection on bookkeeping and having a specialized department execute it were matters of transparency and precision for Heusler. He argued that only by surveying the totality of a debtor's liabilities and assets could payment be effectively enforced. For the confederation, he accordingly proposed the establishment of a bankruptcy authority that "immediately seizes all of the debtor's books and uses them to get an idea of his situation—or, if there are no books, conducts precise inventories and uncovers everything that appears suspicious, which otherwise might remain concealed—and that also has the power to procure evidence and issue and enforce subpoenas."[13] He asserted that applying bankruptcy only to the "mercantile estate" would "no longer be rational," because modern "commerce" no longer exclusively took place among merchants.[14]

But in the opinion of experts, the conditions for such a broad-gauged authority were in no way given in all regions. Cantonal representatives were of the mind that the bill was tailored to the needs of large-scale commerce and thus failed to acknowledge the fact that the majority of creditors' demands involved small sums borrowed to satisfy the needs of "everyday local economic life."[15] They protested that bankruptcy—the immediate, court-ordered resolution of all debts, including those that otherwise would have been due in the future—would threaten farmers with all-too-sudden ruin because their assets could not be immediately liquidated. A second proposal followed the customs of western Switzerland, which for its part largely mimicked France's Code de Commerce. Thus the procedure in Francophone Switzerland prescribed bankruptcy for merchants, while other debtors had their assets seized. In the words of a report commissioned by a Geneva representative, subjecting average people to the same rigidity as merchants was an "amour platonique de l'égalité ou du droit abstrait" that failed to do justice to factual differences.[16] Another bill replicated the laws of the eastern canton of St. Gallen, where bankruptcy followed upon the seizure of assets as collateral; if the latter came to nothing, the former was initiated.[17] And yet another drew on the codes of the canton of Basel-Land, where small sums were collected via asset seizure, big sums via bankruptcy. Its author contended that an estimated 75 to 80 percent of delinquent debts in Switzerland were collected through the gradual liquidation of assets and involved minor sums.[18] The proposal initially set the defining amount at fifty francs, then one hundred. The federal authority charged with assessing legislation stated that with this definition, at least two-thirds of all debt collection proceedings could be resolved through the attachment of assets.[19] But some showed skepticism toward the arbitrarily set limit: How high was appropriate and justified?

Stuck in the morass of trying to fix a hard and fast number for determining when one procedure should be employed and when the other, legislators were finally helped out by the aforementioned commercial register, which came into force in 1883 as part of the new Code of Obligations.

Special laws for trade and commerce were nothing new. The French Code de Commerce of 1807 provided a separate set of laws for merchants and, perhaps most importantly, special courts; as touched on above, the cantons of western Switzerland partially replicated the French rules. The code drew on early modern commercial institutions and usages. In this sense, the postrevolution law stood at once in tension and in harmony with the revolution's principle of equality: trade constituted a special sphere of law and practice, but it was no longer ruled over by the insular authority of guilds.[20] Jurists from around Switzerland grappled with this issue. In his commentary to his draft of a unified trade law completed in late 1864, Bern professor Walther Munziger divided civil law into, on the one hand, national and international commerce law for "cosmopolitans" and, on the other, canton-level family law, marital law, and property law, which he thought were characterized by a "conservative attachment to home and family." Munzinger's text was foundational, but it was not directly translated into law, instead being altered in the run-up to the passage of the commerce law. The position of trade in civil law shifted. Instead of establishing a special legal code for merchants, the 1883 Code of Obligations established a significantly more comprehensive "commerce law" of which trade only constituted one part.[21] The law was passed with little resistance. Legal and economic historians see its development as having been uncontroversial, because all groups' interests were represented in it in one way or another. Even in the polarized atmosphere of the late 1870s and early 1880s, the Catholic conservatives did not oppose it.[22] Still, the controversial topic of debt collection was left out of the law. Only on this question did the contrary positions on exchange relations refuse to give ground.

The key definitions and distinctions in Munzinger's draft law, elements of which were later taken up in the federal debt collection law, revolved around the merchant. According to Munzinger, merchants participated in the "universal and at the same time mobile field" of trade, and their distinguishing attribute was their credit.[23] The merchant's financial situation tracked his constantly fluctuating credit: "The question as to whether his assets are sufficient to cover his debts is very difficult to answer, due to both the continuous change of the commodities in his possession and their value; and so by the time a survey of their value has been completed, the result is no longer correct."[24] Accordingly, the professor deemed it impossible to determine when a merchant was no longer able to settle his obligations. "Because of the constant change, the present moment cannot serve as an indicator for the future; rather, the future is represented by that which one calls the *credit* of the merchant." As long as a merchant had credit, he could always pay off a debt by liquidating some of his fungible goods or taking out another loan. Thus, the factual stoppage of payments was the only reliable index for calling a merchant insolvent and, Munzinger reasoned, should thus serve as the sole criteria for forcing a merchant into bankruptcy proceedings. The merchant's world was one of immediate payments, a logic with its own peculiar temporality.

Temporalities and Spaces of Debt and Credit

The federal law aimed to make uniform the debt collection procedures of the nation-state. But in realizing this aim, it had to do justice to the various, regionally distinct temporalities of loans and payments. Walther Munzinger described the merchant's world as the "universal and at the same time mobile field" of trade. The emblematic expression of this universality and mobility were the bills of exchange that merchants extracted from material assets. Across all of Europe, bills of exchange facilitated the development of a special, rapid, rigid form of debt collection; they served as instruments of debt, means of payment, a currency exchange system, and instruments of arbitrage. In its simplest form, the bill consisted of a contract closed between two merchants that obliged the maker to pay a specific sum to a third party. For instance, if a merchant from Zurich wanted to transfer funds to a recipient in Paris in the eighteenth century, he would seek out a Zurich merchant who had an agent in Paris.[25] He paid his colleague in Zuricher gulden, who then issued a bill for the corresponding sum in French livres. The colleague then sent the bill to Paris, dispatching his agent there to pay out the sum in livres to the intended recipient. The simple financial instrument served as the foundation for complex transactions. Bills of exchange were at the core of loan contracts, were redeemable like a contemporary check, and could be traded as securities or leveraged as collateral.[26] The abstraction of an originating contract created, under certain conditions, a universally exchangeable note. The abstract foundations and rigid repayment conditions of bills of exchange provided considerable fodder for the social imagination. Economists' writings on the instruments revealed ambivalent feelings about market society. Since the early modern period, the myth that Jews invented bills of exchange had become popular.[27] In the nineteenth century, various theories sought to explain what precisely a bill of exchange was.[28] According to the influential theory of Carl Einert (1777–1855), a jurist from Saxony, bills of exchange were the paper money of merchants. They were a cosmopolitan money, he explained, that received their value from the credit— the "celebrity"—of a merchant.[29] In "our paper age," as Einert called modernity, this money could easily overcome the limitations of national currencies.[30] He argued that a bill of exchange was not a contract establishing a debt, because it abstracted from the original, concrete transaction (whether it be a loan or the receipt of goods or services). After all, it was not a specific creditor who had a claim to payment when the bill matured, but rather whoever happened to be holding the paper in their hand. Thus, "the corporeal dimension of the bill of exchange" was a "piece of paper" that had value as money just "like an order for payment, exchequer bill, bank note."[31] This led him to define the bill of exchange as a "promise" made to "the entire public."[32] The abstraction of an original legal transaction elevated the bill of exchange to a universal promise, which had to be instantly redeemable. The smooth circulation of bills of exchange depended on a strict obligation to pay; accordingly, it developed its own, accelerated form of enforcing payments, with short terms and temporary civil-law incarceration. The stringent terms and conditions were limited to the "estate" of merchants, an exclusive "public." "Credit is the soul of trade," Einert wrote. "The merchant estate can only see the rapidity of the process and the unforgiving strictness of its execution in matters of trade as an act of charity, and, in light of the great benefits that he enjoys because of it, every individual merchant can only see his own subjection to this strictness as an appropriate sacrifice."[33]

Accepting the "stringency of the bill of exchange" was a condition of belonging to an exclusive group. In this sense, merchants' customs can be seen as a predecessor of the state regulation of commerce. Beginning in the early modern period, rules on exchange governed payments; the oldest Swiss example came in 1717 in the trade city of St. Gallen. In the nineteenth century, multiple Swiss cantons instituted laws that permitted all citizens to issue, redeem, and swap bills of exchange, often on the model of the Allgemeine Deutsche Wechselordnung (German General Law on Bills of Exchange) of 1848.[34] Characteristic of discussions on the topic after mid-century, one supporter of allowing all people to trade with bills of exchange stated that the Swiss were living in a time "in which all differences of estate are blurred, and life and occupational situations permeate one another in an all-encompassing fashion."[35] Nevertheless, a treaty between the cantons failed because a number of agricultural cantons refused to participate.[36] The social reach of the financial instrument thus remained restricted, with or without formal legal or customary barriers to its use.

When a merchant fell behind on payments, he immediately entered into bankruptcy proceedings and, with that, lost his male civic rights. One draft law on bills of exchange declared that, in issuing a bill, one "risks his political head, that is, his honor, equally significant from both economic and political points of view."[37] Failure to have the constant liquidity necessitated by the brevity of payment periods thus found its fitting form in the one-off caesura of bankruptcy proceedings. On the other hand, the bill of exchange—the "piece of paper" that abstracted from the original deal—constituted a continuous chain that was only broken by the inability to pay.[38]

Various perspectives have been offered on the relation between law, space, and the temporal regimes of capitalism; others have analyzed connections between the simultaneous homogenization and fragmentation of law as an effect of capitalism's radical reordering of time, space, and material resources. For Marxist theorist Nicos Poulantzas, law plays a role in the production of a "serial, fractured, parcelled, cellular, and irreversible space," which characterizes both the factory floor and the map of territorial boundaries of contemporary nation-states in capitalism.[39] Poulantzas identifies the primary time-shape of industrial capitalism as being articulated in the "segmentation and serialization" of assembly-line labor, its leaden measure of time resulting in a "segmented, serial, equally divided, cumulative and irreversible time that is oriented towards the product."[40] Regulated in uniform fashion, but chopped up into segments; geared toward a goal—the production of commodities—but without end: time appears here as a disciplinary metric.

Historical sociologist William Sewell's analysis of capitalist temporality sees the commodity form and endless accumulation as its basic elements. He attributes to the macro dynamics of capitalism a temporality that is homogeneous, cumulative, and even reversible: the "hypereventful but monotonously repetitive" ups and downs of the business cycle only constitute, at the end of the day, metamorphoses of capital.[41] Still, Sewell also acknowledges that capitalism's rise was a contingent historical process and that watershed events have fundamentally altered it. The two interpretations concentrate on different dimensions of capitalist temporality: Poulantzas describes the linear, serial time of industrial production, while Sewell describes the cyclical time of the circulation and reproduction of capital, repetition with difference.[42] The two sides are intertwined, a relationship that the state and its laws seek to make predictable, and both have been historically associated with particular economic groups. The bill of exchange represented a particular state of things: it symbolized the repetitive, homogeneous temporality up until a merchant's inability to pay set in motion a cascade of unknowns. Theorists of the period asserted that the specific temporality of trade justified treating it as its own sphere of praxis that needed its own laws, as a "universal and at the same time mobile field." The abstractness of bills of exchange came into being by way of concrete practices, such as of submitting oneself to the stringent conditions of payment, an act in which the members of an exclusive group agreed to put their civic rights at risk.

Wholly different were the cycles of agriculture. Early in the debate on the federal debt collection law, representatives from agricultural regions voiced reservations about the instantaneity of the bankruptcy system. In contrast to merchants, farmers were not in constant supply of liquid assets. The high court in Bern objected that countryfolk were short on cash in the summer, because crops were still to be harvested and the sale of animals at the autumn markets had yet to take place.[43] Similarly, a report from the central canton of Obwalden stated, "Only in autumn and winter, after cattle, cheese, and other agricultural products have been sold, is cash payment possible."[44] In other words, the agricultural economy lived by its own temporality. A comment from Fribourg underscored the interplay of different actors in it: "surtout chaque chose a son temps, que si on l'agit à contre-temps, on la compromet plus ou moins, ou même on la désorganise."[45] The comment pointed out the absurdity of the bill's first draft: In contrast to merchants, "nonmerchants" like farmers, tobacco growers, cheese makers, and ranchers could not pledge mobile assets without sweeping the rug from underneath themselves, and so, of course, the creditor of a farmer had no interest in repossessing the latter's dairy cows, because only with the cows could the cheese be produced that was necessary to pay off the debt. The letters from those agricultural and western cantons in which bankruptcy rules only applied to merchants all agreed on one point: Farmers had assets—they just couldn't liquidate them in an instant. The letters depicted agriculture as a form of production dictated by seasonal cycles and appealed that demanding immediate payment was thus incoherent. Of course, farmers were familiar with thunderbolt events: animal illness and death and crop failures constantly loomed on the farmer's horizon.

But precisely because agriculture was so fragile, the comments remonstrated, a single crop failure should not mean ruin. Instead, they pled for safety nets to mitigate the impact of a strict creditor's demands. This was combined with a holistic view on agriculture according to which the farm should be understood as indivisible property.[46] Some wrote of the disastrous consequences of making all accounts due at once, underscoring that because plots were multiply mortgaged, it could ruin not only the debtor but could also cause a domino effect.[47] Moreover, as the above-cited report from Obwalden reminded, the price of a piece of property fell dramatically if its forced sale occurred during the summer doldrums.[48] Representatives from French Switzerland employed such arguments in support of a different form of asset seizure that respected the specific quality of farmers' indivisible property, speaking in the name of a broadly defined middle class that they alleged was in danger of sliding into "an already too large class of proletarians."[49] Their fears were fueled by a general shift in the agricultural sector from crops to dairy farming, which required more capital and thus saw farms take on more debt.[50] During the economic crisis of the 1880s, agriculture was a focus of public debate, even though in absolute terms the number of people employed in that sector had only recently begun to drop.[51] Thus a widely held agrarian ideology positioned a diffusely defined "middle class" as a bulwark against the ascendant labor movement.[52]

To the divergent temporalities came ideas about commerce and agriculture's distinct forms of knowledge and their need for distinct types of regulation, with the networked, placeless world of commerce contrasting with rural rootedness. Because creditors were far away and knew little about individual debtors, legislators thought that bookkeeping would make the financial situation of future insolvent merchants more transparent.

Information was a sought-after good among merchants. Advice manuals for merchants, which had seen increased circulation since the late eighteenth century, taught the best strategies for acquiring and disseminating information on a business's finances.[53] One Swiss book put it in plain terms: giving out information was a "touchy and delicate matter."[54] The book used mnemonics to drill into the aspiring merchant a smart "information style" that would strike a balance between legally cautious formulas and the bourgeois ideal of modest speech. Its author repeatedly enjoined readers to respond with restraint to inquiries for information about others in order to avoid discrediting somebody. Because an intact reputation was taken as evidence of credit, a merchant's ability to make payments was assumed up until the moment in which bankruptcy was officially declared. And because the credit of a merchant—who "does business the world over with other people's money"—was constantly in flux, only "compulsory bankruptcy" could bring to daylight all the assets the merchant had available for paying off outstanding debts.[55] In contrast, legislators believed that rural debtors had direct contacts with their creditors. The farmer's real property that secured his debts was visible to all, fixed in place. In localized relations of exchange, creditors could more easily keep an eye on debtors, and the village grapevine made the latter's finances known to everyone. Other jurists, however, criticized this idyllic image of transparent rurality, stating that local business relations, too, were complex, mediated, and opaque.[56]

In sum, the experts claimed in one way or another that there were different economic spheres, but that these spheres were joined through exchange, which compels the historian to inquire into their various positions in the system of economic exchange. The very entanglement that legal authorities thought definitive of the modern economy assigned economic actors to different roles, and precisely because all branches of the economy were intertwined, different, targeted procedures were seen as necessary. The 1880 economic crisis only reinforced existing conceptions of economic differences. Spectacular bankruptcies taught that bankruptcy had diverse impacts that depended on the size of the bankrupt business and the degree of its political influence. The crash of the Schweizerische Nationalbahn in early 1878 had long-lasting repercussions. It thrust four mid-sized cities that had heavily invested in the company onto the verge of bankruptcy, forcing government and citizenry to grapple with the question as to what exactly bankruptcy proceedings for municipalities entailed and how they should be carried out.[57] The Nationalbahn's competitor, the Nordostbahn, also came close to bankruptcy. But in this case, the well-connected finance magnate and politician Alfred Escher exploited his power to negotiate a moratorium on payments.[58] The big investor's ability to win special treatment for his holdings did not go unnoticed. Early labor movement organizations petitioned for protections for small debtors in the future federal law. They also pled that sick debtors who had no source of income should receive individual relief; after all, the Nordostbahn had been afforded moratoriums.[59]

These conflicts illustrate well that the specific nature of economic relations and branches had become a key topic of public debate. The elites, too, emphasized the diverse types of exchange and production and their corresponding temporal rhythms. The *Neue Zürcher Zeitung*, a newspaper supportive of the federal state, criticized the draft bill's one-size-fits-all payment deadlines, which would "treat with the same model the large merchant in Geneva and the smallest farmer in a remote Valais valley," "allegedly because doing otherwise would create inequality before the law."[60] From this perspective, different laws for different branches of the economy did not imply the reinstatement of aristocratic privileges.[61] Rather, it simply meant recognizing the factual complexity of the modern economy, in which differing modes of production, reproduction, and exchange were intertwined, differences that needed to be met with appropriately discriminating rules and not with a blanket approach. One jurisprudential assessment proclaimed that in matters of civil law, "the modern legislator" should not seek to hold fast to the principle of equality before the law, but should instead see his task in "smoothing out certain material legal inequities through the sacrifice of formal legal equality."[62] A journalist siding with the government compared the distinction between merchants and nonmerchants to a river that "pushes out of the way all artificial dams with natural force."[63] In this view, economic practices—and not principles like equality before the law—formed a comprehensive, yet differentiated system of regulating debt.

The Commercial Register: A Novel Cultural Technique

The commercial register implemented as part of the 1883 commerce law provided the framework used by the 1889 bankruptcy law for deciding who should be subject to which procedure. The register established a purely formal distinction. In the words of a leading jurist, a merchant was "anybody" "who is listed in the commercial register, whereby it does not at all matter if he belongs in the commercial register or not."[64] Registration didn't document an already existing status; it created one. The legislative aides tasked with drafting the commerce law avoided providing a substantive definition of what a merchant was, instead opting for flexibility in order to accommodate the shifting needs of the business world. After all, reasoned Basel professor of law Paul Speiser, state officials would always arbitrarily demarcate between who was a merchant and who wasn't; thus it would be much better if "the decision were left up to commerce itself."[65] Certainly, registration was obligatory for a certain class of merchants and corporations (though defining this class, as discussed below, posed insurmountable difficulties too). But otherwise, every person with legal capacity was free to enter their name in the book.[66]

The legal administration of purely formal categories designed with the express purpose of not imposing limitations on "free development" constituted a cornerstone of liberal governance.[67] Liberal governance was not averse to state intervention, quite the contrary. In the nineteenth century, state authorities took active measures to ensure what they viewed as the free circulation of labor power, goods, and information.[68] Material environments and legal arrangements were intended to facilitate certain normalized commercial practices. Historians have elucidated this point in research on the systematization of infrastructure toward the end of the nineteenth century: asphalt streets, gas meters, plumbing systems, postal routes. Economic exchange was also increasingly described with infrastructure metaphors, as the expansive use of the word "Verkehr" (literally: traffic) in nineteenth-century Germanophone economics demonstrates.[69] But strategies to induce people to practice certain behaviors that conformed with the vision of the normalized, "free" movement of commodities and information failed again and again. Both the attempt to wield free trade as a technique of governance and the instability of this venture found expression in the implementation of the commercial register.

The analysis of the mechanics of registering and deleting that brought the category of the "merchant" into being can be helped along by the concept of cultural techniques, which has recently experienced a revival in media studies. The concept of cultural techniques opens up a distinct perspective on basic techniques that organize culture, such as reading, writing, drawing, counting, and calculating.[70] The concept underlines the recursive, procedural dimensions of media and things. In the words of media theorist Cornelia Vismann, cultural techniques give contours and definition to agency. They set sovereignties in motion by shaping subjects whose actions remain configured by the operational assemblage of media and things. The practice of producing a register and inscribing names into it is thus a cultural technique par excellence.[71] The commercial register exemplifies how administrative writing amalgamated representation and production. Its functional analogy with the property title register helps explain why liberal jurists thought of them as counterparts, because both served the purpose of making legally binding titles known to the public.[72] In short, the registers didn't simply secure a particular legal title or status, but fabricated these things themselves.[73]

The "main commercial register" consisted of two books: a chronological record of entries and a register of companies in tabular form. Each company got a page in the latter that rounded out the information contained in the former. A third, "special register" listed persons who were not required to have their names in the register but had applied for an entry anyway.

The tabular format of the register extracted individual actions—such as the delegation of a commercial power of attorney—from their context and fixed them in an easily comprehensible layout.[74] People were deleted from the register when they died, moved away, or filed for bankruptcy; companies were deleted when these events happened to their owner. Deletions were marked in red ink. In the register of companies, entries were deleted by crossing them out; in the record of names, through a new entry. Thus, deletions were not erasures, but new marks. They themselves were a means of itemization. Prescripts prohibited erasures, just like they prohibited all other "edits and marginal notes," and even errors discovered in retrospect could only be corrected through new entries.[75] One of the most important bits of information contained in the register were its deletions, because they often denoted bankruptcies. In a register, one could only cross out, never erase.

Indeed, throughout all of Europe, such systems for controlling economic information flows came into high demand in the 1870s.[76] The register regulated access to publicly available information. But the commercial register was not a new invention. In the thirteenth century, Italian cities kept various types of registers; later on, "Ragionenbücher" were used in the Swiss trade cities of Geneva (1698), St. Gallen (1717), and Basel (1719).[77] In the eighteenth century, city governments instrumentalized these sorts of registers for economic and fiscal policy, and they were increasingly drawn on to answer questions of liability and regulate the credit system.[78] Individuals and corporations listed in the early modern registers were permitted to issue bills of exchange. As forms of incorporation became more and more differentiated in the nineteenth century, certain facts about a company took on new significance.[79] The commercial register contained some of the same information as a company's articles of incorporation: the company's owner, its legal structure, and its initial capital. As a system of information, the register kept precise records on everybody listed in it. When the register was implemented in 1883 as part of the commerce law, 75.7 percent of all businesses listed in it were sole proprietorships that had to be registered in the name of their owner.[80] The federal bankruptcy law tightened things considerably: It mandated that the commercial register be expanded with an alphabetic list of people from the original list for the exclusive purpose of noting whether bankruptcy or asset seizure proceedings should be initiated against them.[81] As a cultural technique with sovereign force, the commercial register ascribed statuses by administering names, affixing them with titles, and publishing the information.

Merchants' wives' assets made up an important part of their businesses' capital.[82] The debates over the status of these assets demonstrate in brilliant fashion the ways in which the commercial register rearranged social relations. When a merchant filed for bankruptcy, his wife's assets enjoyed—at least theoretically—privileged treatment. By asserting her right to retake possession of her dowry, she stood in competition with creditors. In the view of the legislators, however, no privileges should impede the flow of commerce. The epistemic issues and questions of power posed by the special treatment of the dowry are discussed in detail in chapter 5; here I just want to touch on them as they pertain to the commercial register. In some localities, like in the canton of the city of Basel, the register listed all merchants whose marital unions were matrimonial regimes of separate property, thus giving potential lenders a more precise picture of their liquidity and future ability to pay.[83] Opinions were divided over whether and to which extent familial relations could be kept apart from business relations. For instance, which procedure should apply to a merchant who could not pay private, non-business debts: bankruptcy or the seizure of assets? For the federal government, the debtor's legal status as a person was the deciding factor, not the nature of the debt. If it were otherwise, the argument went, private demands could take precedence over a business's creditors, thus violating the aforementioned principle of free-flowing commerce:

> If, for instance, a tailor or cobbler were allowed to seize from a merchant the latter's as-yet unpaid sugarloaves that he had received from

a foreign business, this would be an inconceivably unfair act. By the way, a merchant can always come by credit and money if he is in good standing. If he cannot even scrape together enough to pay off a small household debt, then immediately opening bankruptcy proceedings against him is even more urgent than if he were unable to pay multiple business debts that happened to be due at the same time.[84]

The commercial register was an instrument of laws that privileged commerce. Its identification and regulation of certain persons as merchants thus effectively established the "merchant" as a special legal subject. Labeling a person a merchant reconfigured their social relations in a singular manner: some relations were inferior to others; some took on new significance. For example, the rights of wives were subordinated to the affairs of the business and the names of companies' proprietors were recorded in ink. Entering a person's name in the commercial register produced a title and, by extension, the merchant as a subject. But the circular logic at the root of this formal determination—recall that a merchant was "anybody" "who is listed in the commercial register, whereby it does not at all matter if he belongs in the commercial register or not"—was not so easy to translate into reality as Walther Munzinger's simple, elegant writing would have made it seem. Allowing anybody to register left unresolved the question of who should be explicitly required to register, and lawmakers differed on how to draft a federal regulation that would have provided a more specific definition of which businesses qualified.[85] Some suggested that the mobility of the business's wares or whether or not it issued bonds should serve as criteria. Others sought to avoid such substantial definitions. In the end, the federal legislature opted for an open-ended formulation and tasked the cantonal administrations with deciding the matter on a case-by-case basis. The circular published by the Federal Council illustrates the dilemma well: "Many inquiries concerning the obligation to enroll in the commercial register, mostly from retailers of all branches, cattle traders, innkeepers and restaurateurs, craftsmen, etc. give us occasion to remark that general prescriptions cannot be made on this issue. Even within a single occupation, things can differ so substantially that, in the one case, the person is absolutely obliged to be listed in the register, and in others, no obligation exists." As a consequence, cantonal authorities were supposed to oblige persons and businesses to register as merchants if they fulfilled two conditions: "1) The business of the businessperson is, to a large extent, based on credit, lending, and receiving loans and 2) precise information concerning the business's debts and accounts receivable necessitate reliable bookkeeping."[86]

Thus, the primary criterion for defining the merchant was his credit. In this respect, the nineteenth-century law stood in conformity with eighteenth-century practices, but with a twist: obligated to enter themselves in the register were those businesspeople about whom only accountant's books could offer the knowledge that other businesspersons wanted to have. One might describe this as performance through bookkeeping. An epistemic system set up to determine creditworthiness coupled with extant practices of credit thus staked out the boundaries of the field. Nearly a decade after the commerce law went into effect, however, the debate was still being fought out. Some business circles, and the Verein Schweizerischer Geschäftsreisenden (Association of Swiss Traveling Businesspersons) in particular, bemoaned that the rules were still too vague. As an alternative, they proposed using revenue and the value of a businessperson's merchandise as criteria. In the mind of one representative of the Handels- und Industrieverein (Association of Commerce and Industry), the current stock of merchandise offered a practical measure, because if the businessperson didn't keep reliable books, it was easier to estimate its value than to calculate the business's revenue.[87] In 1893, the foremost association of Swiss business interests thus recommended that a person be required to register as a merchant if their annual revenue exceeded ten thousand francs or their storehouse held over two thousand francs worth of goods.[88] The representative voiced understanding for state officials' desire to protect small business owners from the rigid conditions of bankruptcy to which registered merchants had been subjected since 1892. But from a practical perspective, he continued, the discipline in matters of business and borrowing imposed by the requirement to keep tidy books was a welcome development.

If registering as a merchant had an effect in and of itself, however, the demarcation it drew was porous. Beyond the limitations of the circular definition, the practical administration of the register was also plagued with difficulties. In its first year, the commercial register only listed 31,470 entries; a decade later, it was just 42,719.[89] Moreover, the actual record-keeping practice was not exactly transparent. An investigation conducted on Zurich, the heart of Swiss commerce, showed that the city's register of companies had a backlog of over four years.[90] In 1886, about three years after the commercial register had been implemented nationwide, the Association of Commerce and Industry observed that merchants had little interest in having their names and companies listed, seeing little real benefit for their credit in submitting themselves to the system's cumbersome rules.[91]

In other words, constructing the commercial register as a cultural technique did not automatically lead to its being utilized. Still, media studies asks us to consider the official scripts, with Cornelia Vismann going so far as to assert that prescriptions themselves can serve as evidence for the significance of cultural techniques. The "rules of art" expressed in instruments like the register themselves refer to a "certain practice."[92] Indeed, the rules regulating practices of knowledge can provide clues as to how media and the material constellations to which they give shape help produce these very practices. Nevertheless, some research from media studies tends to overestimate the social significance of official scripts. This book has a different aim. It seeks to draw connections between material constellations and social conflicts, thus analyzing cultural techniques *within* relations of debt rather than relations of debt *as* cultural techniques.[93] Interesting are the contradictions that characterize the historical situation and not just the formal, self-enclosed logic of cultural techniques themselves.[94] In effect, social conflicts and the institutions that employ specific cultural techniques are intertwined with one another. The next section deals with one such social conflict, namely the conservative opposition to the federal law on bankruptcy and debt collection.

Conservative Opposition and "Honor Sanctions"

Conservatives initiated a referendum in the hopes of blocking the passage of what would become the 1889 Federal Statute on Debt Enforcement and Bankruptcy. A heterogeneous social group, the conservatives' base resided in the Catholic, agricultural cantons of central Switzerland that had been defeated in the 1847 Sonderbund War, the western Catholic canton of Fribourg, and rural Protestant areas like Bern's countryside. The referendum was part of the conservatives' more general fight against the federalization of laws, which their liberal opponents criticized as "obstructionist politics."[95] They had been pursuing this strategy since 1871, when federal referendums were enshrined in the constitution, and continued it until they gained representation in the Federal Council in 1891.[96]

The federalization of debt collection laws opened an opportunity for conservative political mobilization precisely because it involved everyday acts of law. At stake in this conflict were conceptions about what constituted legitimate rules of economic exchange. The conservatives' rhetoric centered on the notion of morally sound commerce. This section analyzes their use of this concept and the meanings they attributed to it, as they adapted it to varying contexts and effectively wielded it to turn the arguments of the federal law's proponents against them. The tactic was fitting for the issue, because speakers could claim that their support for either bankruptcy or asset seizure was in the interest of rural municipalities. Their lack of commitment to one or the other was a consequence of the fact that the two procedures did not have clear connotations in the minds of the Swiss. In Lucerne, for instance, delinquent debts were collected through bankruptcy. The influential newspaper *Das Vaterland*, which had been founded during the Kulturkampf, thus agitated against the federal codification of asset seizure.[97] The conservative Protestant *Berner Volkszeitung*—the paper of the Berner Volkspartei, led by prominent representative of the cantonal parliament Ulrich Dürrenmatt—also editorialized against the federal law.[98] While legal reformers in the federal government brushed off the rural economy as simple and straightforward, conservatives countered that it was complex and opaque. They clamored that rural economies would be placed in danger and railed against the way in which the federal jurists drew the line between asset seizure and bankruptcy.

The conservative press was of the opinion that the proposed federal law's hard division between asset seizure and bankruptcy failed to line up with reality, an argument built upon the insight that the rural economy ran on multiple timelines. Businesspeople, they wrote, were in constant contact with farmers and thus needed to conform to the monetary rhythms of agriculture, not the other way around: "In the agricultural regions, merchants have money, just like the farmer who buys goods from them does; in other times, their accounts run low, especially in the summer."[99] The critique was that the new law would subject rural merchants to the same proceedings as those in industrial and trade-heavy regions, with the demise of small-time rural merchants as a consequence. A brochure with the expressive title *Trau! Schau! Wem?* (Trust! Look! Whom?) criticized as hooey the law's proponents' view that rural economies were transparent. It explained that people were no longer living "in a time when one knew the exact assets of one's neighbors"[100] and continued that only the strict inventory conducted as part of bankruptcy proceedings could bring to light a debtor's hidden assets, which might lie "in a bank, perhaps in another name, perhaps in stocks in a foreign company." Beyond this alleged factual benefit, the discrete practice of mailing collection notices was important to conservatives too. They protested that the proposal to seize farmer's assets would have an astonishingly negative effect on farmers' credit, because when the debt collector came over personally to haul things off, everybody in town would see. This would stir up rumors. And even if the debtor was ultimately able to pay off his debts on time, the damage would already be done. The end effect, the pamphlet regretted, would be that farmers in dire straits would seek relief from shady "usurers."[101] "When mobile assets are seized, the debt collector [*Weibel*] comes, a person known to villagers as someone who does not bring pleasant tidings to those that he honors with a visit. The village neighbors learn of this and soon enough they're saying: so and so is giving up his stuff, or at least he's being 'collected on.'"[102] The official debt collectors, who donned titles like "asset seizure sheriff" (*Pfandvogt*) and "debt sheriff," were described in conservative rhetoric as an outside authority coming to meddle in the village's social order.[103] In the canton of Bern, debts were collected not by officials, but by private agents, leading the *Berner Volkszeitung* to fear that the federal law would involve an expensive "army of federal debt collectors."[104] The bill's conservative opponents thus accused the drafters of ignoring the specific, self-regulating logic of regional economies and asserted that infringements on the widely shared ideal of economic independence would be the inevitable result.

The notion of morally sound commerce propped itself up on anti-Semitic demonization, a key element of contemporaneous conservative criticism. In the 1880s, new styles of political anti-Semitism began gaining ground among the bourgeoisie. During the ultimately successful 1893 campaign for a ban on *shehitah*, the trope of Jewish ritual murder was brought in connection with the "Jewish usurer," who was described as a "slaughterer of estates" (*Güterschlächter*).[105] In the diction of anti-Semitic conservatives, the new debt enforcement law played into the hands of usurers, "Jews, and speculators."[106] One article complained that if assets bid on at forced sales had to be immediately paid for in cash as the bill proposed, then "the capitalist, the Jew" would exploit the situation while farmers would be at a disadvantage.[107] Others struck an antiplutocratic tone in lambasting the law as a "product of big industry and big commerce" that would primarily benefit "capitalists and speculators."[108] Thus, alongside the trope of the rural usurer, they also, if indirectly and with less emphasis, employed the trope of "Jewish finance."[109] Anti-Semitic fearmongering was also used to package concerns about the transparency of exchange relations (or the lack thereof). According to Max Horkheimer, Theodor Adorno, and Leo Löwenthal, the construct of the usurer can be interpreted as an expression of doubly distorted modernity. Doubly distorted because on the one hand, the "Jewish usurer" was imagined as the embodiment of the illusory view that "the circulation sphere is responsible for exploitation."[110] In this iteration, the usurer personified the opacity of capitalism and its mysterious demands to do nothing but turn a profit. But on the other hand, the "Jewish usurer" functioned as a decidedly premodern entity. The trope was used to transfer anonymous market forces back into the realm of personalized relations of dependency, which, at the same time, were seen as being a thing of the past.[111]

To sum up, the conservatives disparaged the federal law as the expression of a topsy-turvy world: while petty creditors would be hurt, crafty debtors would go unpunished; while poor debtors would lose everything to asset seizure, "Jews and speculators" would win big. The conflict over the regulation of debt collection that the conservatives fought with venomous anti-Semitism was negotiated in terms of transparency and intelligibility. Conservatives undergirded their opposition to the bill by emphasizing the opacity of rural economies, in effect arguing that the latter did not constitute a "knowable community" of close ties.[112] In this sense, they took a more nuanced perspective on the rural economy than did the reform-minded federal legislators. They thus concluded that the proposed federal law would do nothing to invest debt collection and lending practices with the legitimacy it intended to give them. This point will be illustrated by analyzing a particularly contested issue, namely the "honor sanctions" associated with insolvency.

"Honor sanctions" was the name for the restrictions imposed on the civic rights of male bankrupts. They were not codified in the 1889 federal bankruptcy law, remaining different from canton to canton. In many places, the loss of civic rights became more and not less intense in the wake of the law's passage.[113] In Bern's cantonal legislature, where the conservative Berner Volkspartei sought to strip bankrupts of more rights than they would have previously lost, a law only passed on the fourth round of voting.[114] Bern's honor sanctions law of 1898 prescribed that bankrupt people lose their civic rights for six years and those whose seized assets weren't sufficient to pay off their debts for three. Additionally, the names of these persons were to be published in the official gazette. Their rights could be restored by a judge, but only on the condition that they acquired from their local municipal council official certification that their financial difficulties had been no fault of their own.[115]

The federal law's division between bankruptcy and asset seizure produced new forms of inequality. Until then, honor sanctions were only imposed on bankrupts, but the new law mandated them for insolvent persons subject to asset seizure as well. The number of those stripped of their civic rights immediately surged. A report by Bern debt collection officials criticized the expansion of honor sanctions for making existing local practices more severe.[116] They fretted over the fact that the law put "nonmerchants" in a worse position than registered "merchants," because the latter were granted more time to get it together and their creditors had to expressly demand that bankruptcy proceedings be initiated against them. In contrast, Bern conservatives inveighed against "through-and-through socialist laws" that dictated less severe honor sanctions, claiming that being too lax on debtors would "encourage prodigality."[117] A "petition of Swiss bankrupts," finally, ripped into the canton of Bern's practice of publishing the names of insolvent debtors in the official gazette (which, they emphasized, was distributed to some 2,400 innkeepers), calling it a "system of denunciation."[118] An author going by "friend of the people" noted that registered companies were permitted to reach a settlement with creditors in the run of bankruptcy proceedings, thus leaving their honor unscathed, a benefit not afforded to "nonmerchants." He added that a "capitalist" who had outstanding debts to an artisan or a laborer could arrogate long terms of payment that would cause the latter financial ruin.[119] An association of laborers and craftsmen appealed to Bern's cantonal parliament to not strip the civic rights of men who had "come into economic hardship through no fault of their own." Their petition did not propose any methods for identifying "fellow citizens *not at fault* in their financial distress." Instead, it reasoned that the courts should use their authority to investigate to automatically conduct an examination of each debtor's degree of fault, rather than only doing so on the debtor's request. The alternative, they decried, would be that insolvent persons of the "poorer classes" would remain without rights, either out of "ignorance of the law" or because they would fear "the stress and costs" of applying to have their case reviewed.[120]

The semantics of inculpability helped transform honor and guilt into legal terms, drawing on the distinction common in many cantons between bankruptcies for which the debtor was at fault and those in which the debtor was not at fault. The discourse played heavily on the polysemy of the word "Schuld" (culpability, debt, guilt): debtors who had become insolvent on no fault of their own, the argument went, were morally innocent. Further, a debtor who tried their best, was morally irreproachable, and still fell on hard times should be viewed as legally inculpable. This argument, which will reappear repeatedly throughout this study, took on different guises in varying contexts. At its core was a conception of normalized economic behavior.

The debate over honor sanctions was part of a larger fight over the relation between economic activity and social status. The 1889 Federal Statute on Debt Enforcement and Bankruptcy homogenized debt-collection strategies and the sanctions associated with them, but by leaving the matter of honor sanctions up to the cantons, the law occasioned considerable confusion. Jurist Alfred Brüstlein pled for legislators to be mild with honor sanctions and employ them only to the extent necessary to "cut off credit from persons unworthy of it."[121] This would limit the damage done to their reputation in the economic sphere, thereby doing justice to the "modern view according to which debt enforcement is executed against assets and not against the person." But it was precisely this detachment of the person from their property that conservatives refused to accept. They had different ideas about how the state should deal with insolvent debtors. In the end, the issue of honor sanctions evidenced that the economic effects of the state-enforced collection of delinquent debts were inextricable from the discussions on morality that accompanied the legislative process.[122]

The Object of the Economy

The controversy over the morality of honor sanctions was a symptom of the more general debate over the regulation of debts. At its core lay questions over knowledge and economic exchange. The economic depression that followed upon the Panic of 1873 provided the impetus for an intensified focus on economic exchange in the 1880s in various fields of social discourse.[123] To briefly touch upon a few points here: With the rise of marginalism in the final decades of the nineteenth century, political economy left behind production costs and labor theories of value and recast itself as a science of formalized intersubjective relations of exchange.[124] Further, in the Habsburg Empire, German Empire, and various Swiss cantons, the antiusury laws that had been repealed a few decades previously were brought back into effect.[125] These parallel developments gave rise to an alliance between political anti-Semitism and social-scientific expertise that would have serious consequences.[126] Confronted with processes of urbanization in the everyday economy, small business owners organized themselves in the 1880s to press for more robust protections for creditors. A Swiss branch of the German commercial credit agency Creditreform opened in 1888, bolstering the services provided by the already existing news source for Swiss traveling salesmen and the Bern credit agency Confidentia.[127] The agencies published a "blacklist" of notorious debtors, represented their members in bankruptcy proceedings, and demanded that municipal administrations publish the names of debtors undergoing asset seizure.[128] Finally, debates over futures trading grappled with the role of finance in society.[129] Elevated interest in economic exchange relations went hand-in-hand with elevated awareness of the increasing differentiation of economic life. Economists began to conceive of the economy as a complex sphere of highly specialized forms of production and consumption, which led them to conclude that uniform regulations and avenues for exchange sensitive to these differences were necessary. The Federal Statute on Debt Enforcement and Bankruptcy was one important lever in this double movement of homogenization and fractioning.

This chapter argued that the federal statute aimed to stabilize exchange. It accomplished its aim by further developing a new form of economic subjectivity, the "merchant." The distinction between merchants and nonmerchants was instituted by techniques that molded knowledge into specialized formats. On a more general level, the modern economy was shaped by such techniques as well as by social conflicts over what constituted legitimate relations of exchange. The chapter thus analyzed the connections between practices of legal knowledge, media constellations, and social conflict. As the conservatives' protestations against the federal law reveal, the issue of bankruptcy and debt collection served as a focal point of efforts to reform the system of debt and lending. Conservatives disdained the division between statuses—merchant and nonmerchant—and procedures—bankruptcy and asset seizure—drawn by the federal law. They saw the divisions as obscuring economic relations, not as making them more intelligible. In effect, the fight over "correct" business practices was a fight over transparency in economic life. From this vantage point, the techniques of mediatizing knowledge and the social conflicts over debt and credit were intertwined with one another every step of the way. The federal law functioned to join the two together, thereby absorbing the tensions between the various domains and temporalities affected by it.

What did these tensions look like *before* the adoption of the federal law, when rules and regulations were more rooted in local contexts and "the ground of routine," in the words of one federal jurist?[130] The next chapter takes up practices of debt enforcement between 1800 and 1870, when they had a legal structure very different from that ultimately codified during the rise of the modern economy.

TWO | Law as Local Knowledge 1800–1870

In 1800, the archdeacon of the Grossmünster of Zurich, Johannes Tobler, advised political leaders to heed a "practical maxim" that could guard against a potential revolution: "Forgive us our debts as we forgive our debtors."[1] A "benign hierarchy," Tobler found, expressed itself in such acts of forgiveness, which he believed were becoming ever rarer. He opined that one should treat mercifully those "who owe us money, services, feudal dues, interest, tithes" by, "according to circumstance—but always such that charity governs the choice—extending the payment deadline, reducing the debt, or wholly writing it off." Riffing on the Lord's Prayer, the theologian had a feeling for the business side of paternalistic responsibilities. In forgiving debts, one could "win—in a sense, buy—hearts, certainly not of much expense and yet of inestimable value."[2] In short, debt relief would imply less material cost for the rulers than would the danger of revolutionary unrest. The treatise thus provided an analysis of debts and power in society, contrasting revolutionary reckoning with the social bonds that might be forged through debt forgiveness. The text also sutured the regulation of debts with a diagnosis of crisis. Tobler coined his practical maxim in a time of revolutionary upheaval. In the years between the French Revolution and Napoleon's takeover, many of the hierarchies that the archdeacon sought to help preserve with his advice were abruptly abolished.[3] Plebeian movements and uprisings, French troops traversing the continent, and Switzerland's role as a front in a European war rapidly transformed the relationship between rulers and their subjects.[4] But after the demise of the short-lived Helvetic Republic, which between 1798 and 1803 for the first time imposed centralized, constitutional governance on the Swiss cantons, the practical norms thematized by Tobler regained relevance.[5]

Deferring, forgiving, and restructuring debts were common practices, both between individual debtors and creditors and in various cantonal laws. Tobler's plea for a benign hierarchy seems far removed from the modern economic complex that was codified eighty-nine years later in the Federal Statute on Debt Enforcement and Bankruptcy, with its categorical distinction between merchants and nonmerchants. What did the norms and practices of compulsory debt collection in Switzerland look like before they were fixed in a unified federal law? Debt collection made do with minimal state intervention by drawing on established customs and habits. It was shaped by a series of documents, terms, deadlines, proclamations, and unwritten rules, a situation well illustrated by the following anecdote.

In August 1829, eight women from Oberweningen, an agricultural municipality in the canton of Zurich, filed a complaint with the cantonal administration.[6] The women had been refused the right to estovers because their husbands had declared bankruptcy. They demanded that they be allowed to procure firewood from common land just like the families of "upright men."[7] The municipal council, however, was only willing to grant them and their families half of their normal wood allowance. The women signed their petition with their maiden names. And they were also the ones who were heard by the local government, not their husbands, whose bankrupt status meant relinquishing their gender guardianship over their wives.[8] The fact that the women signed their maiden names indicates that the separation of assets was at play here. In the canton of Zurich, husbands had legal dominion over the assets of their wives and could command these assets at will. But the bonds of joint property were dissolved when bankruptcy was filed, as was the husband's dominion over the property itself,[9] which made possible the unexpected event of women filing an official grievance.[10] The women of Oberweningen directed their charge at the highest authority in the canton.[11] They wrote that the "burden of the house's finances" had been thrust upon them because their husbands had fallen into bankruptcy: "The bankruptcy of our husbands forced us either to take over the properties that our husbands owned [and with them the properties' heavy debts—MS] or to purchase anew our house and home (in order to maintain our households and raise our children with God and honor and in order to burden neither the community nor the public treasury)." The women viewed themselves as dutiful citizens of the community.[12] They had dampened the effects of their husbands' bankruptcy by purchasing with their own funds the men's properties at their forced sale, and in their complaint they emphasized that in doing so they had saved their family from becoming dependent on poor relief. And still, for five years they had been denied their full share of common wood and had thus been "treated as mere half citizens." By writing an official appeal, the women circumvented the actual authority on the issue, as the wives of bankrupt men were generally placed under the gender tutelage of a government-appointed legal guardian.[13] Even though the institution of husbands' guardianship over their wives was legally binding, it was undermined in bankruptcy. In contrast to husbands, third-party legal guardians had to keep accounts of their "ward's" finances; often, however, they were barely literate.[14] The administration tasked with supervising these guardians regularly determined that they had completed in slipshod fashion the paperwork required when they inspected the box containing their "ward's" promissory notes and other securities.[15] In their appeal, the women wrote that the common of estovers was an elementary matter, since almost nobody in the community owned forest land. Until 1800, they reminded their readers, communal wood had been distributed according to need, and later on, everybody received the same amount. But ever since the community had cut down and sold a large number of oaks in 1824, the ration for bankrupt families had been halved.

The municipal councilmen were incensed. The complaint "angered" them all the more, they wrote to the cantonal administration, because the municipality had only sold the oaks in the first place in order to balance out the costs it had incurred on behalf of bankrupt families.[16] Moreover, the principle that bankrupt families could only receive a half portion of common wood had been valid since "time immemorial," because the husband had to forgo his share. The municipal leaders' argument demarcated between community members in enjoyment of their full rights and those who had lost their rights, and they framed their response as a defense of the former group against the women's claims. They countered that it was necessary to set a "low barrier" that, in matters concerning the "enjoyment of civic privileges, separates the upright family men from the bankrupts" in order to ensure that "the poorer, debt-burdened citizen" does not declare bankruptcy "with scornful laughter & visible schadenfreude." The councilmen's response stated that the bankrupt families had put a strain on the municipality's finances, because their insolvency had forced the community to acquire the families' assets during their forced sale only in order to return them to the family at a lower price. And, in fact, in the mid-1820s, the village's books showed deficits; for 1824–25, a note explains that it had to intervene on behalf of a number of bankrupt community members.[17] But the cantonal administration was not convinced. It dictated that the municipality find a compromise with the women and allow them a sufficient quantity of wood. Before composing a response, the canton had petitioned a third party, the *Oberamt* (district office), for their opinion, which was: "Both parties make appeals to old customs, which have, however, undergone fundamental changes over time due to the significant increase in population and the ever-increasing cutting of forests."[18] The district administration reasoned that the bankrupt families must receive their due lot of wood because otherwise they would cut trees illegally and thereby damage the forest.

The common of estovers was a recurring locus of social strife in the epoch of pauperism.[19] In Zurich's rural regions, too, the agricultural crisis reached new heights in the second half of the 1820s.[20] In contrast to other municipalities in the canton of Zurich, Oberweningen did not have a system of "Gerechtigkeiten" or "equitable apportionments," a system that meted out exceedingly unequal portions of communal goods on the basis of purchasing shares.[21] Instead, all community members were granted an equal amount of wood. At the same time, in the first three decades of the nineteenth century, the central cantonal authorities started to more stringently regulate communal woods. The affected municipalities, which often sold timber to cover the interest payments incurred by the gradual abolishment of feudal dues, resisted this fiercely.[22] Interesting for us, however, is less the weight of the wood and more the role it played in a conflict over belonging, rights to the commons, and whether they should be diminished because of debts. The district alleged that the practice of debt enforcement was determined by "old customs," habits that stood outside the letter of the law.[23] The loss of civic rights as a consequence of bankruptcy led to official sanctions, but it also had unanticipated effects: the social construct of "the bankrupt" stripped of his rights contrasted with the bankrupt's wife, who acquired a more prominent legal position in the run of the process.[24] Since the 1970s, scholars of women's history have demonstrated the power and agency that women have historically possessed in familial economies.[25] This insight makes clear that the Oberweningen women asserted themselves as that which they were: active economic subjects. In effect, the debt collection proceedings themselves brought forth legal subjects with a novel complex of restricted rights. On the stage of jurisprudence, bankruptcy could cause confusion. It placed women in the position of having to defend their claims to things necessary for survival, but it also opened up a liminal legal space for them to do so. The women of Oberweningen portrayed themselves as active members of the community. The municipal leaders, for their part, also spoke of the community, if in a different sense. They defined belonging through exclusion, arguing that because the families' bankruptcies had threatened the solvency of the village, their demotion to a secondary status was justified. Moreover, they connected the financial question with a moral one: as quoted above, they wanted to prevent insolvent persons from declaring bankruptcy "with scornful laughter & visible schadenfreude."

Lending, debt, and debt collection in nineteenth-century Switzerland were structured differently than their later homogenization in the 1889 federal law. This chapter seeks to show that the shifting contours of debt did not follow a preordained path. The tension between established local practices and liberal governance resulted in a kind of constructed continuity; a key part of the federalization of bankruptcy law was its adaptation of long-standing, regionally idiosyncratic routines to a federal context, a combination that produced new practices that were not a one-to-one prolongation of the established forms. Instead, they metamorphosed as they were tested out in different arenas. Liberal government and its project of standardizing debt collection procedures did not impose itself upon localities as an external power, but rather derived its own practices from the shifts and contradictions at work within local society. Nevertheless, the relationship between traditional local practices and liberal governance was an uneasy one. Adequately analyzing this relationship and the changes it led to—even those of a gradual nature—necessitates exploring the discontinuities and conflicts it engendered. Interpreting it all from the perspective of the federal law would fail to do justice to the ways in which contingencies and decisions born out of particular experiences ultimately crystallized into or were left out of what later became the uniform rule. I approach this issue by way of two related questions. First, what did debts effectuate? What conflicts did they occasion? What kinds of cultural practices did they give rise to? Second, what effectuated debts? Which procedures brought forth debts as a visible phenomenon? Which constellations of space, time, material resources, and notions of personhood led to debts being conceptualized as a legal issue? And, perhaps more theoretically, of which techniques were debts an effect?[26]

These two lines of questioning guide my study of laws and legal practices as forms of local knowledge, as complexes that join local norms with context-dependent descriptions of reality.[27] Such knowledge was practical, but not autochthonous. A more appropriate name for it would be "pidgin knowledge," a concept coined for the study of colonial and post-colonial history and the manifold "central peripheries" and "peripheral centers" characteristic of colonial and postcolonial exchange relations.[28] In debt enforcement practices in nineteenth-century Switzerland, early modern, agriculturally influenced customs overlapped with modern forms of liberal governance. This chapter paints a panorama of both established and new practices and their interactions in the simultaneously protoindustrial and agricultural canton of Zurich. It explores the administration, deadlines, and paperwork of state-enforced debt collection. The last section then inquires into the image of the bankrupt in the social and political imaginary and the transformations undergone by the social perception of debt and its social, legal, and moral legitimacy. To this end, I focus on a regional authority tasked with supervising and regulating the concrete enforcement of debts. Sources in which legal institutions feature as the recipient of petitions, hearer of appeals, and publicly accountable authority offer a glimpse into the processual logic of debt enforcement and the moments in which it malfunctioned.

Summary Judgments and the Genealogy of Liberalism

Documentation formed the essence of debt enforcement. Certificates, tables, registers, and signatures were its backbone; deadlines gave the process its rhythm. When somebody in the canton of Zurich wanted to collect on a debt from a delinquent debtor, they directed an official, the debt collector, to generate a form.[29] Without checking any further into the creditor's claims, the debt collector sent the form to the municipal bailiff, who had it delivered to the debtor. The latter now had fourteen days to appeal the claim; if they did that, then the matter ended up in the office of the president of the district court. If the debtor failed to act, then, after another twenty-one days, they were issued a so-called certificate of collateral, in which the bailiff wrote down everything in the debtor's household that might be able to be seized in order to satisfy the debt. If the debtor still failed to act, they were, after a further twenty-one days, warned that their assets would soon be realized—or, in Swiss parlance, *versilbert*, "turned to silver"—at a compulsory auction if the creditor so desired. This was the run of "minor debt enforcement," the procedure for claims that did not involve real estate. Small sums could be collected by the bailiff himself. An estimate from 1858 concluded that the majority of claims involved sums under forty francs.[30] Minor debt enforcement, however, could wind up in "major debt enforcement," which is to say, bankruptcy proceedings. Seizure of assets as collateral and bankruptcy were combined in the canton of Zurich; as outlined in the previous chapter, these were the two systems that the federal law of 1889 sharply separated from one another. Claims involving mortgaged real estate (and the interest owed on it) went straight to major debt enforcement and thus initiated bankruptcy proceedings right off the bat. Major debt enforcement did not involve the forfeiture or pledging of property; rather, after a series of deadlines, an official conducted an inventory of the debtor's ownings and published the details of the bankruptcy, a step known as the *Auffallsbeschreibung*.

The iterative, routinized nature of the proceedings made it possible to almost entirely dispense with the intervention of higher-ranking authorities. Officials tasked with collecting delinquent debts managed things from start to finish; judges were rarely involved. Jurists of the time were fascinated at the almost entirely administrative character of debt enforcement.[31] In 1858, Zurich professor of law Friedrich von Wyß counted it among the "oddest and at the same time most important and invasive legal institutions" in Switzerland: "Compulsory execution of monetary claims of all types, usually carried out at the mere request of the creditor, without a court judgment or even a court's knowledge or permission having to precede it, performed by an administrative official, often without judicial participation . . . that is an institution that will cause every jurist who has not become accustomed to it by seeing it with his own eyes from his youth onwards to shake his head."[32] Yet von Wyß concluded that, surprisingly, this system was an exceptionally advantageous, practical instrument for run-of-the-mill legal proceedings. Mundane measures with broad applicability executed by laypeople and low-level administrative officials were the bedrock of the procedures, not case-by-case judicial decisions. Jurists like von Wyß were astonished at the efficiency of this approach to debt collection, which they traced back to long-standing customs. And indeed, the basic elements of the procedure had been around since the early modern period. The laws regulating municipal and property affairs in the canton of Zurich were put on the books in 1715 and were only superseded by the Zurich civil law code implemented in the 1850s.[33] But in the nineteenth century, the meaning and practical expression of these laws shifted, brought on by the repeated updating of handed-down rules.[34] Debt collection relied on self-organization, and in the nineteenth century it took on an emphatically liberal shape.

Historians have researched various aspects of the interrelations of republican traditions and liberalism in Switzerland[35] and have shown how traditions of local autonomy were receptive to a new political culture rooted in the language of rights.[36] The continued significance of the municipality has been identified as a key feature of Swiss liberalism. In matters of poverty law in particular, corporative municipal rules and regulations remained binding even after the establishment of the Swiss Confederation.[37] Rather than being a coherent set of ideas, liberalism has been described as a contradictory flux, exemplified by instances like when women from the educated bourgeoisie tested the limits of liberal rights and had their claims repeatedly denied.[38] Another perspective has been opened up by research on governmentality, which sees liberalism as a specific technique of governance that developed out of new forms of knowledge and expertise.[39] In the canton of Zurich, the liberal turn of 1830/31 combined with an increasingly professionalized administrative staff[40] to bring into being new types of publications that archived the actions of the state, such as the annual report of the high court (which functioned as the supervisory authority of the judiciary) and the Zurich journal of jurisprudence, the *Monatschronik der zürcherischen Rechtspflege*.[41]

New forms of state responsibility lent administrative practices an unprecedented intensity and significance and laid the groundwork for new supervisory authorities. The rationality of liberal governmentality dictated that the exercise of power not be localized in one single core authority. Its guiding principle was to regulate and form subjects while keeping direct state interventions to a minimum.[42] It was rule from a distance, effected through everyday practices and the conscious shaping of material environments. Bland administrative formalities supplanted personal interventions. Accordingly, freedom was not the mere absence of compulsion, but served as a technique of governance, a technique that both demanded and produced self-regulating, reflexive subjects.[43] Constitutive for this mode of freedom was the—often violent—imposition of restrictions on those deemed unfit for self-rule. Understood thus, the universal liberal citizen-subject was constituted through the exclusion of its other: the gendered woman, the propertyless poor, and the racialized subject of colonization.

The exclusions at the foundation of liberal rights had practical consequences in the world of debt. In bankruptcy proceedings, women obtained a novel, if limited status of legal independence, while men lost their civic rights. More restrictive still was the exclusionary treatment of Jewish creditors. A decree from 1804 forbade Jews in the canton of

Zurich from involvement in "all things debt-related, with the exception of mercantile matters," and denied them access to "all registries and protocols,"[44] including the title register. This meant that Jewish creditors could not obtain titles on mortgaged properties, forcing them to resort to individual contracts with debtors to secure their loans with real assets, a situation that placed them at a clear disadvantage.[45]

Liberal governance drew on, modified, and systematized customary practices, rebaptizing them in the ink of newly found expertise. This found expression in the idioms and customs, papers and directives that gave debt enforcement its contours. For instance, the third and last warning sent to creditors before the initiation of bankruptcy proceedings was a form called a *Schreckzettel*, or "terrifying note."[46] After that, the particulars of the case were, in the city, posted in a public square, or, in the countryside, read aloud in the church three Sundays in a row. After the third "church announcement" (*Kirchenruf*), creditors convened to negotiate over the bankrupt's inventoried assets, an event called *Verrechtfertigung* (roughly, "the calling to account") in the canton of Zurich and *Geltstag* ("day of reckoning") in Bern and the canton of Aargau. In order to avoid this, a debtor could pledge part of their future harvest and certify the promise by giving the creditor a "flower note" (*Blumenschein*). Still, creditors holding debts secured with real estate had priority when it came to extracting pledges on unharvested crops.[47] In the canton of St. Gallen, creditors could demand a "fortune note" (*Glücksschein*) that guaranteed that the creditor would be paid off as soon as the bankrupt debtor received an inheritance "or other benefit of fortune."[48] A bankrupt who had paid their debts petitioned their creditors for a "liberation note," which was necessary for having one's civic rights reinstated.[49]

The "church announcement" was a media technique from the Ancien Régime. Back then, the weekly price of bread was read out in church— underscoring that bread came from the Lord—and, after the sermon, an official announced the names of the bankrupt.[50] This froze debtors' assets and prohibited members of the community from entering into financial deals with them. This was an embarrassing experience for the debtor, and the publication of their finances was often coupled with an act of shaming. In the city of Lucerne, bankrupts were put on the pillory on Tuesdays and at the weekly market; a trumpeter hired for the purpose ensured everybody's attention. In 1848, this practice was given up, both because names were now published in newspapers and official gazettes and because this type of shame sanction was seen as disproportionately harmful for persons whose bankruptcy was due neither to "carelessness" nor to "fraud."[51] It was not seldom that debtors skipped town in order to avoid being subjected to the dishonoring treatment. Gregorius Aemisegger (1815–1913), a salesman who wrote down the story of his own life in a still-preserved manuscript, recalled having faced, in 1848, his name being read out in church: "A close relative sent me a seizure note. I had to pledge my things, and only had 24 hours, then my name was supposed to be read out in the church, published in the newspaper, and I would be banned for two years from the taverns and inns." His friends advised him to relocate. It seems that at the last minute, a neighbor who had won the lottery helped him out with a considerable sum of cash. Aemisegger's bankruptcy was compounded with the honor sanction of being banned from the bars, which was the rule not just in St. Gallen, but also in other cantons like Aargau, a "hard law" in Aemisegger's estimation.[52] A novella published in the same year by conservative author Johann Jakob Reithard with the plain title "A Swiss Village Story" tells of a debtor who fears his name being read out in church, plans to flee the village, and is saved at the last moment by an anonymous gift.[53]

An 1805 Zurich law held that the "customary announcement in the church of the debtor and in those of neighboring congregations" would generally reach an appropriate number of people, deeming that publication of names in "the public papers" was only necessary when the debtor "to be called to account" was involved in "noteworthy business, such as in milling, trade, etc."[54] As cultural historians have shown, in many rural areas in the nineteenth century, the acoustic radius of the church bells marked the borders of the municipality: a normative, conservative acoustic sign that, in a time of urbanization, promised bucolic harmony and tight-knit community.[55] Church bells alerted townspeople of dangers like fire and announced rites of passage like marriages, baptisms, and burials.[56] In a certain sense, the church announcement accomplished a similar task, proclaiming the bankrupt's passage into a new legal status. The bells' function of staking out the municipality's borders was, at least in a figurative sense, also fulfilled by the reading of bankrupts' names in church, as the latter was a form of communication based on acoustic proximity that was strictly accessible to those present.[57]

But expanding networks of debt altered these borders in the following decades. Adopted in 1843, Zurich's rules on forced sales dictated that in places where the reading of bankrupts' names in church was still in use "this custom shall be substituted by a different means of publication."[58] In 1845, an article in the opposition newspaper *Der Bote von Uster*, printed in Zurich's industrialized highlands, demanded that the custom be abolished altogether.[59] The municipality of Wetzikon did away with the practice in 1852, when a regional newspaper in the highlands was founded.[60] The extensive distribution of newspapers and official gazettes created new channels and ultimately expanded the circle of those involved in debt collection.

Deadlines, Rhythms, and Authorities

A look at the deadlines that punctuated debt enforcement proceedings illustrates well how everyday habits and state measures were intertwined while at the same time often contradicting one another. During periods called *Rechtsstillstand*, open cases were put on standstill. The periods aligned with religious holidays and agricultural rhythms. In the 1820s, they were movable and determined from locality to locality; the summer standstill began when the knots on the first bushels of rye were tied in a specific plot at the Sihl River, and the autumnal standstill for the wine harvest lasted until the cellar of the main church stopped receiving grapes.[61] Alongside these harvest breaks, things were also put on hold for Easter, Pentecost, the Federal Day of Prayer (after 1832), and Christmas: from the Thursday before Palm Sunday to the Tuesday after Misericordia Sunday, from the Wednesday before Pentecost to the Thursday after it, a total of twelve days around the Federal Day of Prayer, from the Thursday after the twenty-first of December to the first Tuesday after the "twentieth day" (January 12). Other multiday pauses included Pentecost festivities, the first of May, the Autumn Fair, and Saint Martin's Day (November 11). Thus, debt collection proceedings were effectively paused for more than a third of the year. The legal standstills were noted in widely distributed calendars sold cheaply by traveling salesmen.[62] A manual on jurisprudence observed that "so-called sinister debtors" timed their due dates to line up with the standstills, thus winning for themselves a considerable amount of extra time to pay off their debts.[63]

In the 1830s, the dates were fixed and payment periods became shorter. When Zurich's liberal cantonal government passed a new debt enforcement law in 1832, the canton's agricultural municipalities complained that the shortened deadlines would make life more difficult for them. The municipal council of Uhwiesen in Zurich's wine country had already opined in the preliminary debates on the law that the deadlines were "more suited for mercantile people than for agricultural people." The first two years of the law witnessed an increasing number of people fall into poverty in the region, leading the municipal council to protest in the cantonal parliament. Of the abbreviated periods of payment they warned that:

> If we receive no relief in this matter, many of our citizens will have no other choice but to allow themselves to become honorless men, and at that not just of the type that is on the lowest level from an economic perspective, but rather of that type that still owns real property, because the shortened deadline for debt collection [*Rechtstrieb*] is often used by stone-hearted creditors to exploit their debtors' desperate situations and to deviously appropriate the properties pledged to them in the terms of bankruptcy. What is to become of such municipalities that count among their members such a large number of men who, through no fault of their own, are impoverished, propertyless, and *have nothing to lose?*[64]

With its subtly threatening warning that the cantonal government was playing with fire by indirectly creating a population of "*men who have nothing to lose,*" the petition juxtaposed people experiencing "misfortune through no fault of their own" with the "stone-hearted creditor," elaborating that "law-abiding families" had fallen into debt "because of years of bad harvests and hampered sales of the little they did harvest; thus, through no fault of their own." The local authorities were concerned about the municipality's poor relief and demanded extended periods of payment and special moratoriums for farmers in order to ameliorate the crisis.

On a local level, extralegal forces often sought to moderate the pressure. Bailiffs delayed enforcement of claims and were particularly weary of liquidating pledged assets. After Zurich's liberal government instituted new forms of record keeping and judicial supervision over bailiffs, an uninterrupted flow of laments over these delays flooded in. The state's documentation made deviations from the norm more visible. In the Ancien Régime, too, officials had delayed proceedings in times of crisis—like in 1770—by officially declaring moratoriums. Indeed, it was just such merciful practices that archdeacon Tobler admonished governments to adopt in his turn-of-the-century "practical maxim."[65] The very identity of the liberal government, however, was to declare such habits the vestige of bygone eras.[66] But the bailiffs didn't let up. In the 1840s, a government report determined that only a minority of officials enforced debts by the book.[67] They delayed liquidating pledged assets or claimed that the debtor couldn't be found, which, especially in small municipalities, aroused the suspicion of the cantonal administration.[68] Beginning in 1855, Zurich's eleven districts were required to publish statistics on officials who had been reprimanded for such derelictions of duty.[69] In the following year, no fewer than three thousand complaints were filed, with a particularly high quotient in the canton's northwestern agricultural areas.[70] But the district courts rarely enforced punitive fines against the officials. The district of Andelfingen ultimately came to prefer a different strategy, implementing a bonus for model civil servants.[71]

Why this obstinate custom of delay? In contrast to the wishes of the liberal cantonal government, the bailiffs adhered to a logic of local authority guided by local interests. Drawn-out proceedings kept people off the poor relief rolls, which were seen as a burden on the municipal treasury.[72] In the case of the eight women from Oberweningen discussed above, the municipal council emphasized the cost of bankruptcies for the municipality. When in 1849 the cantonal administration questioned official debt collectors on this point, they responded that it was "in the interest of the creditor to not liquidate pledged assets to the letter of the law," because a settlement between debtor and creditor would generally lead to better results. Jolting a debtor out of the fragile web of repayments would, they explained, trigger a domino effect. With reference to the economic crisis of the late 1840s, they continued that "in many cases, it was not possible for the bailiff to liquidate assets in the manner dictated by law if he did not want the debtor to have his credit completely revoked, particularly in times like the present one."[73] It was in the local interest to not let debtors suffer such a loss of credit. But the cantonal authority saw things differently. In the interest of "our canton's credit system," it insisted on the speedy execution of creditors' claims.[74] The cantonal administration found that enforcing the individual self-discipline that stood at the foundation of stable commerce would "increase the credit of our canton and inspire trust in our laws," but only if the local authorities acted "with care and professionalism" and strictly punished officials who broke the rules.[75] By setting the maintenance of stable exchange relations as the primary goal of policy, the canton was adhering to one of the key principles of liberal governance.

The deadlines set by debt collectors can only be properly understood when viewed in conjunction with the more general rhythms of debt payments. The dizzying quantity of credit relations corresponded with all kinds of different modalities of payment. First, there were the generally applicable dates of payment, when wages and outstanding invoices were paid and messengers were hired to request payments: Saint Martin's Day,

May Day, and the end of the year. On these days, the demand for cash rapidly increased, which led to supply problems before the establishment of the Swiss National Bank in 1907 plugged the hole.[76] Everyday, uninsured consumer loans formed another branch of debt. The "bread nexus" was subject to special conditions. For instance, a manual from 1796 stated that married women were directly liable for debts on staples for the period of a year, after which the debt was annulled.[77] In the nineteenth century, the courts reaffirmed that married women could take on debt in order to nourish their families. For instance, in 1878, Zurich's high court permitted to go into effect a decree that bound husbands to pay debts their wives had incurred to satisfy "normal daily needs."[78] In contrast, and similar to gambling debts, debts to the innkeeper had a precarious special status, with no laws regulating them in the canton of Zurich.[79] In Bern, too, limited legal means were available to innkeepers seeking to collect on debts.[80] Debts could be agreed upon in informal writings, such as in a signed IOU called an *Obligo*. Still, promises of payment in writing often necessitated pledging assets as collateral, and pledges had to be notarized. The most prevalent instrument of credit in the canton of Zurich was the *Schuldbrief,* a type of mortgage note or security backed by real estate.

The transformation of credit instruments like the mortgage note and the rise of new financial institutions exerted a profound effect on debt collection. The mortgage note was a mix between the medieval *Gült*—a perpetual payment of money or goods by a free peasant to a lord that was common in central Switzerland—and the pledge of real estate as collateral common in Francophone Switzerland.[81] In contrast to the *Gült*, nonpaying debtors sacrificed not just the pledged asset, but all of their assets, and in contrast to the simple mortgage, the mortgage note could be exchanged with third parties. The creditor received a contractual "note" promising payment at a maximum interest rate of 5 percent (which, however, was rarely reached due to the large availability of capital).[82] The mortgage note had a legally regulated term of six years. After the expiration of this period, the creditor could no longer demand payment in full, but could only either sell the note to a third party or continue to collect the accruing interest.[83] In theory, the debt persisted in perpetuity. Up through the end of the nineteenth century, mortgage notes that had originated in the seventeenth century were still in circulation. They functioned as means of payment, were auctioned off, and were used as collateral to secure loans.[84] A report commissioned during the debates over whether to establish a cantonal bank in Zurich in the 1860s determined that mortgage notes constituted the most common financial instrument in rural areas.[85] The year 1853 was a watershed moment. Zurich's *Aufkündigungsgesetz* made it possible for both creditors *and* debtors to terminate the mortgage note contract, through immediate payment on the part of the latter and demand of immediate payment or debt forgiveness on the part of the former.[86] This increased the liquidity of mortgage notes, initiating a massive mobilization of the capital that had until then been locked up in them. At the same time, the spectrum of monetary papers and those who could issue them expanded. Mortgage notes now competed with railroad stocks and bank bonds as well as with papers issued by the Bank Leu, which had originally been established during the Ancien Régime to facilitate the export of capital and house the city's treasury and which, after the passage of the 1853 law, functioned as a primary motor of the mortgage industry.[87] Commercial banks founded as joint-stock companies like the Bank in Zürich (1837) and the Schweizerische Kreditanstalt (1856) issued bonds.[88] Ever since the first savings bank was opened in the canton of Zurich in 1805, the trade in bonds and other debts had been growing. But in the opinion of one economic historian, the savings banks were transformed in the 1860s from instruments of philanthropy into "rational credit institutes."[89] Personal loans rooted in real estate lost their long-standing monopoly on the market, which created new impulses to enforce obligations of payment.[90]

Finance became a bone of political contention. The "Democratic Movement" was the name adopted by a motley opposition group of agricultural, petty bourgeois, and proletarian forces that successfully agitated for revisions to Zurich's cantonal constitution in 1869.[91] Like similar campaigns in other Swiss cantons, the movement had a regional focus. But it was one part of a global constellation of the 1860s that included the cotton shortages caused by the American Civil War and a worldwide wave of democratic mobilization. The expansion of representative democracies in Europe and the fight against slavery in the United States were the most impressive events of this moment.[92] The Democratic Movement posited that the unprecedented ease of transforming real estate into liquid assets served the interests of a new "monied aristocracy," a trend they thought could be reined in by creating a public cantonal bank.[93] Whatever their differences, the opposing parties agreed on one point: that the new institutions had drastically sped up the tempo of payment deadlines. The sources drawn upon here make it difficult to precisely discern which new means banks had to enforce creditors' claims. Evidence of banks' resistance against increased regulation can be found in the

St. Gallen Credit Institute's demand that the canton of St. Gallen allow
it to offer stronger protections to creditors who made asset-guaranteed
loans, barring which it declared that it would stop dealing with movable
collateral.[94] New types of retail businesses also altered the rhythms of
everyday debts. Consumer cooperatives, an important institution of the
Democratic Movement, insisted on cash payments in their stores.[95] In
general, the financial sphere swelled considerably in the 1860s, which
found expression in the stricter enforcement of new payment deadlines.

In order to understand the social relations between creditors and
debtors, it is important to have a clear grasp of the local institutions
that creditors appealed to for support.[96] With their great latitude in
matters of debt collection and their in-depth knowledge of local affairs,
municipal bailiffs had substantial power in the towns and villages.[97] In
the above-mentioned fictional work "A Swiss Village Story" by Johann
Jakob Reithard, a bailiff tries to use his insider knowledge to profit off of
the fate of an unlucky debtor.[98] The extent to which official debt collectors were attacked, however, is hard to determine. Still, a council order
from 1812 stated that people who insulted or assaulted bailiffs would reap
severe consequences.[99] The sources drawn on here only contain anecdotal evidence of attacks against debt collectors, though such instances
seem to have hardly been rare in the canton of Zurich.[100] Thus in the
town of Birmensdorf near Zurich proper, the three grown sons of the
farmer Hafner stood at their front door and threatened the bailiff, who
had come to seize their father's goods, bringing along a policeman "as
protective accompaniment" out of caution. The officials had no choice
but to retreat, and later that evening the sons hunted the creditor down
and beat him up.[101] The bailiffs (*Gemeindeammänner*) filled their posts as
a supplemental job and fulfilled various tasks, which is why they resisted
taking on new responsibilities.[102] In comparison, in the years around
1800, being a full-time debt collector (*Schuldenschreiber*)—which ranked
higher in the administrative hierarchy—was lucrative work. Debt collectors' income was primarily drawn from fees, which were prohibitively
high, as petitions from 1830–31 protesting the costs associated with debt
collection evidence. The fees had to be paid by debtors themselves.[103]
Most people who applied for the position of debt collector already held
some kind of state office: low-ranking judges, bailiffs, school teachers,
municipal clerks.[104] As qualifications for the job, applicants emphasized
their abilities to do paperwork, legible handwriting, and knowledge in
filekeeping acquired in previous office work. Then there were the virtues
of the public servant, frequently accompanied by pleas that the appli-

cant be allowed to fill the position because they had a family to feed.[105] Middle-class status was not just a customary requirement for assuming the post, however; it was also an economic requirement to gather the support needed to pay the high security payment, which, at mid-century, ranged from twelve thousand to sixteen thousand francs.[106]

Controversies over hiring practices also show how liberal governance was not always synonymous with centralization. The web of jurisdictions became more tightly interwoven, geographically and institutionally, over the run of the nineteenth century, and their relations were cause for political debate. The resulting spatial organization of Swiss debt enforcement fits well with the theory that ruling at a distance is a constitutive aspect of liberal governance.[107] Until Zurich's liberal turn in 1830–31, debt collectors were located at the center, fulfilling their duties from the city of Zurich. The first section of the relevant 1803 law decreed, "Debt enforcement should be central and should emanate from the capital city throughout the entire canton."[108] To this end, a supervisor and four administrators were employed. Much of the indignation over debt enforcement was directed at the centralized management of debt collectors. In 1832, new rules delegated the authority over debt collectors to the canton's eleven districts,[109] thereby satisfying the demands made by a number of petitions sent in during the change in government in 1830–31.[110] Alongside grievances over the high fees, the social and spatial proximity of debt collectors was an important point in many petitions. The revisions to the constitution won by the Democratic Movement in 1869 transferred the duties of debt collectors to the bailiffs. The idea was that by filling the office with locals, more sensitivity would be shown toward cases of hardship and administrative costs would be reduced.[111] Of the 158 petitions sent to the members of the convention to revise the canton's constitution, 40 of them—a full quarter—thematized debt enforcement.[112] The new division of debt collection jurisdictions followed a logic that treated localities as "natural," self-organized units, relegating the central authority to a supervisory function. The 1889 Federal Statute on Debt Enforcement and Bankruptcy revised the jurisdictions again for the newly instituted debt collection offices. The jurisdiction over debt enforcement gradually became equally spread, minimizing the role of the central authority. In the end, the 1889 federal law combined rule from a distance with a valorization of local authority. The federal administration worked not *against*, but *through* local offices, reconfiguring the organization of debt collection and the power vested in local authorities in order to optimize the machine of liberal governance.[113]

The Bankrupt: A Personification of Crisis

The shift toward liberal governance in multiple cantons in 1830, the protest movements of 1839–41 and their use of religious language, the founding of the Swiss Confederation in 1848, the revisions to the constitution instigated by the Democratic Movement in the late 1860s: all of these events represented conflict-ridden turning points in governmental rationality.[114] I already touched upon the petitions that piled up in these moments and would now like to take a closer look at the ways in which these petitions formulated issues of debt and social status. The petitions' rhetoric centered on the figure of the bankrupt. The bankrupt was a personification of crisis in two senses: first, bankruptcies increased in frequency during the economic crises that ignited these political transformations. Second, in a more metaphorical sense, the bankrupt served as an image that facilitated more general thoughts about crisis—a character in the political imaginary that condensed multifarious fears, demands, and meanings.[115] Invested with emotions for people from all walks of life, the image of the bankrupt helped political actors elevate crisis into an object of knowledge.[116] The image was used in various contexts in order to diagnose social issues and mobilize political energy. A liminal figure itself, the metaphor of the bankrupt made it possible to forge a novel perspective on economics and its crises, a perspective situated at their constitutive margins.

The bankrupt was, in the words of texts on constitutional law, the opposite of the "upright debtor."[117] Of the 270 petitions that reached Zurich's cantonal government during the liberal transition of 1830–31, 75 of them discussed debt enforcement. The Cantonal Council of Zurich had encouraged citizens to send in such letters of grievance, whose catalog of topics was often predetermined by local elites.[118] One petition from Wetzikon observed that the fees assessed during debt collection represented "for poor people one of the most oppressive burdens that have ever been imposed in a state." "[I]n order to retain his civic honor as his most precious possession," it continued, "a poor man" would do all he could, which was why, the author argued, the fees must urgently be reduced.[119] The threat of being stripped of one's civic honor was an iteration of "civic death" (*bürgerlicher Tod*), a powerful metaphor for fears of losing independence and rights. Such fears went beyond the citizen's privileges of political participation: civic death connoted a form of subjectivity that was the antithesis of bourgeois identity. Bankruptcy had been associated with civic death since the early modern period.[120]

Aspects of the fear of being buried alive that flourished in the late eighteenth century were also baked into the metaphor.[121] The fusion of legal status and death opened up on another semantic web, that of the "social death" of slavery. The *mort civil* was the most severe punishment in the Napoleonic Code Civil; it was related to galley slavery, but was rarely used.[122] In a more figurative sense, the metaphor of civic death told a story of experiences at the margins of civil society. It brought together economic and personal failure, implying that suicide was the only option left for the bankrupt. In turn, suicide came to be valorized as a heroic act of despair, real death cancelling the symbolic civic death. Bankrupts from the upper class did commit suicide from time to time. For instance, in 1829, after the collapse of the Finsler Bank and Trading House, Staatsrat Hans Jakob Hirzel was found frozen to death on Zurich's Üetliberg with a dose of morphine in his blood.[123] But outside of the seldom spectacular act, civic death was utilized as a rhetorical tool to denounce circumstances viewed as unacceptable and unjust. A vivid example of one such charged speech act can be found in an anonymous petition from around 1868: "A bankrupt in the canton of Zurich is dead in all relations. Not all bankrupts are negligent or slovenly. Most who go bankrupt have tortured themselves over the difficult experience."[124] The author emphasized how bankrupts did their best to continue to care for their families and excoriated the legal punishments imposed by bankruptcy. Those who criticized the existence of civic death sought to make clear that bankrupts took active steps to better their situation but were continuously thrust back into a position of passivity by legal restrictions. In short, the talk of death was a rhetorical sign of life.

Liberal jurist Friedrich Ludwig Keller (1799–1860) labored to deflate the powerful, popular metaphor of civic death.[125] Doubtless, he wrote in 1833, bankruptcy was an event with "far-reaching and partially irreversible consequences for the entirety of the bankrupt's personal life."[126] And, he admitted, while there was "some truth" to the notion of civic death, bankrupts were indisputably in possession of their rights: Swiss law did not permit slavery, not even as a form of punishment.[127] For instance, Keller continued, bankrupts could acquire and inherit property, build wealth, and take on debts. The only difference between the bankrupt's ability to do these things and those of others was that the bankrupt's creditors always had access to his assets. On this point, Keller took the position that the bankrupt's assets should "be visible to all eyes, permanently,"[128] arguing that this was why bankrupts were forbidden from pledging their real property as collateral for new loans. Similar to Jews, bankrupts had "no access to the title register." Thus, although bankrupts retained their civic rights and their capacity to make legal decisions for themselves, they had, by becoming bankrupt, sacrificed much of their ability to enter into legally binding relations. Keller's text supported keeping detailed records of bankrupts' assets and finances in order to ensure that they were not liquidated for purposes other than the payment of creditors' claims. On the other hand, he wrote, bankrupts lived in constant uncertainty, as creditors might put forth new, more onerous demands. The bankrupt, in his words, "should be in perpetual service" to his creditors, "so to say with body and property," until accounts "have been completely settled."[129]

The starkest manifestation of the social anxieties embodied by the bankrupt was his loss of marital gender guardianship over his wife. Recall the dispute between the municipal council of Oberweningen and the wives of bankrupt men discussed at the beginning of this chapter. Gender hierarchies were turned on their head as the "rightless family men" faded into the shadows of their wives, who now donned the legal pants.[130] Political petitions took on the nexus of bankruptcy, citizenship, and masculinity. In her research, historian Toby Ditz analyzed the connections between bankruptcy and precarious masculinity among the business elites of the early American republic, where the loss of professional reputation was associated with emasculated subjectivity.[131] The discussions of citizenship in petitions written by bankrupt Swiss men struck similar tones. The writings defined the politically mature masculine subject through his dominion over his wife and children, implying that a man's sovereignty was rooted in his position as head of the family. Being stripped of this symbolic aspect of male sovereignty went hand-in-hand with a real loss of power. As outlined above, the agency over a wife's property was taken away from the husband and was placed under the gender-tutelage of a state-assigned guardian. This imposed "outrageous injustices" on his wife and children, remonstrated a leaflet sent to the cantonal government in 1840, all while the bankrupt was "not permitted to say anything" because he had "forfeited his rights to God, heaven, and soul and his rights of municipal citizenship."[132] The exceptional situation created by the loss of masculine authority gave rise to remarkable events, such as the case of the women of Oberweningen, who signed their protest as "Gemeindsbürgerinnen," citizens.[133] The assets with which the wife entered into marriage represented one of the most difficult and heatedly fought over items in the classification of the bankrupt's finances (chapter 5 deals with this issue in detail). The *Frauengut*, as the dowry was known, was also put to strategic use in the complex social negotiations that followed out of the bankruptcy proceedings of wealthy citizens.[134] When Zurich's Finsler Bank and Trading House—which had close ties to the cantonal government—went bankrupt in 1829, the two Finsler brothers sought to reach an out-of-court settlement with their creditors by offering to pay them twenty cents on every gulden owed. Moreover, they promised that their wives would forfeit their dowry, valued at about sixty thousand gulden, if the creditors agreed to this "accommodation." But if they did not, the brothers threatened, their wives would exercise their legal privileges, which would ultimately force the creditors to accept a meager eight cents on the gulden.[135] In other words, the dowry was wielded to make the creditors an offer they couldn't refuse.

Rhetorical uses of the image of the bankrupt spoke not only of marital hierarchies, they also framed bankruptcy as a threat to political order in the state. An example is given by the leaflet composed in 1840 discussed above, which was addressed to Zurich's new government.[136] In September 1839, an alliance of the rural underclass and conservative elites had forced the liberal government from power.[137] Alongside disputes over the place of religion in public life—the "Züriputsch" was occasioned by the naming of controversial theologian David Friedrich Strauss as professor at the University of Zurich—the pauperized workers of the Zurich highlands demanded amnesty for the Luddites who had burned down a factory in Uster in 1832 and been sentenced to be chained to the prison walls. In light of the upheaval, the petition voiced the hope that the new government would grant "innocent" bankrupts the same amnesty sought for the arsonists of Uster.[138] The plea put the republicanism of the new government to the test. In many monarchies, it argued, those who "through misfortune" have fallen into bankruptcy were viewed as having been "punished enough" by the loss of their property and continued to enjoy "the same rights and freedoms as their fellow citizens": "Why not then in free Switzerland, in the free canton of Zurich?" In 1848, a moment of economic crisis and European revolutions, another petition exploited the government's fears of unrest in its own territory in order to demand a moratorium for debtors deemed morally blameless. It stated that, in the case that this demand was not met, bankrupts' concerns "could, as a consequence of the current times and the dominant zeitgeist, sooner or later be unleashed in a serious form."[139]

Bankrupts constituted one of the groups of men stripped of the right to vote. In the years leading up to confederation in 1848, petitions to restore their rights gained in urgency. These petitions treated economic

status and social classification as one and the same by pointing out that
the current system made the bankrupt's poverty into the direct cause
of his exclusion from political life. In coupling the issue with civic participation, the critique of debt collection and existing bankruptcy laws
found a new avenue of attack, shifting the debate to different terrain
and forcing more general ruminations on the meaning of citizenship
in the liberal state. The move from a conflict over everyday economics to a discussion on citizenship invested the demands of bankrupts
with new rhetorical weight. But it also increased chances for consensus
by overshadowing the contentious economic aspect of the issue, thus
opening space for novel solutions. In this sense, the conflicts over debt
enforcement had a politically moderating effect. An example of this can
be found in Johann Jakob Treichler's (1822–1906) work in the canton
of Zurich in the mid-1840s. Treichler was the editor of the newspaper
Noth- und Hülfsblatt from the canton's pauperized highlands, a region
of weavers and factory workers. When he held lectures on "socialism,"
rumors circulated that he was planning to convene a communist popular assembly.[140] In order to inhibit repressive measures, he published a
manifesto titled "Political Principles" in February 1846. Its first demand
was the "right to vote for citizens dependent on poor relief and for bankrupts who had not become bankrupt through illegal actions,"[141] a wish
undergirded by the argument that nobody should lose their civic rights
in perpetuity. Another part of the manifesto distanced the author and
his demands from calls for collectivization and revolt, pleading instead
that all men be allowed to participate in the affairs of the state. Thus,
far from being an "absolute other" to consensus-based, procedural state
politics, the bankrupt as a personification of crisis helped cultivate a
specific notion of the citizen-subject. This became apparent during the
founding of the Swiss Confederation in 1848. Though universal male suf-
frage was proclaimed for the new state's first elections, the right to vote
was in practice unequally distributed because it was made conditional
upon restrictive residency rules in the various cantons and municipalities. Even on the federal level, in the year 1854 almost 20 percent of adult
Swiss men were barred from casting a ballot.[142] The requirement that
citizens be "capable of honor" effectively made property ownership a
condition of participation in state political life. Bankrupts' campaigns
for the right to political participation countered this. In the city of Basel,
a self-organized association of bankrupts pleaded—unsuccessfully—to
be allowed, by way of exception, to take part in the vote on the ratifi-
cation of the federal constitution in September 1848: "The bankrupt's

heart beats just as warmly for the fatherland as the heart of the citizen in full possession of his rights."[143]

It's unsurprising that talk of economic misfortune became more frequent during periods of crisis. The collapse provoked a certain rhetoric, but at the same time, the rhetoric worked to make visible the contours of crisis. It identified a wide-reaching, exceptional situation independent of individual deeds or misdeeds. The fundamental assumption made by those who described a situation as one of crisis was that stability was the norm; thus they tended to draw a hard distinction between norm and crisis, and they declared the distinction to be systemic.[144] The diagnosis of crisis fused together objective circumstances, subjective action, and normative ideas. The claim that crises and their effects lie beyond individual influence and could thus lead people to suffer "misfortune through no fault of one's own" was reinforced by statistical information produced by state administrative bodies. The number of such official institutions increased between 1848 and the late 1860s. Their quantitative reports on economic fluctuations—such as improved statistics on bankruptcies— provided media that could be used for political ends.[145]

As early as 1848, petitioners supported their claims with published information. In that year, for instance, one petition referenced the "terrifyingly unceasingly increasing mass of bankruptcies of which today's official gazette, for example, already counts *fifty*."[146] It is consensus among historians that the Democratic Movement of the 1860s was initiated and held together by a novel use of media communications. The movement took advantage of newly available administrative record-keeping techniques to imbue debt with a more gripping visibility,[147] and, in turn, bankruptcy numbers played a key role in their campaign to revise Zurich's constitution. For one, the absolute number of bankruptcies had dramatically climbed. The economic crisis of the 1860s followed a boom period during which many farmers had taken on debt. In 1867, the statistics on bankruptcy compiled by the canton's high court began distinguishing between broadly conceived social groups. In his study on the social dynamics of the Democratic Movement, historian Martin Schaffner demonstrates that bankruptcy equally affected farmers, skilled laborers, and the group consisting of "factory workers, wage laborers, domestics, and journeymen." The last group represented, in 1868, 9.6 percent of all bankruptcies, considerably less than the farmers at 25.4 percent and skilled laborers at 26.2 percent, which was probably because unskilled laborers had too few assets to justify bankruptcy proceedings.[148] Schaffner's analysis helps explain the rise of a popular movement that brought together "all discontents."[149] What's more, bankruptcy statistics were at the time widely perceived as barometers of the canton's economic health.[150] Statistics, in short, put debt as a social fact in black and white and made them into a visible problem. Thus, in 1867, an opposition newspaper wrote that it would bring together the last eight statistical reports of the canton's high court into a "little picture" that

> will show if the canton's general social welfare is increasing or decreasing. As the content of the image we choose the annual bankruptcy numbers, and then only include the bankruptcies that were not voided, but were executed. If a high number of bankruptcies were a sign of fortune, then the canton's fortunes would have increased sixfold over the previous eight years; for the time being, though, we will assume that it is a sign of the opposite and see in these numbers a seriously unsettling tumor on the canton's body.[151]

From the selectively reproduced bankruptcy statistics, the newspaper deduced a judgment about the "canton's general social welfare." That the canton's welfare was in poor shape represented an irrefutable fact for the authors, "a seriously unsettling tumor on the canton's body" that necessitated political action. Positioning bankruptcy as a danger to social welfare helped reframe the heated debate over the legitimacy of debts. After all, social welfare could now be measured through techniques of statistical quantification, which endowed the economy with a degree of facticity that placed it beyond the influence of the missteps of individual bankrupts. Those sympathetic to the plight of bankrupt persons argued that if the economy constituted its own objective sphere with its own laws and forces, then personal moral failure could be ruled out as the cause of at least some bankruptcies. This claim, however, gave rise to a related question. Under which circumstances *could* insurmountable debts be seen as the fault of the debtor? Or, in other terms: When did the liberal citizen-subject bear responsibility?

The Shifting Objectivization of Morality

A petition filed shortly after the founding of the Swiss Confederation in 1848 evoked the recently achieved national unity in order to speak "in the name of a large number of economically unfortunate fellow citizens" who had been "thrown down into voicelessness." It bemoaned the fact that the relevant article of the constitution placed "all those affected into the same category": "the merchant gone bankrupt on account of mishaps, those who have suffered this fate because of revengefulness, even wickedness, or because of a bagatelle, those who have squandered large sums or have otherwise acted foolishly, costing their creditors many thousands of guldens."[152] The author explained that the causes of bankruptcy were many, and not all involved the fault of the debtor: creditors could make malicious claims intended to harm their debtors and morally upstanding merchants could be struck by misfortune. The petition concluded that the government should "wholly abolish civic death" and classify bankrupts according to their degree of personal fault, distinguishing between those who were at no fault, those who were legally incompetent, and those who were personally responsible. The petition illustrates that bankruptcy implied an intensive process of social classification, and further petitions implored the government to make adjustments to the logic of classification. Still, it is important to note the limited nature of these demands. None of the sources consulted here called for a general moratorium for insolvent debtors and none of them sought to do away with the classification of debtors altogether. Rather, all supported case-by-case relief for individuals who had suffered economic misfortune at no fault of their own. They framed their arguments in terms concordant with the system of bankruptcy and its alterations of debtors' legal and economic status. Their reformatory energy was simply dedicated to gaining more differentiated treatment.

Twenty years later, in the 1860s, representatives of the Democratic Movement again moved for revisions in how bankruptcies were classified. One petition delivered to the constitutional council urged that a new law be passed to make it easier for a "family man" who had fallen into bankruptcy due to "adversity and bad times" to regain his civic rights and rights of gender tutelage over his wife.[153] When a "thorough investigation and inventarization demonstrates" that a "businessman of lesser means be in such a situation (on account of misfortune)," then "such a family man" was surely more "desperate and miserable" than all others. In such cases, the petition argued, creditors should not have limitless claim to the assets of their debtors. The quantifiable "inventarization" provided substantial justification for giving relief to the rhetorically loaded "family man."

The concept of an independent economic system whose workings lie beyond the control of the individual increasingly featured as the key premise of arguments that some debtors fell upon misfortune through no fault of their own. In no way new was the notion that one could suffer economic misfortune through no fault of one's own; indeed, historians of economic life have found it in early modern sources.[154] In liberalism, however, it took on a new form. After debating the issue, the Zurich constitutional council decided to revoke the civic rights of bankrupts for a period of one to ten years, depending on their degree of personal fault; previously, only paying off one's debts in their entirety was enough to have one's civic rights reinstated.[155] But the lawmakers balanced out this mitigation by expanding the class of debtors who could lose their rights to include those whose bankruptcy had been annulled on account of their reaching an out-of-court settlement with their creditors. One commentator believed that the intention was to prevent people from having their slate wiped clean too easily. Some opined that the Democratic Movement that led to the new constitution of 1869 was standing up to the "system," as the powerful financial interests gathered around the "railway baron" Alfred Escher were called, and that the idea was to ensure that members of high society couldn't wriggle their way out of their liabilities through backroom deals.[156] The rule sought to establish a universal standard for how debtors were to shoulder the obligation of indebtedness. Judges were now responsible for determining the bankrupt's degree of fault. In their discussions on criteria of judgment, the constitutional council used keywords like "fraud," "foolishness," "carelessness," "licentiousness," and "idleness."[157] This was the moral language that also guided the decisions of the poor relief administration.[158] Thus, on the one hand, there was the production of statistics as objective facts about society,[159] and on the other, the case-by-case assessment of individual circumstances, causes, and reasons before a judge. Making it easier for bankrupts to have their rights restored, in sum, did not put an end to honor sanctions for economic shortcomings. Instead, it synthesized the facts of statistics and the principle of individual responsibility into an increasingly objectified form of moral evaluation.[160]

This last point fits well with some scholars' observation that toward the end of the nineteenth century, new categories and forms of objectifying the social and the welfare of society came into being.[161] Jacques Donzelot sees in the rise of the category of the "social" a transformation of political rationality.[162] The concept opened up a middle road that at once held high the sovereignty of the people as a key part of the social contract while at the same time dispelling revolution by officially acknowledging the existence of social inequalities. The category of the social prescribed reform, not revolution, offering a means to de-escalate conflicts through a *depoliticized* politics. Relatedly, François Ewald argues that the ascension of "risk" to the key term of insurance and its probabilistic procedures was the decisive moment in the genesis of welfare law.[163] In the emergent welfare state, insurance was the most striking medium of societalization. Christian Topalov interprets the development of the concept of the unemployed, the *chômeur*, as the product of a fight over classifications.[164] In the years after 1880, conflicts, methods, institutions, and projects were dedicated to addressing, in one way or another, unemployment as the converse of the by-then normalized form of work: wage labor. What these three authors have in common is a focus on the epistemic dimension of statistics, an issue that this chapter has sought to shine some light on. The statistics on debt enforcement and bankruptcy, however, showed marked differences to the aggregates, averages, and probabilities that Ewald and Donzelot discuss.

The petitions advocating for bankrupts' rights have to be situated in their proper historical context. While the invention of the social was rooted in the logic of shared risk and distributed responsibility, the notion of the bankrupt's blameless misfortune did not dispense with the moral imperative of identifying individual blame. Formulated with Ewald's words, the blameless bankrupt was entrapped in the "liberal diagram."[165] The called-for relief for debtors who had fallen into bankruptcy through no fault of their own was confined to an individual diagnosis that entailed evaluating the bankrupt's moral fortitude and giving them a chance to prove their innocence.[166] The concept of blameless misfortune and the progressive objectivization of the social in the late nineteenth century converged in the construct of an objective, factical system called the economy that stood outside the influence of the individual. Analogous to Topalov's findings in his study of liberal poor relief (with its category of the able-bodied poor), bankruptcy rules in Switzerland came to recognize a larger, more differentiated set of causes of bankruptcy that included some objective events like market downturns. Still, what remained decisive in the determination of blameworthiness were the individual combination of factors. The codified system of classification and the identification of causes served to facilitate a precise diagnosis of the singular case; the latter's assessment by a judge constituted the core of bankruptcy proceedings. Distinguishing objective causes from subjective missteps was part of a drama in which the tensions inherent in liberalism's conception of itself were played out. On the one hand, it acknowledged contingent events that took place in a secular, highly differentiated society, and on the other, it asserted individual responsibility as an irreducible truth.[167]

This closes the circle begun by theologian Johannes Tobler's "practical maxim": "Forgive us our debts as we forgive our debtors." Instead of a paternalistic creditor forgiving debts on a case-by-case basis, the liberal state installed judges to conduct a case-by-case evaluation of debtors' morality and finances. My point here is not to draw a direct line to the logic of shared risks in the fin-de-siècle period analyzed by Ewald and Donzelot. Indeed, in his discussion of how government and insurance administrations objectified particular social relations, Topalov notes that the recognition of particular causes as justified developed asynchronically from one authority to the next. Still, remarkable is the way in which an 1880 letter that petitioned the cantonal government of Lucerne to adopt a "classification of bankrupts" spoke not only of misfortune, but also of "contingencies." The petitioner wanted debtors to have the opportunity to "prove that they have really become insolvent on account of misfortunes and relations that are no fault of their own. The current legislation does not yet consider such contingencies. . . . The classification of bankrupts [would] shield from total dishonor, immorality, depravation, and squalor those who have become bankrupt or insolvent because of misfortunes that are no fault of their own."[168] Bankrupt people appealed to the government to grant them the right to demonstrate through evidence that they had behaved in a normal, economically sound, morally irreproachable manner. This was not the political rationality of an insurance system working with aggregates. Rather, bankrupts and their advocates themselves both conceived of the actions of the individual as the foundation of a reasonable attribution of culpability. But the other irreducible element put forward by petitions that demanded the government classify different types of bankrupts was the existence of an objective, factical system called the economy. This particular bridging of the individual and the general opened up a new field in the conflict over debts, paving the way for the distinction discussed in chapter 1 between seizure of assets as collateral and bankruptcy that was ultimately codified in the 1889 Federal Statute on Debt Enforcement and Bankruptcy. The process that resulted in this distinction was not determined in advance, however. The history of debt enforcement followed a broad pattern in which local demands combined early modern customs with principles of liberal governance to give birth to new procedures.

THREE | Theoretical Interlude

The Anthropology of Debt

A "Paradox of Society"

Debt has posed a conundrum for social theory since its very beginnings. In 1887, Ferdinand Tönnies called the financial instrument known as the "obligation" a "paradox of society."[1] In *Community and Civil Society*, the foundational text of German sociology, Tönnies distinguished between two forms of social existence. He defined "Gemeinschaft," or "community," as an irreducible bond that joins individual members into a unit, giving as examples the family, home, and village. "Gesellschaft," or "society," was something entirely different: a relationship between individuals that is constantly being reproduced. If "community" is an organism, then "society" is an artifact. Tönnies concluded that the circulation of money and the exchange of commodities were the constitutive practices of "society," whose members only interact through one-off contracts. The "obligation," in his eyes, concentrated in itself the totality of the relations found in the trade of commodities, and it transformed the intersection of two individuals' needs and desires from a momentary encounter into an enduring relationship. The enduring nature of the credit obligation constituted "something that transcends Gesellschaft." In the obligation, "a lasting 'bond' is created, in contradiction to the very conception of Gesellschaft—a 'bond' which unites not objects but persons."[2] This meant a "paradox" in Tönnies's theory of "society," flipping it on its head: dependency instead of unfettered exchange, bonds between persons and persons instead of between persons and things, a transaction determined by legal regulations and not by the free flow of money.

My point is not to wholeheartedly affirm Tönnies's theory, but simply to offer it as an illustration of a broader historical trend, an expression of the increased focus on relations of economic exchange in the 1880s that was touched upon at the end of chapter 1. At the same time as Tönnies was developing his distinction between community and society, the view that "the economy" constituted an objectively existing complex guided by its own laws was becoming widely accepted. As explained at the end of chapter 2, bankrupt debtors, too, increasingly referred to the economy as an objective fact. In order to tie together some of the arguments developed thus far, the current chapter draws on some theories from cultural anthropology. The survey begins with Marcel Mauss's *The Gift*, published in 1923/24, nearly four decades after Tönnies's book. After a selective reading of Mauss's essay, I then proceed to the concept of the "moral economy," concluding with some remarks on how these theories inform the empirical analysis in the rest of this book. Theory gives orientation to the historical narrative and offers tools for untangling the "paradox of society" that Tönnies observed in the debt relation. This intermediary chapter thus serves as a transition to the last three chapters, which tackle problems of subjectification, classification, and person-thing relations in the world of debt.

The Gift and Its Effects

Marcel Mauss's text on the gift provides a theoretical apparatus for conceiving of debts as a social relation. My reading couples Mauss's ideas with Karl Marx's assertion quoted in the introduction that debts constitute a relation in which "man's *moral* existence, man's *social* existence" are at stake.[3] Mauss's text is profoundly paradoxical, his argument at once complex and simple. He took rituals from Oceanic, Northwest American and medieval Icelandic societies and epics and legal tomes from ancient India and republican Rome as evidence of a generalizable pattern. Giving, receiving, and the obligation to give back constitute a chain of transactions that Mauss called the "system of total services" or "*total* social facts,"[4] because they fused legal, moral, religious, economic, familial, and aesthetic relations. The norm of giving, accepting a gift, and giving a gift in return that Mauss repeatedly found in otherwise divergent contexts led him to conclude that these activities composed the bedrock of social relations as such. The gift in Mauss's theory is a fundamentally relational instrument of power and obligation. The aspect of obligation, in turn, made the gift economy into a debt economy. From his perspective, the principle maintained its validity in rituals of generosity and in feuds, in Western social insurance systems and in Polynesian swaps.

Mauss's *The Gift* is open to at least two interpretations. The first places primary weight on reciprocity (a word that, for its part, does not feature in Mauss's own vocabulary).[5] On this reading, gifting and gifting in return form a symmetrical pattern, a systematic unity with no remainder. Claude Lévi-Strauss thought that the triad of giving, receiving, and giving in return constituted a structure that transcended and enveloped each of the three constitutive acts, explaining that the various modes of the transfer of gifts and the endless diversity of objects exchanged are "reducible to more fundamental forms."[6] Mauss, in the structuralist's take, perceived a "*constant relation*" between phenomena, a web of functions that precede individual attributions of meaning and empirical forms and actions.[7] Lévi-Strauss's reading thereby positioned Mauss as a progenitor of his own project of structural anthropology and extrapolated from the three-step gift exchange a universal grammar of the social as such. Born out of this reading is the notion that a society reproduces its unity through the unity of its practices, the triad of giving, receiving, and giving in return that is always already one. The use of this heuristic allowed Lévi-Strauss to enter into dialogue with historians who shared his interest in repetition.[8] Historian Gilles Postel-Vinay, for instance, applied the anthropologist's theory to the widespread practices of saving, borrowing, and spending savings that defined, throughout the life cycle, the relations between creditor and debtor in rural systems of lending.[9] Lévi-Strauss's position was supported by Émile Benveniste's writings on linguistics, which described how in varying families of languages, words like "borrow," "loan," and "lend" always come in pairs and trace their roots back to a different, superordinate semantic register, namely that of favor and obligation. Thus, in the end, these words belong to the dictionary of power.[10] "Lending and borrowing are two aspects of the same transaction as the advance and repayment of a given sum, without interest," and are "organically linked by their polarity."[11] German linguists of the nineteenth century also discerned the parallel between the words "*borgen*" and "*leihen*." Grimm's *Deutsches Wörterbuch* explicated that "our *borgen* denotes the mutual relation of obligation between creditor and debtor . . . and *borgen*, like *leihen*, expresses *mutuum sumere, accipere* as well as *mutuum dare*,"[12] continuing that the context determined which one of the two meanings was intended. For his part, Mauss too thought that things, people, and actions in the economy were "homonyms and synonyms," concluding that "all in all, it is one and the same."[13] Thus these perspectives, too, treat the exchange of gifts as a unified, general structure.

The constant confusion between people, things, and actions in exchange relations forms the focal point of the second line of interpretation, which focuses less on the "one and the same" aspect. This reading is made plausible by the French armchair anthropologist's own elevation of reading to the status of a research method.[14] Mauss's translations were more like paraphrases: sometimes he condenses a source into a quote that makes his point more effectively, sometimes he adds a line from a magic spell, sometimes he complains about the translation of a passage from the *Edda*, refusing to allow his inability to understand Old Norse to get in the way.[15] While his desire to squeeze his countless, multifaceted sources into a theoretical schema led Mauss to shut out other potentially viable interpretations, he tirelessly endeavored to integrate and elucidate new, divergent sources.[16] "Ceaselessly shifting" is a description that applies well not only to his approach, however, but also to his object itself.

First, the gift obscures the boundary between people and things; it "represents an intermingling," animating things and objectifying people.[17] The recipient is obligated by the gift and thereby forced into a particular position. To explain the automobility of things, Mauss pointed to the Maori word "*hau*," which signifies the power that inheres in a valuable (material or immaterial) thing or "*taonga*." (Lévi-Strauss reproached the master for succumbing to "a mystification" by adopting an indigenous theory, a contamination clearly unconscionable for the author of *The Savage Mind*.)[18] Second, and related, Mauss treated things themselves as compounds made out of all kinds of heterogeneous relations.[19] Not only do gifts forge a bond. The thing transacted itself embodies a relationship: "The thing itself, given and committed in the pledge, is a bond by virtue of its own power."[20] A residue of the person rubbed off on the "token," and in pledging an object, the recipient of the gift also pledged their honor. Thus, Mauss observed that rather than coagulating into a structure, the divisions between gift and return gift, person and other, were unstable. From this perspective, *the gift* is always already poisoned and *le don* is blended with the "dose, dose of poison."[21]

Mauss's remarks on the ambivalent nature of things underscore the importance of contexts and procedures. Although Mauss tended to see "homonyms and synonyms" everywhere he looked, his richly sourced book bears witness to the diversity of expressions and practices associated with the gift. The differing values of words were not lost on inquisitive minds of the nineteenth century either. Although the Grimm brothers noted the parallel between the verbs "*borgen*" and "*leihen*," they also qualified that:

> In New High German, the word *leihen* dominates, but in such a way that between the two words [*borgen* and *leihen*—MS] there is a difference. *Borgen* only concerns movable things, not immovable things; one says "*ein gut leihen*" [to loan out a property] . . . to *leihen* a house, a field, not *borgen;* in contrast, to *leihen* money, clothes, a horse is the same as to *borgen* it. But *borgen* also has the additional connotation of something that has remained unpaid or nonpayment, while *leihen* connotes reimbursement; thus, *leihen, entleihen, lehnen* are nobler than *borgen*.[22]

As a general term, "*leihen*" could denote immovable and movable things, while the more specific "*borgen*" could only denote movable things. And because "*borgen*" evoked the notion of unpaid accounts, the Grimms ranked it lower. Thus, the pair movability/immovability is inscribed into each of the distinct terms and the evaluations attest to cultural mores.

Analyzing the entanglements of persons and things requires sensitivity toward contexts and configurations. In her book *The Gender of the Gift*, Marilyn Strathern draws on her fieldwork in the highlands of Papua New Guinea to demonstrate how categorizations such as "woman," "man," and "thing" only appear in particular situations, noting that the same is true of the attribution of gender to things, persons, and body parts.[23] Thus for the inhabitants of Mount Hagen, just as the body is a record of mutual relations, so too does a thing only become a thing through interaction; otherwise, it lacks substance. Piecing together the contexts in which persons and things interact and take on specific qualities can also aid in our understanding of legal procedures that turn assets into collateral and set out the terms of a debtor's liability, like those analyzed in chapter 6 of this book. According to Strathern's research, the object of the gift exchange is only constituted in the relation between donor and donee.[24] Debt is formed not by ownership or its absence. Instead, the two parties' perspectives on the object mold it into a thing with specific qualities that can be exchanged.[25] Donors force upon donees the gift as an obligation of debt, which makes the donor superior because they have alienated a part of themselves.[26] The superiority of the creditor or donor, in turn, leaves the recipient with a lack: the gift tears a hole

when it arrives. It is a manifestation of a negative balance. From this perspective, debt appears not as a derivative phenomenon, but as something
with its own positivity; debt brings forth an asymmetrical, nonreciprocal
relation that remains unstable throughout its duration. This reading of
The Gift and its implications can be summed up in three points. First,
the gift animates things and reifies people. Second, this process is registered by those involved, occasioning value judgments. Third, the transaction itself charges the objects of gift exchange with tension, because
it attaches their status to operations that function in binaries like alien-
able/inalienable, movable/immovable.

Mauss exerted considerable energy in framing the relation created
by the gift as an elementary constituent of sociality. If one interprets the
gift not as something that can be isolated in pure, a priori form, but as a
phenomenon always bound up with specific contexts and practices, then
the analytic distinction between premodern reciprocity and the utili-
tarianism of modern industrial capitalism loses its rigidity.[27] Historians
and anthropologists have demonstrated the significance of gift giving in
early modern Europe just as much as in capitalist economies.[28] Others
have established that with colonial conquest and capitalist relations, the
exchange of gifts did not decrease, but increased.[29] European practices
of consumer credit in the nineteenth century have also been placed on
a continuum between gift exchange and commodity exchange.[30] Gift
giving has not been left behind as a vestige of the past, but has instead
transformed over time. In an influential article, Jonathan Parry argues
that only in societies that conceive of "society" and "economy" as two
separate spheres can there develop an ideology of the pure gift.[31] In
expanding markets, too, gift giving has more than a supporting role
to play, as studies on philanthropic organizations in neoliberalism and
their moralization of the social have shown.[32] In short, the deep symbolic
significance of economic transactions does not disappear in capitalism.

The purpose of my selective reading of *The Gift* and of those influenced by Mauss's text has not been to claim that gift giving is a transhis-
torical structure. Quite the opposite, the gift offers historians a heuristic
fiction for conceiving of debt as a complex, multifaceted relation.[33] This
heuristic fiction reveals some similarities between Mauss, the scholar
of exchange in archaic societies, and Karl Marx, the "source from the
field" of liberal capitalism. Commodity and gift are not the same (and
are often viewed as mutually opposing fictions), and a history of debt
would be best advised to refrain from hastily jumping into the history of
the theory of the commodity.[34]

But two basic assumptions picked up in the above reading of Mauss can also be found in Marx, if in a different context, namely that of capitalism, the world market, the division of labor in the factory regime, and the development of social practices that themselves are rooted in abstractions. The first is the assumption that there is a generalized structure that encapsulates and regulates individual relations of exchange without itself having any inherent meaning. From this perspective, people's actions are not reducible to their significance or utility in intersubjective relations; instead, they are determined by an individual's position in a structure. Consequently, the structure is only perceptible in its effects; it is not a force that influences relations "from the outside."[35] The second common assumption is that the symmetrical relation of exchange brings together radically incommensurable elements and thus contains a fundamental asymmetry.[36] According to one particular reading of Marx, this is the domination of labor as an abstract category over the actual labor of the living worker, the rule of the dead labor of capital over living labor. It is this asymmetry that makes social relations appear as things to those involved in them.[37] The confusion and conflict that results out of the reification of people and the personalization of things are problems inscribed into the social relation of capital. A particular history of systemic regulation—the aim of the present study—should seek to connect both suppositions: that concerning the relation between a structure and its individual articulations and that concerning situatedness in context, confusion, and conflict.

Moral Economy and the Logic of Confrontation

Focusing on conflict brings into sharper contrast the ways in which historical actors conceived of the problem of debt. Marcel Mauss's theory of debt as a complex relation can help us tease out the various values wrapped up in debts. Anthropologist Janet Roitman inquired into "how debt can be a mode of either affirming or denying sociability" in her project of parsing the types of value judgments made about debt in central Africa.[38] In a related analysis of value judgments about debt, sociologist Ute Tellmann employed the concept of the moral economy, a notion that is currently experiencing a renaissance in multiple disciplines.[39] Tellmann is interested in how heterogeneous categories of evaluation and measurement are intermixed when people assess debts and their meaning in various contexts. The "moral economy" is a highly suggestive notion that aims to provide a novel perspective on the economy.

Moreover, "moral economy" is one of the few concepts coined by a historian that have found resonance in other disciplines.[40] For our purposes, it can help us better grasp what was at stake in the complex forms of legitimation involved in struggles over debt.

In his 1971 essay on the "moral economy of the poor," E. P. Thompson argued against reducing the food riots of eighteenth-century England to "rebellions of the belly."[41] Instead, Thompson sought to demonstrate that the riots had been triggered by what the rural poor deemed violations of nuanced conceptions of justice and legitimacy. In a society only partially structured by the antagonism between wage labor and capital (in Thompson's words, urban industry was characterized by a "cash-nexus," the countryside by the "bread-nexus"), the food riot appeared as a "total social fact."[42] The protesting poor legitimized their actions in various ways. They selectively championed the cultural meanings of bread, related notions of taste and health, and traditional repertoires of the politics of provision. In the interplay of confrontation and consensus, which enacted norms and duties in complex relations between social classes, two factors are of particular interest: the dimension of conflict and the performativity involved. The moral economy of the poor cannot be boiled down to appeals to paternalism. Rather, the dynamic process of making claims set in motion its own particular logic, proving the more general point that the "moral assumptions of another social configuration" expressed in movements like the food riots are historically specific.[43] For this reason, many have read into Thompson's text (sometimes with the intention of writing it off) a romanticization of a lost world of morally "embedded" economic relations.[44] One need not share this take to ask whether the concept of the moral economy belongs to a specifically early modern normative universe. In a later article, Thompson clarified that he had not written about an economy decoupled from markets, but had simply sought to capture the effects of the collision between popular expectations and ideas and the concrete conditions of food markets.[45] Indeed, it is more fruitful to study how such moments of confrontation blossomed their own logic rather than to pit predefined notions like "moral" and "political" economy against one another. Applying Thompson's concept to wage-labor struggles in the *Vormärz* period, Ahlrich Meyer identifies the moment when the underclass's rhetoric latched onto old-standing rights as a moment when capitalist accumulation and valorization were undergoing a shift, a juncture that transformed calls for a right to subsistence into revolutionary demands.[46] It is an example of the "unevenness" in capitalist development, when received practices and traditions undergo abrupt updates. Unexpected, unpredictable acts can burst forth out of such confrontations, but they need not be spectacular like riots. Accordingly, the concept of the moral economy has been expanded to apply to everyday practices of resistance and to signify notions of what is just or appropriate in particular material contexts.[47] In his survey of the history of the concept since the publication of Thompson's 1971 article, anthropologist Didier Fassin argued that "moral economy" should be used to study the conflicts (*"les enjeux et les conflits"*) between various systems of affects, values, norms, and duties.[48] He reasoned that the concept could be extracted from its original source in early modern underclass agitation and be used to shine light on the various moral economies of particular societies, without, however, losing sight of political conflict. A critical anthropology of moral claims can thus analyze historically specific qualitative values that assess "what is good" and classificatory norms that assess "what is appropriate" in a given system of social rights and duties.[49] The idea is not to attribute moral worth to one's own research, nor is it to treat morals as the fundamental guiding principle of historical actors. The point is to describe the conflicts in which the divergent moral vocabularies of different groups clash.[50] This take on the concept of moral economy supplies historians with a tool capable of picking apart the epistemic aspects of historical conflicts, the shared or opposing epistemologies of groups, and the collectively held values that endow these epistemologies with force.[51] The following chapters emphasize the significance of material conflicts, an issue that sometimes falls to the wayside with more metaphorical uses of the term "economy." I am less interested in models that solely highlight the strife between moral views.[52] Moral economy as a heuristic concept brings the economy into the discussion by identifying opposing views on the system of material provisions and these views' expression in moments of increased social tension.

Subjectification, Classification, Persons, and Things

This book dissects the meanings attributed to debt in nineteenth-century Switzerland by undertaking a historical analysis of the particular systemic rules that framed them. Debt enforcement brought together multiple, often contradictory practices and ideas. The discordant social positions that were articulated in debates over debt elucidated thus far include the legal category of the merchant that was codified in the 1889 Federal Statute on Debt Enforcement and Bankruptcy; the multifarious personal statuses and types of bankruptcy proceedings in the period before the federal law, when moralists promoted the maxim "forgive us our debts as we forgive our debtors"; the spatial reach of media techniques like announcing debtors' names in church; and jurists' arguments that bankrupts could not be considered civic dead because slavery did not exist in Switzerland.[53] This chapter's theoretical ruminations highlight three consistently present issues that unite the diversity of facts discussed thus far.

The first concerns subjectification. The concept of moral economy was originally developed to describe collective action.[54] Debts, however, affected individuals, displacing them from the space of collective exchange.[55] Studying debt as a moral economy thus does not imply treating it as a homogeneous form of subjectification; rather, the idea is to identify particular aspects of the demands and obligations that defined the debt relation.[56] The moral economy of debt constituted a repertoire of appeals and justifications; it hardly rose to a collective class struggle. Liberal governance subjectified debtors by judging their economic hardships as the effect of individual ineptitude. Recent ethnographic studies have shown how debts knot together diverse obligations and aspirations that cannot be translated into a single, uniform catalog of debtors' demands, complaints, and experiences.[57] Moreover, poor people's "economy of makeshifts" is not divorced from institutions, as the market incorporates and targets their needs, social networks, and cultural practices in various ways.[58] Debts have the power to bind, as Mauss's *The Gift* teaches. In situations both historical and contemporary, institutions have tempered this power into a mechanism for exerting control over labor power, opening up a spectrum of compulsory action that evades the simple duality of freedom and slavery.[59] Reflecting on the "fetish character of debt," Michael Taussig pointedly wrote: "in answer to the question, What makes a man a man?, the answer lying closest to hand is his debt."[60] Succinctly put, history tells us that indebtedness has not crystallized into homogeneous experience. Still, in each historical context, legal procedures subject debtors to generalized rules that create distinct legal statuses. Thus, in Switzerland, bankrupt persons petitioned judges and other officials to adapt a homogeneous scheme for assigning and defining this status, as detailed in chapter 2. They claimed that their fate had been caused by a higher-order economic system—above all its crises—and they drew on the liberal state's statistics as evidence. Thus there is a compelling case to be made for the hypothesis that debts had some uniform effects on debtors. And yet, as chapter 4 will demonstrate, on the level of individual subjects, the exercise of power did not lend itself to a general pattern.

The second point is classification. One reading of Mauss suggests that the gift positions people in a system, because the obligations it produces tie together all members of society, who, in giving in return, constantly reproduce the gift structure. The enforcement of debts, too, had a system. Bankruptcy proceedings were a matter of "making up people," as Ian Hacking described the invention of statistically derived entities in modernity. In the nineteenth century, state authorities expanded and refined in an unprecedented fashion their regimes of categorizing people and distributing them into definite positions.[61] Pigeonholing people in a classificatory system by labeling them a bankrupt or a merchant involved cutting them off from some relations and placing them into new ones.

Historians have analyzed in detail the conceptual apparatuses that made possible such acts of classification.[62] Their elementary categories and operations constituted particular forms of knowledge that can be studied with the methods of historical epistemology, which historian of knowledge Hans-Jörg Rheinberger defines as the study of "the conditions *under* which, and the means *with* which, things are made into objects of knowledge. It focuses thus on the process of generating scientific knowledge and the ways in which it is initiated and maintained."[63] Others like Ann Stoler have taken a more "worldly" approach to historical epistemology that goes beyond the formal theorization of historical forms of scientific knowledge.[64] The hemming in of the economic uncertainties bound up with insolvency can be understood as capitalist epistemic practices par excellence. Because debt enforcement connected various categories of social knowledge, the moral judgments applied during bankruptcy proceedings acquired epistemic meaning, as detailed in chapter 5.

The third point concerns the status of persons and things. While the gift reifies people and animates things, law does as much to structure this chiasmus as it does to confuse the borders separating the two, fabricating persons and things and making one stand in for the other.[65] Jailing debtors was a particularly striking method of metamorphosizing people into collateral, while the seizure of assets breathed life into objects. As will be discussed in chapter 6, both posed inextricable problems for the liberal imagination and its fundamental principles of freedom and property ownership. What's more, converting a thing into a collateral asset or a "token" that facilitates a transaction gives that thing itself an inconsistent status.[66] In this conversion, the movability and immovability of a thing and a person's ability to alienate it were negotiated. Pledged assets condensed an entire social relation into an object, while at the same time transmuting an object into a social relation. A pledged object is not necessarily a commodity, but commodities are, like collateral, always things. In the special commodity called the "obligation," Ferdinand Tönnies observed a force that also characterized the collateral asset. This force was a "'bond' which unites not objects but persons," a bond that Tönnies thought constituted a "paradox of society." The following chapter takes up some of the written narratives about the obligation of debt in nineteenth-century Switzerland and the often overwhelming experiences to which they bore witness.

FOUR | Debt and Subjectification in Narrative

Narratives are intrinsically linked to subjectification through debts. The common features of narrative and debt are clear: like narrative, loans and debts open up their own temporal horizon; like a tragic plot, enforcement is an aftershock of failure; like all literature, debts are tied to systems of writing. More noteworthy, perhaps, are the game-changing effects imagination exerts on the relation of forces that is debt. It suggests lines of flight and solutions, offers reassurance and orientation. Adding imagination to the mix of time and pressure sediments into a scene of subjectification. The aim of this chapter is to demonstrate the unpredictable paths that subjectification could take in the nineteenth century.

The connection between debt and acts of writing has long been an object of historical analysis.[1] Some studies focus on the habituation of practices that fell in line with dominant ideas about economic rationality, thereby framing subjectification as a translation of normative discourses into action. Others focus on technologies of the self and training.[2] This chapter charts a different tack. It does not dispute the dominance of certain conventions dictating debt relations. Instead it delves further into the problem articulated in the previous chapter: identifying debts with persons and assessing the meaning of those debts were often unclear and contested processes. My understanding of subjectification homes in on unpredictable circumstances, the intermittent shocks of power's prod, and individuals' reactions to it. I am less interested in the formation of coherent identities, because debt enforcement, time and again, educed moments of disidentification. Subjectification takes place in the gap between the rule-guided procedure of assigning a particular status to a person and the unforeseeable, heretofore unexperienced consequences that this status effectuates in their everyday lives.

This chapter analyzes three examples: the diaries of popular author and one-time cottage weaver Jakob Stutz (1801–1877), the stories of Gottfried Keller (1819–1890), and the political theory of communist Wilhelm Weitling (1808–1871). Statistical representativeness is not the purpose here, but neither are the examples arbitrarily selected. They are exemplary in the sense that they give expression to a particular formation of subjectivity generated by a constellation of factors specific to mid-nineteenth-century society in and around Zurich. To repeat: the chapter aims not for representativeness, but at tracing something singular, not in the sense of being spectacular or unheard of, but in the sense of being shaped by a specific constellation.[3] Thus the chapter's approach follows the impulse—if not exactly the methods—of microhistory by working with the principle that "Any document, even the most anomalous, can be inserted into a series. In addition, it can, if properly analyzed, shed light on still-broader documentary series."[4]

The development of new forms of lending and credit in the nineteenth century went hand-in-hand with new forms of writing about the economy. Economic journalism, romantic literature, the banknote: the appearance of these new, specialized genres helped people accustom themselves to a new type of market-centered value.[5] Another rich example are didactic tales like those found in the "physiologies." At the same time as urban social reporting was becoming established as a genre—and rural "children of the people" like Jakob Stutz were showing a bourgeois audience its "other"—the "physiology" genre satirized the archetypes of the new economy.[6] In his 1842 *Physiologie du créancier et du débiteur*, Parisian writer Maurice Alhoy presented a panoramic view of the people and places of the modern metropolis and its economic relations, complete with dodgy debtors, unscrupulous creditors, and a veritable underground industry of debt collection that turned the debt collector into a full-fledged dandy.[7] This didactic urban satire investigated the tactics and habits of streetwise economic subjects. The rural stories of Jeremias Gotthelf (1797–1854) were composed with a similarly didactic impulse. In his 1846 *Der Geltstag oder die Wirthschaft nach der neuen Mode* (The day of reckoning, or the new style of economics), he made an innkeeper and his wife the target of moral condemnation not only because inns were generally perceived as the hangouts of a potentially uproarious crowd, but also because the economy of innkeeping was tightly bound up in arrangements of lending and debt, both with suppliers and with customers.[8] The antimodern Gotthelf encapsulated his judgment about the state of rurality in a story about bankruptcy.[9] The short stories *Avons-*

nous payés nos dettes?, written in Lausanne, shine yet another light on the everyday economy of lending and borrowing. In one story, a couple—a laborer and a seamstress—go broke because the seamstress's customers fail to pay on time. Elegant madams could afford to leave open debts with the socially inferior tailor, while an impoverished neighbor has to hide her children's clothes from the bailiff come to seize everything she's got. A young middle-class couple has to learn how to manage money and cut back on the extravagant *dîners*. Paying one's debts on time, the collection allegorized again and again, was made possible by the virtue of budgeting. Such writings nudged their readers to adopt a gendered mode of self-conduct. After mid-century, these types of advice writing expanded into children's literature.[10]

Diaries are another important source for studying relations of debt. Scholars of early modern writing have concluded that the era made little distinction between personal diaries and accounting and that economic transactions were often described in detail as social events.[11] After the early modern period, however, diary writing underwent a shift. Around 1800, at the same time as more stable networks of lending and credit were being institutionalized, the concept of an autonomous self came to permeate all disciplines. This self's private writings served to confirm her identity and set her apart from the external world of society.[12] In liberalism, the self stood in contradistinction to society. While liberalism placed less weight on status and reputation than did the old order, the debtor's character gained in significance in contemporaries' imaginations.[13] In this sense, liberalism was obsessed with introspection, which found articulation in the self-observations jotted down in diaries. Research on ego-documents have interpreted this notion of the intimate self not as an authentic expression of the person's "inner essence," but as a historically specific conception of what it meant to be a person, which was trained through practices of writing.[14]

Autobiographical texts about bankruptcy and debt provide yet another source that offers insight into how people became entangled in webs of obligation. Recollections in hindsight often framed bankruptcy as a key turning point in the "biographical illusion."[15] One example is the autobiography of Zurich banker Gustav Anton Schulthess von Rechberg (1815–1891). In 1883, he wrote a manuscript for his children in which the 1865 collapse of his bank occupied a central place.[16] A Protestant in the Pietist tradition, Schulthess used the language of religion to justify his economic failures. On the one hand, the bankruptcy—made public, but then reversed five months later and settled with an agreement to pay 30 percent—appeared to him as a test of faith.[17] On the other, Schulthess juxtaposed his Christian virtues with the principles of the business world. He described his economic ruin as an effect of his unwillingness to engage in ruthless business practices and his time-consuming volunteer engagement. In a kind of inversion of Bernard Mandeville's dictum in *The Fable of the Bees*, according to which private vices can produce public benefits, Schulthess's text deduced the public malady of bankruptcy from his overflowing private virtues.[18]

In the nineteenth century, writing about debts meant actively translating a social relation into the language of personal experience. In relations between creditors and debtors, prospects of receiving payment were estimated, expectations formulated, reactions anticipated, a series of actions undertaken by both parties. After all, creditors, too, were bound by rules. The next section deals with the situation of a creditor caught in the murky zone between solidarity and blackmail.

A Creditor under Pressure

By the time Jakob Stutz's niece implored him to help her pay her debts in March 1852, the relatives' monetary relations with one another were already a complicated matter.[19] With no less insistence did Stutz reproach his nephew and brother-in-law, as his diary testifies:

> This morning, during the most intense storms, Annalise came to us from Matt and asked if I would lend them 50 gulden so they could settle with their creditors—she said her sister Barb in Fehraltdorf and my sister Anna, too, each promised 25 gulden for this purpose so that she could get out of compulsory debt collection [*Rechtstrieb*] and retain her dowry of 400 gulden. I certified to her in writing the sum I would pay out. What else was I supposed to do? And yet I hardly know where I can get this sum. What pains me the most is that I can be certain that all this money is thrown to the wind, that my nephew and the others will not change their deleterious habits in conducting their household affairs, and besides that, they have debts of more than 300 gulden in interest and everyday expenses—without the money owed to me about 200 gulden.[20]

Stutz's niece, Annalise Lattmann, exploited her familial relations to reach an "*accordement*," a settlement with her creditors. She seemingly intended to recover her dowry, which she had pledged, presumably to cover a debt of her husband. Whatever the events leading up to her asking Stutz for help may have been, the point was to "get out of compulsory debt collection." The sum she requested was considerable: fifty gulden converted to 116.65 francs after the introduction of the franc as Switzerland's currency, which took place that year. For comparison: fourteen francs were the weekly earnings of a family of six cottage silk weavers in the Zurich highlands, who, in the eyes of the poor relief administration, were "not to be considered poor," but whose children were still too young to work. The weekly earnings of two parents who weaved white cotton cloth amounted to seven francs.[21] Jakob Stutz did not have much money, but he was single. If one breaks down his earnings for the year 1853, his weekly income came to about 9.41 francs, a little higher than that of a worker in a spinning mill.[22]

Jakob Stutz's belief that he had no alternative but to give Annalise Lattmann support is expressed in the rhetorical question: "What else was I supposed to do?" Although he felt that he was obligated to help her, he was reluctant to do so, even deeming the act senseless, money "thrown to the wind." Transferring money to his relatives was at once a value judgment about their "deleterious habits in conducting their household affairs." In the end, Stutz exerted himself to calculate the precise sum of his nephew's outstanding debts. Whether he succeeded in this is unknown, but it's clear that he was committed to closely monitoring his relatives' financial situation. What was the context of these transactions in which the interpretation of others' behavior stood front and center?

Jakob Stutz, a former teacher, cottage weaver, and domestic servant, was a so-called "people's poet" who lived among the cottage workers of the Zurich highlands.[23] For a time a relatively famous author, he was, in contemporary parlance, homosexual. Before he moved to Sternenberg in 1842, the place where he grew up and where two of his sisters lived, he had lost positions in Zurich and Appenzell and was once arrested because of his sexuality. In 1856, he was sentenced again and banished from the canton. While in Sternenberg, Stutz lived a modest life on the margins, but he was not isolated from the village community. A few young people who aspired to get an education grouped around him there. The most famous among them was certainly the popular author Jakob Senn (1824–1879), whose brother Heinrich Senn's (1827–1915) diaries from 1850 on have been preserved.[24] Stutz's own diary, whose entries from 1846 to 1856 were consulted for this analysis, bears witness to the pauperization of a place that experienced firsthand the collapse of the protoindustrial cotton textile trade.[25]

Located in the heavily industrialized Zurich highlands, Sternenberg had undergone a protoindustrial boom that tapered off after the gradual construction of factories in the 1840s. The economic crisis and the hunger crisis of the late 1840s put the final nail in the coffin, and Sternenberg started losing residents.[26] A mobile labor force moved on. A long-standing custom of preindustrial underclasses, this mobility clashed with the nineteenth century's rising factory landscape and the shift toward a more stationary population defined by its location within the nation-state, thus causing anxiety among the authorities.[27] A few of those who stayed looked for new kinds of work, like in silk and straw weaving,[28] while others moved closer to nearby factories.[29] Most took on debts in order to mitigate the one-two punch of rising consumer costs and falling prices of the products of their labor.

Headed by initiatives to teach people how to properly budget, a new body of knowledge about how to deal with money developed in the first decades of the nineteenth century.[30] Much of it drew on customary practices and ideals, but it was inserted into a new institutional framework. At the same time, the moralization of poverty secured its place in the discourse on money. As a leading figure of the Swiss savings bank movement put it in a writing on Zurich's highlands, pauperism was "mass poverty with an overwhelming tendency to immorality."[31]

Savings banks were a beloved project of bourgeois philanthropy. The institutes compelled people to conform to the expectations of the market economy, thus functioning as a decidedly liberal solution to social issues.[32] They were primarily used by godparents making gifts to newborn children and domestics saving bits at a time.[33] Children's savings accounts meshed well with liberal desires to instill in children a forward-looking mindset focused on self-interest. But more than anything, savings banks were a site of interclass contact.[34]

Stutz's program of popular education transplanted long-standing ideals of asceticism into new institutions. He founded a savings bank for children and a cooperative for savings, lending, and wholesale purchasing in a region whose everyday economy of lending and borrowing was characterized by deferred payments, divvied up assets, leasing, and pledging.[35] The "people's poet" Jakob Stutz garnered the interest of a bourgeois readership whose social, cultural, and political universe was opening up to the concept of "the people."[36] In his role as a mediator between classes, Stutz attracted recognition from bourgeois personalities and philanthropic associations, in turn gaining distinction in his village.[37] The educational associations and local financial institutions

organized by Stutz were sites where the middle class focused their energies on "the people." Stutz's struggle for recognition also had practical
effects on his own ability to lend and offer aid; after all, just like debtors,
creditors too had to submit to a particular set of norms.

In early 1846, Stutz founded "an association of men with the name
Schillingverein [Shilling association] that has an economic and an educational purpose."[38] Its members were obligated to deposit a shilling
once a week; after a year, the consumer cooperative was able to start
making purchases. The financial association had the additional benefit
of securing the author an audience, because the weekly meetings made
it possible "to connect a sort of reading circle with it so that these simple people can also get some spiritual nourishment," which, in practical terms, meant that Stutz "read something to them." Moreover, the
Schillingverein functioned as "a kind of lending bank, where one can
help one or the other out of a bind."[39]

Stutz also set up a charitable foundation, which served as the bedrock for his children's savings bank. In 1848, the foundation acquired
increased institutional validation: teachers, municipal councils, and
poor relief now collected donations for it; a pastor hired to restructure
the bankrupt municipality of Sternenberg joined as its director; and
the whole arrangement was incorporated into the district savings bank
and administered by the schools.[40] This "rite of institution," which took
place at a school and placed Stutz on the same footing as village digni-
taries, conferred upon the venture official blessings.[41] Stutz's financial
initiatives were intertwined with a search for symbolic power, and his
diary served to keep ledgers of both his social and economic capital, for
example, when, at year's end, Stutz tabulated how many letters he had
sent and received alongside a description of how thriftily he had lived
that year.[42]

Without conscious reflection, yet with systematic rigor, Stutz worked
to make himself an indispensable member of the village community. One
aspect of this was his effort to fashion himself as a model of frugality in
the household. His monthly paper *Ernste und heitere Bilder aus dem Leben
unseres Volkes* (Serious and cheerful scenes from the lives of our people)
published articles on the successes of the savings banks and didactic stories like "Auf welche Weise manch' reiche und arme Leute zur bösen
Zeit sich einschränken wollen" (The ways in which some people poor
and rich know to restrain themselves in bad times).[43] In the youth club
that Stutz founded, presentations were held with titles like "Was heißt
Armuth und wer ist arm?" (What is poverty and who is poor?).[44] Stutz

repeatedly preached the virtue of frugality and thereby distinguished himself in the village.[45]

Village society and familial relations enforced a system of expectations; their preferred forms of communication—rumors and chitchat—were decisive for the construction of reputations and records in the nineteenth century.[46] Rumors were a discourse in which many participants tested out varying versions of the truth. They produced apparent facts through social interaction: who reacted how to which rumors and who sought to justify themselves, offer new facts, or register a different perspective—all of these questions fed into what would ultimately become the official version of the events.[47]

In the sources researched here, slander, while generally remaining below the level of civil suits, exerted powerful effects.[48] Because reputations were negotiated in rumors and village chatter, the latter carried incredible weight for a person's credit, and because a person's reputation was decisive for their credit, any damage done to it could result in fatal social and financial isolation. Rumors affected not only debtors and their credit; they were unpredictable and could also stir up problems for creditors. The village rumor mill spat thorns in all directions, as Stutz had to learn the hard way.

"Of course they asked me first, because the good people always believe that I have plenty of money," Stutz wrote in March 1846 after a relative in Augsburg fell ill and asked him for money to travel, a favor Stutz granted only after considerable hesitation.[49] In the entry, Stutz recalled that two decades before, he had already lent them one hundred gulden, had hardly received half the interest payments, and then ultimately ended up reducing the debt. Now he was being asked to shell out another thirty gulden. If he demanded that the already outstanding debts be paid, the relative would "pay with curses and scolds."[50] His niece Annalise Lattmann's appeal for help discussed above was another complicated matter. Rumors accused him of treating her "coldheartedly." The accusation of coldheartedness seems to have gone so far that Stutz saw it necessary to explain his actions to a municipal bailiff. As it happened, however, the bailiff and the debtor—Stutz's nephew and godson Hans Jakob Lattmann—interpreted Stutz's explanation as demanding that the fifty gulden he had promised to Annalise Lattmann in writing be returned to him. Hans Jakob Lattmann and another relative immediately wrote to Stutz that he ought to keep his promise.[51] All in all, a misunderstanding, albeit one that led to further rumors and fueled the ongoing conflict.

Criminally convicted for his homosexuality, Stutz was particularly vulnerable to malicious rumors.[52] In 1852, Hans Jakob Lattmann black-mailed him, and after Stutz was convicted again in 1856, Stutz maintained that he had been extorted.[53] When he visited his sister in Wängi (canton of Thurgau) in spring 1853—among other reasons, in order to get away from defamatory talk against him—the reception was frosty, because relatives had spread a rumor that Stutz gave preference in his financial assistance to a favorite student while leaving his own family members out in the rain.[54] When he returned to Sternenberg, he reflected on the money owed to him and its implications for his social relations:

> I think that some unpleasant things will affect me and believe this because I had to file for debt collection proceedings against my cousin Lattmann for a sum that he owed to the Schillingverein in Matt. Now he will certainly thoroughly badmouth me, just like his in-law Furrer in Sternenbach, whom I was supposed to have lent 25 francs, which however I did not have, and even if I had been able to give it to him, I certainly never would have gotten it back, because he budgets in the most backwards manner.[55]

His function as an official in the cooperative he had founded exposed him to "unpleasant things," because when somebody owed money to the Schillingverein, he was the one who had to apply for the debt to be collected on. In doing so, however, he ran the risk of being slandered. Refusing to loan his relative Furrer money—same issue. He judged Furrer's household economics against his own standards about what constituted good budgeting in order to assess whether he would ever see his money again.[56]

Indeed, the normative concept of the household supplied the blueprint with which Stutz evaluated his surroundings. But the symbolic gratification he enjoyed by setting up small-scale financial associations like his "penny bank" had a flip side in that he was now repeatedly asked for "gifts." He who promoted thrift and asceticism could be accused of miserliness. Stutz, too, spread rumors about others. Deprecating statements and the refusal to lend money were attentively registered by those around him, and whoever fell out of his good graces was likely to be cut off by others too. Accordingly, Lattmann complained that he couldn't borrow from anyone because Stutz had "robbed him of his credit everywhere," as Stutz noted in the summer of 1853.[57] Thus reputation and rumor also governed practical interactions among relatives.

At their core, Stutz's conflicts stemmed from power relations in the family and village community. The transfer of property played a key role here. Hans Jakob Lattmann sought to push debt-burdened real estate back and forth between family members. The story stretched back two generations. In 1843, Hans Jakob's father went bankrupt. His wife, Stutz's sister Elisabetha, purchased the property with her 300 gulden dowry, allowing the family to remain on the property; in the act, however, she assumed responsibility for the property's roughly 2,400 gulden in debt. Of these debts, 600 gulden had been lent by Stutz himself in 1836.[58] Thus, beyond the fact of the bankruptcy, things remained as they had always been, and creditors stopped bothering the older Lattmann. This accorded well with local authorities' strategy of doing everything in their power to not divide up familial estates, lest family members become dependent on the public purse.[59] When Stutz's sister Elisabetha died in 1849, her son Hans Jakob inherited the estate and with it its debts. Stutz opined that Hans Jakob Lattmann would "hardly be able to escape bankruptcy."[60] After dispatching to Stutz's address a series of demands for help backed up with or-else threats, Lattmann auctioned off the indebted property in pieces, which allowed him to evade bankruptcy. Among the buyers was Stutz, who acquired a meadow.[61] A few days later, however, Lattmann repurchased a large portion of the estate.[62] What Stutz hadn't understood at the moment of the auction, as he later noted, was that by purchasing the meadow, he assumed legal responsibility for the entire property's debts. If Lattmann were to go bankrupt and the other buyers were not able to pay the outstanding interest, then Stutz would have to jump in and pay it himself.[63] The financial liability imposed on him by the situation angered Stutz all the more when Lattmann left town. Lattmann disappeared only for a week, first claiming that he was traveling as a salesman and then that he was going to Naples to be conscripted.[64] He managed to find somebody who wanted to buy the estate and returned to Switzerland.[65] By selling the property again, Lattmann escaped bankruptcy for a second time, and he and his family moved into a rental. But even after the move, he didn't cease demanding that Stutz give him financial assistance. On multiple occasions, he surprised Stutz by showing up at his door (in Stutz's estimation, inebriated), demanding money, and threatening him.[66]

Debts owed to friends and family could put considerable strain on relationships, and sudden, unforeseen events could throw them into disarray. In August 1856, as he sat in jail awaiting trial, Stutz too violated the conventional scripts governing relations between debtor and creditor by sending an ultimatum to his former pupil Jakob Senn demanding the immediate repayment of a loan. Even more, he demanded double the amount that Senn had borrowed from him a year previously: one hundred francs instead of fifty. Stutz commissioned a law clerk to pen the collection letter. In one fell swoop, he wrecked the trust that the brothers Jakob and Heinrich Senn had had in him. Jakob Senn perceived the excessive sum as an act of extortion, because if he took his erstwhile teacher to court, "the world" would learn of "his labyrinthine relation to Stutz," the jailed homosexual.[67] He rebuked Stutz in a reply (the letter has not been preserved). Shortly thereafter, the law clerk commissioned by Stutz wrote to Senn that the demand for payment had been made in error. In a letter Stutz wrote to Jakob Senn a few days later, he only mentioned the issue in passing, calling it a misunderstanding. But the Senns read the letter as the work of "a fraud."[68]

The episode is recounted in Heinrich Senn's diary, which describes it all with an exactitude that seems eager to justify taking it as a reliable source. He copied word-for-word Stutz's letters and the highly formal language of the two letters from the law clerk, and an "explanatory introduction" sought to lend the transcriptions an air of authenticity.[69] Entries from June 1855 also record the origins of the debt: Jakob Stutz had traveled from his home in Fischenthal to Sternenberg, where Stutz acquiesced to his request for fifty francs, a loan certified with a simple, signed, noncollateralized IOU. Heinrich Senn commented on the events: "Jakob [Senn] wanted to avoid borrowing money here in the area. It is not pleasant to always have one's creditor before one's eyes, especially when the creditor is not capable or worthy of trust and is not capable of being delicate, going easy, and maintaining confidentiality."[70] Thus, Jakob Senn wanted to borrow outside of his immediate social surroundings because he wanted his debt to be discreet following a general principle of avoiding everyday contact with one's creditor. Moreover, Heinrich drew up a complex set of qualities desirable in a creditor: discretion, understanding for the debtor's circumstances, and a willingness to not be all too strict with deadlines. Only by practically demonstrating these qualities would the lender Stutz prove himself "capable and worthy of trust."

Heinrich Senn described having a debt to somebody as both a close personal relation and as a relation of unequal power. He thought that a reasonable person would enter into a relation of dependency with a lender only after assessing how they would react to a late or missed payment, if they would be forgiving, and if they even had the resources necessary to do so. Even as the loan was made, Stutz had not entirely passed the test. In retrospect, Heinrich Senn described as "remarkable" something Stutz said to Jakob Senn, which Heinrich later wrote out in verbatim in dialect with underlines:

> "Yes, for sure, I'll give you the money, you all can give me interest on it like anybody else." [Ja fryli, eu gib ich scho Geld, ihr chönd mer jo s'Zeisli (d. Zins) devo ge wie en andere.]!! This statement made a bad impression on us then and later events have proven that Stutz had no better intentions for us than with "anybody else," despite the fact that he always prided himself on having made so many willing and unwilling sacrifices for relatives and friends and enemies.[71]

The Senns had expected to *not* be treated just like "anybody else," but with amity. At least in hindsight, the routine insistence on the regular, punctual payment of interest seemed like an affront after the creditor had himself erroneously demanded double the amount he was owed. The indiscriminately businesslike treatment seemed particularly unfitting for a lender like Stutz, who portrayed himself as a do-gooder. Jakob Senn (or rather his brother Heinrich, who reported on the events) employed a semantics of "trust" to articulate the essentials of his relationship with his handpicked creditor. By suddenly having a law clerk demand "repayment as soon as possible," Stutz violated the brothers' expectations.[72]

Thus, creditors, too, were observed and evaluated. As studies on debt and credit have demonstrated, rural borrowers cherished the anonymity of the city when they needed to borrow larger sums.[73] In the early modern period, borrowers took out smaller debts with multiple lenders in order to conceal the extent of their obligations.[74] In the nineteenth century, new financial institutions depersonalized debt in a new way, which suited the interests of both debtors and lenders: in the power relation between them, both parties sought to use connections to their advantage and at the same time avoid dependency.[75]

In conclusion, how can these episodically recounted financial relations of Stutz and the dependencies to which they gave birth "be inserted into a series"?[76] Debtors and creditors alike observed and were observed, a complex open to unanticipated contingencies. In the face-to-face relations narrated here, Stutz's debtors had some wiggle room that they generally exploited. Susceptible to blackmail on account of the criminalization of homosexuality, Stutz was a unique lender, but the norms that his relatives latched onto were widely accepted. Rap-a-tap-tapping on the hard-and-fast expectation of familial solidarity, Stutz's relatives took advantage of a central system of social obligation. On the other side, Stutz's use of the language of economic efficiency when lecturing his relatives can be interpreted as a strategy to transfer an irresolvable conflict onto a different terrain, the economic language functioning as a means of distancing oneself from intractable familial difficulties.[77] Thus, rather than adhering to a single, traditional script, those involved legitimated their actions in differing ways.[78] In keeping a diary, people attempted to conceptualize their financial relations as social relations. Heinrich Senn's entries on his brother's loan from Stutz served as a method to document a sequence of events, while Stutz's diary seems to have functioned for him as a means to disentangle himself from the demands of his relatives.

But every drama has its setting. The village, the self-conscious people's poet, and the crisis of early industry in Sternenberg all coalesced into a narrative that could not have taken place elsewhere. In the "strategies of binding and retraction" between debtors and creditors, the former sought to escape the latter's control; but at the same time, the latter also sought to unburden themselves.[79] The leverage debtors had against Stutz on account of his personal situation would not have existed if they had owed money to a new, modern financial institution. Still, the border between institutional lending and private loans was porous, with institutions often founding themselves on interpersonal relations. The tight-knit social relations of the village and its impenetrable power relations didn't necessarily pose a problem for institutions. Quite the opposite.[80] Stutz's engagement with savings banks is just one example of the interconnections between local personal relations and impersonal financial institutions. When Stutz was jailed in the summer of 1856, the symbolic capital accrued through his philanthropic engagement became a liability, as rumors began to circulate that he had illicitly made personal use of his foundations' charitable accounts. In a letter to Jakob Senn written from his cell, Stutz explained that he was compiling a list of his largest donors and benefactors in the hopes of proving his innocence, thus seeking to disprove with the evidence of memory the village rumor mill's mode of producing evidence.[81]

A Spectral Realm of Shadows: *Seldwyla* Revisited

When Pankraz the whiner, the protagonist of the eponymous novella, returns to Seldwyla and sits down to recount his fifteen years abroad, his listeners are made up of "a bunch of old bankrupts . . . so that Pankraz— whose neighbors gathered around him all belonged to this estate— saw himself surrounded by a whole troop of curious and comfortable bankrupts, like an ancient hero in the underworld surrounded by the approaching shadows."[82] Describing the "bankrupts" as specters caught in the limbo of the small-town economy, the first short story of Gottfried Keller's collection *Die Leute von Seldwyla* (1856, The people of Seldwyla) captured in narrative form the image of civic death discussed in chapter 2.[83] Fiction played an active role in translating the legal status of civic death into a lived social experience.[84] The writings of the officially con- secrated Swiss author—Gottfried Keller was already deemed a "national poet" during his lifetime and reverence for him has only increased since his death—have been read as compact articulations of elementary scripts of nineteenth-century bourgeois identity, of a class whose interest in new forms of enterprise was accompanied by anxieties about the potential for failure and bankruptcy intrinsic to the new risks.[85] Although the meta- phor of civic death originated in the early modern period, thus predat- ing the liberal concept of the self, fears of losing independence and sta- tus acquired a distinct force in liberalism.[86] At stake was the autonomy of the masculine bourgeois subject; a self who was *in charge* of his status, his autonomy was built on the foundation of property ownership and, conversely, was threatened by fragmentation through insolvency.[87] The uncertainties brought on by debt offered ample stuff for the literary imagination. As I aim to show, however, the palette of perspectives in Keller's bourgeois realism belies the notion that middle-class subjectivity fit into a single homogeneous mold and thus provides the historian with a compelling source for understanding contemporaneous feelings about and perceptions of debt and bankruptcy.

Not least of all, Keller's biography itself familiarized him with what it meant to be in debt. The history of the novella collection *Leute von Seldwyla* documents the precarious situation of a fledgling foreign author trying to make his way in Berlin's literary market.[88] Keller financed his life in Germany on a stipend. But it had long run dry when he tried, in 1855, to play the publisher of his debut novel *Der grüne Heinrich* (Green Henry), Eduard Vieweg, against competing publishers in the hopes of getting an advance for what he initially proposed to be one volume of short stories.[89] Keller first worked out a deal with another publisher, but he abruptly broke off negotiations when he received his advance not in cash, but in bills of exchange bound to strict conditions.[90] He canceled the contract and went back to Vieweg, which meant having to pay back the initial advance of 300 talers.[91] In a letter to a patron with whom he was also in the red, he wrote that he had been left with the choice of either "walking into the bills of exchange prison" or again putting off his patrons with promises instead of real progress. He added that Vieweg "lies like a Jew."[92] Yet in late 1855, as *Die Leute von Seldwyla* was at the presses, Keller proposed to Vieweg a second volume of stories in order to finance his trip back home, which he intended to write on the "basis of real events."[93] Using realistic narration as a bargaining chip in the negotiations failed to win over Vieweg. Keller's mother sent about 600 talers to her son, who, upon his return to Zurich, took out a loan for 1,200 Swiss francs, retracted his offer to Vieweg, and sought out other publishers for the planned second volume. In December 1856, he signed a contract, but it would be another eighteen years before this volume was finally put out by another publisher.[94]

Keller's haggling and his offer of realistic stories based on archival research should not be naïvely treated as interpretive master keys. Keller's realism was not documentary, but lived on reality effects, details that create a "referential illusion" that slides between the text and the world outside it.[95] Agreeing to be paid with risky papers, confidentially pleading to be allowed to make deferred payments, skipping town, and planning to cancel a contract in the hopes of winning concessions: all are practices that stitched together the narrative texts, the book market, and the experiences of the author's readership. From this perspective, the "circulation of social energy" created constellations inside and outside the literary text that were thematized in the stories of *Seldwyla* and rang familiar to its readers.[96]

Bankruptcy features most prominently in Keller's final novel, *Martin Salander* (1886). This section focuses on *Seldwyla*, but it concludes with a discussion of the novel, which offers a hindsight perspective on the mid-century issues that inspired *Seldwyla*. The first volume of the collection fuses—more jarringly than *Martin Salander*—language and finance.[97]

Published in a first volume with a foreword, the five novellas of *Die Leute von Seldwyla* from 1856 recount happenings from a fictive city "somewhere in Switzerland." They tell of a diverse cast of characters and events: the aforementioned adventurer Pankraz; a young couple, the son and daughter of two feuding farmers; a clever mother who raises her son in the absence of her bankrupt husband; three friends who seek the hand of the same woman; and, in a story labeled as a "fairytale," a cat who deflects an evil magic spell back at the man who cast it. Consistent throughout is the attention paid to the characters' interactions with the town's economic system.[98] Seldwyla is a world in which bills of exchange without material backing float freely. This modern system of signs referring to nothing but other signs contrasts with the town's layout: still surrounded by walls, provincial, dull, a place at once restless and monotonous in which, despite rapid change, everything stays the same. In the "Author's Preface," it is described as a place where the people "love a change of opinion, and even of principle," which is spurred on by the cyclical "scarcity of the coin."[99] The town's economic driving force is an "aristocracy of youth," who make "use of their profession solely to constitute an admirable contraction of debts."[100] Living on speculation creates a paradoxical situation in Seldwyla, whose "community is rich, while its citizens are poor . . . and properly speaking no one knows what they have lived on for the last few hundred years."[101] As soon as a member of the young elite grows older, he goes bankrupt and "remains hanging on in his native town as a weakling and one driven forth from the paradise of credit," or, like Pankraz, "he will enter foreign military service."[102] Banished from the paradise of credit and youth, the city's bankrupts are forced "to take to some kind of business." They "are the busiest folk imaginable" and the only ones in Seldwyla who do productive work.[103]

In Seldwyla, values economic and otherwise have no substance, but nobody desires that they should either. The constantly fluctuating model of governance brings the denizens to "the last stage of lassitude and ennui as regards public affairs." This feeling motivates them to toss together an administration of "old stagers of the 'rest and be thankful' type . . . who failed some thirty years ago, and since then have quietly reinstated themselves" and whose lone qualification consists in being employed by the church's poor relief.[104] The preface to the second volume from 1874 sketches an image of "prosier and more monosyllabic" commerce: "Instead of the bloated and bulky pocket-book of former days, with its I.O.U.'s and its bills of exchange for small amounts," the Seldwylers "now sport elegant little notebooks, in which they briefly jot down their orders in shares, bonds, cotton, or silk."[105] "And in place of the plebeian and jolly bankruptcies which were formerly in vogue, only highly respectable accommodations with eminent foreign creditors are in fashion now."[106]

The town's system of finance becomes more advanced and the language necessary to document debts is reduced to algebraic signs that abstract from the material behind them. While the circulation of signs in the debt business made the fiction possible—the novellas of 1856 are said to consist of "a few quaint odds and ends, curious quips and pranks, such as happen in between"—transactions of a second order—only "briefly jotted down"—threaten to make the narrative "prosier and more monosyllabic."[107]

Seldwyla tells the stories of debtors beyond the binary of bankruptcy and civic death. Insolvent people actively participate in the fictive town's economic life even though they could lose their property from one day to the next; they are elected to office even though their rights are returned to them not publicly, but in an unceremonious act. Each novella undermines the notion that economic rules follow clear and distinct principles. This fits well with the observation that mid-nineteenth-century fiction—and particularly the new genre of novels about merchants—undertook an "expansion of economic thought."[108] The homo economicus was driven not so much by greed as by the impulse to perceive everything through the lens of self-interest, converting it all into various types of currencies. The proliferation of currencies and values both literal and metaphorical posed problems for assessing the worth of things, and the capacity to distinguish between currencies and their differing registers of worth (or learning how to do so) was at the core of *Seldwyla*'s critique of knowledge.[109]

"The Three Decent Combmakers," more so than any of the other moral stories, begins with an explicitly moral maxim. It tells of three journeymen who only look out for their own self-interest, in matters both financial and romantic. Their issue, the first lines tell us, is that their "vacuous justice" sucks the marrow out of the principle "And forgive us our debts, as we also forgive our debtors!"[110] Their rectitude is "vacuous" "because they never contract any debts whatever and cannot stand the idea of debts," a stance that flips the meaning of the moral nearly identical to that championed by Johannes Tobler from an expression of the hope of salvation into a bit of small businessman's wisdom.[111] The three combmakers are goal-oriented, but joyless. They save and try to increase their earnings and profits by switching from the register of business dealings to the register of romantic pursuit. When the youngest of the three gets the idea to seek the hand of Züs Bünzlin, a laundress's daughter with an inheritance coming to her, the other two copy him. Züs Bünzlin stages a competition, because each of the three "is as worthy to win me as are the others."[112] *To be worthy to win her* requires knowledge about what constitutes worth in the first place. Sitting in the grass with her suitors, Züs puts their minds to the test. She commands that each imagine that three copies of her desire to wed each of the three men, "so that I in a manner of speaking would exist ninefold, and that they all were regarding you with love-lorn eyes, and were desiring to possess you with great strength of feeling."[113] The game is precisely calculated: She promptly chastises Dietrich when he pronounces that "I should indeed like to see you hover around here not only threefold but a hundredfold, and to have you look at me with love-lorn eyes and to offer me a thousand kisses!"[114] It would be advantageous to have her because "she possessed as her own undoubted property a mortgage of seven hundred florins":

> This valuable bit of paper she kept in a highly varnished trunk. There, too, she had the accumulated interest money, her baptismal certificate, her testimonial of confirmation, and a painted and gilt Easter egg; in addition to all this she preserved there half a dozen silver spoons, the Lord's Prayer printed in gold letters upon transparent glass, although she believed the material to be human skin, a cherry stone into which was carved the Passion of Christ, and a small box of ivory, lined with red satin, and in which were concealed a tiny mirror and a silver thimble.[115]

Instead of a sum of abstract numbers on paper, Züs Bünzlin's assets are things. She is not a capitalist, but a hoarder, of a particular sort, certainly. Her treasures are not objects of value that speak for themselves. Rather, many are pawned pledges that she obtained from erstwhile lovers and indebted customers.[116] In short, they are objectified expressions of personal relations.

But she, too, is incapable of distinguishing between different types of value, because her possessions are, as the lengthy enumeration exaggeratedly underscores, just a bunch of junk. Ultimately, finding a way out of the impasse experienced by Züs and her suitors requires understanding the differences between various regimes of worth. The imperative of forgiving debts thus reveals itself as the imperative to ensure the continuity of social relations by distinguishing them from other forms of value. The "vacuous justice" of the combmakers is precisely their incapacity to do so: they see in Züs, as in everything else, only money value, and she puts their lack of wit on full display.

In Seldwyla, productivity only enters the scene once bankruptcy has been filed and the men decamp. The protagonist of the story "Regel Amrain und ihr Jüngster" (Regel Amrain and her youngest son), Regula Amrain, holds onto her dowry when her husband, the owner of a rock quarry outside Seldwyla, goes bankrupt and skips town. She takes over the business and switches it to "real production instead of paper push-ing."[117] She raises her son in accordance with her own "lineage,"[118] which is to say, in a wholly non-Seldwylian style. Her influence leaves a lasting mark on her son's character: in one scene, he dresses in women's clothes and attends a party of careless women who have "a ton of secret debts"[119]; in another, his mother has to pay his bond after he is thrown in jail for taking part in a "free troop mission,"[120] the name for the armed bands who rampaged against neighboring Catholic cantons in the tumultuous 1840s. Finally, after they have their finances together, his mother sends him to a campaign rally, where he denounces the re-elected munici-pal governor "because he himself is bankrupt and civically dead."[121] The proclamation shocks the governor into grimacing "like somebody who has been buried for a thousand years and is resurrected."[122] Fritz's uprightness, only possible because he was raised without a father, ulti-mately paves the way for intergenerational reconciliation. When his father returns from America, where he worked up a small fortune, he is warmly received by his wife and son, and the "lineage" of Regula Amrain "flourished" after her death.[123]

Legal templates promised stability in bourgeois society.[124] But fiction homed in on how they could fragment a person's sense of self. Keller's texts explore this issue pointedly in their descriptions of the relation between contracts and characters' fates. His narratives reveal how fictive constructs like contracts fill in characters' lack of knowledge and thereby inform their actions. But when their decisions run aground in the narra-tives' real world because they have no way to verify things, the truth that every contract is more complex than its literal reading becomes apparent.

The story "A Village Romeo and Juliet" revolves around this issue. The generic hybrid is at once a miniaturization of Shakespeare's trag-edy and a bestowal of Shakespearean laurels upon a newspaper report about a double suicide.[125] The children of two long-feuding neighboring farmers fall in love. The feud had come about because the farmers Manz and Marti plowed, bit-by-bit, a piece of fallow land that lay between their properties, appropriating the respective sides as their own. Manz buys at an auction the side that Marti had already partially plowed. It then turns out that the piece of land had an owner all along, "the black fiddler," who, however, lacks the certificate of baptism necessary to take posses-sion of his inheritance.[126] This missing document is the absent cause of the whole story, in the run of which the two farmers come to appear to one another "as a sort of lightning rod of evil itself."[127]

The civil suit mutates into a feud and neither farmer "desisted until both were completely ruined."[128] When the two meet again while fishing—another instance of taking free goods—Manz stands "upstream and alone, like a wrathful shadow of Hades."[129] Marti eventually falls into poverty, as he "had had one section after another of his property sequestrated by orders of the court," until he finally dies.[130] While Seldwyla's bankrupts are living shadows, law-abiding property owners are killed by legal troubles. The collection of novellas depicts the threshold to civic death not only as chock full of holes, but as a porous enclave within the field of legality itself.

Seldwyla grapples more intensively with the world of finance than does Keller's explicitly finance-themed novel *Martin Salander* (1886). The novel has been interpreted as a document of the crisis of liberalism in the 1880s and as an expression of estrangement over the unfettered capitalism of the "speculation game."[131] I'd like to take a different approach, showing that the novel deals less with a disjointed financial sphere and more with traditional modes of exchange. The novel tells the story of a former teacher who becomes a successful merchant in Brazil and then loses everything twice, first due to a personal surety, then due to a failed bill of exchange. He goes back to Brazil, sets things straight, works his way back up the ladder, returns to Switzerland, and becomes a well-liked politician. He hesitatingly allows his daughters to marry twin brothers, attorneys who turn out to be crooks and later flee the country. The unhappy marriages come to an end, while Salander's business is taken over by his discerning son.

During a sociable evening, Martin Salander cosigns on a loan for his old friend, the banker Louis Wohlwend. A decision made only because of his social relations with Wohlwend, the deal proves tough to navigate: custom dictated that Salander remain sober and contained, but he also needed to be ready to respond to an appeal to his magnanimity.[132] Cosigning for another was based on ideas of masculine honor and might thus be seen as traditional, but contemporaneous observers associated it with modern banks. By the 1880s, cosigning had become a cause of considerable worry.[133] In an article in the *Zeitschrift für Gemeinnützigkeit* (Journal for the common good), one author argued that it had "taken on a heretofore unseen volume," because the new banks often demanded a cosigner as an additional guarantee on loans.[134] Evidencing the constant dialogue between literature and the nonliterary world, the article refers to the then new novel *Martin Salander* as the most illustrative example of this real social issue. In the novel, the wife's household economy has to compensate for the loss brought on by the male economy of honor,

because "suddenly Want, like the Grim Messenger, arrived."[135] While
Martin is away, Marie Salander runs an inn and redeems her reputation
of frugality to buy bread on credit.

The dowry, a seemingly traditional asset form, drives the novel's
plot. Marie puts hers on the table so that her husband can liquidate his
business without declaring bankruptcy.[136] Future mother-in-law Amalie
Weidelich boasts that each Salander daughter is "worth a half million
apiece."[137] When the daughters catch wind of this, they protest that they
are not "produce to be sold at the market!"[138] When bankruptcies happened, the nominally privileged dowry became an object of contention
that spawned other transactions. Wohlwend, for instance, defrauds his
creditors by declaring assets that might be attached to pay his debts as
belonging to his spouse's dowry.[139] The sons-in-law want their new wives
to wear luxury clothes every day "as if they were Oriental slave girls,"
which eats into the interest on the dowry.[140] After the twins are arrested
for fraud, the Salander parents attempt to reclaim whatever movable
assets are left from their daughters' dowries; the cash, however, has
already been frittered away.[141] Thus, in both plot lines, the economy of
the dowry and household prop up the masculine business world.

But to what extent are these business machinations of the modern
speculative sort? Salander's enterprise recovers from its first collapse by
exploiting slave labor (itself invisible in the novel) on Brazilian planta-
tions.[142] The plantation produces hard commodities like "sacks of cof-
fee," "cigars," and "Paraguayan tea."[143] At the same time, Wohlwend's
company Schadenmüller & Comp. is stripped down to nothing more
than an "empty office" with no credit by the time it goes bankrupt.[144]
Banks are also depicted as hollow shells, as when a colleague asks
Salander where he had cashed a bill of exchange: "Certainly in the 'Big
Trunk'? Or in the 'Old Chest'? Or in the 'New Chest'? These are the
newest nicknames for our banks."[145] But it would be too simple to reduce
the novel to a black-and-white conflict between a self-standing finance
sphere and a real economy that "did not speculate."[146] Not just because
Keller's novel does not engage in this critique, which became a popular
interpretation of the causes of the economic crisis in the 1880s. Keller
certainly did this, as his castigation of "paper pushing" makes clear.[147]
But his reproach didn't stop there.

Alongside Wohlwend's fraud, the main criminal doings in *Martin
Salander* are executed not at the stock exchange, but through the
manipulation of rural property records. The banal property market—
not out-of-control stock prices—is the stage for the sons'-in-law double-

dealings. Isidor and Julian cheat people by reselling expired mortgage notes. In one rural district, the real estate system is overhauled, old entries deleted, and new titles issued. Isidor's position as an attorney means that the "millions" involved in the overhaul pass through his hands. He exploits the situation "by speculating with only a few hundred thousand in order to try his luck on the stock exchange."[148] But the core of the scam consists in the manipulation of the title register. This style of corruption sporadically shocked rural real estate markets throughout the nineteenth century, and its primary features didn't have anything to do with high finance.[149]

The novel's insight was to elucidate the connections between such long-standing, local-level schemes and the globalized world of finance. Historians interested in economic cycles have read in *Martin Salander* an expression of the sense of disorientation that took hold of society in the 1880s.[150] Others have interpreted it as an early critique of modernity that grappled with the destructive consequences of disjointed, semiautonomous spheres of the economy.[151] Still others have described Keller's criticisms as a form of "bourgeois regression," because they framed the systemic crises of capitalism in the language of morality.[152] This last point certainly holds water, but it leaves open the question as to the precise source of Keller's moral scorn. The lack of orientation in the face of the erosion of values is the essence of the matter, because the novel narrates the travails of a person in a world that has become opaque to him. The novel tends to attribute this loss of orientation and transparency, however, not to the wildness of the finance industry, but to the crumbling of paternal authority. Corruption, fraud, and the subversion of state power are the threats, not imperialist globalization per se (after all, the latter makes Salander a rich man twice over).[153] The critique of finance is not much more pronounced in *Martin Salander* than it is in *Seldwyla*. The lively bankrupts of Seldwyla exemplify not the nadir of civic death, but the ever-present possibility of renegotiating things, because in the town's paper economy, everything is always in flux. Even the scoundrel Louis Wohlwend from *Martin Salander* is "juristically speaking, an interesting subject."[154] In both texts, bankruptcy denotes not an end of values and signification, but a beginning of something new that is neither a *tabula rasa* nor the mere continuation of the old. In short, Keller depicts bankruptcy as a catalyzer of contingent events.

The semiotics of debt opens the stage for fiction in general, just as the two prefaces to the *Seldwyla* volumes open the stage for the novellas. People who don't take on debt or don't have debt inhibit narrative.

But the signs of debt and indebtedness refer to social relations as their signified. Subjects have to be able and willing to recognize and honor different sorts of values and situate them in the proper register; short-circuiting the currency of money with the currency of love is a problematic act. The ability to do so, however, necessitates orientation in one's social space and knowledge of one's place in it. What is satirized in the cartoons of *Die Leute von Seldwyla* is described in *Martin Salander* with disillusioned realism as a "swindle."[155]

Walter Benjamin saw in Keller's liberalism a respect for civil law that filtered knowledge of its shortcomings through humor. He wrote that in Keller's work, humor "is itself a kind of judicial system," a "universe of enforcement without verdict, a universe in which both verdict and pardon express themselves through laughter."[156] Debt enforcement, too, adhered to the principle of "enforcement without verdict": it was a purely administrative procedure that required no judge. In Keller's liberalism, such standardized measures made it possible to ward off catastrophe. They also laid the groundwork for open-ended plots: in Keller's literature, things run their course, but they're never brought to an absolute conclusion. And yet, characters always have to be prepared to make assessments of things in their interactions with others. While Keller doesn't demand absolute, existential decisions from his characters, he shows how they are compelled to constantly adapt to the situation at hand. Keller's liberalism was rooted in the idea that drawing the line between legitimate and illegitimate debts was not easy. But for all that, the line didn't cease to exist. Instead, he made it the task of the individual to judge. The alternatives to intelligently judging, of course, were the "speculation game" and "swindle," but less because subjects were tricked into it by some external force and more because they themselves lost orientation in a dizzying vertigo.

Debt as Dispossession: A Theory of Pauperism

While Keller tracked incremental change, Wilhelm Weitling put the conception of "'ideas' as events" to the test.[157] A dressmaker from Magdeburg, Weitling has often been described as a "utopian" or "craftsman's communist." He joined the *Bund der Gerechten* (Coalition of the Just) in Paris in 1837 and wrote his main works in Switzerland between 1841 and 1843.[158] The theory of pauperism articulated in these works sought to make sense of the precarious circumstances of the early industrial underclass, a population whose day-to-day survival heavily relied on an informal economy of loaning, borrowing, and pawning.[159] Debts and assessments of their significance played an important role in this economy of makeshifts, which knew no Archimedean point. In contrast to other versions of early socialism, Weitling neither valorized labor nor was he fixated on the money form. He was interested in production, reproduction, consumption, and circulation to an equal degree.[160] His ruminations on property took the lack thereof as its more elementary form.

Weitling's texts should not be fetishized as an authentic expression of life in poverty, but as a genuine contribution to social theory. A millenarian thinker, Weitling invested his politics with a specific temporality that banged together divergent temporal regimes: the actualization of communism, for him, was necessary right here right now.[161] He did not dream utopian dreams filled out in detail, but instead was a vessel of the "utopian impulse," of the desire to break with things as they are.[162] Debt figured prominently into this particular theory of utopian temporality.

The downtrodden and wretched peopled the stage of Weitling's *Evangelium eines armen Sünders* (Gospel of a poor sinner) (1843). A mother, for instance, who "sighs": "Again I return with empty basket and empty stomach . . . the neighbor lady won't lend me anything, the baker won't give me bread on credit, the pawnshop will loan me nothing for these rags. . . . Dear God, have pity on us poor creatures and send us a merciful angel who will save us from this poverty."[163] But the narrator's interjection, repeated to rhetorical effect over the book's first pages, provides a counterpoint to this prayer by asserting: "We poor sinners will not wait." Rather than waiting for a salvatory event, the "poor sinners" "hope" that a time will come when "nobody will need to borrow from a neighbor, when no more pawnshops are necessary and no landlord collects rent."[164] Wilhelm Weitling's treatise invests his miserabilism—the graphic depiction of underclass miseries—with a rebellious engagement by adopting the viewpoint of the "sinners," by which is meant everyone with debts.

Weitling's ideas should be compared and contrasted with other socialisms of the era. Credit systems were a key aspect of many early socialist utopias, which viewed them as a tool to help organize labor and society.[165] After the July Revolution in France, the number of pamphlets promoting novel forms of lending exploded. In Paris, the short-lived republic of 1848 aided the organization of some projects and, temporarily, garnered state support for them. In Germanophone Switzerland in the 1840s, such initiatives failed in the face of active state repression and weak financial backing; the 1850s witnessed the first cooperatives.[166] Weitling, however, set his sights not on credit, but on debt; not on speculative visions of the future, but on the policies being enforced in the present. His revolutionary fervor flowed out of an antagonistic analysis of society. He thought debt was theft, and his notion of debt as lack makes his work interesting for a study of how debt subjectifies individuals.

Switzerland was a favorite place for journeymen to work and pass through; in 1840, around ten thousand German journeymen were residing in the various cantons.[167] The journeyman's economy was well acquainted with begging and borrowing, but also with official modes of exchange structured by institutionalized gifts.[168] The German journeymen's political associations in Switzerland constituted a small, heavily fluctuating, linguistically and politically isolated group whose members were in constant conflict with the authorities and always threatened with arrest and deportation.[169] In the summer of 1836, a wave of expulsions hit political organizations, compelling the politically engaged journeymen's associations to move to the less repressive western cantons.[170] In 1841, the members in Francophone Switzerland counted three hundred, and under Weitling's influence their numbers may have doubled; estimates for Germanophone Switzerland count another two to three hundred members.[171] Having already published in Paris the booklet *Die Menschheit wie sie ist und wie sie sein sollte* (Humanity as it is and as it should be, 1838, early 1839), Weitling edited the newspapers *Der Hülferuf der deutschen Jugend* (The German youth's cry for help, 1841) and *Die junge Generation* (The young generation, 1842/43) in Romandy. The papers had runs of about a thousand issues, with around half going to Paris and London.[172] In 1842, Weitling's most influential booklet, *Garantien der Harmonie und Freiheit* (Guarantees of harmony and freedom), was printed in Vevey; as with his earlier booklet, it was published with the help of subscriptions and donations. In the spring of 1843, Weitling traveled to Zurich, worked for a tailor, and established contact with the German publisher-in-exile Julius Fröbel, who held Swiss citizenship.[173] In Zurich, Weitling's propaganda competed with the German cultural organization Eintracht, with about two dozen of their members joining the Coalition of the Just.[174] While living in the city, Weitling wrote *Das Evangelium des armen Sünders* and was arrested for the incendiary text in early June.[175] He spent just under a year in a Zurich jail cell. Member of government Johann Caspar Bluntschli sent him novels by conservative author Jeremias Gotthelf, such as *How Uli the Servant Becomes Happy*, and forced him to copy various writings.[176] "'How Uli the servant becomes happy,' that is, how he becomes happy as a servant. The title says it all," Weitling wrote. Copying, he recalled, distracted his intellect in a way that manual labor would not have: "Working as a tailor or cobbler is better for the free mind; one can speak, sing, and think while doing it." In late May 1844, Weitling was deported to Prussia, which he left to travel, via Hamburg, to London.

Weitling's writings repeatedly criticized classifications of people and the institutions that administered these classifications; residency permits, passport checks, and, above all, the *Wanderbuch*, a special type of passport for itinerant workers, were all targets of his ire. The itinerant worker's passport recorded information about the bearer's behavior at work, previous convictions, and debts. It had to be presented to the authorities and could be confiscated, thus prohibiting a journeyman from continuing his trip.[177] This instrument of control outlived its original function in guilds and became a feature of the emergent nation-state's passport system. In 1828, Weitling himself finagled his way to a journeyman's passport issued by Hamburg, which enabled him to travel freely and escape military service.[178] Weitling's indignation at banal societal mechanisms of discipline and control is detailed in an article he wrote in *Die junge Generation* that listed things useful, pleasant, and harmful to humans. Alongside jails, he deemed harmful "the foreigner's offices with their files, passports, and worker's passports; the file libraries in courts and town halls, the tax register, testaments and certificates; . . . all the labors of merchants, shopkeepers, soldiers, innkeepers, lenders, servants, customs officers, court bailiffs, etc."[179] His main theoretical work, *Garantien der Harmonie and Freiheit*, demanded that "all IOUs, promissory notes, and bills of exchange" be immediately declared "null and void." He energized his revolutionary call by arguing, "There will come a time when people will no longer plead and beg, but demand. When this time comes, one will ignite big fires with bank notes, bills of exchange, certificates, tax lists, rent and lease contracts, and IOUs."[180] The destruction of paperwork symbolized the desire to abolish the practices of record keeping, control, social status, and subordination elemental for the reproduction of class society.[181] Weitling's rhetoric lived on extreme terms. *Die junge Generation* regularly published stories from Switzerland, describing them as scenes from the "front" of social conflict. One narrative from Zurich, for instance, cast a harsh image: "Here in the towns on the lake, hardship snarls with bared teeth. One hears people say here and there: this cannot go on another two years."[182] A dispatch from Aargau relayed, "Poverty is gradually gaining the upper hand here. Never before have there been so many bankruptcies, the jails are stuffed to the brim—remarkably, with poor people—not a single rich person can be found there."[183]

Contemporary society's "system of usury," in which "the just must beg for his bread,"[184] was characterized by things like opaque "money and commodity huckstering." Just as despicable as "increased prices for basic goods and decreased wages" was the "adulteration of products."[185] During the early days of the labor movement, the conviction that merchants were middlemen who exploitively inserted themselves between production and consumption was widespread.[186] While Weitling shared this view, he did not consider commerce worthy of special theoretical reflection. Similarly, and in contrast to other labor movement thinkers, finance did not hold a special place in his social critique. He was fascinated little by speculation and finance, arguing that at the end of the day, speculation just pushed to the extreme the ongoing "theft" that was the exploitation of labor power by appropriating, through interest, "a piece of the plunder" for itself.[187] He didn't rail against finance as the cause of hardship, just as he resisted the temptation to pit productive labor against wheel-spinning financiers. In the "money system," he wrote, property was the concrete manifestation of the principle of plunder, and the accumulation of commodities and money in one place produced lack and poverty in another. It brought forth asymmetrical relations by appropriating the work of labor power and keeping poor people from getting what they needed. The "money system" was a zero-sum game in Weitling's theory. Unequal distribution perpetuated the unrewarded toils of the poor, because "poverty is a lack, and wealth is a surplus; it originates and maintains itself through constantly raking away everything that laboring poverty produces."[188]

The metaphor of "raking away" recalls Marilyn Strathern's studies on debt relations discussed in chapter 3, which show that debt leads to the extraction of time, energy, and goods from debtors. The primary achievement of Weitling's theory of pauperism was to describe debt as the obverse of wealth, which, for its part, was always bound up with the production and perpetuation of poverty's constitutive lack. Debt as the flipside of wealth had its own positivity. An article with the title "Die Werthfälschung im heutigen Geldsystem" (The counterfeit of value in today's money system) conceived of money as the "metal bars" that separated labor from consumption, a separation that Weitling viewed as the condition of possibility of the accumulation of riches on the one side and the lack thereof on the other:

> Thus, one has made of the money system metal bars, a separator between labor and consumption. The poor people, the whole popu-

lation, hunker down before the bars, hustling and bustling, and when they've gathered together a little pile, the gate opens up and the rich claw it in; a little crack stays open for the workers through which they squeeze two fingers and take back a piece of their work, which is put in piles for them, and if one complains, the bars are shut in his face and more patient scrapers are allowed to push him aside.[189]

The lack of money caused by plunder left debt as its only remainder. Thus, Weitling concluded, debts were a subjective manifestation of money. Debts imposed the power relation of money upon individuals and reinforced the network of money through the absence thereof. Money as a medium of exchange perpetuated indebtedness and constituted "a debt that can only be paid off in heaven."[190] Another article on the question "What is money?" signed with the pseudonym "Saphir" pithily capped off the investigation with a more novel question, asking "But what is no money?"[191] "No money is a thing that fills all empty pockets and that everyone who has nothing in his hand can grasp with his fingers. No money is a quiet beckoning of nature to accrue debts and a loud command to not repay them."[192] The absence of money in empty pockets is depicted as a tangible presence, a social relation with its own plasticity that forced upon those in possession of it the imperative to take on debts and not pay them back. Weitling's repeated discussion of theft and plunder shocked commentators more than anything else he wrote.[193] He saw a contradiction in the criminal prosecution of theft: when petty thieves who stole out of hunger were tossed in jail, he argued, the formal equality before the law birthed factual inequality, because rich people would never commit such crimes of hunger and fines would hardly scathe them anyways. Weitling failed to see the difference in the "distinction between usury and theft, between vagabondage and idleness."[194] He asserted that the offense of theft had been brought into the world through the institution of private property,[195] and he saw evidence for the arbitrariness of the legal definition of theft in the fact that debts were enforced through asset seizure and bankruptcy: "The man who comes into my house to seize my things, is he not a thief?"[196]

The critique of property as theft, as Proudhon's oft-cited motto from 1840 proclaimed, was just one side of Weitling's theory.[197] His works also extensively explored theft as a counterstrategy of the underclasses. In Russia, for instance, Weitling observed that "among the lowest classes, theft is held as an act of bravery; one becomes great through it, like our young people when they succeed in cheating a usurer."[198] Some of the "scenes from the front" in Weitling's newspaper also recounted dramatic stories of bands of thieves.[199] A series of letters confiscated by member of government Bluntschli stirred up emotions: in them, people sympathetic to Weitling called on him to not declare that theft was a revolutionary principle in his next piece.[200]

How could the money system be overcome? *Die Menschheit, wie sie ist und wie sie sein sollte* explicitly rejected socialist proposals for state-run banks, reasoning that they would be financial flops, even if they had commercial arms, and would, perhaps more importantly, never be able to transcend the "spirit of usury."[201] Weitling took a class-based stance that championed equality above all else, thus contrasting with approaches like that of Charles Fourier, who was less concerned about abolishing inequality than ensuring a minimum of general welfare. Around a decade after Weitling's writings appeared, Charles Fourier became popular among socialist initiatives in Switzerland. For example, Zurich socialist Karl Bürkli translated a tract by Fourier and in 1851 he campaigned to found a bank on Fourier's model.[202] Although Weitling admired Fourier, he chucked his proposals. In an 1842 consideration of some French projects that issued paper money redeemable at cooperative markets, Weitling accused Fourier's followers of acquiescing to "the authorities and the approval of the money men." After all, building a *phalanstère*, as Fourier's utopian palaces were called, cost a lot of money. The Fourierists had, in his words, "only a system, but no principles, at least not radical ones." They perfected their particular type of association, but they did it at the expense of equality. Likewise, Weitling had no time for savings banks, dismissing their key tenet of the individual pursuit of wealth as dividing workers from one another rather than fostering solidarity.[203] Weitling saw his rejection of these instruments of bourgeois philanthropy validated in their own programs. As a booklet published in Zurich with the title *Bete und arbeite!* (Pray and work!) formulated it, the purpose of savings banks was to keep their customers from falling for the "crazy idea of communism."[204] In the community of the "just," Weitling countered, petty concerns about individual needs and comforts would be relegated to the past. "Don't save up for the future," he wrote in the *Evangelium des armen Sünders*, because "converting at least one other person to the principle of the community of goods every 14 days" was "the best savings bank."[205]

Weitling's politics of communalization focused on the present. While socialist systems of credit like Fourier's were founded on a model of a rationalized future, Weitling grasped utopia as "realizable—here and now," only speculating on the future to have "a point of orientation, something external to the ordinary course of events from where he is on the lookout ready to take the leap."[206] The refrain of *Das Evangelium des armen Sünders*—"We poor sinners won't wait"—encapsulated the temporality of Weitling's work. The abolition of private property in the name of equality was the substance of this demand for the present. It was the core of Weitling's concept of communism as the communion of community members, which was rooted in his interpretation of communion in Christ as something to be practiced in the world.[207] He believed that sharing common goods should have priority and thus sought to avoid all the nuanced forms of condescension characteristic of philanthropy and its symbolic acts of exchange. Charity was rejected because poor people who had nothing to give could not practice it;[208] the handouts of the rich were regarded as a mockery.[209] Achieving egalitarian relations, he explained, was much more difficult than rehearsing the old inequalities of largesse and thankfulness.[210] The danger that "the support could become a venom for the friend" if others heard about it was persistent. "Thus, what the Christian lends he should treat as a gift and he should refrain as much as possible from borrowing from like-minded persons, but should read in their eyes their affliction and offer them help."[211] Members of the community, Weitling posited, should not expect anything in return for their gifts; the community of the just was constituted by nonreciprocal acts of gifting.

On the same note, though, he warned against overtaxing the generosity of others. While this caution was rooted in the economic precarity that defined the situation of the community's members, it followed out of the more general desire to nip in the bud the subjugation and inequality produced by generosity. Of Weitling's twelve rules for the "propaganda period"—his name for the limited community of already-convinced communists that could be brought into being without further ado—four dealt with borrowing and lending. One maxim asked members to buy a round for a friend experiencing "hardship."[212] Another summed up the main idea: "If you lend somebody something, don't expect to get it back," which was complemented with a command to debtors: "If somebody lends you something, remind him regularly of the amount in order to show that you have not forgotten." Finally, members had to guard against borrowing too much from others in the community, which was best accomplished by the alternative method of "forcing your hardship onto the shoulders of our enemies as much as possible, so that our energy is not exhausted." Avoiding disputes in the community was of utmost importance for those who rejected the poison of generosity, Weitling articulated, which implied taking advantage of bourgeois philanthropy in moments of need. On the whole, Weitling's conception of exchange placed considerable responsibility in the hands of community members, fusing individual action with social relations and a large-scale willingness to give with the confidence that others would be sparing in their asks.

While Weitling thought that the individual communist should break with the expectations of reciprocity, he thought that on the level of social life as a whole, the organization of exchange and giving would involve equivalencies. Weitling sought to supplant money with "commerce hours" (*Kommerzstunden*), labor time performed in excess of the community's six-hour work day.[213] This surplus work was to be compensated with the "maximum possible freedom of each and every person."[214] Thus, in Weitling's theory, economic equality as a necessity imposed by the dictates of natural law did not stand in contradiction with individuality.[215] Every member of the community could use their accumulated "commerce hours" to acquire goods to satisfy their individual "desires." "Prices" followed the movements of supply and demand, but to give an example, "a gold necklace" amounted to "50–100 work hours, a bottle of champagne 12–18."[216]

Each community member would carry a personalized book containing four types of entries: the owner's overtime "commerce hours," their regular hours worked, their state of health, and, on the opposite page, the things they had "purchased" with their extra hours.[217] Money and similar notes of exchange could be hoarded and turned into objects of speculation. In contrast, the personalized book—whose owner could be identified by a picture and description on the first page—had to, "despite all exchange, always remain in the hand of its owner and at the same time serve as a diary of his desires and abilities."[218] This "diary" could be stamped at the inn, which was just as simple as paying in cash or on a tab. The books were at once a "passport, certificate of baptism, certificate of residence, qualification paper, certificate of apprenticeship, bill of exchange, receipt, record of transactions, diary, school transcript, entry ticket, letter of recommendation, collection plate, currency market, calendar; it is a reflection of all of the individual's mental and physical needs, their portrait, their biography—in short, the entire ego of the individual as it has never before been represented."[219] This grandiose rationalist fantasy cast the utopian system of credit as a giant knowledge bank for administering subjectivity, economy, and social planning.

Thus, the instruments like the journeyman's book that Weitling had criticized in other contexts resurfaced in his imagined society. Perhaps most remarkable is the way Weitling conceptualized credit and debt as *describable* social relations: because his system did away with money as a general medium of exchange, everything was written down. This system of tabulation painted an "image of the individual," as if a person could be summed up by the information collated in the book. The knowledge bank was not just gigantic. How to decipher it and live by it was also supposed to be instilled into every individual person. Thus it constituted a total instrument of subjectification, taking on substance through entries documenting direct relations of exchange. Weitling did justice to the need for a general medium of exchange, but he stripped it of the anonymity characteristic of money. In effect, the communist's theory of utopia was thus at once a reflection of and commentary on the social content of the everyday economy of makeshifts in the nineteenth century.

Debt and credit continued to occupy Weitling after he left Switzerland. After a falling out with the *Bund der Gerechten* (which was renamed *Bund der Kommunisten* soon after) in 1846 and a year in the United States, he returned to Germany during the revolutionary year of 1848.[220] In Berlin, the Prussian parliament was debating an ultimately unsuccessful moratorium on payments owed on real property. Prompted by the economic crisis, the proposal aimed to safeguard debtors from eviction for a period of three years or, in a watered-down version, to ensure help from the state in cases where a debtor received notice. With renters in mind, Weitling petitioned legislators to expand the relief to the "propertyless." Moreover, he asserted that because democratic states were identical with the people, they could act as "central merchants" and "rescue all sources of income from the nets of capital."[221] It was this kind of thinking, of course, that led Weitling to design his own system of credit in the first place. In combination with the power of a revolutionary democratic state, Weitling thought that money—"the axle around which the entire political and social state machine turns"—constituted a means to combat the capitalists and their corporations.[222] But the counterrevolution took the day and in 1849, Weitling accepted an invitation from a labor union to return to New York, where he published the newspaper *Republik der Arbeiter* (Workers' republic) and worked together with a "labor association." While the possibility that a democratic state might be established in Germany in 1848 convinced Weitling to revise his opinions about state-run banks and state-socialist money, he directed his energies toward self-organized cooperatives in the United States.

The workers' association began drawing up ideas for an exchange bank in 1850, but it never got past the planning phase. Indirectly, the project brought together the theories of American currency reformers with those of leftist Ricardian Owenists.[223] The bank was supposed to distribute exchange notes to its members—that is, laborers and small business owners—that would function as a parallel currency and to centralize commerce by establishing a combination marketplace-warehouse where members could deliver and sell their products. The plan was to transfer the bank into state hands down the road and turn the exchange notes into state-backed paper money.[224] The Communia commune in Iowa, which was founded in 1847, bore the brunt of the financial burdens, and in 1851 the project's organizers began viewing it as the key balustrade of the bank.[225] The workers' association invested money in Communia. When internal strife hit the commune, conflicts over its debts were a primary bone of contention.[226] In June 1856, Communia was officially dissolved.

Debt's potential to eat away at the future is illustrated pointedly by a tidbit out of Weitling's own life. In New York, Weitling began keeping a book of memories for his children with the seamstress Dorothea Caroline Louise Tödt, whom he married in 1854. Wanganschi Weitling, named after an eleventh-century Chinese reformer, was born in 1855. In 1858, the couple began keeping records about the development of Wanganschi and their five other children and reflecting on the progress of Weitling's studies in astronomy. But in the 1860s, entries on outstanding debts piled up. The family started a small business producing vests, but after paying the rent, tuition for their children, and other expenses, they had about seventy-seven dollars left over every month to pay off debts of about 3,400 dollars.[227] Unsuccessful applications to patent a machine for sewing buttonholes that Weitling had worked on intensively swallowed up the money. And shortly after the family moved into a less expensive apartment, they were being threatened with eviction.[228] The debts taken on to provide a better future ended up eroding the present. The book concludes with anti-Semitic rants against Karl Marx, fury against the "filthy Jewish neighbors" at the new place, and irritation that he had been forgotten by the labor movement.[229]

Weitling's experience should be interpreted in the context of pauperism. Pauperism was a concept that interwove mass poverty with the vocabulary of moral unrest; it was "demoralized poverty," "poverty as a type of behavior."[230] It positioned the pauper as a figure of absolute abjection standing outside law and rationality, thus constituting its own anthropology.[231] A pastor's account from 1817, a year of famine, offers an early example. Pastor Salomon Schinz from Zurich's highlands described the "class of humans" that were paupers and factory workers as a genuine "race of beggars" no longer "accustomed to strenuous labor and ruggedness," thereby shifting between terms of "race" and "class."[232] He identified the defining attribute of these people as their having taken on debts that could not be paid off with harvests, but only "by the spinning wheel or loom."[233] Thus the moral shortcoming of the pauper was less their lack of property and more that they lived in a state of perpetual indebtedness. The economy of makeshifts, driven by low-level exchanges like the ever-criticized purchase of clothing on credit, lacked the structure people like Schinz valued.[234] He thus demanded that marriage between propertyless people be prohibited, which, until 1874, it was in some places.[235]

Various avenues to challenging the diagnosis of pauperism were open. Weitling's class-based politics sought to extend the social reach of communism to include not only craftsmen, but also unskilled laborers.[236] Singing the song of the impoverished early industrial masses was motivated by a struggle for basic needs. Weitling attacked the moral language of pauperism by adapting it to his own ends. Refusing to separate the material from the symbolic, his critique of morality led him to posit contrary morals that motivated the composition of the *Evangelium des armen Sünders*. His descriptions of misery and hardship were thus not simply kindling for the political fire, but also constituted a novel epistemological strategy that promised to produce its own unique knowledge. In other words, the affective charge of Weitling's texts followed out of an antagonistic point of view. Thus the direness of his writings should neither be debunked as fiction nor praised as a naturalistic eyewitness account of things as they were. His concentration on misery enabled the production of knowledge that went against the dominant truths of thinkers like the "rich philosopher Malthus" and the Malthusian politics of people like Pastor Schinz.[237]

Religion, the number one medium of morality, provided the language that Weitling harnessed to paint the picture of a contradictory society that failed to practice what it preached. Weitling himself was indifferent toward Christianity.[238] He saw the communion of the apostles as a model for his own secular community and religion as a means to rupture hegemonic norms and unleash the "hermeneutic contradiction."[239] Weitling's theory conceived of pauperism as an expression of a complex of forces. From this vantage point, he defined debt as theft, as a relation that condensed all kinds of social issues into a single nexus. In his account, the "money system" reached its apex in debt and for that reason had to be abolished. At the same time, Weitling's image of an ideal society preserved a system of exchange and record keeping that retained debts in a certain sense. The labor money of "commerce hours" was thus less a substitute for money than an attempt to describe the social relations of the everyday economy of makeshifts in their totality.

Writing about Debts

Jakob Stutz's diary, Gottfried Keller's literature, and Wilhelm Weitling's theory of pauperism offer a series of distinct perspectives. The financial problems that Stutz got wrapped up in revealed debts as open-ended relations of forces. Stutz the lender didn't have the means to compel even his family members to pay him back, nor did he have to reckon with just one single type of the traditional norm of solidarity. Stutz's family members thumped on norms when asking him for help, but this wound up in processes of surveillance and countersurveillance, in efforts to employ and dispel rumors, and generally in a search for ways to manipulate the social rules to one's own advantage. Keller's *Seldwyla* depicted bankruptcy not as rock bottom, but as something subject to constant renegotiation. Debts make stories possible, but the self-interest that subjects pursue in their exchange relations necessitate that they cultivate the capacity to properly draw distinctions. Every individual had to distinguish between good and bad debts, a task with moral overtones. Weitling's concept of debt as the subjective iteration of the "money system" and the positive embodiment of lack drew on the experiences of the underclasses' economy of makeshifts. Attacking debt meant defending the right to sustenance, which is why in Weitling's eyes, the subjectification process instigated by debt sowed the seeds of revolt. Keller and Weitling's anti-Semitic invective projected the difficulties of debt onto a boogeyman, thus attesting to the continued presence of that script, and the haste with which they engaged in this invective reveals just how quickly people could be carried away by such distortions. The three examples in this chapter were individual, perhaps unusual cases that are not representative in the statistical sense. : Placed side-by-side, these social experiences—the proto-industrial complex of relations in the diary, the fiction of the national poet, the communist theory and its promotion of uprising—escape easy categorization. I aimed to elucidate *instances* in the process of subjectification without undertaking something like an analysis of larger configurations such as the genesis of the bourgeois subject, the homo economicus, or—of more recent vintage—the "entrepreneurial self."[240] The bankrupt was never an emblem of an epoch, but neither were bankrupts the throwaway people of the nineteenth century's rapidly growing economy. Subjectification through debts ushered in processes that were more nuanced than a clean-cut concept of subjectivity allows for. I in no way claim that the three examples exhaust the full spectrum of what was possible, but they are rich nonetheless. Perhaps these exceptional cases show that fictional, first-person, and theoretical writings should not be shut out from the get-go, but should instead be made a part of historiography. At any rate, the singular experiences I wanted to describe were not necessarily spectacular. It could be that many people had such experiences.[241] In the next chapter, I explore this issue by inquiring in depth into the concrete classification of debtors in order to more precisely understand the system of classification and disidentification that was debt enforcement.

FIVE | Bankruptcy and Social Classification

What made up the "estate of the bankrupts"? The day laborer Rudolf Hunziker proved to have a strong opinion on the question when, in September 1854, he petitioned the mayor of Basel to have his civic rights restored: "Six years have now passed," he wrote, "since I left a highly respectable business and soon thereafter was thrown into the deepest hardship. Added to that was the loss of my civic rights & honor as a consequence of my bankruptcy."[1] His letter detailed the efforts he had taken to work himself out of bankruptcy. After holding out for "four breadless months," he "assiduously" toiled as a day laborer at a large store in the city, "often through the entire night." He later won "the *trust* & respect" of his superiors. The thirty-six-year-old emphasized that he had paid off all his creditors and had never had to draw on poor relief to support his family. "But now, Herr Mayor, respected sirs," Hunziker continued, "one blemish still afflicts my innermost being & poses a great hurdle for my future—namely, the loss of my civic rights."

In Basel, all insolvent persons—not just merchants—were subject to bankruptcy proceedings. Both bankrupts and the authorities spoke of "the bankrupt estate" or "estate of bankrupts." Those who were not citizens of Basel—in 1854, about two-thirds of the city's population—risked losing their residency permit.[2] For every case, Basel civil courts were tasked with sending a short report to the government and assembling a *Konkurskollokation*, or schedule of claims: a list of creditors' demands that were ordered by priority. The government administration, in turn, often ordered the person in question to be interrogated by the police. In order to be rehabilitated, bankrupts had to prove that they had paid back all their creditors. But some debts had a special status that allowed for exceptions, among them the debtor's obligations to their family. Rudolf

Hunziker, for instance, had not replenished the money he had borrowed from his three children's baptism gifts in his dire straits. Nevertheless, the administration's recommendation that his rights be restored stated that such intrafamilial debts were "generally in a different category from the demands of other creditors."[3] Not all claims were equal.

Rudolf Hunziker spoke of external hardship and deep inner pain, of an external "blemish" that afflicted his "innermost being." He clearly perceived civic death to be the principal consequence of bankruptcy, and he dedicated all his energies to recovering his civic honor and returning to the community of legally capable persons. This interplay of external and internal also featured in Karl Marx's analysis of debt as a relation that went to the core of "man's *moral* existence, man's *social* existence, the *inmost depths* of his heart."[4] But was Hunziker giving expression to a widely shared set of norms? The transcript of the police interrogation of cobbler Rudolf Vest, which took place in 1857, speaks a different language. The peculiarity of the situation warrants quoting it at length:

> 2nd question: It seems that your name has been published a few times?
> Answer: A few times?
> 3rd question: Yes, a few times.
> A: Twice, yes.
> 4th question: Is your name currently published?
> A: No.
> 5th question: But you are bankrupt.
> A: That is no longer true; you are in error.
> 6th question: The civil court wrote to the city government that your creditors are missing 852 francs from you & we have been given the task of discussing this matter with you. Now, if we are talking about Rudolf Vest the cobbler, then we are talking about nobody other than you who is sitting here before us; because there *is* no other Rudolf Vest the cobbler. Can you tell us how you went bankrupt?
> A: I've been asked this before and the last time nobody called except Mr. Deputat Laroche.
> 7th question: Because they knew they weren't going to get anything.
> A: You can't say that. The situation is such that Mr. Deputat got what he wanted.
> 8th question: Why did you go bankrupt then.

A: Because I was sick multiple times & because of unemployment.

9th question: Show me your hands!

A: (he does it).

10th question: There is not the least sign there that you do any kind of work & certainly no shoes have been made by these hands in a long time. It thus seems that you do nothing at all; that you earn nothing by doing nothing is of course natural & completely normal.

A: When I have work, I work. I take commissions from laudable volunteer firefighters and it is not appropriate to deliver with filthy hands.

11th question: You will certainly not dispute that you are nothing more than a dawdler.

A: That is certainly not the case. I currently have work.

12th question: For whom & since when?

A: A pair of boots for Mr. Guntern . . . since last week.

13th question: He should have had them already if you would work?

A: One first has to have the money to buy leather.[5]

In contrast to Hunziker, Rudolf Vest contested the authorities' accusations. He stonewalled the interrogation. He even denied that he was bankrupt—an unambiguous administrative fact, it might seem. But there is more to this than his stubborn persistence. The police officer accused Vest of a dearth of morality, and, not unsimilar to Hunziker, the defamations latched onto a bodily attribute, Vest's apparently clean hands. But Vest denied it all. The officer interrogated the bankrupt man with little information to go on, a lack of certainty emblematic of the uncertainty of the status of bankruptcy itself. As a result, the interrogation ran off the rails. The authorities complained that Vest did not want to take responsibility and they criticized the meager preliminary report supplied to them by the civil court administration, a summary-justice authority tasked with bankruptcies.[6]

The interplay between inside and outside discussed by Hunziker and parried by Vest was part and parcel of the process of subjectification through social classification. The previous chapter grappled with three individual instances of subjectification through debt and bankruptcy. This chapter analyzes the relation between the qualities ascribed to bankrupt persons by others and those persons' ideas about themselves.

In doing so, it reveals the repercussions that such ascriptions had for people in Basel's economy. In particular, it illuminates the techniques and schemata that assigned people to the "estate" of bankrupts.

This chapter draws on 151 police interrogations, about 340 short reports about bankrupt persons that the civil court administration sent to Basel's cantonal government, and a dossier of 38 petitions for rehabilitation filed by bankrupt persons in the 1840s and 1850s.[7] The court reports were intended to guide the police in their interrogations of bankrupts suspected of manipulating their assets or carelessly falling into bankruptcy. Identifying "carelessness" as the cause of bankruptcy demanded ascertaining "whether prodigality, boldly ambitious business undertakings, poor management" (which included large purchases of wares or large loans while knowing one was unable to pay) or "sloppy bookkeeping" were "really" the cause.[8] But that was not the only purpose of these reports to the government. As the head of Basel's judiciary put it in 1867, they offered the authorities insight "into an important part of public life," which included "business matters, credit . . . co-signing, merchants, and much more; in general, into the lives and activities of a considerable number of families, both of citizens and long-term residents."[9] The reports about bankrupts gave the government administration a detailed picture of the city-canton's economic life. The building blocks of these reports were categories both moral and economic, which courts, police officers, and bankrupts themselves employed to explain the economic failures of bankrupt persons.

In their research on codification and classification, sociologists of knowledge and historians of statistics have inquired into the conditions that influence state apparatuses' decisions to subsume individual cases under general classes and the techniques they have used to do so. Analyzing the rigidification of a code into a standardized taxonomy reveals that "one can no longer contrast . . . universal and scientific" (or, in this case, economic and juridical) "knowledge contained in a scholarly project to other forms of knowledge said to be indigenous, local, partial, nonsystematic, or action-oriented."[10]

When the courts in Basel labeled an insolvent person a bankrupt, they engaged in practices of knowledge crafted to pinpoint the precise moment of economic failure and to quarantine the cause to ensure it remained the issue of an individual. What went into the methods of gathering knowledge about cases? Which vocabularies did the authorities and bankrupts use? What kinds of inconsistencies contaminated these methods and semantics? A useful tool for studying these questions is sociologist Luc Boltanski's concept of operations of qualification. Operations of qualification determine what should be acknowledged as fact in a given situation; they are particularly refined in institutions. Operations of qualification involve comparing the situation at hand to a standard, attributing a meaning to the situation, and deriving consequences from it.[11] These acts of judgment and evaluation take place in a social environment in which heterogeneous forms of justification and legitimacy exist side-by-side. People draw on clashing, often conflicting registers to justify their actions depending on the institutions involved and the position they occupy in the situation.

When the Basel authorities described a case of bankruptcy, they wrote with standardized codes. The primary script was a narrative of individual economic downfall, which was generally traced back to a series of causes. The individual diagnosis was a definitive aspect of this type of knowledge. How the authorities constructed narratives shifted over time, and the stories they pieced together out of their categorizations and causal explanations were either confirmed, contradicted, or—in rare cases— directly disputed by the bankrupt person. Practices of classification were not just a numbers game of calculating debts and assets, generating protocols, and evaluating accounting books. Narratives played a decisive role in authorities' reports and thus had an epistemic value. Historians of knowledge have analyzed the rhetoric and narrativity of calculative practices.[12] More fundamentally, however, narratives in general—discussions, rumors, the recounting of life events—constituted central aspects of knowledge production.

Finally, it is important to study the ways in which investigations into bankrupts were regularly frustrated. They were plagued with gaps, their models built on the sand of uncertain knowledge, their taxonomies never entirely fitting. The constant lack of information not only hindered officials' investigations, it limited their use value. In her study on colonial practices of classification, historian Ann Stoler, building on the works of Lorraine Daston and Peter Galison, developed the concept of "epistemic anxieties" to capture colonial authorities' doubts about their own resources and abilities.[13] Her discussion of Dutch rule in Southeast Asia underscores that colonial common sense was a leaky ship. Colonial practices of knowledge, though violent and powerful, were generally incoherent and fragmentary. Their project of identifying and enforcing "racial essences," of course, was vastly different from the everyday practices of bankruptcy proceedings administered by low-level bureaucrats in an early-industrial Swiss city; Basel police officers were not talking to a colonized "other" when a bankrupt person concealed some silverware from the bailiff inventorying their assets. Nevertheless, the concept of epistemic anxieties is helpful here, because officials worked in an epistemic gray zone. They belonged to communities of expectations and tried to make sense of the uncertainties of an economy shot through with contingency. Moreover, classifying somebody as bankrupt was a practice of foundational epistemic significance in liberal capitalism.

The following section outlines the contexts, institutions, and actors involved in bankruptcy proceedings in Basel between 1840 and 1867. After that, I analyze the practices and logics that informed the authorities' observation and assessments of bankrupt persons. The chapter then considers the other side, laying out debtors' own explanations of their economic fall. Two closely related sections consider how the normative concept of the household figured into these explanations and how the wife's dowry had a contradictory status as property, which underwent profound changes over the run of two decades. The chapter concludes with an analysis of the factors that motivated bankrupts to petition to have their civic rights restored.

The "Estate" of Bankrupts

Between 1840 and 1870, Basel was a small but rapidly growing city-canton. The population increased from 28,067 in 1847 to 40,680 in 1860 to 47,040 in 1870. After the agricultural regions were split off into their own canton in 1833, the city-canton encompassed the city plus the rural municipalities of Riehen, Bettingen, and Kleinhüningen.[14] Although becoming a citizen was gradually made easier in the years between 1840 and the beginning of the new century, only a minority of the canton's population were citizens in the period studied here. In 1860, 28.7 percent of those living in the canton were foreigners, and in the city, there were 11,000 citizens of the canton, 16,000 residents from other cantons, and 11,000 from abroad.[15] Residency statuses distinguished between the expensive-to-obtain full rights,[16] long-term residents, and short-term visitors.[17]

The city's economic structure was bifurcated: on the one hand were the export-oriented, capital-intensive silk and finance sectors and on the other the more conservative trades, dominated by guilds and focused on work within the canton.[18] Joining a guild continued to be a requirement for occupations like bakers and butchers well into the second half of the nineteenth century. This system bound the city's master workers together in political allegiances in a canton dominated by industrialists and commercial bankers, a structure that achieved an extraordinarily stable configuration of power.[19] The guilds ruled over multiple facets of economic life. For instance, up until the canton's constitution was revised in 1876, they were tasked with administering gender tutelage over unmarried women and the wives of bankrupts, as discussed in chapter 2. Silk weaving industrialized rapidly: while 1,500 people worked in silk-weaving factories in 1843, there were over 6,000 by 1860.[20] It was clearly the canton's main industry, and yet in 1850 it only accounted for 20 percent of its gross income. The machine industry was also on the rise, though it was dominated by small businesses until the 1870s. A large part of the canton's economy in the years studied was local small-scale commerce.[21] The city increasingly attracted migrants, though only a small number of them found work in industry, with most adapting to the circumstances and performing a series of jobs.[22]

The silk-weaving industry expanded and became the motor of the canton's economic ascent. Its success relied to a considerable extent on the roughly 13,000 cottage weavers in the surrounding areas, which allowed it to quickly increase or decrease volume as needed in a volatile market largely driven by fashion trends.[23]

The crisis of the late 1840s was attributed no longer to crop failures and rising grain prices, but to industrial business cycles.[24] The number of bankruptcies shot up. While 0.35 percent of households in the city were bankrupt in 1840 and just 0.21 percent in 1843, 0.88 percent (for a total of 51) went bankrupt in 1849.[25] Things stabilized in the 1850s, with the exception of one year that charted 0.85 percent (56 completed bankruptcies). During the crisis of the 1860s, the number again tripled. So, in 1866, a whole 2 percent of the canton's households were in bankruptcy (170 completed bankruptcies) and 1.58 percent (for a total of 136) in 1868.

These numbers on the cases of insolvency serious enough to warrant bringing bankruptcy proceedings to a conclusion (and not broken off because the debtor was able to pay or renegotiate their debts), however, were only the tip of the iceberg of outstanding debts, which were often dealt with through unofficial settlements. The tools used by the authorities to identify insolvent persons also fail to communicate a clear-cut account. The primary instrument for keeping records on bankruptcies was the register of bankrupts. Created in 1806, the record served not the production of statistics and the aggregation of social knowledge, but the identification and surveillance of individual bankrupt persons.[26] Bankrupts were placed in alphabetical order, their names filled out by the date they entered bankruptcy proceedings and, in many cases, their occupation. Such registers provided key economic information and were kept throughout Europe.[27] This information, however, was not stable. Only allowing for a single occupation was a basic inadequacy of the records, as proven during police interrogations, where most bankrupt persons explained that they worked varying jobs. Beginning in 1847, the canton's appellate court began compiling statistics on bankruptcies.[28] The court was primarily interested in the bankrupt's occupation and status as a citizen or migrant, and in a "special group," namely women. More than 90 percent of bankrupts were men. The categories under which the court subsumed bankrupts' occupations shifted over time. In 1861, there were eighteen sweeping occupational classifications, which was cut down to eight by 1870. The "craftsmen," which also counted people like bakers and butchers, always formed the largest group. Only in 1864 was the catch-all category "retailers" introduced. The third-largest group were "merchants," the fourth "day laborers," the fifth "factory workers," then "employees, officers, civil servants."

It is important to take a critical perspective on the administrative logic that informed the statistics while combing through them for socio-economic data. Still, despite this reservation, I would like to note some elementary information about Basel's bankruptcies from the court's statistics and the bankruptcy register. Retailers and craftsmen, like bakers, butchers, delicatessen workers, tailors, and cobblers, were heavily represented. But protoindustrial silk weavers, day laborers, employees in retail, coachmen, washerwomen, dressmakers, and pattern designers in weaving factories also had their fair share.

Many bankrupts had fallen on hard times while making a transition, such as retailers who had yet to find footing and build up a reputation, sometimes because they were new in town and could not fall back on family.[29] They were caught between customers who paid on credit and suppliers who, after a while, demanded payment.[30] The baker Jakob Henz, who lapsed into bankruptcy because of a flour bill, was a typical example: "In 1838, as I was pursuing my occupation as a baker, I could not pay a creditor as fast as he wanted, because I also had to extend credit; thus, I was not only subject to debt enforcement, but because this creditor was so strict, I was run out of my business and became bankrupt and then many of my creditors suffered losses."[31] Crisis hit hardest people who were not sufficiently established in the network of mutual obligations and protections.[32] The cobbler Rudolf Vest, whose interrogation in 1857 was discussed above, had already been subject to interrogation once when he slipped into bankruptcy for the first time in 1845. Back then, he was less obstinate and explained how he had started a business with little means and "even had to borrow and pay interest on my bed and everything."[33] An order for leather from a French supplier that turned out to be of bad quality had left him wrapped up in a lawsuit. Added to that were illness and that Vest was single and a boarder, all problems that robbed him of his ability to pay his bills. Too few reliable business relations, life events like illness, and marital status were ever-present topics in the stories of bankrupt persons, a point that I will return to.

Being bankrupt did not automatically mean being a pauper. It is true that in the 1840s, about a fifth of all cases reported by the courts concerned people who had no assets at all, most of whom were simply too poor to pay back their creditors. But the small subset of bankrupts who were interrogated by the police were often involved in real estate deals, and the sums they owed were often considerable. This, for sure, has much to do with the source material itself, as the government had a stronger interest to learn more about such financial situations. Perhaps the insights gleaned from their work contributed to the court's call on the government to impose restrictions on real estate purchases when the crisis of 1847 hit.[34] The downward spiral of rising bankruptcy rates and falling home prices was a general index of crisis.[35] The most frequent explanation bankrupts gave for their insolvency were meager earnings on a forced sale (whether it be ordered as a result of bankruptcy or done out of general duress). In a certain sense, they lambasted the market as a mechanism without memory, while they themselves remembered full well their past expenses and efforts and sought to make something out of them for the present and future.[36]

The Language of Moral Judgment

How did the court administration scrutinize bankrupts in their reports for the government? The authorities' knowledge was always piecemeal and uncertain, its information often patched together from rumors and others' negative statements. Another reason they lacked solid information was the simple fact that in the 1840s, a quarter of the insolvent persons on the list had left the canton. Again and again, they surmised that their bankrupt had *probably* settled in America, the primary destination for European emigrants in the 1840s that also functioned as a symbol for places far far away. For instance, "a lack of employment and a bad conscience" pushed former teacher Niklaus Feßler to depart for

America with some of his family;[37] the wagonmaker Joseph Sprich moved to America in spring 1847;[38] the glassblower Hieronymus Friedrich Holzach left behind wife and children and made off for the States;[39] the barkeeper Jakob Schneider secretly sailed away with his second wife— "according to our information" to America—abandoning his children from his first marriage in a Basel orphanage;[40] and the butcher Rudolf Jeremias Christ, who had lost his wife and children, had also, "according to our information, emigrated to America."[41] One-time civil court servant Heinrich Tschientschy "suddenly left office, family & home and went to America."[42] Of the saddler Eduard Rebsamen the courts wrote that he, "according to our information, emigrated to America,"[43] just like Urs Victor Pfirter, a carpenter who moved to America with his family,[44] and Richard Trappet, a goldsmith who did the same.[45] Thus, the flight of Johannes Bader—a butcher who, "according to our information, paired up with a woman" and left behind his wife and children "in order to settle in America"—was in itself nothing unusual.[46] Unusual in Bader's case was that he returned to Basel shortly thereafter and "to a certain extent tried to make good on his missteps" by promising his creditors 20 percent of the original owed sum, "which the relatives of his wife will pay on the condition that his creditors entirely free him of his obligations."[47] Former clerk Leonhard Matzinger-Weck established a gas lamp business in Amiens, fell into insolvency, reached a settlement with his creditors, returned to Basel, managed "to build up credit and trust" despite his notorious lack of assets, started dealing weapons "during the uprising in Baden" in 1849, went bankrupt again, and then left with a considerable sum of cash "to America, according to our information."[48] In another case from the 1840s, the authorities assumed that suicide was the reason they couldn't find their man: "Häring has disappeared without a trace; one supposes that he threw himself into the Rhine; he had set his household on a more splendid base than his estate and his income allowed; and through his economic hardship he succumbed to the temptation to use for his own purposes money that he was supposed to administer for others."[49]

The concealment of assets was another source of uncertainty for the authorities, and its very possibility was a constant cloud on their horizon. "Defrauding," "delaying," and "sale" of assets could occasion criminal investigations. But the police often didn't follow up on leads because they either lacked important information or because the assets involved simply weren't worth it. When the insolvent Abraham Sixt concealed some household goods, silverware, and cash in the Basel suburb of

Allschwil before he was about to enter bankruptcy, his wife apparently said, "you don't have to be so dumb, you have to hide away your things." At least this is what an anonymous informant told the policeman tasked with investigating the Sixt family. When the officer served Sixt with a summons to appear at an interrogation, he looked in at the bankrupt's kitchen, reporting that he had "seen it only poorly equipped with old stuff, just like people who don't have much left." But he still wasn't certain, because he didn't have a search warrant: "I could also see into the living room through the open door, but there too I saw nothing worth mentioning, just a table in the middle; admittedly, I could not see into the entire room."[50]

Insolvent debtors not only often appeared poorer than they actually were. Sometimes, they donned the trimmings of wealth in order to retain their credit and acquire loans. This was true of Samuel Barth, who was accused of "giving the appearance of wealth by possessing a carriage."[51] In another case, when a neighbor secretly informed on an insolvent person for hiding their assets—namely sheets, blankets, clothes, and a small kitchen table—a delivery man was called in to testify. He had been sent to a house, he recalled. Whether it was that of the suspected family he could not say, because a girl, not an adult, had handed him the suspicious package. The girl also led him to the delivery address, which he had now forgotten. The content of the package was soft, at any rate, but he couldn't remember any more details.[52]

Still, the lack of reliable information didn't hold the courts back from attributing a definitive cause to every single case of bankruptcy. In the 1840s, their reports adhered to a logic of individual responsibility and fault. The following two decades witnessed a shift in this language. While they retained their focus on the individual's life, they increasingly considered a broader range of causes that could plausibly explain why someone went bankrupt. Every change in thinking on this issue was accompanied by conflicts in the administration over the methods of gathering knowledge, documenting evidence, and reporting on cases.

The highly standardized reports of the 1840s relayed a narrative whose two primary components were laziness and lack of good housekeeping: "This bankrupt could have avoided his bankruptcy if he had budgeted better and worked harder," read the briefest formula.[53] "Hardworking" and "household management" were personal attributes rooted in production and consumption, consistent earnings and frugal spending, seemingly distinct spheres of economic life. But in the eyes of the authorities, they were closely related. Budgeting had a productive side; work necessitated virtues rehearsed in the household. They were not juxtaposed and categorized as masculine and feminine, but together forged an ideal of normalized economic behavior that balanced "home" and "work" while retaining their gendered hierarchy.[54]

Failures in domestic life were often associated with accusations of alcoholism, "debauchery," and "living beyond one's means."[55] Not a negligible number of bankrupt persons seem to have opened inns before falling into insolvency.[56] While opening an inn represented a precarious form of economic independence that could be risked with limited initial capital—assuming one could buy from suppliers on credit—the courts interpreted such business decisions as having their source in the bankrupts' alcoholism and "carelessness," thus blurring the boundary between work and home.[57]

The "unwillingness to work" signified inconsistency, a lack of concentration on one's tasks, and a lack of timekeeping skills: "This bankrupt made a living as a decorative weaver," the administration wrote of Jean Maas-Day, who came from Haute-Loire, "and sold wares given to him on commission; it seems that he more belongs to the class of *aventuriers* than to that of hard-working people who exclusively stick by the practice of their occupation."[58] A report on a hatter played the same tune: "This bankrupt is not exclusively dedicated to his occupation, but is often away on trips, where he presumably spends more than he earns."[59] A carpenter had similar issues: "Unwillingness to work and perhaps a lack of customers—for which he is to blame—are the causes of the bankruptcy."[60] Negligence and "lack of business knowledge" were additional causes of economic failure.[61]

The reports documented individual mistakes and bad habits, the latter a diagnostic category that combined notions about nature, social life, and individual personality.[62] Conceiving of bad habits as a factor of "second nature" and "individual self-control" implied that the individual could make the decision to give them up. Thus bad habits were a moral issue, and coupling them with economics was a specifically liberal move. In some cases, the courts' reports referenced immoral conduct that had tarnished the person's reputation. This conception of immorality was involved in the interplay of society and self, inside and outside exemplified in Rudolf Hunziker's complaint that he was afflicted by an external blemish that affected his "innermost being." Judging a person immoral was based on objectionable actions performed in a social context. Disrepute often stemmed from extramarital affairs or sexual transgressions, such as when master builder Ludwig Caldre got divorced after a year of marriage "in the wake of his immoral turn."[63]

Because reputation was such a delicate matter, behavior condemned as immoral could have direct economic consequences.[64] But reputation could not be easily quantified, and identifying immoral acts was not an unambiguous matter either. The administrative solution lay in describing objectionable behavior as acts of deception.[65] Fraud could be criminally prosecuted, but it was difficult to pin down, because determining an act as fraudulent necessitated first forming an accurate picture of a person's creditworthiness in the eyes of others. But even when they suspected fraud, the authorities only had limited latitude to investigate it. The courts insisted that there must be a way to get at debtors like Oscar Häring, "who in total insolvency nevertheless constantly borrow small and large sums," because this activity was nothing but "fraud."[66] Crystal clear, on the other hand, was the case of tobacco factory worker Christoph Heckendorn. Heckendorn "deceitfully" convinced the "relatives of his wife to pay out to him five years in advance the annual pension of 1,000 francs to which his wife had claim." As soon he had the 5,000 francs in his hand, he made off with it, abandoning his wife and children.[67]

Astonishingly, the court administration's reports from the 1840s rarely mentioned illness, disability, or old age as causes of bankruptcy (which stands in stark contrast to the explanations offered by the bankrupt persons themselves discussed in the next section). The one cause that the 1840s reports never acknowledged were economic crises. During the crisis year 1847, when the number of bankruptcies saw a rapid uptick and philanthropic initiatives in Basel organized soup kitchens to serve about five thousand people,[68] the courts closed their report with the words: "Although many of these bankruptcies find their cause in the distress of the times, the prevalence of careless bankruptcies makes it appropriate to take a stricter approach to those at fault as our laws demand."[69] Thus the focus was again directed toward individual missteps that translated into bad reputation. The authorities saw their task in documenting individual behaviors, comparing them with a moral standard, and intervening when deemed appropriate.

But the authorities' perspective shifted in the run of the 1850s. The sources suggest that the change emanated from a different approach to acquiring knowledge. On August 23, 1855, Alexander Hill, a twenty-nine-year-old butcher, was interrogated in vain:

Question 1: When did you become bankrupt?

Answer: I cannot say exactly.

Question 2: Your debtors tried to collect on you a year ago?

A: I don't think it has been quite a year.

Question 3: You didn't have any assets then?

A: No.

Question 4: So, your creditors are going to lose the entire sum, and that at 443 francs.

A: Yes.

Question 5: Why was it that you did not own anything?

A: I just had no property, that's all.

Question 6: Have you never earned and saved something?

A: I was sick for a long time and earned nothing.

Question 7: What do you do now?

A: I work for wages for Frau Ryhiner-Streckeisen and Herr Dr. Iselin; next Monday I will have work at the White Mansion.[70]

On the same day, the police dispatched a complaint to the cantonal government. They were aggravated by the fact that the meager information provided by the courts regularly put the interrogating police officers in a dilemma, because they did not know what exactly they should accuse the bankrupt of.[71] In January 1855, the court responded to an inquiry that for the case in question, they "really didn't know what more to report & the person could not be reached."[72] The chief of police thus demanded that the civil court administration conduct preliminary interrogations of bankrupts before the police took over. The head of the civil court administration, however, rejoined that bankrupts were "pretty unknown" to the court officials and that it was not uncommon for the schedule of claims to be compiled at a hearing in the absence of the person in question.[73] Acquiring more information was difficult, he continued, and increasing the number of authorities conducting interrogations would only cause further confusion. The government ultimately decided to order the court administration to note in their reports whether they thought that a criminal investigation or police interrogation was necessary and also to note cases caused by an "unfortunate combination of various circumstances."[74]

The shift in practices of documenting and attributing causes was not occasioned by one single event. And thirteen years later, the court reports were still being criticized as "totally aphoristic notes."[75] Nevertheless, the sources make it possible to retrace the gradual metamorphosis of reports and police interrogations. The reports from the 1860s briefly recount a chain of events that, in the authorities' estimation, had led to the bankruptcy. In some cases, the diachronic series of events supplanted the earlier list of character flaws. The reports were now based on files on individual bankrupts with records that began with the schedule of claims.[76] Alongside disputed assets or claims made against the person, the statements of the bankrupt person themselves were recorded in the files, so long as the bankrupt person had been present at the hearing where the schedule of claims was compiled. Issues like sickness, multiple children, and heavy competition found their way into the reports with a frequency markedly higher than before. The officials also increased their interest in bankrupts' bookkeeping habits. "The bankrupt does not keep accounting books," a report on the owner of a textile business stated (who actually did keep books for others, but not for his own business), "he considers this to be unimportant for such a small business like his. The bankrupt is a hard worker, but without order in his affairs."[77]

It is not as if moral failings disappeared as an explanation altogether. In the 1860s, too, there were reports on housewives of "ill repute" and craftsmen who lost their customer base after a scandalized divorce.[78] But instead of stereotypical blaming, the reports narrated stories of individual entanglements. Still, these stories, too, were reduced to a small number of causes and critical points of no return. For instance, the report on the sixty-eight-year-old widow Margaretha Vogt states that she had to support her daughter because the latter's husband had gone bankrupt; it also mentioned that the senior had worked as a silk weaver, that her deceased husband had suffered a long illness, and that she had been hosting boarders ever since his death. During the hearing for the schedule of claims, however, she emphasized not these facts, but her relations with her creditors. From one butcher she "got very bad meat, thus the boarders started to leave; I wanted to pay him if he would have had patience. Since the beginning of the year he has set the collectors on me. My landlord Langwirth also asked him to have patience with me."[79]

The spectrum of explanations expanded, but personal failure still stood front and center. Despite the shift away from an emphasis on character flaws and moral shortcomings toward objective factors, the consistent feature of the reports was their fundamental epistemology of individual diagnosis.

In 1867, the court administration began filing their reports in tabular form. The high number of bankruptcies seems to have been one reason for this shift in notation. Nevertheless, when they deemed it necessary, the court administration appended a narrative account of the case: "Mere tables with few words with very general content in the 'remarks' column do not substitute the previous, in-depth, personally nuanced reports."[80] Finally, in 1876, the court administration discontinued sending reports to the government on the grounds that their limited resources only allowed them to compile "incomplete information with vague evidence." Importantly, in the 1860s, the court administration started sending suspicious cases directly to the police, thus surpassing the administrative roundabout to the government counsel, who until then had to order the police to conduct investigations of individual cases.[81]

The Loss of Credit

It should come as no surprise that bankrupts told a different story of their hardships. Conflicting narratives featured in many interrogation records. Each session began with the question as to whether the bankrupt person knew how much their creditors would lose because of their bankruptcy; they rarely gave the correct answer. Proclaiming ignorance may have been tactical, but the generally low sums that they guessed also indicate the existence of differing versions of the events. The court administration wrote that it was pointless to mail bankrupts the numbers in the schedule of claims, because they would only come up with an excuse for each entry: "The extraordinary expanse of bankrupts' 'negative imagination' makes it such that they can never be brought to understand and admit the material correctness of their creditors' losses without disputing the correctness of the claims."[82]

The bankrupts' versions of things framed the events differently: the claims had already been paid, creditors had promised that they could defer payment. The schedule of claims extracted open claims from the web of social obligations. The bankrupts, however, did not assess the situation in terms of abstract numbers. They saw themselves as active subjects in the economy still capable of providing services in return and asserting their own claims.

On the whole, their narratives took a distinct form. They recounted their biography as one determined by superindividual systems and events. Doubtlessly, the accounts were "enforced narratives": they were structured in line with the standardized questions posed by the police and adhered to a logic that Carolyn Steedman calls "autobiographical injunction." In such a "history of expectations, orders and instructions," bankrupts sought to appear upright and conforming.[83] One requirement of these highly scripted narratives was to tell an individual story that identified similarities with those of others, a story demonstrating that one had not done anything of note. Bankrupts, in short, employed a rhetoric of mundanity.

"My experience is like that of many others, I returned to my occupation," stated the above discussed Rudolf Hunziker during his police interrogation.[84] He told how he had bought his father's house for 9,500 francs and only got 7,250 from the house's forced auction. In contrast to the court reports, bankrupt persons regularly referred to general economic crises, such as those of the 1840s and 1860s.[85] Falling house prices and terminated loans on real estate were the constant elements of these narratives of bankruptcy suffered at no fault of one's own. The superindividual crisis provided the context, while the narratives sought to concretize its meaning for the individual by articulating the specific impact it had on them. The junction of general crisis and individual relations, in short, engendered the loss of credit.

"Credit" was not a matter of one-off financial transactions, but the state of being of a person with a particular reputation in a particular economic situation. This social complex was defined by that person's interactions with suppliers, business competitors, customers, and family members, who all had their own expectations of the debtor and sought to assert their claims in different ways. The interrogation protocol of a thirty-year-old cobbler named Friedrich Hodel, a divorced father of four, is exemplary:

> In 1838, I established myself here [in Basel] in the Gerbergasse with ideas that I brought with me from Paris, where I worked for a while as a lead cobbler at a reputable shoemaker and retailer. At the beginning I had no money of my own and had to supply my shoemaker store on credit . . . and so the rough beginnings put me in debt; I had the unconditional trust of the tanners here, but their bills started piling up. . . . In the first years I did indeed realize that I had not built up my business in the way necessary here, but I could no longer change it and was already in dire straits; many commodities sat on the shelves and I had to sell them at a loss; moreover, I lost customers here and there; and finally, marital difficulties disrupted my family life and hindered me.[86]

In response to the police officer's rebuke that he should have budgeted smarter and worked harder, he stated, "[I]n later years, as I lost more and more customers and came under increasing economic pressure, my earlier natural aversion to the cobbler's profession returned, and I openly admit that my ambition cooled off and I did as many others in my same situation would have done; but I did not act carelessly, nobody who knows me would say that." Hodel's depiction of his business's beginnings was contradictory, at once burdened by heavy debts and propelled by easy credit. The narrative then meandered to a recounting of his own apathy and pressure from creditors, combined with a shift in sentiments toward his occupation and a general loss of ambition.[87] Hodel also noted the "trust" he enjoyed from his suppliers. While this word seldom appears in the sources consulted here—and when it does, it is usually in a very ambivalent sense—the basic phenomenon it describes sums up what it meant to have credit.[88]

Having good credit necessitated fulfilling two conditions: having a solid customer base that reliably paid and having the support of business partners. One cobbler regretted that his customers were "people of lower class . . . from whom one had to wait a long time for payment & then in the end never received."[89] A sturdy reputation among suppliers, in turn, enabled one to withstand tough times. For example, during an interrogation, a debtor stated that he would have slipped into bankruptcy earlier if it hadn't been for a respectable distributor treating him, a merchant who otherwise had "integrity and an honorable manner," with so much "mildness & consideration."[90] A tailor was confident that even his bankruptcy had not compromised his reputation: "I have sought to retain so much trust from my customers that I currently can again employ eight journeymen."[91]

But credit was a resource that could dry up quickly. In the above-cited interrogation, Friedrich Hodel reported on being "in dire straits." In some cases, debtors blamed the rapidity of debt enforcement and complained that they had simply run out of time.[92] When an interrogating police official accused an insolvent mason of having "exploited gifted credit up until the last minute" and "piling debts upon debts," the mason retorted that he had "not abused my credit frivolously," but had been "at once from all sides pressured" and could no longer sustain himself.[93] Bankrupt debtors often translated their credit situation into personal relations when they felt the heat of creditors' claims, as with a debtor who emphasized that the creditors from abroad who were now insisting on immediate payment had first "importunately" flooded him with commodities.[94] An insolvent merchant read "ruthless" demands to pay "quickly" as a malicious act against him as a person.[95] Conversely, the

Jenga tower of unpaid loans threatened to collapse when others did not pay, when creditors came knocking to collect on another's debt one had cosigned on, or when a business partner skipped town.[96]

Creditworthiness depended on public appearances. "Nobody can accuse me of carelessness; to the contrary, I always had credit," a debtor told a police official, offering his financial reputation as evidence of his moral fortitude.[97] Bankrupt persons repeatedly underscored the significance of public reputation, a point particularly relevant for the inn, a plebeian public space.[98] The inn was a place where free time and work overlapped.[99] Inns were often discussed in the police hearings because the authorities disliked them for a number of reasons. They were potential sites of upheaval, not least of all during Basel's constitutional crisis of 1846, when, out of fear of being overthrown, the conservative government sent undercover informants to listen in on pub talk.[100] Moreover, alcoholism counted among the lapses and vices that the police believed explained some bankruptcies.

Banning someone from the inns, as discussed in chapter 2, was a rare yet particularly damaging sanction, because it cut the debtor off from appearing in public. In 1849, the blacksmith Jakob Christoph Grey went bankrupt, and his wife and kids had to depend on poor relief. The police made public that he was banned from the inns.[101] He begged to be spared this dishonoring punishment, fearing the "shame and disadvantage that it would have for me." Grey did not defend himself against having his civic rights stripped, promised to cooperate with the police, and to not visit inns. But, he rejoined to the interrogating officer, he had never been "kicked out of an inn as a drunk or a non-payer or for staying too late." When accused of being drunks, other bankrupts claimed that someone had slandered them. They demanded witness reports, insisted that they had never been seen in a drunken state or been arrested by the police, and, in general, constantly referred to public appearances.

Claims and Expectations in the Household

The investigating authorities and bankrupts themselves repeatedly spoke of the household, marital relations, and family economy. The household—a problem, an argument, a normative concept—played diverse roles in the bankruptcy records.[102] A precarious domestic economy offered bankrupts an opportune explanation for general financial failure, because, as women's historians have long known, budgeting was women's duty.[103] Johannes Haering, a sixty-five-year-old gunsmith, proclaimed that his wife—and, after her death, his daughter—had been responsible for his finances. Thus, he asserted, he really had no clue as to the causes of his bankruptcy: "I really don't know, all kinds of debts must have been growing for a long time, how and from where, though, I cannot tell you; when she was alive, I gave my wife my monthly earnings of about 36 francs for the household budget, and since her death two years ago, I give my earnings to my daughter and don't concern myself with it any further."[104] Shifting responsibility to a soberly calculating housewife—who, excluded from the masculine honor economy, was thus knowledgeable of "the truth of prices and open accounts"— was more than an exculpatory rhetorical trick.[105] More than a few bankrupts told of marital difficulties, drawing a straight line from domestic "disturbances" to economic turbulence.[106] Others blamed their insolvency on their inability to rely on unpaid domestic work on account of being single or a widower.[107] Benedikt Rebsamen, whose wife had filed for divorce because of his alcoholism—and in all likelihood domestic violence—justified his economic situation with the lapidary remark: "my wife should just return to me so that the household can be kept more economically than it can be without a housewife."[108]

The gendered division of labor and knowledge, the men essentially argued, made it impossible to properly manage finances without a housewife. Bankrupt men described again and again the opacity of household economics. Quarryman Joseph Kuhn claimed that he had little notion of household accounts after his wife's passing. Not only had she sent off portions of his earnings to her family "out of ill-advised precaution." She had also accrued debts to pay for luxuries that Kuhn claimed to have known nothing about before her death.[109]

Household issues stood under the microscope of official scrutiny. Moral shortcomings, a favored explanation of bankruptcy among officials, were brought to the public eye during divorce proceedings. Of the wigmaker Rudolf Karli, court officials wrote that he had "long had a shattered domestic life" and a "bad moral reputation."[110] In his own defense, Karli traced the source of his bad reputation back to his "evil marriage." What exactly made the marriage "evil" remained unclear, though Karli's own violence toward his wife was the likely culprit and not anything she herself had done; at least he found no occasion to say anything bad about her during the hearing. Nevertheless, he found that he had been defamed for his divorce, particularly after he started a relationship with another woman and had a child with her while still not yet allowed to remarry.[111]

We've heard how the authorities interpreted bad budgeting as the cause of some bankruptcies. But what of the cases when debtors presented their good household budget and family life as reasons to excuse them? By describing themselves as caring family men, interrogated bankrupts played on the polysemy of a normative concept that they knew the authorities certainly shared. Does this mean that the values applied to the household differed from those valid for markets and contracts? Perhaps that with the increasing separation of wage labor and reproduction, the home and family were becoming emotionally warm shelters against the cold, calculating world of business? As Karin Hausen's classic essay on the topic elaborates, this interpretation—along with its assumptions about the gendered division of labor—was widely shared among the nineteenth-century haute bourgeoisie.[112] But it should not distract from the constant intertwining of monetary relations and family life.[113] Flying in the face of the assumption that home and business were totally separate spheres, the budgeting and accounting performed within the home were monetary activities that were invested with considerable significance by both bankrupt persons and the bankruptcy authorities. The complex of duties and needs that constituted the household were multifarious, mixing together financial, social, and familial values. Thus when they depicted themselves as responsible family men, bankrupt persons grabbed for the "household," or "home," because the notion evoked authority and duty, referred directly to the fact that they had dependents, and suggested that they had a well-earned place in a gendered hierarchy.[114] Bankrupt men emphasized that they had lived within their means: "I have conducted my household affairs in a very economic manner, sometimes things were very tight."[115] It seems only natural that debtors often highlighted their efforts to support multiple children or care for a sick wife. Less banal, however, is how bankrupt men positioned the fulfillment of these duties in a normative framework that demanded that one support one's family "with honor."[116]

The narratives spoke of the family as a network of needs, activities, and expectations.[117] Debtors asserted their role as breadwinners. The point was less to simply remind the authorities that family and business life were interrelated and more to note the pressure put on them by family members, thus providing further justification for the bankruptcy. In-laws who exploited being a cosigner by constantly demanding "return favors"; the debts of a father or son that one had to take on ("it is correct, my son could have acted better"); businesses that had to be run after the death of an uncle or other relative, even though they weren't profitable were all put forth as burdensome duties that sapped the individual debtor's time and energy.[118] To be classified as a bankrupt diminished a person in the value system of the "family man." Thus one bankrupt wrote in his rehabilitation petition that having to place his daughter in an orphanage pained him so greatly because it put him "on the same level as those family men . . . who throw themselves and their family into misfortune through carelessness and prodigality."[119] Shining light on one's virtues as a family man and breadwinner thus constituted a key trope in bankrupts' defenses.

Some reciprocal services and duties that made up the web of the family were only partially represented in a bankruptcy's balance sheet. Although Rudolf Hunziker admitted that he had not yet replenished his children's baptism gifts, the authorities restored his rights on the grounds that Hunziker had worked off his monetary debts to his children in other ways. To repeat the authorities' reasoning: the children's belongings stood "in a different category from the demands of other creditors."[120] How property and claims were classified in the process of generating the schedule of claims was a delicate matter. Who could claim what from whom for what reasons was a question that shook the cage of intrafamilial power relations, a point most prominently exemplified by the dowry.

The Dowry: A Contentious Form of Property

The dowry posed more daunting issues in bankruptcy proceedings than any other class of property. It linked marital bonds, domestic gender hierarchy, and the interests of the wife's family. Jurists of the time situated it in a gray zone between bankruptcy law and marital property law.[121] Its liminal status resulted from the fundamental tension between contractual relations and the sanctified idea of the household. The husband had legal authority over the dowry, which made it possible for him to put it forth as a guarantee for a loan, on the condition that his wife gave her written assent in the accompaniment of a legal guardian.[122]

Records on bankruptcy hearings often contained discussions of how bankrupt men had established their businesses with their wife's dowry. Like unmarried women and widows, the wives of bankrupt men stood under the legal guardianship of a third party. In Basel, the guilds played a central role in the administration of gender tutelage. Since the early modern period, when women often appeared alone in court, the guilds had expanded their power on this point.[123] As a study on the canton of Basel-Landschaft demonstrates, gender guardianship had divergent, class-specific effects. While bourgeois women were relatively free to dispose of their assets at will, women of the lower classes were subjected to strict regulations.[124] But in the city of Basel, the guilds also sought to exert their authority over wealthy women. They wielded the enormous sums of money under their administration to further their own financial and political interests.[125] Only a small minority of women enjoyed the exceptional right to freely control their assets.[126]

When her husband entered bankruptcy, a woman had a privileged claim to her dowry. In the schedule of claims, she was ranked lower than taxes and other fees owed to the state and lower than creditors who held promissory notes secured with real estate or other assets, but she was ranked above other creditors who held unsecured debts. Moreover, women could take possession of their movable assets so long as they hadn't already been realized. Studies on the history of the dowry have illuminated how this seemingly premodern institution opened up spaces to maneuver for women.[127] From a legal perspective, the dowry could be interpreted as a loan granted by a woman to her husband. Thus, the dowry provided leverage to women, whose rights were otherwise restricted. In a special sense, the dowry was the property of an individual woman.

When it came to actualizing the leverage afforded by the dowry during bankruptcy proceedings, however, serious limitations were imposed on the woman's position as a "creditor" in Basel in the run of the nineteenth century. Interpreted as a loan to the husband, the dowry did not have the same status as claims made by other creditors, a fact evidenced by the shifting rules for the rehabilitation of bankrupts. In order to have their rights restored in Basel, debtors had to prove that they had paid off all of their creditors with their own money; in the first half of the nineteenth century, this rule was made increasingly stricter. By 1849, declarations from creditors that the debts had been settled were no longer sufficient: Debtors now had to provide documentation that they had actually paid the debts.[128]

But the rules on the replenishment of the dowry went in the exact opposite direction. Already in 1827, the court administration drew a remarkable conclusion when considering one bankrupt's petition for rehabilitation. The debtor had paid off his creditors, but was not able to restore his wife's dowry. Nevertheless, the administration recommended granting his petition, reasoning that "The relation of a woman to the assets of her husband consists in the fact that she is not a creditor *in relation to him;* she only retains a privilege *in relation to other creditors.*"[129] Thus his wife found herself in the paradoxical situation of not being a creditor and at the same time being ranked higher than other creditors on the schedule of claims. As a loan extended within the household, the dowry had a special status. This principle was written into law in 1867.[130] The argument was that marriage bound the wife to the fate of her husband. The economic motivation for this intervention into the meaning of marriage and the dowry, however, was to satisfy the complaints of commercial creditors. If creditors couldn't know if a borrower was speculating with his wife's dowry, then they also couldn't be certain that she would not assert her privileges in the case that the debtor went bankrupt. The uncertainty this caused posed, in the words of lawmakers, "a serious threat to the security of commerce."[131]

Edited by Basel jurist Andreas Heusler, one of the first drafts of a proposed federal law on bankruptcy and asset seizure granted privileged status to only 50 percent of the dowry's value. The canton of Basel-Stadt adopted this rule in 1884, though at the same time women were still permitted to demand that their marriage be organized as a matrimonial regime of separate property, if with some restrictions.[132] The 50 percent rule was set in stone by the federal bankruptcy law as it was passed in 1889. Thus the security of commercial creditors was increased at the expense of married women's property rights.[133]

Property has always been a social relation in a field of forces, a notion made pointedly clear by the dowry's position at the juncture of liberal-capitalist contract law and hierarchical gender relations. A look at a specific case underscores the contentious nature of this special type of property. After his mother's death in 1845, Abraham Wertenberg inherited about 7,000 francs. Four years later, the former tailor, who had also worked for a time as a policeman, petitioned to have his rights restored after having them stripped as a consequence of an earlier bankruptcy. This wasn't the first time: in 1845, he had petitioned to be rehabilitated, but the court administration determined then that he had only paid off domestic creditors and not foreign creditors.[134] In the new petition, Wertenberg claimed that he had now been able to "satisfy" all his creditors, but this time around, too, he had not paid them all back.[135] The officials tasked with the case nevertheless recommended that the request be granted. The creditors who had declared themselves satisfied despite not receiving payment were an uncle of Wertenberg's wife, who forgave the erstwhile tailor's debt of 518 francs, and a group of creditors who dropped their claims to a few dozen francs. The court considered the uncle's claim as belonging "not entirely to the same category" as those of other creditors, and because it represented the largest sum out of the settled debts, they were willing to fulfill Wertenberg's wishes and restore his rights.[136] First, however, they asked the opinion of the Safran Guild, which administered the dowry of Wertenberg's wife. The guild voiced reservations. The "personality of the petitioner," they worried, gave little reason to be confident that the dowry of about 6,400 francs would not be entirely consumed if he were allowed access to it, thus bringing him into "even greater deficits."[137] They added that the danger of dependence on poor relief and the interests of the wife's family (who remained unnamed throughout the entire procedure) spoke against restoring her husband's rights.

When the authorities told Wertenberg that the guild would continue to administer his wife's dowry, he fought back against this "vote of non-confidence" and demanded that he, as a rehabilitated man, should have complete control over it. The transcription of Wertenberg's discussion with the court quotes him as saying: "With such a restriction, he would still be a fettered man & would be hindered by these shackles in every independent step he might take to secure his existence."[138] The court finally recommended that Wertenberg's petition be denied on account of his fussiness. Shortly thereafter, though, a resolution was found. He submitted a new petition for rehabilitation in which he argued that expensive retreats at spa towns to cure his wife's lengthy illness had contributed to the "devastation" of his finances.[139] He declared himself willing to forgo his rights to her dowry, pleading that just 1,000 francs of it should be set aside for him to start a new business. Thus, he was warranted prohibitory rehabilitation. But just three months later, the court learned that Wertenberg had swindled control of the whole dowry from the guardian and gone back to his old ways at the inn.[140] When the guardian found out about it, he demanded that Wertenberg cough it up, only to discover that 1,800 francs had already been squandered.[141] The court administration reported that they summoned Wertenberg and, after a few quarrels, convinced him to hand over the money the next day. But the clerk recorded that when he showed up the next day he started acting like a madman: he denied having admitted to anything, pulled all kinds of papers out of his hat, made new offers, and departed saying "he wanted to wait and see, he wouldn't allow himself to be harassed" and have his "rightful property" wrenched away from him.[142]

The dowry—particularly when it reached sums like in Wertenberg's case—was an object of fierce conflict. Wrestling over it involved stak-

ing out positions (such as when Wertenberg referenced his wife's taking
to the spas as a reason why his business failed), designating special statuses (such as when the uncle's forgiven claims were placed in a special
category), and exercising administrative discretion (such as when the
court allowed Wertenberg to control 1,000 francs of his wife's dowry).
Determining how to distribute and delegate the dowry involved fights
over values, claims, and accomplishments. The example also highlights
the significance of marital gender hierarchies for men's identities as
economic subjects and illustrates the underside of the elementary role
that economic independence played in the constitution of liberal legal
subjectivity.[143] Male sovereignty, acquired through economic agency, was
often established in the husband's legally guaranteed authority to control his wife's property, which served as its touchstone. Finally, the narrative offers insights into how state institutions exercised their authority
over bankrupts to discipline and control their economic behavior.

Male control over a wife's dowry was a particular expression of masculine sovereignty. Our understanding of the latter's historical genesis can
be aided by new research on the social history of kinship relations. The
tendency to reduce women's control over their own property is an index
of more general shifts in models of familial ties. According to David
Sabean and Simon Teuscher, over the course of the nineteenth century,
the bonds of marriage gradually gained the upper hand over the wife's
family of origin.[144] In step with the expansion of capitalist relations, the
significance of horizontal marital ties increased as that of the vertical
family line sunk. Viewed through the lens of social class, the capitalist
family regime was characterized by smaller, more close-knit familial networks. This shift supplanted the many-branched familial relations that
defined the clientelism of the Ancien Régime. Homing in on the intersection of class, family, and financial relations shines new light on the
gender relations of the household. From this perspective, the husband's
increasing control over his wife's dowry was one step in this process of
reshaping familial relations.[145] It also contributed to an uptick in newly
started businesses in Switzerland in the nineteenth century.[146] This was
made possible by a potpourri of fragmentary, incoherent, yet formalized
laws that codified conflicts over power in the home.

Rehabilitation and the Varieties of Social Experience

According to jurists, a debtor's petition for rehabilitation represented his
attempt "to be reinstated into his position as a person with civic rights."

The conception of rehabilitation as being *reinstated into* a particular status in a system of socially codified agency is an apt description of liberal subjectification. How did debtors themselves perceive these processes of classification? Which categories and distinctions were significant for them? And what were the future perspectives that motivated them to work to escape bankrupt status?

The sources offer a picture not of homogeneous ideas about civic honor and morality, but rather of an enduring, cacophonous debate between debtors, creditors, and state institutions over the practical significance of the loss of rights. Losing and recovering one's civic rights did not involve some abstract notion of citizenship that was vested with the accoutrements of bourgeois identity. Even when the founding of the Swiss Confederation in 1848 set off a wave of different nationalistic activities,[147] bankrupt persons in Basel did not place the right to vote at the top of their petitions, but instead articulated both narrower and broader concerns and aspirations. Chapter 2 detailed how the bankrupt functioned as a personification of crisis in the social imagination, skillfully deployed by political movements to lend urgency to their demands. But the claims of individual debtors were much different.

Of the petitions for restoration of rights filed in Basel between 1840 and 1866, the year that the rules for rehabilitation changed, 116 were granted.[148] This amounted to less than 10 percent of bankruptcies in the same time period. Many bankrupts never got to the point where they could reasonably file a petition, while others saw no point in bothering (which I will come back to). Those who tried often asserted male honor as their motivation; one subset of this argument were the depictions of oneself as an upstanding family man, as discussed above. Rudolf Hunziker, for instance, wanted "to be able to act as an honorable citizen."[149] Jakob Lüdin, too, pled that he be allowed to announce the "restoration of his civic honor and make it public in the cantonal gazette," because he was "quietly and honorably" laboring to support his family.[150] Benedikt Cyprian petitioned for "the honors and rights granted to an upright man."[151]

In many cases involving debtors without Basel citizenship, the threat of deportation was the most pressing reason to apply for rehabilitation. In his petition from 1851, Johann Ludwig Hagemann listed a number of fateful events: he had been baited by a merchant to travel abroad and returned with empty pockets; he had cosigned on too many loans; multiple family members suffered from illnesses; his home along with four expensive looms had burned to the ground. Added to these "misfortunes of no fault of my own," which, Hagemann stated, he had nonetheless been able to overcome thanks to his industriousness, came a disastrous blow: "namely, the revocation of my residency permit here."[152] If they demonstrated considerable effort, debtors had some room to get their residency permits extended. Heinrich Thommen, a worker at a silk-weaving factory, couldn't manage to pay off all his creditors. But because he only had fifty francs left to pay, the authorities refrained from deporting him and restored his civic rights about six months later.[153] Cantonal institutions, however, kept a close eye on debtors who they believed might draw on municipal poor relief. Even if a noncitizen paid off all his debtors and had his rights restored, law enforcement requested that the immigration administration monitor them if they had no money. Silk weaver Johann Jakob Grieder, for instance, paid his creditors, but after it was all said and done, his only property was the bedding that could not be legally seized from him. This evoked the concern of the authorities.[154] Even a creditor weighing in with the authorities on the debtor's behalf and partially forgiving their debts was sometimes insufficient to help them get their rights back.[155]

Familial relations were often the key to rehabilitation. Historians have identified the desire to pick oneself up by the bootstraps and get out of a pickle on one's own volition as an element of bourgeois ideals, expressed in genres like the Bildungsroman.[156] But individuality as the primary mode of bourgeois subjectification should not be overestimated. Applications for rehabilitation in Basel, at least, demonstrate the paramount importance of familial relations for escaping the "state of bankruptcy." Inheritance was often the only way to stock up enough assets to pay off creditors.[157] Authorities sought to prohibit bankrupt persons from taking on new debts to pay off old ones, but they generally expected family members to aid their indebted relatives. For instance, the authorities found it acceptable when a bankrupt person appropriated the inheritance of his stepdaughter to get the ball rolling on his rehabilitation petition (even though the two were no longer on speaking terms) or when an unmarried mother offered to reduce the child support that her child's father was obligated to pay her.[158] Maintaining an overview of convoluted familial relations and complicated intrafamilial transfers posed a challenge for the authorities. At the same time, debtors did not passively wait around to have their applications accepted. Officials complained that some creditors badgered their creditors to sign onto an abatement. "It is not uncommon," the judicial authority[159] tasked with assessing petitions determined, "that bankrupts who want to be rehabilitated assail their creditors with pleas that at least a part of the debt be forgiven and receive on account of the latter's goodness documents stating that the debt has been paid, even though it has in fact not been or not in whole."[160] This spurred them to check whether the creditors' letters of support were legitimate or not, which involved evaluating documents, reviewing older court proceedings concerning the person, researching their familial relations, and interrogating both creditor and debtor.[161]

Finally, the petitions for rehabilitation reflect a wide range of approaches to indebtedness. Being classified with the symbolically loaded term "bankrupt" undoubtedly affected debtors' personal identity and social relations, as this chapter has sought to show. Similarly, the practical effects of bankruptcy could be far-reaching, such as being expelled from the city. And yet, it seems that the status and the legal sanctions coupled with it often hindered bankrupts little in their everyday affairs. Still, taking the petitioners at their word supports the conclusion that punishments like being banned from inns hurt some bankrupt men more than the loss of their civic rights.

The merchant Franz Schaub explicitly requested that the news that his rights had been restored not be published in the cantonal gazette, because he believed that this would start people talking again and bring him into "discredit." Schaub had been in Paris when he entered bankruptcy proceedings and, upon returning to his business, was again treated by others as an "upright citizen."[162] The judicial council thus deemed Schaub's wish legitimate, but the government's adviser rejected the request.[163] J[ohann?] Meyerhofer-Glatt, a cattle and horse dealer, successfully continued his business after exiting bankruptcy and only filed for rehabilitation when he felt the time was right.[164] Jakob Lüdin, on the other hand, claimed that he wasn't even aware that bankruptcy proceedings had been initiated because he had moved away from Basel, and that "when I later learned of the effects of the proceedings, it was too late to do something about it."[165] Friedrich Ungerer never found out that the petition he had filed in 1853 had been rejected. Two and a half years later, the aging tailor's progressing deafness impeded his ability to work with others and thus forced him to set up shop on his own, which led him to apply for rehabilitation again. Only then did he learn that his first attempt had failed because he hadn't sent in the proper documentation on time.[166] Little in the way of generalizable conclusions can be drawn from the examples. I note them not to disavow that the ripple effects of bankruptcy transformed lives, but to underscore the multitude of attitudes and experiences wrapped up in the classification. The sources evidence not a comprehensive, coherent set of norms, but a spectrum of situations and context-specific effects that debtors dealt with and perceived in various ways. The social status of being bankrupt was more nuanced than the standard of homogeneous bourgeois values suggests.

Bankruptcy and Epistemic Anxiety

In 1867, new sanctions for bankruptcy went into effect in Basel. The purpose of the new law was to mitigate the punitive effects of bankruptcy. It was passed in response to a rapid increase in bankruptcies, with comments to the law's drafts noting a fourfold rise over just a few years.[167] It permitted out-of-court settlements, reduced the loss of civic rights to ten years in most cases, and allowed bankrupts to argue in civil court that they had fallen into bankruptcy through no fault of their own.

The commentary on the bill made the case for more nuance in how bankruptcies were classified. It gave legislative form to the processes of differentiation and categorization discussed in this chapter. It is worth quoting the legislators' views at length:

> One has indeed long felt that treating all bankrupts the same is not in harmony with the principle of justice. There are clearly fundamental differences to be considered here. People go bankrupt due to external factors, a decline of their occupation, overheated competition, loss of accounts because of misfortune, co-signing, illness, or entering a bad business on the basis of false information. Finally, there are poor people who, culpable or not, are pursued by others and brought to bankruptcy. Others, in contrast, go bankrupt because they lazily and indifferently let things run their course, lacking knowledge of their business and the ability to run it efficiently. They enter into fraudulent deals or allow themselves to be swindled by others without further contemplation. Among them are to be counted those people who carelessly handle other people's money or their wife's dowry, and finally the slovenly people who just refuse to work.[168]

In short, the range of causes demanded a corresponding range of classifications. Still, as discussed in the previous chapters, the legislators consistently focused on the individual run of events that had led to bankruptcy. Perhaps causes like "decline of occupation" might be seen as more objective than others, but even the seemingly superindividual "overheated competition" was a matter of judgment. At any rate, nowhere in this text is there a generalized conception of aggregate factors that we might call structural. Subsuming singular events *as such* under one of a series of causes was the epistemology that informed the classification of bankruptcies.[169] This seems to explain why the authorities attributed such significance to narrative accounts and why they continued to do so for such a long period. Because the epistemological foundation of classification was the individual case and its unique causes, narratives acquired epistemic value. But this method of processing knowledge reached its limits once a certain number of bankruptcies was exceeded. This chapter retraced the gradual reduction of reports to tables, though the tables, too, were still infused with narrative elements. By allowing debtors to petition for milder treatment, the 1867 law shifted the burden to bankrupts to prove that their bankruptcy was of no fault of their own. Put succinctly, it played to their ability to spin a narrative about their insolvency. They were guided by the same moral pragmatism as the court reports, but the positions were now swapped. Legislators tasked civil courts with hearing the pleas, not only because bankruptcy was not a matter of criminal law, but also because criminal courts could only make judgments about individual actions. Investigating the causes of bankruptcy, however, was not a matter of a single act, but concerned many of the debtors' actions in many spheres of life.[170]

"Civic death" was a powerful metaphor for experiences at the margins of civil society, including the experience of bankruptcy.[171] The language of inside and outside used by Rudolf Hunziker to describe bankruptcy as an external "blemish" that afflicted his "innermost being" illustrates well the cultural assumptions that structured perceptions of bankruptcy. The role played by reputation and loss of credit in the bankrupts' own narratives also reveal subjectivity as an interplay between others' thoughts about a person and that person's thoughts about themselves. Public appearances and interactions with commercial partners carried serious weight here. Without wanting to deny the power of "civic death" as a metaphor, the chapter sought to illuminate the sheer plurality of social experiences of bankruptcy. Active debtors looked for ways out, while the state often appeared as an unknowing authority (which did, however, *have* authority). The classifications that divided up the "estate" of bankrupts were contested, as was the process of winning for bankrupts more nuanced treatment before the law. The narratives surveyed here displayed concerns that fell outside the rigid bourgeois values of economic independence and being a citizen of the state. Petitioners fretted over keeping their residency permit, maintaining their masculine authority in the family's gender hierarchy, and retaining a good reputation among certain people. Belonging to the "estate" of bankrupts did not connote an inability to act in society. Perhaps the partial, patchwork nature of this "estate" is well captured by the fact that, ironically, only few bankrupts took advantage of the opportunity to exonerate themselves offered by the 1867 law.[172]

Morality assumed a special status for bankrupts, because it joined together personal identity and social life. The moralism of the authorities should be understood less as a dated cultural bias and more as the underside of economic relations. Their normative judgments exerted real economic effects, damaging reputations and thus establishing serious barriers to bankrupts' ability to restore their credit. Bankrupts' narratives of losing credit and the authorities' moral reproach stemmed from diametrically opposed positions, but they also filled one another out. In the end, morality was inseparably bound up with the calculative, technocratic side of bankruptcy enforcement.

A particularly significant element of the moral codex was the household, its gender hierarchy, and the household budget. They were weaponized in various ways by debtors, their wives, creditors, and the authorities. At the juncture of private and public expectations, the household and its budget were put forth as evidence to both confirm and contest value judgments about bankrupts' missteps. A foundational element of the household was the dowry, with its uncertain, regularly redefined status. Morality consistently informed the authorities' judgments and decisions and constituted a key component of their epistemic practices. It helped determine how they labeled bankrupts with a particular status or if they were willing to grant their petitions for rehabilitation. Constantly being confronted with a lack of reliable information challenged the authorities' capacity to develop a comprehensive account of the complex social and financial relations of individual debtors. Morality thus provided the schema that bridged their efforts to subsume a qualitatively singular situation under a general normative standard. The authorities' formalized catalog of vices and aberrations can be seen as an expression of epistemic anxiety, an index of the problems that hampered their efforts to gather knowledge. Their moral judgments contributed to the genesis of an entire "estate," that of the bankrupts. And yet they were made on shaky ground. Over the course of the period studied here, the authorities integrated more factors into their considerations and took a more nuanced approach to identifying causes. Still, they never renounced morality in favor of more objectified forms of knowledge. Instead, morality and knowledge were closely intertwined for the entire period. Morality offered "semantic security," while at the same being incoherent.[173]

The introduction quoted Karl Marx's statement that debt—a relationship in which promises were exchanged in place of money—concerned "man's *moral* existence, man's *social* existence, the *inmost depths* of his heart" by turning "man himself into *money*" and making money "*incorporated* in him."[174] This chapter addressed debt as a relation between people, seeking to demonstrate that it was bound up in constant confusion. The next chapter goes a step further by arguing that the confusion caused by debt also involved relations between people and things.

SIX | Collateral

Confusion over Persons and Things

During a lecture held in 1893, Alfred Brüstlein, one of the architects of Switzerland's Federal Statute on Debt Enforcement and Bankruptcy, argued that legislators should adhere to the "modern view according to which debt enforcement is an act carried out against property and not against the person."[1] His appeal sought to shift policy away from stripping rights and reputation from persons whose seized assets were insufficient to cover all their outstanding debts. As discussed in the first chapter, the various "honor sanctions" imposed as a consequence of insolvency differed from canton to canton, even after the passage of the federal bankruptcy law. This chapter grapples with what it meant for debt enforcement to affect "property" and "the person": What was the purpose of this distinction and why does it seem to have not been a matter of common sense to adhere to "the modern view"?

Brüstlein's statement staked out a clear position in late-nineteenth-century Switzerland's confusion over what exactly the object of debt enforcement was or was supposed to be: did it affect the status of the debtor's property? Or did it affect the status of the person themself? This chapter addresses how various rules and practices blurred the boundaries between the category of the thing and that of the person. A key site of contention in person-thing relations were the objects seized as collateral for unpaid debts. In contrast to bankruptcy, asset seizure, or attachment, was the more common legal means to collect debts in nineteenth-century Switzerland. As touched upon in chapter 1, sources from the 1880s estimate that around 75 to 80 percent of all delinquent debts in Switzerland were pursued through asset seizure. In asset seizure proceedings, an official levied as collateral a quantity of the debtor's assets valued at the amount owed in order to ensure payment; only in exceptional cases were the assets realized at auction.[2] Asset seizure involved first and foremost the exchange value of things. But the procedure also invested things with social and political meaning, a point that attracted the interest of debtors, government officials, and legislators alike. Finally, the materiality of the objects put a mark on the procedure itself. Making an object into collateral represented an at once banal and confounding relation between persons and things. How to seize assets as collateral and which assets could be attached were questions that posed constant problems for those involved in the various aspects of debt enforcement: How should assets be separated from one another, where should they be stored, to whom should they be transferred, and when and how should they be liquidated (or, in contemporaneous parlance, "made into silver")? The collateral object was a conundrum both for legal minds and for everyday economics. Could the state lock a person in jail in order to enforce a debt, thus effectively turning that person into collateral? The fungibility of money and the materiality of property were another issue, as was the constant need to define which goods should be protected from seizure because they were indispensable for satisfying the bare needs of survival. All these issues were crystallized in the status of the collateral asset.

The chapter deals with movable goods seized in the collection of debts not secured with real property, certainly the most common type of debt at the time.[3] In the everyday economy of the underclasses, things had diverse values and functions. During the eighteenth century, the remuneration of many workers bore aspects of a gift economy, in which allowances of food, lodging, and used clothes made up a considerable portion of payment. The purchase of expensive clothing was seen as a form of investment that could be pawned in emergency situations; moreover, an elegant appearance promised to increase one's credit.[4] Maligned by upper-class observers as "luxury," fancy clothes were a means for underclass people to present themselves as successful members of the market economy and thus be allowed to participate in it in the first place.[5] This "culture of appearances" held personal distinction up high, but it also had practical material effects.[6] Looking back at his life, an itinerant worker wrote that in the period around 1860, he had to always make sure he did not look too shabby in order to have a chance at getting day labor.[7] In the nineteenth century, servants, maids, journeymen, and farmhands continued to be paid in kind, despite the progressive expansion of wage payments. Second-hand stores were demoted to marginal significance only at the end of the century, when cooperative stores and, at least in large cities, department stores became more common. Before then, reselling one's stuff was always considered a viable option to shore up one's finances.[8] In rural areas, the underclasses also purchased used goods at compulsory auctions triggered by bankruptcies.[9]

But over the run of the century, the status of objects and their availability underwent fundamental shifts. Clothes manufactured with industrially woven cotton decreased in value, and the expansion of wage labor increased access to new goods like jewelry and pocket watches. Factory labor in the rural regions altered patterns of saving; previously concentrated in the ownership of house and land, money was now being invested in originally bourgeois, urban furnishings like dressers, mirrors, and printed portraits. Movable goods were not bound to urban environments, however. The possessions of small-time farmers, too, entered into circulation through pawning, asset seizure, and bankruptcy.[10]

The status of things as a medium of thought—"thinking through things"—also underwent a profound shift in the nineteenth century.[11] The industrial division of labor produced the "immense collection of commodities" that, in the eyes of one observer, defined "societies in which the capitalist mode of production prevails."[12] The varying positions on this reorganization of people and things are plenty. From the perspective of some Marxists, the abstraction inherent to the concept of exchange value eviscerates the objects produced and exchanged by people, which ultimately results in the reification of interhuman relationships.[13] Another perspective focuses on the multiplication of things caused by the commodity form's rise to dominance.[14] As historical studies of consumption have shown, Europeans, motivated by new commodities, invested their desires and practical skills into acquiring an ever-larger amount of things, which became available on a hitherto unknown scale.[15]

The flood of movable things also impacted the concept of property over the course of the century. In liberalism, humans and things were sharply separated as subject and object.[16] But the hard distinction opened up new modes of relation between them, one being the bond forged by the concept of "property." Defined in the Napoleonic Code as absolute sovereignty over a thing, property signified a strong relation between a person and an object.[17] The strict conceptual distinction between persons and things was the condition of possibility of the system of liberalism, in which the person demonstrates their ability to act *through* the possession of property. Liberalism elevated the property relation to an inviolable bond deserving of rigorous protections.

The expropriation of goods thus hit a soft spot in the juridical mind. In liberal culture and law, the sanctity of the home and objects like clothes were granted special status, because they were seen as constitutive of the person themself.[18] The construction of personhood through objects was not limited to middle-class subjects. As complaints of theft filed by the rural underclasses demonstrate, the dispossession of everyday items not only restricted a person's practical capacity to act, but was also "painful far beyond the material loss."[19] Property as absolute control over a thing also collided with those things' use value, as expensive everyday tools like wash basins were often used collectively.[20] These issues complicated attempts to identify an object's owner during asset seizure proceedings, and the official act of attachment had consequences for many people.

This chapter details these relations between people and things in four steps. First, it draws on anthropological theory to understand the ways in which collateral functioned as an object of knowledge for legislators and officials. It then moves to the incarceration of debtors and the debates over the abolition of debt imprisonment, analyzing the reasons why treating a person as collateral ultimately fell out of favor in liberalism. The third section tackles the shifting definition of "indispensable goods" that were to be legally sheltered from attachment. The chapter wraps up with a comparison of various forms of pawning, while paying particular attention to how bourgeois commentators were unsettled by the unstable connection between persons and collateral assets represented by it.

The Epistemology of Collateral

When the Federal Statute on Debt Enforcement and Bankruptcy established the key distinction between bankruptcy and asset seizure as the law of the nation-state, Alfred Brüstlein appealed "to the Swiss people" with a "word of enlightenment." In a pamphlet promoting a "yes" vote in the referendum held on the law in 1889, he lambasted the absurdities that had "grown out of the routine" of long-standing customs.[21] Common in central Switzerland, the "reprehensible" practice of immediately handing over seized property "to the creditor at an arbitrarily assessed value in lieu of payment" rather than auctioning it off appeared to Brüstlein as a relic of the past. "In earlier times, when all loaning took place between neighbors and collateral assets comprised everyday things, cattle, tools, etc., this might have been appropriate; in today's world, it is a true scandal."[22] The modern economy was driven by the conversion of things into exchange values, relegating the swap to the margins. Not determining the price of seized things through an auction, he believed, made it nigh impossible to state their value. "How is a municipal official supposed to correctly estimate the value of collateral materials, paintings, artworks? He will always go too high or too low." Without the general medium of exchange, these things had no place in the complex modern economy: "And what is a Bern merchant supposed to do with an old dinghy docked on Lake Lucerne placed in his possession; what is the Zuricher recently reported on in the papers supposed to do with the heap of dung in the canton Schwyz that was granted him in place of payment?"

Brüstlein's heated rhetoric underscores the problems posed by collateral as an object of knowledge. The historical epistemology of collateral presented here analyzes how historical actors conceptualized the collateral object as a unit that helped produce and arrange knowledge. In contrast to bankruptcy, which distributed a debtor's assets to creditors all at once, asset seizure was an extended process that involved the assessment and apportionment of individual assets one after another. Bankruptcy collected all assets as a single homogeneous estate and distributed it among the creditors; asset seizure did not. Sometimes called "minor bankruptcy," asset seizure did not settle the claims of various creditors by giving them their share of a whole. Instead, it allocated one creditor an object or objects seen as equal in value to the debt owed, then moved on to the next creditor, then on to the next.[23] In nineteenth-century Swiss legal doctrine, the right to collateral complemented a property right accrued in the debt relationship: If the debtor violated their contract with the creditor by failing to pay, the creditor obtained a right to the debtor's property.[24] In other words, a seized asset—and the laws that regulated its status—was a secondary obligation that functioned as the fulfilment of a primary obligation, namely that of the loan. The seized asset was thus a hybrid of contract law and property law (*Sachenrecht*, the "law of things"), occupying a liminal space between a contractual obligation (repayment of a loan) and a transfer of property (from the debtor to the creditor).[25] As an object, it oscillated between debtor and creditor. Thus, the relation constituted by the collateral asset is well captured by Marcel Mauss's classic description of the gift: it animated things and objectified people.[26] The imprisonment of debtors, as we will see, was a particularly striking example of this movement between persons and things that fixated people and liquidated assets.

In the nineteenth century, the objectification of persons and the animation of things recalled earlier legal traditions loaded with philosophical implications. In the law of the early Roman Republic, "nexum" designated the act by which a debtor put himself and/or his children up as collateral.[27] The "nexum" led the philologist and philosopher Friedrich Nietzsche (1844–1900) to identify the subjugation of debtor to creditor as the genealogical origin of morality. The Roman Law of the Twelve Tables (451 BCE), with its principle of equivalency, provided that insolvent debtors be lawfully cut to pieces by their creditors, at least that was how a fascinated Nietzsche saw it, as did Swiss jurists.[28] In Nietzsche's words, the debt relation was the elementary expression of the human as "the calculating animal as such."[29] The barbaric corporal punishment, intended to inscribe a debt in a person's memory, "bred," in Nietzsche's words, man into an animal "with the prerogative to promise."[30] Creditworthiness—the value of a person's promise—was backed up by the debtor's body itself. Nietzsche saw in the act of pledging one's own body the most elementary operations of evaluation and judgment.

But beyond debt imprisonment and the violent images evoked by nineteenth-century thinkers' ruminations on Ancient Rome, pledged property in Switzerland exerted pressure both on people and on other things.[31] Asset seizure reorganized relations between humans and things, while, in a more figurative sense, the seized assets contributed to the "partibility of the person" as well.[32] Transactions were what transformed a thing into collateral.[33] Constitutive of collateral was not the thing with its various qualities, but the complex process that stamped upon it a specific status. Consider anthropologist Annelise Riles's analysis of the techniques of collateralization used by contemporary financial institutions to back their transactions. Although they cannot be directly applied to the practices of low-level authorities pursuing delinquent debts in nineteenth-century Switzerland, Riles's insights are interesting for the present study, because she demonstrates that collateral is an object of knowledge produced by documents and legal procedures. Collateral provides a shortcut solution to an epistemic riddle. Banks save themselves the trouble of tiresomely assessing the risk of every single transaction by implementing a routinized procedure that offsets it with a holding of proportionate value.[34] The collateral asset absorbs the entirety of relations that constitute it. By closing the gap between promise to pay and payment, the object encapsulates relational knowledge.[35] The praxis of asset seizure was an everyday heuristic that shortened a procedure. While the officials administering bankruptcy exerted themselves to obtain information, as discussed in chapter 5, asset seizure did not necessitate lengthy assessments. The impounded asset simply represented the value equivalent to the debt owed. In that respect, collateral brought closure.

The reduction of complexity necessitates standardization, which is accomplished through forms, books, and systems of notation. Analyzing the processes and codes that informed how entries were made in legal documents like records of seized assets rather than the content of the entries themselves offers telling insights.[36] An idea of the processual logic of asset seizure can be gleaned by looking at the structure of seizure records, which, in the canton of Zurich, were kept by municipal bailiffs.[37] The records were logged on standardized, printed templates that packaged events and objects into uniform categories. Of the ten columns, the three before the last thematized the public auction of seized goods, which marked the end of each case. There was a column for the date on which the creditor's motion to have a debtor's assets publicly auctioned posted, another for the date the debtor was notified that the auction would take place, and a third for the date that the auction took place. The first six columns registered a case number together with the date of seizure, the date the notification of impending seizure had been issued, the debtor's name, the creditor's name, the sum of the latter's claim, and an inventory of the seized goods. Another column was reserved for "remarks" on matters like whether the proceedings had ended or the statute of limitations on the right to seize assets had expired or how much the auction had earned. The columns on the auction remained empty in the vast majority of cases, because proceedings were often ended before an auction was necessary. Nevertheless, it was the endgame plotted out by the standardized record sheets. Documents with their preprinted forms set up standardized distinctions and structured time by anticipating events. The seizure records accomplished the latter with the vanishing point of the final auction and the former by recording, numbering, and estimating the monetary value of particular things.[38]

While bankruptcy wiped the slate clean, asset seizure held collateral on a provisional basis until the debt could be paid or a settlement reached.[39] Only in the rare auction were collateral objects converted into money.[40] Collateral temporarily covered for the debt, bridging the gap between promise and payment. It functioned on the basis of the legal fiction that the creditor was actually in possession of the value of the collateral assets for the duration of the proceedings. By working as if the future payment had arrived, the fiction suspended the need to perform the complex assessments of value and divisions of property that characterized bankruptcy. But the procedure was stunningly opaque, as this chapter elucidates.

Although the focus here is on movable property, a brief look at state-administered assessments of the value of real property helps illustrate the epistemological problems involved. Like the commercial register discussed in chapter 1, the state-administered assessment of property values had a twofold function: it served the fiscal interests of the state by providing the basis for the more efficient taxation of landowners, and it provided a basis for lending, borrowing, and the extension of credit by delimiting a collateral object and its exact value in a standardized fashion.[41] The assessment of property values and their registration in a cadaster was thus a fundamental element of the liberal regime of private property. Throughout the entire nineteenth century, reformers saw the precise assessment of the value of real property as a solution to the structural financial issues faced by agriculture, because they thought it would make it easier for farmers to take out loans.[42] The concept of collateral produced new objects, such as real property eligible for mortgage, and the distribution of mortgage titles recalibrated relations in the expanding world of things. Contemporaries perceived the advent of property assessments as a further step in the extraction of exchange value from anything and everything. In an 1867 article, the *Schweizerisches Volksblatt vom Bachtel*, the voice of the opposition Democratic Movement in the canton of Zurich, analyzed increasing wealth as an effect of the increase in home equity loans:

> It is . . . a remarkable fact that holds true in all places: on average, it is not the municipalities with the most valuable property that are mortgaged least of all, which in itself would seem to make them the most prosperous municipalities; rather, the rule is that the higher the debt, the more valuable are the properties. On average, the sum of mortgage debts has followed in line with the sum of equity, a sign that our society has the tendency to *collateralize everything that can be collateralized.*[43]

The possibility of extracting equity from real property led the author to identify wealth with the assessed value of property. New methods of borrowing against real property altered the financial situation of property owners. Diagnosing the spirit of the times, the article discerned a tendency to "*collateralize everything that can be collateralized.*" Thus, assets were

acquired by way of an interplay between the present and the future per-
fect, property owners taking on debt by maximizing the collateral value
of their real estate. The *Volksblatt* viewed the phenomenon with ambiva-
lence. The crisis of the late 1860s had been preceded by a period of
prosperity that witnessed large-scale property speculation, leading many
farmers to take on considerable debt. The crisis was triggered by falling
grain prices caused by the import of wheat from eastern Europe, which
then caused property values to sink, all while interest rates rose because
new financial instruments like bonds issued by the Bank Leu were more
attractive investments than were mortgage loans.[44] That the temporality
of collateral was inherently unpredictable was proven when the assessed
value of the now pledged real estate plunged.

During debt collection proceedings, too, the conversion of assets into
collateral was a tricky issue that boggled the minds of many legal experts
because it necessitated sequestering the tangible thing from the relations in which it stood. Reducing the complex utility of a thing to a sheer
number value brought forth new problems; collateral closed the gap
between payment and obligation, but it also created new imponderables.
Straddling the line between contract law and property law, it evoked per-
ilous uncertainties. When, by whom, and, above all, for how long would
the asset be attached? The creditor's right to collateral was limited in
many instances. The complexity and instability of debt relations were
reflected in the collateral thing, because it was at once rooted in the
concept of property as absolute control over a thing (the collateral asset
had to really belong to the debtor) and it simultaneously undermined
this concept (the temporarily expropriated thing was not in control of
the debtor, but suspended between debtor and creditor).[45] In short, collateral was supposed to stabilize the debt relation by conceptually disen-
tangling property, but through the back door it created more, not less,
entanglement. The basic problem at work—the objectification of people
and the animation of things—was expressed most pronouncedly in debt
imprisonment.

The Body as Collateral in Debt Imprisonment

On September 5, 1864, Anna Jäggli of Aussersihl lodged an official complaint with the Zurich high court, protesting the issuing of a warrant for
her arrest. By that point, the conflict with her creditors had reached a
boiling point. The district court of Zurich had authorized an application
to have her arrested that had been submitted by a butcher from Wiedikon

named Mr. Morf and by one Heinrich Maier from Aussersihl. The former demanded 110 francs and 10 centimes, the latter 80 francs. Added to that was a claim of 20 francs from a third creditor, Mr. Wiederkehr, who also threatened Ms. Jäggli "with execution," a threat that, she wrote, "he made in earnest . . . as he has already once demonstrated."[46]

Zurich's district court had issued Morf and Maier a *Wortzeichen* (an idiomatic Swiss expression that literally translates to "word sign"), or debt warrant. Valid for one year, the certificate permitted a creditor to demand the arrest of a debtor at any time.[47] Anna Jäggli failed to appear at the hearing where the certificate was granted, a fact that was used against her. At the hearing, she would have had a chance to explain her situation, because under Zurich's debt enforcement law of 1851, judges had complete discretion in deciding whether to grant a creditor's petition for the debt warrant.[48] By failing to appear, Mr. Maier wrote to the high appeals court, she had "unconditionally acknowledged" the legitimacy of his claim.[49] Anna Jäggli stated that she had forgotten to inform the district court of Wiederkehr's claim, and she retorted that she was "unaware" that she was required to appear at the hearing on the first of the two arrest warrants, where she could have perhaps negotiated "installment payments."

Nevertheless, in her complaint, which she filed with the high appeals court in a timely manner, she evidenced precise knowledge of the procedure. Her letter used the juridical concept of "undue hardship" to describe the arrest warrants issued to her debtors and pointed to a passage of the 1851 debt enforcement law that required the courts to consider "the particular situation of the debtor." An expert commentary on the law opined that courts should refrain from ordering arrest in situations where the debtor cannot "satisfy the creditor even if they had the best intentions of doing so." Such situations included illness, old age, and, in special cases, insufficient income. The latter was only legitimate grounds to rule out arrest, the commentary qualified with reference to four precedents, if the debtor had a family to feed.[50]

Anna Jäggli tirelessly sought to demonstrate just that: She stated that she did not earn enough and that she, a single mother, had to care for her son born out of wedlock and her sixty-four-year-old mother. Her only source of income was putting up boarders. She wrote that recently she only had three boarders instead of eight or ten; moreover, "two Italians with significant bills" and another boarder had failed to pay, costing her fifty-seven francs. After listing a series of extenuating circumstances—the precarity of her income source, the general economic crisis that had set in by 1864, and the financial burden of caring for others—she stated that she was unable to ask family members for help, but that she also was not drawing support from the state. And despite all that, she maintained, she had tried her best to pay her debts: of the eighty francs owed to Heinrich Maier, she had already paid fifty in four installments.[51] The district court, however, interpreted these payments as evidence that the debtor should indeed be able to pay off her debts bit by bit. Countering this conclusion, Jäggli's letter to the appeals court explained that she had only been able to pay the installments by making "considerable sacrifices." She ended her letter by arguing that allowing her to defer making payments was absolutely necessary, because otherwise, her mother and child would have to depend on poor relief. She pled that the high court might "suspend execution of the warrant for 2 to 3 months so that I can pay the rent and so that my mother and son are not forced to ask our home municipality for support, which would occur if the warrant is issued."[52]

The high appeals court gave the two creditors an opportunity to state their position. The butcher, Mr. Morf, did not, but Heinrich Maier did. In his statement, he opted against succinct legal language, complaining instead how he believed the debtor was trying to hoodwink him. For fifteen months, he wrote, Anna Jäggli had been coming up with one excuse after another to delay payment: "But if she had just paid a few francs instead of lyingly promising payment, the debt would be paid off by now. It is clear that this person has the intention of paying nothing more; otherwise, she would have personally asked me to grant her lenience in payment instead of filing this petition for relief resp. complaint. But, as I said, she just wants to pay with lies."[53] Thus, he continued, he had seen no alternative but to deposit ten francs with the district office to cover the costs of holding his debtor in jail, which would have been sufficient for about ten days.[54] Creditors were required to advance the costs of jailing before enjoining the debtor to pay these costs themselves. Heinrich Maier gave weight to his consternation by asserting that he would have afforded Jäggli the chance to pay in installments if she had only asked him directly, and his repeated accusations that the debtor was dishonest bolstered this. The rhetoric had a legal purpose, because the aforementioned commentary on the 1851 debt enforcement law stated that arrest could be used against debtors who failed to pay "out of carelessness or ill intent."[55] Two weeks later, however, Heinrich Maier relented and said he was willing to wait until the beginning of February before he would call for Jäggli's arrest.

This case was typical for a number of reasons. In the canton of Zurich, very poor debtors were the almost exclusive target of debt imprisonment, which always involved small sums; the jail term was always short, Zurich law limiting it to no longer than six weeks.[56] The result of the negotiations was usually installment payments and only a fraction of the debt warrants were ever actually executed. Still, the threat of debt imprisonment loomed in the Zurich of the liberal era. Anna Jäggli's case from 1864 was part of a last wave of the special debt warrants issued to creditors before revisions to the canton's constitution in 1869 abolished this legal instrument. The practice of imprisoning debtors was rarely treated as controversial and its abolition found few opponents. A jurisprudential essay written in 1870 pointedly summarized the general position: "It is evident that in Switzerland as everywhere else, the imprisonment of bodies will soon have its time."[57] In 1874, a revision to the federal constitution outlawed debt imprisonment altogether, after the cantons had already taken this step.[58]

Only for the brief period between 1851 and 1869 did the Zurich court administration annually publish how many debt warrants had been issued in the canton for the year. In the 1850s, the numbers spanned from 491 in 1859 to 781 in 1851; in the 1860s, they increased drastically.[59] The peak year was 1866, with 1,041 cases, an outlier to the average 836 annual issuances between 1860 and 1868, the last full year that the debt warrants existed (the median was 858). In 1864, the year Anna Jäggli filed her appeal, creditors had been granted permission to order the arrest of their debtors 858 times, the median for the 1860s.[60] What was the purpose of this legal instrument? Did it serve to punish, to force payment, to deter people from nonpayment, or to facilitate the authorities' investigations of delinquent debtors? To what extent did debt imprisonment treat a person as a monetary value, and to what extent did it place limits on such treatment? In more abstract terms: which modes of knowledge, of calculating values, and of constituting subjects were at play here?[61]

The history of modern debt imprisonment says much about the broader cultural history of the economic.[62] Throughout western Europe, laws abolishing it were passed around 1870 (in actual practice, however, doing away with it proved messier).[63] Some historians have situated the problem of jailing debtors as part of a secular process in which the association of insolvency with moral failure gave way to the calculative logic of economic risk.[64]

In Europe, the extent to which merchants should be subject to special laws was a question that found divergent, provisional, and always contested responses. In France, where debt imprisonment was abolished three times and reinstated twice between 1793 and 1867, only *négociants* and *commerçants* could be locked up for outstanding debts, a rule that unleashed a decades-long public conflict over who exactly was to be considered a merchant. These debates negotiated the status of commerce in a postcorporate society.[65] In England, where the per capita rate of jailed debtors presumably was higher than in any other west European nation, efforts to reform debtors' prisons targeted indigent debtors.[66] During the eighteenth century, the debtors' prison was an ambiguous space that afforded male debtors—often with considerable means— the chance to escape the claims of their creditors at least as much as it served to compel them to pay their debts. In contrast, the reformed debtors' prison was a punitive institution that sought to hammer market discipline into the minds of the incarcerated.[67] In 1869, England did away with debt imprisonment for larger sums, while making permanent its role in the pursuit of small sums.[68] Consequently, only working-class debtors were locked up and the new debtors' prison largely ceased to interest the social imaginary.[69]

The shift in significance was important in campaigns to abolish debt imprisonment. Contemporaneous discourse read debtors' prisons as an upside-down world where the rules of civil society didn't apply.[70] In this parallel universe, imprisoned debtors were removed from productive activity, were subjected to elaborate initiation rituals, and bore the brunt of an economic regime that combined luxury and abject poverty. A debtor once incarcerated in a Breslau jail wrote a pamphlet that he called a "cry of distress to our lawmakers": "In this little world that is thrown together out of so many different social elements, in this microcosm, into which the differences between elegant and humble, educated and uneducated from the big world spill over in abundance, the common fate brings forth a contact between persons that the macrocosm isn't acquainted with to the same degree."[71] He criticized that in the debtor's prison, "the ethical universe comes into contradiction with itself," because it afforded "a private man a place to house his serf and officials to imprison and surveil them."[72] In the estimation of prison reformers, debt imprisonment revealed the barbaric kernel of debtor-creditor relations, a relic that had to be civilized.[73] In the long formation process of prisons as punitive and correctional institutions, debt imprisonment came to be seen as a vestige of the past, as a scandal, or as a casual measure against underclass debtors hardly worth the mention.[74]

I note shifting views on the subject in Europe in order to outline the context in which developments in Switzerland took place. On the one hand, Swiss legal experts compared and commented on other countries. On the other, the charged discussion in Europe contrasted with the near complete lack of debate on debt imprisonment in Switzerland, a lack worth analyzing. For sure, the limited debate can be partially attributed to the low number of debt prisoners, but not entirely. The parenthetical tone of the discussion in Switzerland was indicative of the commonly held opinion that such practices need not conflict with liberal forms of legitimation. The existence of multiple models of debt imprisonment in Switzerland also made it easier to downplay the issue.[75] For instance, the mercantile city-canton of Geneva aligned itself with French law and reserved debt imprisonment almost exclusively for merchants. Thus, for all intents and purposes, the canton adhered to the separation between merchants and nonmerchants that was first federally codified in 1883 with the commercial register and applied to insolvent debtors in the 1889 Federal Statute on Debt Enforcement and Bankruptcy.

The objective of imprisonment in Geneva was to hold an insolvent merchant as collateral while investigations into the debtor's property ran their course in order to make sure that they did not conceal assets. In the 1810s, jailed debtors in Geneva spent on average about fifty days in lockup; in the 1820s, it was about two months. The averages, however, conceal the fact that more than a third were released after two to five days.[76] Heidelberg jurist Carl Joseph Anton Mittermaier remarked upon the parallels to the French system: Practically speaking, debt imprisonment was rare and the actual duration of incarceration short; in France, Mittermaier noted, debtors were usually released after fifteen days.[77] Mittermaier thought worthy of imitation Geneva's distinction between debt imprisonment as a means of punishment and as a means of insurance, judging the latter to be legitimate and purposeful.[78] Over the twenty-three-year span between 1825 and 1848, 213 debtors were jailed in Geneva, 123 of whom were foreign merchants. In each year, however, the *tribunal de commerce* issued 600 to 700 arrest warrants for insolvent debtors. Thus, here, too, the number of actual arrests was much lower than the number of warrants. Proponents of Geneva's *contrainte par corps* believed it had an "*effet préventif utile.*" They reasoned that only in a market based on strictly enforced, uniformly observed rules could credit flow freely, and that the high frequency of international transactions with bills of exchange in the canton necessitated that its laws not trail behind those of other states.[79] Opponents cautioned that the practice would regularly impact people who hardly qualified as merchants, rejecting it as an abusive punishment that only served to deliver "unfortunate debtors who acted in good faith" into the clutches of misfortune. They raised the principle that human freedom was categorically incommensurable with commercial bondage: "a man's liberty cannot be put at commercial disposal, even if he entered the commercial relation voluntarily."[80] In Geneva, debt imprisonment was largely used to enforce payment of bills of exchange, which is to say that it intervened into a fast, volatile, and intricate mercantile sphere whose complexities it intended to break through and whose tempo it sought to slow down.

In Zurich, things were very different. Over the first half of the nineteenth century, debt imprisonment in Zurich metamorphosed from a step in the evaluation of a debtor's assets to a means to coerce the penniless. Toward the end of the eighteenth century, the administration used the expression "*Wortzeichen*" (the warrant granted to creditors to demand the arrest of the debtors discussed above) interchangeably with "*Signallement*" (physical identification).[81] This language was retained well after the fall of the Ancien Régime. The legal codex adopted by Zurich in 1715 described the debt warrant as a means to prevent debtors from fleeing or concealing assets and defined it as a warrant for the arrest of a merchant. In the eighteenth century, this "means of deterrence" was supposed to discipline hardheaded debtors who "accepted neither judgment nor warnings and always showed themselves to be disobedient," as the text of the 1715 law read.[82] In a retrospective analysis written in 1821, a legal expert reflected on this passage's relation to the concepts of reputation and a merchant's honor. He wrote that the purpose of the law was to spare creditors the trouble of having to encounter in everyday affairs their fraudster debtors, "who freely and unhindered walk around before their eyes," which would cause the creditor to suffer "mockery alongside loss."[83]

From 1715 until the early nineteenth century, creditors would request that delinquent debtors be jailed while authorities compiled an inventory of their assets. The debtor could secure their release by officially declaring bankruptcy, because laws prohibited incarceration for bankruptcy. This usage of the debt warrant was gradually altered in practice: creditors increasingly had debtors arrested who owned no valuable assets whatsoever.[84] Subsequently, more creditors applied for permission to have debtors arrested and instrumentalized this capacity as a coercive tool. A notable implication of this practice was that filing for bankruptcy no longer freed one from this form of intimidation. In 1812, this reorientation of creditors' ability to apply for the arrest of debtors was codified by a legal decree.[85]

Although the available sources unfortunately reveal little about the district courts' work in matters of civil law, there is reason to surmise that creditors frequently applied for debt warrants in the 1830s and the following decades.[86] In 1851, the law was amended to leave the decision to issue debt warrants up to the discretion of the district court president. This enabled courts to begin considering mitigating circumstances, such as Anna Jäggli's status as an indigent single mother. By mid-century, the debt warrant in Zurich had been transformed into a coercive instrument against debtors who had already entered bankruptcy proceedings. It was also wielded against debtors who lacked the funds to cover the costs of bankruptcy and whose creditors refused to advance the money necessary to do so. Finally, creditors used it against debtors without permanent address who had no assets that could be seized.

In 1856, the canton's judiciary called the arrest permits a "necessary evil," writing, "Experience shows us that some people, before they allow themselves to even temporarily be deprived of their freedom, would prefer to exert themselves to satisfy their debtors; certainly, a large number of debts would go forever unpaid if our laws did not have provisions for debt imprisonment. Creditors generally declare themselves ready to accept moderate installment payments and the courts take them by their word in this offer."[87] Other jurists underscored that the acceptance of installment payments did not diminish the creditor's right to demand arrest at a later point in time. When a creditor conditionally deferred arrest by agreeing to installments, the judge did not alter the debt relation in any way, because the creditor's claim to the money owed remained intact.[88] Thus creditors could leverage the debt warrant to put pressure on debtors well outside the instrument's limited legal applicability.

The expanded use of debt warrants corresponded with a systematization of the territorial jurisdictions of courts and law enforcement. By creating district courts and district jails in the 1830s, Zurich's liberal state intensified existing forms of regional administration, and in the 1850s the canton expanded the district jails' sphere of authority,[89] which now incarcerated debtors arrested at the behest of their creditors.[90] Instituting a tightly woven network of penal institutions with varying geographical and legal jurisdictions was the liberal state's response to a key demand of the prison reform movement.[91] Like in the rest of Europe, reformers in Zurich insisted that prisoners be housed separately on the basis of nuanced classifications of the offense committed.[92] As early as 1826, an article pled that the construction of different types of jails was the only way to do justice to the differences between prisoners. The author was particularly concerned about the unclear status of imprisoned debtors, who had, after all, not committed a crime.[93] The requirement that creditors put forth the costs of housing their imprisoned debtor (like in Prussia, France, and Russia) was not an invention of the "lean" liberal state.[94] Legal experts in the nineteenth century were well aware that this rule had been adopted by the Federal Diet of Switzerland in the sixteenth century.[95]

Zurich's cantonal head of prisons understood district jails as "essentially just holding cells" that did not need to provide the comprehensive religious services, forced labor, and "discipline" imposed on prisoners convicted of crimes.[96] Representatives of the cantonal high court tasked with supervising the prisons, on the other hand, criticized that no system was in place to make imprisoned debtors perform "adequate labor" with which they could work off the costs of holding them.[97] The city of Zurich had two district prisons: the penitentiary in Selnau for serious crimes and, located on the property now occupied by the university, the Berg jail, where jailed debtors went.[98] The Berg jail also housed a large number of people arrested by the police for offenses like drunkenness, begging, and violating residency laws who were generally only held there for a night.[99] In 1864, the year that Anna Jäggli would have been locked up in Berg had her creditor not agreed to have her arrest deferred, 1,625 persons arrested by the police passed through the jail's cells. The next largest groups were considerably smaller: 48 imprisoned debtors, 42 convicted criminals, 38 arrested for failing to pay municipal fines, 21 in pretrial detention, and 12 people on poor relief.[100] During that same year, creditors made 331 requests that their debtors be arrested, but in the majority of cases, like that of Jäggli and her creditor Maier, a settlement was reached before the warrant was executed.[101]

What conclusions should be drawn from these statistics? Complete data for incarceration numbers for all of Zurich's district jails is only available for 1867, when 174 people were jailed for debts, again just a fraction of the 999 judicially granted debt warrants.[102] The ratio between debt warrants issued and actual arrests, however, fluctuated considerably. For instance, in the Pfäffikon district in 1868, no fewer than seventeen of the thirty-eight debt warrants issued were carried out, the arrested debtors spending between two and nineteen days in jail.[103] Just as well, the proportion of imprisoned debtors in district jails' populations dif-

fered considerably from district to district, though they always constituted a minority outnumbered by the criminally convicted and persons
in pretrial detention. The low numbers of people locked up for debts
makes finding an appropriate point of comparison difficult. The general
categories "criminal offender" and "pretrial detention" used by the statistics on district jails comprised a range of different offenses. The proportions are different when one compares the numbers of imprisoned
debtors with the numbers for particular offenses. In the Horgen district
in 1868, for instance, 13 people went to jail for debts, and 25 spent time
in pretrial detention for theft, as did four for fraud, four for embezzle-
ment, four for disturbing the peace, five for bodily harm, two for arson,
three for abortion, one for stealing wood, and one for fraudulent bankruptcy.[104] So while the 13 debt prisoners constituted a small though not
insignificant minority of 10 percent among the total 142 persons jailed
in Horgen,[105] they were the second largest group when the comparison
focuses on those in pre-trial detention and breaks them down into individual offenses. In 1867, 5,305 people entered municipal jails in the canton of Zurich. If one subtracts the 2,918 people briefly locked up after
being arrested for begging, public intoxication, or not having residency
papers, the 174 debt prisoners make up 7.3 percent of the remaining
2,387 jailed persons.

But perhaps the numbers of jailed persons aren't a good point of
comparison. Perhaps the ratio of completed bankruptcies to debt imprisonments gets closer to the point. In 1864, the year Anna Jäggli appealed
her arrest, forty-nine debtors were imprisoned in Zurich's Berg jail and
sixty-six people completed bankruptcy proceedings in the district of
Zurich city, the latter number higher than usual on account of the rever-
berations of the American Civil War. In this comparison, the number of
debt imprisonments appears more significant.[106]

In the end, debt prisoners undoubtedly made up a small fraction
of the people held in Zurich's district jails; debtors threatened by their
creditors with arrest sought to propose a plausible settlement and those
who did get locked up were generally freed after ten days or so. The debt
warrant was a marginal instrument that hardly stirred the social imagination. Still, the threat of arrest was ever-present for indigent debtors.
Though its strictly juristic significance was limited, it put pressure on
debtors to quickly agree to installment payments out of court. Agreeing
to pay installments, however, did not give the active debt a new legal
status. In effect, the debtor's promise to pay installments and the actual
payment thereof functioned as a placeholder for their body on the stage

of jurisprudence, because the liberal doctrine closely associated a person with their property.[107] As the treatment of a person as collateral for debt found increasing application in the second third of the nineteenth century, out-of-court settlements to pay in installments substituted for the collateral person. Debt imprisonment did not just offset money with bodies. As a coercive tool to force payment and an instrument to facilitate the authorities' assessment of a debtor's assets, debt imprisonment established complex equivalencies between bodies and sums owed. To wrap up this section, I would like to consider one of the few writings of the time that criticized these equivalencies as incoherent.

The "Dissertation über das Wortzeichen" was a roughly forty-page manuscript composed by former Zurich mayor Conrad Melchior Hirzel (1793–1843), probably in response to Zurich's 1842 debt enforcement law.[108] Hirzel addressed three aspects of the issue: He analyzed the legal foundations of the debt warrant, customary practices of using it, and its deterring effect. He concluded that the debt warrant undermined bankruptcy proceedings' logic of evaluating assets and settling debts, condemning the issuance of warrants for debtors who had already entered bankruptcy as a "striking inconsistency." He thought that the exclusive legal justifications for jailing debtors were the "suspicion that assets are being concealed" or when a debtor not yet in bankruptcy proceedings was considered a flight risk. But, he argued, consistency demanded that bankruptcy end the possibility of arrest,[109] because bankruptcy was not a criminal act, but the end station of economic ruin, which was caused by "a stroke of fate, the problems of the times, private issues, or the weakness of human nature."[110]

Thus Hirzel found that allowing creditors to demand the arrest of debtors crassly contradicted the practices of knowledge constitutive of bankruptcy. By issuing a warrant for the arrest of a debtor who had already passed through bankruptcy, the "harmony and consistency of the various parts of our laws are destroyed."[111] If the debtor was penniless, bankruptcy simply established the "absolute impossibility" of payment, and arresting them would change nothing about that.[112] If the debtor did have assets, bankruptcy proceedings sought to equally distribute their value among creditors. Essential to this fundamental aspect of bankruptcy was that the debtor's assets were treated as a homogeneous mass of value and the creditors as a homogeneous group of claimants.[113] Allowing a creditor to threaten arrest and thereby arrogate a privileged position for themselves thus wrecked the whole logic of bankruptcy: debt imprisonment not only "dissected" the debtor as a person (epitomized by the violent image invoked by the Roman Twelve Tables), but also disintegrated the class status of creditors' claims. He complained that the vulturing of a "vengeful creditor" would throw the bankruptcy into disarray, launching the debtor into "the dark fate of an anxious, fugitive, outlaw life."[114] He concluded that the canton's juridical practice was a mishmash, and he pointed out that from time to time, arrested persons were even made to suffer corporal punishment.[115] Subjected to the "arbitrariness" and "private revenge" of a creditor, the bankrupt was, "in the fullest sense of the word, placed outside the protection of the law."[116] Far from being an instrument of the law, issuing arrest warrants on behalf of creditors devolved into lawlessness.

Hirzel wrote with the rhetoric of civility. He cast arrest warrants issued on behalf of creditors as an expression of untamed emotions, which led him to deny their legitimacy as a "means to prevent and deter from bankruptcies."[117] The threat of arrest only pushed debtors further into insolvency, making them ready "to risk even the most desperate acts" in order to "stop the wheel of their fortune from rolling away" from them. It encouraged debtors to be secretive about their situation until bankruptcy broke out, "like a long-constrained fire, all the more destructively."[118] Hirzel was convinced that deterrence could only be achieved through consistent, uniform legal procedures, and he described arrest warrants issued on behalf of creditors as being closer to a "sellable object that could be haggled over."[119]

As a one-time mayor, Hirzel was well-versed in the nuances of public appearances. He chose to condemn the barbarity of debt warrants in the language of class, writing that they were "rarely used among the educated estates" and only held appeal for brutish people unconcerned that using the instrument would gain them a reputation as a "hard-hearted and capricious man."[120] Greedy extortion and unharnessed vengefulness could force the most upstanding debtor into a situation that ensured that "dishonesty would gain the upper hand over honesty,"[121] because debt warrants promoted clandestine agreements between the debtor and their unscrupulous creditor. Such agreements disadvantaged other creditors, thus creating an atmosphere of opacity and distrust for all.

Hirzel's intent was most likely to shine some light on the murky legal situation of the early 1840s, to analyze the relations between the laws on the books, and to draw jurisprudential conclusions from the analysis. He observed inconsistencies on multiple levels: Equality before the law was threatened by private revenge; the methodical coherence of bankruptcy proceedings and the practices of knowledge underlying them was threatened by creditors elbowing their way through; bankruptcy's goal of providing security for "public credit—the soul of all commerce"[122] was threatened by the incentive to be secretive. Thus, Hirzel opined, debt warrants rested on a false equivalency indicative of a lack of clarity in the legal edifice. For sure, the detention of debtors placed individual bodies and sums of money in a problematic relation to abstract norms of freedom and property. But Hirzel drew a distinct conclusion from this problem. He did not believe there was a fundamental categorial incommensurability between bodies and collateral. Rather, he was concerned that treating them as equivalents could lead to unpredictable consequences, which risked derailing the epistemic validity of the bankruptcy proceedings: confusion instead of clarity and forceful passion instead of predictability.

It is important to note that Hirzel's critique was only aimed at the imprisonment of persons who had entered official bankruptcy proceedings. He believed that debt imprisonment was an appropriate tool for investigating a debtor's assets *before* they filed for bankruptcy. In a sense, his discussion highlights the casualness with which Zurich authorities issued and executed debt warrants, an attitude that stuck around to the end, when lawmakers abolished the practice in 1869 without much noise. Hirzel doubted the effectiveness of arresting persons declared bankrupt by a judge. But he held it an effective measure to force indigent debtors into making installment payments. Debt warrants encouraged negotiations and actions that stood outside the legally recognized debt relation. One key feature of liberalism's rule from a distance was that actual enforcement was supposed to be seldom necessary. The threat of jailing somebody to coerce them to agree to pay was a wholly different function than bankruptcy's inventorying of assets and restructuring of debt. In sum, while treating the body as collateral was a secondary feature of debt enforcement, it opened up an extrajudicial space of action with its own logic and purposes.

Indispensable Things

The mistakes that plagued the paperwork involved in turning objects, titles, and animals into collateral are highly revealing. Administrators tasked with conducting inventories were baffled by objects that had been pledged multiple times, borrowed, or lent out.[123] Tangible things were not the only types of collateral. Accounts receivable could also be pledged, transmuting them into transferable values with the same status as movable goods. The pawn shop set up by Zurich's cantonal bank in 1871 issued certificates that ascribed the right to a pawned object "just like a warrant or bill of lading." The certificate could be transferred, so that if its receiver later became unable to pay their creditors, the bankruptcy court could seize the certificate itself.[124]

In one case that illustrates well the levels of abstraction involved, judicial reviewers suspected the bankrupt former vintner Heinrich Surber of concealing his book of accounts receivable ("which admittedly contained multiple dubious entries") to the detriment of his creditors. Surber credibly testified in court, however, that before entering bankruptcy—when he would have lost the right to transfer his assets and books—he gave the accounting book to a creditor to cover a debt of ninety gulden and had in no way intended to harm his other creditors.[125]

In Zurich, the seizure of assets as collateral was wrapped up in the entangled economic relations of the protoindustrial putting-out system of cottage labor. Among the goods circulating in rural areas were semifinished textiles. Determining their owners was a complicated matter, and thus so was seizing them as collateral. In 1842, a coalition of bailiffs petitioned that raw materials that belonged to an employer who had commissioned work from a debtor be excluded from the inventory of that debtor's assets. They named things like, "for example, cloth for clothes, silk etc., because otherwise the cloth given to the tailor to be sewn or the silk given to the weaver to weave must be seized—however objectionable this might be for the owner of the objects—without, nevertheless, providing any advantage to [the indebted worker's] creditor; saying this is unnecessary, the point speaks for itself."[126] In principle, seizing assets as collateral meant expropriating them. But the seized object was only transferred from debtor to creditor virtually and on a provisional basis. In effect, it belonged to neither, existing in a liminal state. As granting a right to somebody else's property, the laws regulating collateral and pledging were subject to considerable limits; the collateral object was an equivalent for the amount owed only in a restricted sense. To draw an analogy, as a token, collateral fused the open debt and the payment thereof in a similar way that coupons regulated the flow of commodities.[127]

Creditors could request that officials depot the collateral assets, but often enough, a lien was placed on them and they remained in the debtor's possession. The official storing of animals, however, posed particular issues. The bailiffs' petition pled that seized animals be placed in the possession of creditors: "Very often, a bailiff must take objects like animals into custody for which he has no place to store and can thus only keep with great effort & costs, while it is more likely to be possible for the creditor to keep the things in an appropriate fashion. Thus, so long as putting things in the creditor's possession poses no danger for the debtor, which the bailiff will certainly be able to judge, doing so would be purposeful to avoid costs that, if they arise, the creditor is obligated to pay."[128] Lawmakers got twisted up in complicated questions over whether this or that object should be considered a movable or immovable asset, particularly when it came to the machines of the cottage industries like looms, spinning machines, and lace machines, which were permanently installed in workers' homes.[129]

But the confusion didn't stop with animals and perishable goods and the murky status of protoindustrial raw materials and machines bolted to the floor. The status of monetary claims like wages also posed difficulties. In 1855, Zurich's high cantonal court heard the case of a laborer in a weaving factory who had been forced into asset seizure proceedings by a creditor. The bailiff ordered the garnishment of the entirety of his wages, both those earned but yet to be paid and those not yet earned. When he informed the factory's owner, the latter protested that he would fire the laborer if his wages were garnished, arguing that "the factory head cannot be made into the director of the affairs of his workers' creditors" and that he gave his workers advances of five francs a week to cover their costs of living.[130] Asset seizure collided with the relation between boss and worker and the long, seasonal payment rhythms dominant at the time.[131] This complex of claims and counterclaims made it difficult to isolate an object as collateral. It seems that the threat of dismissal constantly impeded attempts to garnish wages, because bosses were not prepared to settle their accounts with laborers through the mediating instance of a debt collector.[132]

At the same time that legal practice was declaring tools, animals, and titles as collateral in individual cases, the law was also establishing protections for certain kinds of objects. Still, it is remarkable how the protections were long restricted to tangible objects, a situation that was only changed by the 1889 Federal Statute on Debt Enforcement and Bankruptcy, which added, with qualifications, wages to the list of things that could not be seized (without, however, providing a hard-and-fast definition of what constituted a minimum level of subsistence). In a sense, the law treated the minimum as being embodied in the protected things themselves. This constellation reproduced liberalism's clear separation of subject and object, protecting things seen as necessary for providing for oneself and one's family while refraining from defining subjective needs, which were viewed with suspicion because of their plasticity and potential inability to be satisfied.

The valorization of objects expressed here was, however, not an invention of liberalism, but stemmed from early modern agrarian customs. Zurich's 1832 law on debt enforcement stated:

> The following assets cannot be seized as collateral:
>
> a) The hymnbooks of the debtor and his wife; the hymnbooks and schoolbooks of their children.
> b) The clothes of the debtor's wife and children. Moreover, the indispensable clothes of the debtor himself.
> c) The clothes and weapons necessary to perform compulsory military service.[133]

In 1842, baptism gifts given to children by their godparents were added to the list.[134] They, too, were more than just private gifts, because godparenthood reached beyond the boundaries of the nuclear family.[135] In 1851, the list was again expanded to include tools and objects distributed by the poor relief authority and objects deemed essential for the prevention of fires. It also added "indispensable bedding," which included pillows and blankets, but not bed frames and mattresses, which could still be seized.[136] Finally, Zurich's 1851 debt enforcement law for the first time protected from seizure an object necessary for sustenance, namely, the "fertilizer necessary for cultivating the debtor's land."

The concept of indispensable and therefore nonattachable basic goods initially only applied to asset seizure proceedings. In bankruptcy, a debtor could lose everything. In the canton of Zurich, the protections of objects were only extended to bankruptcy proceedings by the private law codex of 1854/56 and the bankruptcy law of 1857. Around the same time, the concept was also expanded to bar debtors from pledging on their own volition the particular set of legally protected objects. Before that, jurists were uncertain whether a debtor could, for instance, freely pledge their only bed. In 1848, the Zurich district court decided in the negative, explaining that "if the mere permission of the debtor were sufficient to expropriate the last things he had," then it would be too easy for creditors, "at least the ruthless ones," to put undue pressure on their debtors.[137] The 1889 federal law, however, reversed this decision by allowing debtors to pawn everything they owned.

The set of things covered by the concept of indispensable basic goods remained constant until the passage of the 1889 federal law.[138] Zurich's restrictions were relatively thin when compared to other cantons, which often excluded tools, farm animals, and a reserve of food from the things that could be seized as collateral.[139] The federal law significantly expanded the list, which led a court newspaper to deem its "social aspect" as "much more important than all personal liability insurance laws, accident insurance laws, and alcohol laws combined."[140] On this point, the law followed the related laws of the German Empire and France, the latter having already served as the model for the Francophone cantons. Beyond the things already listed, protections from seizure now applied to certain home items and kitchen utensils, the tools needed by a debtor and their family, tools and books required to perform their occupation, a two-month supply of food and cooking fuel, monetary and nonmonetary support from poor relief, health insurance, and aid societies, and a choice of either one dairy cow, three goats, or three sheep along with a month's worth of feed and straw.[141] As early as the drafts of the law composed in 1875, lawmakers had concluded that it was "in the interest of creditors to leave debtors their tools, which they use to work not only for themselves and their family members, but also in order to pay their debts."[142]

In another draft of the law, the Federal Council wanted to exempt a portion of wages from garnishment. The draft protected 150 francs of income for most debts, while proposing that for debts accrued for the "procurement of absolutely necessary things" such as food, creditors be permitted to garnish a debtor's wages down to only 50 francs a month.[143] But the bill could not win majority support in the Federal Assembly. The upper chamber then lowered the general protection down from 150 to 100 francs, to which the lower chamber responded by tossing out the idea of a definitive limit altogether. In a report from 1885, Basel professor of law Paul Speiser and the Association of Commerce and Industry spoke out against limits on wage garnishment.[144] According to Speiser, the Federal Council's bill would have made it impossible to collect the delinquent debts of day laborers and factory workers, which would in turn deprive everyday creditors of the underclasses like innkeepers and grocers of security. The law, he claimed, would lose its disciplinary force because "people who know they are shielded from all legal consequences easily become immoral, foolishly take on debts, and unlearn the desire to pay debts even if they are able to pay. A good debt enforcement law should also educate the people; with too much mildness one ruins their character." When the federal law came up for a vote in 1889, the conflicts over protections for certain asset classes flared up again.[145] The *Neue Zürcher Zeitung* saw the expansion of protections as an act of "humanity" and argued with the language of civilizational progress: While "[y]ears ago," indigent debtors in Switzerland were put in the "debt tower," and in dark times, some peoples even forced a debtor "along with his family into slavery," more recent times subscribed to the notion "that the debtor should not be pushed down beneath a certain standard of living and that his existence must remain humane."[146] On the other side, merchant circles repeated Speiser's fears that the large number of assets exempted from asset seizure would make it impossible to collect on the delinquent debts of underclass debtors. They complained that the state's coercive power would be wholly diminished if the law essentially protected the whole of a worker's assets from seizure by creditors. At an event on landlord-tenant laws, the "already infamous Article 92 of the debt enforcement law" (which listed which objects were protected from asset seizure) was discussed.[147] A magistrate judge criticized that "with the mass of things excepted from asset seizure, 70 percent of current claims will certainly be impossible to recover."[148]

Thus the limitations on asset seizure dealt more generally with the regulation and normalization of certain aspects of everyday exchange. The politics of the minimum that informed the debate unfolded as the state was implementing new institutions tasked with observing, shaping, and intervening in the social.[149] Part of their work was to make social practices mesh with the unified nation-state.[150] During the debates over the federal law in the 1880s, a complex network of knowledge production came into being that was made up of state administration, the sciences, philanthropic and civil society organizations, chambers of commerce, and organizations of the workers' and women's movements.[151] A key instrument for shaping perceptions of what constituted "social facts" was statistics, whose increasingly nuanced methods were put to use by various organizations to collect data on the entire nation.[152] The economic crisis increased the elites' need for statistical information to guide their decision making.[153] Although politically contested, statistics ultimately established itself as a dominant method of collecting information. Statistics provided ammunition in arguments during the heated class conflicts toward the end of the nineteenth century, while at the same time claiming to neutrally communicate indisputable facts.[154] The concept of minimum basic needs advanced to a key social category.[155] The debate over how to define them centered on the unit of the household. Interested parties latched onto scientificized research on the budget of the proletarian household to support their arguments, thus turning the assets of underclass households into a topic of serious discussion.

At the same time, the economic crisis of the 1880s churned up criticism of market liberalism. Its "centrifugal force" was attacked with the rhetoric of Christian corporatism, agrarian ideology, and anti-Semitism.[156] Liberal proponents like Carl Hilty, too, distanced themselves from laissez-faire and "Manchester theory."[157] The qualitatively new period of growth that had been gaining steam for a few years by the mid-1880s was viewed by liberal thinkers as evidence of their vision of progress, but anxieties about another crisis persisted.[158] "The standards for what constitutes a humane existence are increasing," wrote the *Neue Zürcher Zeitung*—a paper that supported the state—in the feature article on "humanity in the debt enforcement law." "In fifty years," it hoped, "the general welfare, morality, and education of our people" will be further "progressed."[159] Laws like the bankruptcy law were considered "social" legislative projects by analysts of the time,[160] while laws conducive to commercial exchange were passed with the ultimate goal of regulating society. Thus, to take one example, the deadlines set by the law that marked out the road from insolvency to the compulsory auction of seized assets privileged agriculture. When a farmer couldn't pay their debts, a creditor could only request that their land be auctioned six months after a lien was placed on it, and their right to demand the auction expired after two years; for movable goods, they had to wait one month before demanding an auction, a right that expired after only one year. The intention was to "protect" rural property "because of its social significance." Most debtors would be able to quickly recover after asset seizure, it was reasoned, "but the farmer without home and hearth sinks to a proletarian."[161] Against this general discursive backdrop, legislators working on the 1889 debt enforcement law also expanded the list of protected objects and exempted a portion of wages from seizure.

But even after the law went into effect in 1892, Swiss lawmakers could never agree to define a hard-and-fast minimum sum protected from wage garnishment or attachment of assets. They argued that in contrast to Germany, the restrictions were intended to ensure a narrowly defined "minimum subsistence level"; in no way were they intended to allow a person to retain the "standard of living customary for their estate."[162] The increasing prominence of wage labor in the late nineteenth century might lead one to believe that indispensable basic goods would have been supplanted by abstract sums of money in lawmakers' definition of what would enable people to meet their "minimum basic needs." But that was not the case. On the contrary, the restrictions on asset seizure for the most part applied to tangible things. As a law dissertation from the time put it, guaranteeing the possession of certain tangible objects "fixed as the norm a middle standard of life, naturally measured according to fairly low needs."[163] From this the author drew the conclusion that useful tools and the like could not be substituted with a sum of money: If a person had no stores of food for a period of two months (which, except with farmers, rarely happened), they could not insist that an equivalent amount of money be exempt from seizure.[164] Images with biblical themes could, in principle, be pledged, but not "actual pictures of saints"; wedding rings were definitely exempted.[165] A frock coat couldn't be seized from a traveling salesman, but it could be taken from a farmhand.[166] Sewing machines that did not provide their owner's main source of income were initially an issue of debate, but they gradually came under protection,[167] as did laborers' pocket watches.[168] Exempted from seizure were also one chair per member of the household, a wardrobe, a washbasin, beds for all adults, and in one case, a sofa as ersatz for a children's bed.[169] The lists of objects normalized specific employment, familial, and social constellations. But the norms were fodder for humor, too. During the law's first months, satirical newspapers wrote about wily debtors who swapped everything they owned for nonattachable stuff right before the bailiff came knocking.[170]

In many respects, the law's policy on wage garnishment followed common practices. Before its passage, debt collectors generally let laborers keep a portion of their wages in order to not rob them of "their necessary means of subsistence."[171] The law afforded debt collectors considerable discretion in determining how much of a debtor's wages were "indisputably necessary."[172] This gave rise to criticism that the law's openness on the point had "more than doubled" the workload of magistrates.[173]

As mentioned, the federal debt enforcement law did not define a minimum that was to be exempted from wage garnishment. The seizure of wages did not simplify creditors' access to debtors' assets by translating them into the homogeneous general medium of exchange. Rather, it caused new complications, because the seizure of future wages often proved impossible due to many debtors' shifting, temporary employment. Moreover, the authorities justified the limited restrictions on wage garnishment by claiming that if it were otherwise, proletarian debtors would never be able to buy on credit or get loans. Workers in seasonal jobs like masons had particular need of credit in the winter, which was generally given to them because lenders knew they would earn money in the coming summer. Basel's cantonal court found that the fixed amount of 150 francs that the Federal Council proposed to protect from wage garnishment exceeded the monthly wages of an average construction worker, which they believed would lead to a situation where "nobody would grant him credit merely on the basis of trust in his good will."[174]

The authorities took varying approaches to determining how much money could be garnished. In privileging certain claims, however, they drew on the moral vocabulary of useful things.[175] For example, a court newspaper reported on a case that came before the federal high court a year before the federal debt enforcement law went into effect.[176] A worker at a machine factory, married with seven children, earned 57.60 francs every fourteen days. His wages were garnished to pay off a debt incurred for milk and rent, with the debt collector deciding that 100 francs a month would be enough for the family to get by. The worker challenged the decision, but the court refused to hear it on the grounds that recovering debts "for objects essential for life" like bread, milk, or rent necessitated stricter conditions than for other things. In effect, this meant that underclass households, who primarily took on debts to buy food and clothing, could more easily have their wages garnished. In the words of the paper, they were "treated worse than the wealthy man" who buys "cigars, wine, books, luxury objects" on credit.

In her history of the "technopolitics" of living standards since the French Revolution, Dana Simmons writes that the determination of what constitutes the bare necessities has always been "a political act."[177] The debate over which goods were indispensable and basic enough to warrant protection from asset seizure is a prime example of this. In the 1830s, the liberal government of the canton of Zurich counted a small number of qualifying objects that included schoolbooks and hymnals, weapons and armor, and, a bit later, tools necessary to prevent fires. These objects were, in a sense, communal objects, the juncture at which the household linked up with the community of state subjects. Zurich's lawmakers opted to define this limited set of indispensable goods in order to escape having to grapple with the more confounding question of indeterminate, potentially limitless needs. The discourse had shifted by the time the 1889 federal debt enforcement law was passed. In the 1880s, too, the debate on indispensables focused on tangible objects. But by then, jurists were willing to try and determine what constituted a need. Even though legislators disagreed about how to define basic needs, there was consensus that the issue could be talked about, a change in common sense facilitated by the expansion of statistics. Needs had become objectified to an extent sufficient to be a deciding factor in the discussion on which objects were indispensable. Nevertheless, the thereby expanded definition of indispensables remained murky. On the one hand, legislators opted to narrowly circumscribe the set of indispensable objects by refusing to establish a minimum income that could not be garnished. On the other, the exchange of things in the underclasses' economy of makeshifts posed its own special issues.

The debates on basic needs in the 1880s increasingly scrutinized this economy of makeshifts. Observers of the time agreed that the revolving cycle of swapping objects for money was one of the foremost difficulties facing the late-nineteenth-century proletarian household. Purchasing things on the installment plan, renting furniture and clothes, buying food on credit, borrowing money in hard times, and pawning assets were the common practices of this precarious economy. Migration to the cities was complemented by an economy of movable assets, and the fact that most everything they owned was mobile enabled poor families to skip town or move into a new residence to escape debt collectors.[178] Many different perspectives were taken on the mobile assets of the underclasses, but they converged in the common goal of bringing some order to the heterogeneity of proletarian relations of exchange. Among them were the organizations to protect creditors that began to consolidate commercial interests in the 1880s.[179]

Alongside such initiatives, the debate on subsistence spurred on scientific analyses of the underclass economy. Here, too, approaches diverged. The politics of defining the poverty line could lend legitimacy both to restrictions on what a person was allowed to consume and to demands that the state guarantee a certain minimum level of subsistence.[180] Statistician Carl Landolt's 1891 study on the budgets of ten working households in Basel falls into the latter category.[181] Mined by generations of social historians because of its richness and detail, the study documents the families' poverty not only on the basis of their income and food expenses. It also demonstrates that the households had little more to their name than an inventory of tangible assets, which Landolt described as "a measure of the degree of a family's neediness or prosperity."[182] On the basis of this measure, he categorized households as "very poor," "poor," "average," and "relatively well-off." The first three levels meant that, alongside insufficient nourishment, the families had "no possessions except for household items."[183] Furniture, kitchen utensils, brooms, and the like constituted a remarkable portion of the impoverished families' assets, their market value much greater than the clothes, jewelry, watches, and pictures in their homes, not to speak of cash.

Why did exchange among the underclasses seem so opaque? And that to the extent that it complicated both attachment for the purpose of collecting debts and the identification of proletarian households' economic situation in the first place? Landolt's study shows how the everyday economy of makeshifts escaped the grasp of reformers' methods of observation. He advises his reader to treat his tabular data on food purchases with caution, "because in some cases, food was purchased on credit, and the purchase was only entered into the accounting book either in the next month or even only after the loan was paid."[184] Irregular income, moreover, often forced families to buy nonfood goods on credit.[185] Landolt saw buying on credit as a common, yet precarious, "dubious last resort," while the installment plan businesses that transferred property rights only after the last payment had been shelled out exploited debtors' precarious situations.[186] Animated objects, tangible things that were sold and pawned, and purchases on installment that placed buyers in disadvantageous relations of power, these were the elementary features of the proletarian economy in the eyes of social reformers. The economy of makeshifts necessitated that workers combine multiple sources of income to get by, a problem in the eyes of many. Proposals for solving it were manifold.[187] In patriarchal style, Carl Landolt promoted the primacy of the male breadwinner in order to put a check on the omnipresence of women's labor, which generated income that was, in reality, indispensable for proletarian households. Conservative voices, in contrast, criticized not only the gender of sources of income, but also elected to focus on the economy of makeshifts itself. A pamphlet printed in Cologne titled *Die Ausbeutung der Arbeiter* (The exploitation of workers), which was also distributed in Switzerland, narrated in dramatic language the fates of indebted laborers whose very coats had been seized off their backs. In gendered diction, the text bridged moral politics and the politics of consumption.[188] Ignoring issues of labor and wages entirely, it blamed the "destitution of everyday life" on the consumption practices of women and their alleged susceptibility to fall prey to installment plan schemes, peddlers, and lottery dealers.[189] It cast the bailiff's knock at the door as the denouement of a drama begun by transactions with seedy characters. The pamphlet's author concluded with a plea for restrictions on the scope of asset seizure. He painted a bleak picture of the alternative: The living spaces of working families would become "dreary and bare, and the most naked poverty and hunger" would move in; "discontent in the family" would break out and the man would flee "to the barrooms."[190] In his "distress," the debtor was diminished to a toy of unscrupulous creditors. And in the end, debt enforcement turned human into thing: "Imagine a fragile object on a ledge. It is shifted back and forth and is hardly damaged. But on the ledge, the smallest movement is enough to send the object crashing to the ground, where it shatters. This is the situation of people who have arrived at the limits of their fortitude, to which belong a large number of those people who have lost home and hearth."[191] In the account of this reform-minded observer, the economy of makeshifts not only perpetuated a dizzying quantity of swaps. It also reified people. The loss of tangible assets literally turned the debtor into a fragile thing. The perception that debts and indebtedness ultimately came down to a crisis in people's relations to objects was just one aspect of the ongoing confusion between the category of things and persons that characterized debates on debts and debt enforcement. This is particularly apparent in the controversies over pawning.

The Pawnshop: A Trove of Movable Assets

In one and the same breath, critics considered the nexus of pawned objects and liquid money to be both a relic of the past and a spawn of urban hypermodernity. Pastor Johann Ludwig Spyri puzzled over pawnshops, "an institution of the Middle Ages that, oddly, protrudes into our time, which is based on wholly different principles."[192] Spyri, a proponent of savings banks and one of the most prominent representatives of the elite liberal perspective on the "social question," found a historical precedent for pawning in the charitable *montes pietatis* of medieval Italy.[193] Spyri thought that pawning was anachronistic because, in contrast to the Middle Ages, capital in his day had "become more liquid" and was even accessible to "those of lesser means." At the same time, he thought that pawning was a necessary evil in the "large world cities," defined in his eyes by anonymity and staggering inequality. Spyri pointed to Paris, where summer's end transported "20,000 parasols" into the pawnshops, which thus housed twenty-eight million francs of "dead capital, so to speak."[194] As a consequence, the pawnshops devolved into "institutes that support waste and frivolity," where "cheap trinkets" were exchanged for petty cash.[195] Only in the cities that were "slowly taking on a cosmopolitan character" might Switzerland have any use for them, he opined.[196] In short, Spyri condemned pawning as a liminal practice from a bygone era that turned things into fossilized capital and fostered quixotic desires.

The history of pawning in Switzerland involved in equal parts the practical functioning of pawnshops and the moral castigation of them. Privately organized, publicly oriented philanthropic, institutional pawnbrokers sought to undermine private pawnshops by offering more attractive options for short-term hardships. But a hurdle to combatting pawning was its relative invisibility, an issue aggravated by the common opinion that it had a marginal status in modern liberal capitalism. A business directory from 1885 lists 71 pawnshops in Switzerland, though it passes over several large-scale operations.[197] Compared with the country's 210 savings banks, the pawnshops were clearly in the minority.[198] Yet despite these reservations, the sources make it possible to identify two distinct waves of energetic discussion on pawning. In the 1860s, the expansion of finance induced bourgeois philanthropists to debate the meaning and purpose not only of savings banks, insurance, and securities, but also of pawning.[199] Then, in the 1880s, stricter regulations on pawning were passed as part of more comprehensive antiusury laws.

Switzerland's first official pawnshop opened in 1856. Called the "movable goods loan bank," it was established by the Creditanstalt St. Gallen, which in itself was a regular bank.[200] In 1864, the Basel Handerwerkerbank (Craftsmen's Bank) set up its own pawnshop. The Gesellschaft für das Gute und Gemeinnützige (Society for the Good and the Common Welfare) was initially supposed to cofound it, but they ultimately decided against participating for reasons that I will come back to briefly.[201] Zurich's cantonal bank followed with a pawnshop in 1871. The St. Gallen pawnshop was temporarily liquidated in 1875, but in 1884 it was restructured as a joint stock company insured by the guarantee of the Gemeinnützige Gesellschaft (Society for Common Welfare).[202] The pawnshop in Basel could no longer cover its operating costs after new regulations were passed there,[203] so in 1884, it too was reorganized as a joint stock company partially run by the Craftsmen's Bank and the Society for the Good and the Common Welfare.[204]

Supporters of pawnshops described them as offering temporary help in emergency situations, allowing people to squeeze through tough times. From the perspective of social history, pawning was more a phenomenon of prosperity than of economic crises: in boom periods, it expanded, while in crisis periods, it contracted, the reason being that people generally only pawned their things when they anticipated taking them back.[205] If an object was not retrieved within a year, the pawnshop would auction it off. Over the first three decades of its existence, the pawnshop run by Zurich's cantonal bank auctioned, on average, 7.3 percent of pawned objects (in Basel, the number for the 1890s was similar, at 7.8 percent),[206] meaning that 92 percent of objects were bought back within a year. Not destitution, but the modest affluence of having more things was the industry's driving force.

Both private and charitable pawnbrokers offered loans of between 75 and 80 percent of the value of gold and silver and between 60 and 75 percent of the value of other items.[207] Interest rates varied according to the period of the loan (the shortest being fourteen days) and the amount loaned (as little as two francs). The Zurich bank's pawnshop charged 12 percent APR for the smallest type of loans; Basel 18 percent. Borrowers also had to pay a set fee each time they pawned something. In Basel, for instance, the fee for a fourteen-day loan of five francs was fifteen cents.[208] The Basel pawnshop defended itself against critics by emphasizing that, legally, they were allowed to charge twice as much, while at the same time complaining that many potential customers still preferred the more expensive private pawnbrokers because they felt that those businesses were more discreet than the philanthropic institutions. Anonymity was a key concern for the charitable pawnbrokers. Zurich's pawnshop traced a drop-off in customers back to the canton's 1879 law requiring that they take down lenders' names; in Basel and Bern, reports told of lenders hiring people to pawn their stuff for them so as not to be seen at the pawnshop.[209]

What kinds of movable assets were being pawned in Swiss cities? At Basel's charitable public pawnbroker, watches and gold and silver jewelry made up, on average, 44.3 percent of pawned objects.[210] Clothing followed with 32.3 percent, bed frames and mattresses at 11 percent, with furniture and kitchen utensils in last place at 3.9 percent. Watches and jewelry were not only pawned more than anything else. They also accounted for 65 percent of the money loaned by the philanthropic pawnshop, while clothes only accounted for 11 percent of it, followed far behind by bedding (5.5 percent) and furniture (3.8 percent). And while household items made up a large portion of the assets held by the statistically analyzed family budgets discussed above and were seized more than any other category of goods, people tended to pawn more personal objects less crucial for everyday life.

Critics liked to decry pawning as a backwards practice, but the objects pawned were distinctly modern, as epitomized by the pocket watch. A liberal device par excellence, lightweight and worn close to the body, the watch helped the self-regulating subject conform to the dictates of punctuality on their own volition.[211] In contrast to clocks, pocket watches were initially something of a luxury item, but with the advent of machine production in the 1870s, their prices sank.[212] The watchmaker Roskopf out of La Chaux-de-Fonds aimed to put a twenty-franc watch on the market, which amounted to about a week's earnings for an industrial worker. Pawning centered on movable objects that could easily be removed from their context of use, had high exchange values, and were owned by the borrower. The ownership status of pawned things had to be absolutely clear, because pawnshops were always under suspicion of dealing in stolen goods[213] and because they were not allowed to take things given to protoindustrial workers by those commissioning work from them. When the Basel Craftsmen's Bank announced its intention to open a pawnshop, its representatives took pains to emphasize that they would not accept silk or other "raw goods" from weavers.[214]

The sums of money made liquid by pawned assets were small and were getting smaller all the time. Loans between two and five francs made up 26 percent of those paid out by Basel's philanthropic pawnshop in 1886, a number that would increase to 50 percent by 1902. In the years immediately before and after 1900, the average sum went from about 20 francs to sixteen. The urban underclasses, in other words, increasingly only resorted to pawning when borrowing very small sums of money, and they did it with things that lost value over time. The rise of industrially produced commodities at the end of the nineteenth century—"cheap trinkets" in Spyri's mind—both increased the availability of things like watches and clothes and lowered their exchange value at the pawnbroker's.[215]

Proponents and critics alike believed that the pawnshop's business model relied on the pawned assets' use value being higher than their exchange value.[216] They saw the difference between subjective use and objective value as the determining factor in the status of assets, whether they be seized as collateral to pay off a debt or pawned by families.[217]

Like in the morality-infused debates over indispensable useful things to be protected from asset seizure, Spyri wrote with the language of morality to argue that certain things should not be pawned. He reasoned that "the more necessary an object is for the family's subsistence, the less willing the [pawn] institution is to accept it as collateral; in contrast, the more an object has the character of comfort, even luxury, the more pawnable it should appear." This principle was intended to ensure that the household's "only bed, which often has to suffice for many family members, does not end up in the pawnshop."[218]

Subjective values were objectified in collateral. In an article on debt enforcement law, a German jurist began with the old wisdom that "two cords of wood" constituted an "indispensable reserve for poor people in a hard winter," thus making it more valuable for them than it would be for a "millionaire." He continued that the seizure and auctioning of their assets confused two different types of value: "It is a peculiarity of forced auctions to destroy the subjective value, the notion of which the example has just illustrated for us, because they do not acknowledge this subjective value. At any rate, the creditor only receives a sum that corresponds to the objective value of the thing minus the costs [of seizure and auctioning—MS] or in many cases less."[219] While the laws protecting certain assets from seizure distinguished between subjective needs and objective claims, between real and false necessities, analysts of the time observed that pawning obscured the line between subjective needs and objective means.[220] This was a cause of serious concern for bourgeois, reformist critics, a point worth studying in more detail.

For the Society for Common Welfare, pawning threw time and things into disorder. One writer saw in the establishment of pawnshops an attempt to make "the classes of little means" wealthier, which struck him as an "alchemical endeavor": "You're not going to find gold in the cauldron if you don't put some in there first."[221] Spyri, too, implored that "overstretched credit" could unleash many "calamities," teaching that "happiest is the worker who needs as little credit as possible."[222] The philanthropists of the Society for Common Welfare were of the opinion that a family's movable assets should exclusively be used to private ends, which fueled their objections against pawning as an impermissible misuse of things. Moreover, they warned that borrowing money against pawned goods was little more than pocketing anticipated yet unpaid income.[223]

Pawned assets could be used neither by the borrower nor the pawnbroker, making them into "dead capital."[224] Brokers' habit of lowballing assets' values further reduced pawning's economic rationale.[225] Pawned objects were also "unproductive" because their temporary uselessness inhibited the "classes of little means" from investing in sensible business activity.[226] The same author welcomed cooperatives like the Schulze-Delitzsch Associations, which enabled workers to save and generate capital collectively. He also defended extending credit on the guarantee of a cosigner as a way to shrink the gap between poor and rich, explaining that such credit might salve "the discontent that is secretly gnawing away at modern society."[227] But the raw dealings of "cold, dead pawnshops" destroyed such "mutual support."[228]

Proponents from Basel's Craftsmen's Bank took the opposite position that pawning put the household's assets to productive use. Sure, they admitted, as private use objects, the things made the family's everyday life easier. But they did not bring in any income: "A clock on the wall shows the hour, but generates no profit; a parasol in one's hand protects them from the sun, but hardly generates profit; a table, a chair, a desk, a wardrobe are nice, but they don't increase their owner's gains; a painting, a knickknack might please the eye, but they don't increase our income at all."[229] The pawnshop, though, transformed these things into productive value. It didn't remove capital from circulation, proponents said. Rather, pawning "really produced something."[230] Their argument was implicitly grounded on the premise that underclass households were well able to make their own decisions to do without certain things in times of illness or unemployment. Underscoring their claims with numbers from a weaver family's budget, they continued that savings banks were not a "panacea."[231] And they added another argument that worked with the concept of the minimum level of subsistence: if a household spent all their income on essentials, then "the little bit of capital resting in their movable assets" was the only way for them to obtain credit.[232] Finally, they claimed that pawning would provide some relief to the merchants who extended credit to these families for their purchases.[233] Thus their argument aimed at stabilizing exchange well beyond the underclasses.

Bourgeois philanthropists often did not articulate why exactly they deemed the status of pawned objects to be unacceptable. Indirectly, however, their efforts sought to control the underclasses' consumption behaviors. They insinuated that an object's transformation from a private, emotionally significant possession into a financial guarantee endangered the disciplinary functions of time and self-abnegation. A principle of liberalism is that subjectivity is constituted through property ownership. But the way pawning redeemed objects for value undermined this principle by displacing objects, thus undermining their role in constituting subjectivity. In doing so, it threatened to blur social boundaries, not the least boundaries between classes.[234] This helps explain why bourgeois philanthropists often stressed the symbolic aspects of pawned assets. A common trope were descriptions of the pawnshop's storage facilities with its piles of objects, like the "20,000 parasols" wintering in Paris. These displaced objects roused the philanthropists' imaginations, because they put on display for all to see the distinction between the object's particularity and its exchange value as a commodity.[235] But because the things stored on pawnshop shelves did not disappear, the phenomenon was difficult to grasp, occasioning the perception of it as being at once an uncanny medieval relic and an expression of modern, urban anonymity.

The Things of Liberalism

The "acceleration of economic life that is instigated by money," wrote a perceptive analyst of social issues around 1900, created a world in which, for the first time in human history, "furniture [*die Möbel*], like capital, has become mobile."[236] In the last part of *The Philosophy of Money*, Georg Simmel reflected on how money impacted the world of things. Simmel defined money paradoxically as an absolute means. By encompassing "an increasingly larger part of reality," the universal abstraction of money enabled "subjectively differentiated forms of life" and "the full development of personal differences on the basis of this levelling material."[237] "Gauging values in terms of money," the universal measure of value "has thus enforced a much greater precision in the comparison of various contents of life."[238] By establishing equivalency between all things, money not only inserted itself between people exchanging with one another, but it also came to dominate the relation between people and things themselves: "Our interest in them is disrupted through the medium of money, their own objective significance becomes dissociated from our consciousness because it is more or less excluded from its proper position in our constellation of interests by their money value."[239] At the same time, money placed virtually everything at people's disposal. Money generated a "dual process" of simultaneously producing and eliminating distance that expanded the "associations of interest in which the spatial distance of the interested parties is absolutely negligible."[240] Credit represented the epitome of this dual process, because "the bill of exchange or the concept of money debt in general represents the values of distant objects," which "are condensed . . . in the bill."[241] This oscillation between proximity and distance driven on by money's unification of utmost generality and hyperindividuality also had a temporal dimension in Simmel's account.[242] The common metaphor of "liquid" money captured how the "insubstantial nature of money . . . enables it to support the systematization and tempo of life wherever the level of development or personal trends press for it."[243] While inflation accelerated the pace of life, the mobilization of what had previously been immobile symbolized the temporal power of money.[244] The modernity of a society, according to Simmel, could be determined by whether the "tempo of life" was determined by real property or money: "But where the acceleration of economic life that is instigated by money has asserted itself, it seeks to impose its rhythm upon the resistant form of landed property."[245] Thus the medium of money not only moved things, it also created new objects.

Simmel's diagnosis should be read in its historical context. He wrote at a time when everyday discourse was increasingly occupied with the exchange of things and relations between persons and things. This chapter sought to trace several steps of this historical trajectory. Using assets as collateral posed intractable issues for liberalism's concept of subjectification, because it at once reinforced and undermined the division between subject and object. Asset collateral fused together questions of freedom, property, and agency. It expanded individuals' latitude in economic affairs, but when their assets were seized, this increased freedom flipped into its opposite. It followed the movement between objectified persons and animated objects described at length in Marcel Mauss's analysis of the gift, and it obscured the question of what was a gift and a gift in return, who was giver and who recipient.

The seizure of assets as collateral branched off of a debt that preceded it. In this respect, asset seizure was a moment of closure, bringing a chain of claims and objections between creditor and debtor to a conclusion.[246] The encapsulation of a social relation in an object ultimately served to stabilize credit relations. In turn, it made it possible "*to collateralize everything that can be collateralized*," which characterized the spirit of the times in the opinion of the *Volksblatt vom Bachtel* article cited at the beginning of the chapter. Asset seizure was a simple administrative resolution to the problem of collecting delinquent debts, placing it in contrast with the complexity of bankruptcy proceedings.

Asset seizure, however, was a highly unstable end. Collateral, a hybrid object that straddled the line between property law and contract law, embodied the unpredictability of debt relations. It animated objects and reified persons, confusing the boundaries between the category of the person and the category of things. Debt imprisonment literally turned the person into a collateral thing themself. Though it was initially supposed to be a means to prevent debtors from skipping town and to allow officials to inventory a debtor's assets, nineteenth-century Zurich witnessed its transformation into an instrument to coerce debtors into agreeing to pay what they owed in installments. Liberal governance rarely had to resort to using it, but the very threat was a constitutive aspect of its function. The *Wortzeichen*, or debt warrant, had a fitting name, because it was precisely that: a performative symbol, a declaration that exerted effects outside the court of law.

The conundrum that asset collateral posed for liberal epistemology also became apparent in debates over which objects should be legally protected from seizure. The limits on how much could be expropriated from a person were defined in terms of objects, not abstract money value. By enumerating a set of indispensable things, legislators narrowly circumscribed the rights of debtors subject to asset seizure. The 1889 Federal Statute on Debt Enforcement and Bankruptcy expanded these rights at a time when the concept of a minimum level of subsistence was becoming a key category of social-political debate. Still, the entanglements of everyday economics gave birth to new uses of asset collateral. Wage garnishment forced legislators, reformers, and others to confront the question of how to deal with assets that didn't yet exist, while raw materials and partially finished goods supplied by an employer and tools necessary for work raised further issues. The underclasses' economy of makeshifts evoked the concern of bourgeois commentators, who disapproved of pawning. They illustrated their chagrin by pointing to the freely pledged objects stored at the pawnshop: things of private use, they were now reduced to their abstract exchange value. Social reformers worried that this state of things unsettled the constitution of liberal subjectivity in property, befuddled by a phenomenon that appeared to them at once crudely medieval and uniquely cosmopolitan. Simmel's turn-of-the-century claim that the increasing mobility of things characterized his age is historically symptomatic, one further moment in liberalism's ongoing discombobulation over the status of persons and things and the validity of values, claims, and obligations.

Conclusion

In 1800, archdeacon Johannes Tobler postulated his "practical maxim": "Forgive us our debts as we forgive our debtors."[1] In 1893, federal jurist Alfred Brüstlein spoke of the urgent necessity for lawmakers to adopt the "modern view according to which debt enforcement is executed against assets and not against the person."[2] Separated by nearly a century, both statements represent attempts to understand the relationality of debt and make a practical impact on it. But they are not connected by an over-arching sweep of progress. In the nineteenth century, debt and indebt-edness were topics mired in ever-shifting contradictions, which cannot be ironed out in a neat linear narrative. This book thus undertook to analyze the various ways in which objects, temporalities, and spatial prox-imities and distances shaped debt relations. This conclusion will round out the study by noting some turning points.

The guiding distinction between bankruptcy and asset seizure set in stone by the 1889 Federal Statute on Debt Enforcement and Bankruptcy helped to integrate divergent temporalities of debt into a nuanced, yet unified system. This synchronization was made possible by the commer-cial register, a cultural technique that had been developed for a different purpose a few years before. The register created two classes of persons on the basis of a purely formal distinction: merchant or nonmerchant. The category of the "merchant" was structured by a new spatiotemporal order, and the register laid the foundation for new techniques of con-trol and measurement. Thus it contributed to the construction of "the economy" as its own, autonomous sphere of action with its own laws, a common topic of social analyses in the late nineteenth century.[3] But the commercial register showed cracks from the very first day: it suffered from irresolvable questions of how to define who should be required to register as a merchant, and few people entered their names. Before the federal law went into effect, the tensions between different spheres of exchange and different temporalities were resolved by other means. In rural and protoindustrial regions, distinct rhythms were orchestrated by deadlines, all sorts of papers and forms, and publications like the reading of delinquent debtors' names in church.

In the 1830s, the institutions of the liberal state sought to implement new modes of accountability by commissioning reports based on statistics. But the new knowledge underscored how local authorities delayed debt collection proceedings in order to protect the local treasury from bankrupts, who would inevitably draw on poor relief. The increasing willingness to imprison penniless debtors after 1800 also stood in contradiction to the liberal principle of governance from a distance. Although debt imprisonment was a marginal practice, its use as a threat ramped up until it was finally abolished in 1870.

Political events like Zurich's liberal turn in 1830, the founding of the Swiss Confederation in 1848, and the revisions to cantonal constitutions won by the Democratic Movement in the late 1860s all were politically charged moments in which unresolved questions concerning the legitimacy of debts fueled debates on the fate of the body politic. Male civic rights were publicly debated and expanded, occasioning bankrupts to petition for relief from the "honor sanctions" imposed on them. Still, the bond between economic misfortune and moral failure remained strong in political discourse. The legislators who wrote the 1889 federal law also couldn't agree on a uniform rule for honor sanctions, thus passing the issue along to the cantons. But the law did change the conditions under which bankrupts could apply to have their rights reinstated. Between the crises of the late 1860s and that of 1880, the notion that the economy constituted its own, superindividual totality gained credence. This bolstered individuals' claims that their economic distress was due to "no fault of their own." The epistemology of rehabilitation, however, remained one of individual diagnoses, and relief continued to only be granted on a case-by-case basis. In 1800, Tobler's maxim "Forgive us our debts" asked creditors to show their debtors mercy. By the 1870s, in contrast, judges were responsible for assessing the singular mixture of moral lapses and contingent strokes of fate that led to a debtor's insolvency. Thus the moralization of debt did not disappear; the subject positions just changed.

The increasing objectification of the social exerted an influence on contemporary conceptions of crisis.[4] People explained their situations by pointing to a crisis that affected not just them as individuals, but everybody around them. The liberal state and its paperwork provided the material foundation for the polemical claims made by the Democratic Movement of the 1860s.

But beyond what contemporaries thought of crisis, economic crises also kicked off transformations in how debts were collected. One example was the Basel authorities' decision to change their record-keeping practices in the face of a stark uptick in bankruptcies in the 1860s; another was the decision to relax the conditions under which bankrupts could have their rights restored. But while the liberties of bankrupt men were expanded in the late 1860s, married women's property rights were curtailed. In this sense, the crisis of the late 1860s marked a turning point, as did that of 1880.

From this perspective, capitalism does not have an inner essence, but is rather a specific calibration of practices. The "unevenness" of modern capitalism has made the seemingly insignificant and everyday into the preferred locus of reflections about society, a point that has both methodological and historical implications.[5] Georg Simmel is a prime example. Mundane events form the essence of his writings around 1900, which serve as the chronological endpoint of this book.

This study, too, focused on the unevenness of debt collection—across regions, times, economic spheres—and its unremarkable everydayness. It is a particular history of systemic regulation that traces the concrete aspects of debt enforcement proceedings and demonstrates how a superpersonal, formal legal framework was created through individual interventions. The summary justice that was compulsory debt collection consisted of a mass of individual confrontations between debtors and creditors, confrontations that were both situated in a pre-existing legal framework and that themselves helped to shape it. Debt collection brought to daylight the frictions defining the fundamentally relational phenomenon of debt in liberal capitalism.

The analysis might permit a remark on discussions about the history of capitalism. Recent studies on capitalism have tended to focus on elites or on particular branches like commerce or finance, grappling with how capital was organized in certain historical periods and how it impacted society.[6] But research on the history of capitalism can learn much from the richness of everyday practices, as this book has sought to do. This means refraining from giving preference to certain economic problems or social spheres and instead analyzing capitalist relations of exchange and the conflicts, colliding moralities, and epistemic uncertainties that characterize them. Out of this shift in perspective follows a different historical narrative, one that does not start with ready-made concepts like capital or labor, but instead engages with the contradictions that lie at the foundation of these economic concepts in the moment of their historical emergence.

The processes of formalization and standardization that constituted debt enforcement were not a simple dependent variable that just sort of rose up out of history's automatic, all-encompassing forward movement. This study avoided using epochal concepts like industrialization and commercialization as handy explanations of complicated phenomena, all while not dispensing with the heuristic value of a general concept like capitalism. It aimed to strike an analytic balance between the particular and the systemic, the singular and the regulated. Debt collection did not follow a single inescapable template or logic, but it was also not a chaos of competing practices. Rather, the history of debt collection reveals how divergent practices and contingent forces were patched together into a rule-guided system.

Just to recapitulate one concrete manifestation of this pattern: The most important aspect of debt enforcement was that it required little state intervention. Modern liberal governance set forth early modern, agrarian customs. Policies on debt and indebtedness reveal how Switzerland only partially experienced the kind of expansion of the state undergone by other European countries in the nineteenth century, where state institutions came to permeate ever more parts of society. Bourgeois jurists committed to the "free movement" of money, commodities, and information ranked the legally sanctioned enforcement of debts high on their list of priorities. A German encyclopedia on statecraft from the 1860s sought to persuade its expert readership of the superiority of the "wholly unique Swiss institution" of debt enforcement, because the Swiss procedures were "more energetically" carried out in a manner "more suitable to the common good" than they "generally are in Germany."[7]

The article underscored debt enforcement's low costs and the simple, routine nature of administering it, which usually obviated a court date. The author inferred greater implications from this, claiming that it would loosen restrictions on credit: "Simple enforcement [of debts—MS] in connection with such a simple bankruptcy procedure is without a doubt the main reason why in the respective cantons real property, even that of small farmers, has obtained very great credit, which is elsewhere rarely to be found."[8] Integrating in a practical way even the "small farmer" into the liberal project, debt enforcement reveals a new aspect of liberalism, which, by placing customary practices in a different constellation, did not have to change these practices much to ensure that they would have effects on other aspects of economic life. At the same time, the history of debt collection reveals liberal governance as ready to pounce with coercive means at any time, pointing to an element of force and coercion in liberalism's rule from a distance that has often gone unremarked. Thus this study delved into the forms of resistance, the contradictions, and the entanglements that constantly threw sand in the gears of debt enforcement. Indeed, debt collection in its essence was a matter of confrontation, because debtors and creditors clashed over unpayable debts. This confrontation did not neatly adhere to class lines and generally appeared more as a disturbance than an articulated struggle.

The compulsory enforcement of debts conjoined economic exchange with symbolic values. The bankrupt was threatened by civic death and was cast in the social imaginary as a personification of crisis, particularly of the status of the male citizen subject. But the "civically dead" male bankrupt was not banished from the community of citizens, though he may have represented the opposite of what it was supposed to be. Rather, the metaphor of civic death articulated the limits of this community and its inherent inconsistencies, making crisis into a political problem for the state. Far from being the other of civil society, the image of the bankrupt enabled people to grasp what crisis really meant. Thus, by tracing the contours of the conflict, the social-imaginary representation of the bankrupt also contributed to political containment, consensus, and hegemony. The stories told by individual bankrupts, though, were quite different from this collective narrative. The bankrupts interrogated by the police in Basel were certainly not "dead" in any sense of the word, but actively sought to renegotiate favorable terms for themselves with their creditors. They resisted the authorities and tried to retain their residency status rather than apply for the right to participate in state politics. Some were hardly interested in their legal status at all. Again and again, the tipping point was when the bankrupt's loss of civic rights turned into a question of the marital gender hierarchy. Being stripped of his civic rights implied being stripped of his legal control over his wife and thus of his control over her dowry. This swept the rug from beneath men's self-identity as a property owner, undermining a key legal and cultural construct of liberalism. Conversely, bankrupts' wives made unexpected appearances on the stage of law. Women's increased visibility and capacity to act revealed fissures in the domestic gender hierarchy and the masculinity built upon it. And because both law and culture were cast in the image of this hierarchy, incoherency was the net effect of this friction.

There was no definitive typology of what it meant to be a bankrupt, and the same is true of subjectification through debt. Just like debt itself, subjectification is a *relational* phenomenon that resists standardized typologies. The subjectivity of the debtor was molded by paperwork, deadlines, agreements, and other objective elements that structured the debt relation. A clutch of cultural techniques—from premodern customs to the modern formal category of the merchant—interlinked in the production of subjects. But subjectification was not a one-way road to conformity, because its disciplinary procedures opened up space for unpredictable events. This point is most clear in chapter 4's analysis of individuals' narratives. The case of philanthropist creditor Jakob Stutz illustrated how debts in Zurich's pauperized protoindustrial highlands could impact multifarious social relations. The stories of Gottfried Keller tell of how complicated legal procedures allowed subjects to renegotiate their obligations to creditors and others, but at the cost of a loss of orientation. In his world, the individual subject's capacity to judge was responsible for keeping them from falling victim to "swindle" and the like. Debt was the catalyst of Wilhelm Weitling's communist political theory because it permeated many aspects of life and survival, far removed from the instances of consensus and hegemony mentioned above. Weitling described debt as the subjective realization of the "money system." The techniques of identification and interpellation employed in debt enforcement regularly flipped into their opposite, dissociating persons from their identities and capturing them in unintended situations. Generally speaking, debts put the liberal subject in a sticky situation. Warnings against casually entering into the bonds of indebtedness spanned from Benjamin Franklin's famous tirade—so dramatically quoted by Max Weber in the *Protestant Ethic*—to fears of the dangers posed by the expansion of cosigning in Switzerland in the 1880s. These admonishments did not condemn debts as a death sentence for subjective autonomy that was to be avoided at all costs. Rather, they insisted that people exert caution precisely because debts constituted an omnipresent feature of the economy of precarity. Debts were not an exceptional experience of the liberal subject, but a quotidian relation that had to be approached alertly.[9]

Similarly, subjectification did not produce conformity. When people reflected on their position as debtor or creditor, they generally drew on established schemata. Moralization, however, often led debtors to defend themselves with a whole range of different arguments. The bankrupts interrogated by the Basel police, for instance, depicted themselves as "able family men," guessed low when asked about the losses their creditors would suffer, and skipped town to avoid dealing with the administrative procedures altogether. But bankrupts did not always have to draw on topics only tangentially related to debt. They often exploited the incoherence of social norms to their own benefit.[10] As the study of the messy status of the dowry—a form of property that straddled domestic life and contract law—shows, the laws themselves could be contradictory.

Taken to their logical conclusion, the complexities of debt collection cut to the core of relations between subject and object, persons and things. It sought to mold them into the liberal regime of private property, but in the process it repeatedly brought forth new problems. When things (and, until the 1870s, human bodies) were seized as collateral, they lost their clear status as somebody's private property, which caused a conundrum for concepts of property and its constitutive function for liberal subjectivity. In the 1880s, a time when the expropriation of assets to settle debts was being criticized more and more, efforts to protect things and persons from the effects of debt enforcement gained in urgency. Most, however, failed. The study thus focused less on the various institutions that formed subjects and more on the collisions between these institutions, which wrapped subjects up in confusing situations, in which sometimes a subject lost their subjectivity, paradoxically existing as a *non*subject, so to speak.

The relationality of debt placed debtors and creditors together in a shared space, but it was by no means homogeneous. Institutions both solidified and fragmented debtor-creditor relations, while media like paperwork simultaneously created new forms of visibility and opacity. Epistemic riddles abounded for debtors, creditors, debt collectors, and legislators alike. Some concerned classification, as when officials tried to describe bankrupts' fates in terms of moral failure and economic misjudgment, while others stemmed from the confusion that collateral caused in relations between persons, things, and values.

Ultimately, confusion was the epistemological end product of debt enforcement. This conclusion is not contradicted by the fact debt enforcement was an elementary, generally smooth-running practice of capitalist relations of exchange. The stability of debt enforcement was built on shaky foundations, a problem that this study explored. The period analyzed here was capped off by Switzerland's 1889 Federal Statute on Debt Enforcement and Bankruptcy, which established consistent, federally codified practices. Inconsistencies were embedded in the divergent procedures that existed prior to 1889, which, in the words of one federal lawmaker, had all "grown out of routine."[11] Debt enforcement injected a qualitatively new degree of reliability into everyday economic life in the nineteenth century. But as it solved one issue, it created a whole slew of other problems by serving as a constant source of confusion.

Notes

Introduction

1. Staatsarchiv des Kantons Zürich X 347 (6), Schmähschrift gegen Altschuldenschreiber Schinz (Pasquil against debt collector emeritus Schinz).

2. The episode took place in 1842, about three decades before—according to Michel Foucault's periodization—the sodomite as an "aberration" was distinguished from the homosexual as a "species." See Michel Foucault, *The History of Sexuality, Volume 1: An Introduction*, trans. Robert Hurley (New York: Pantheon, 1978), 43.

3. A more extensive treatment of this case can be found in Mischa Suter, "Schuld und Schulden. Zürich 1842," *L'Homme: Zeitschrift für feministische Geschichtswissenschaft* 22, no. 2 (2011): 113–20.

4. This section draws heavily on Richard Dienst's analysis of the historicity of the debt relation: Richard Dienst, *The Bonds of Debt: Borrowing Against the Common Good* (London: Verso, 2011), 149–50.

5. See Chris Gregory, "On Money Debt and Morality: Some Reflections on the Contribution of Economic Anthropology," *Social Anthropology* 20, no. 4 (2012): 380–96.

6. Giovanna Procacci, *Gouverner la misère: La question sociale en France 1789–1848* (Paris: Éditions du Seuil, 1993).

7. On precarity as a persistent feature in the life of large swaths of the population, see Robert Castel, *From Manual Workers to Wage Laborers: Transformation of the Social Question*, trans. Richard Boyd (London: Routledge, 2017).

8. The current version is translated in Stephen V. Berti, *Swiss Debt Enforcement and Bankruptcy Law: English Translation of the Amended Federal Statute on Debt Enforcement and Bankruptcy (SchKG)* (Zurich: Schulthess, 1997); see further Cédric Ballenegger, *Le droit vaudois des poursuites, 1803–1891* (Lausanne: Bibliothèque historique vaudoise, 2013); Yves Le Roy, "Le choix des voies de poursuites à la fin du xixe siècle, en particulier dans le projet de loi fédérale sur la poursuite pour dettes et la faillite du 23 février 1886," in *Le Droit commercial dans la société suisse du xixe siècle*, ed. Pio Caroni (Fribourg: Éditions Universitaires Fribourg Suisse, 1995), 259–303.

9. *Schweizerisches Idiotikon. Wörterbuch der schweizerdeutschen Sprache*, vol. 14, s.v. "Trib," (Frauenfeld: Verlag Huber & Co., 1987), 64–166.

10. *Deutsches Wörterbuch von Jacob Grimm und Wilhelm Grimm*, s.v. "Trieb," accessed May 11, 2018, http://woerterbuchnetz.de/cgi-bin/WBNetz/wbgui_py?sigle=DWB&mode=Vernetzung&lemid=GT10661#XGT10661.

11. *Grosses vollständiges Universal-Lexicon aller Wissenschaften und Künste*, vol. 23, s.v. "Natur-Triebe," (Leipzig, 1740), 1225–26; Johann Friedrich Blumenbach, *Über den Bildungstrieb und das Zeugungsgeschäfte* (Göttingen, 1781).

12. *Deutsches Wörterbuch von Jacob Grimm und Wilhelm Grimm*, s.v. "Triebfeder," accessed May 11, 2018, http://woerterbuchnetz.de/cgi-bin/WBNetz/wbgui_py?sigle=DWB&mode=Vernetzung&lemid=GT10702#XGT10702.

13. Marc H. Lerner, *A Laboratory of Liberty: The Transformation of Political Culture in Republican Switzerland, 1750–1848* (Leiden: Brill, 2012); Gordon A. Craig, *The Triumph of Liberalism: Zurich in the Golden Age, 1830–1869* (New York: Scribner, 1988); Oliver Zimmer, *A Contested Nation: History, Memory and Nationalism in Switzerland, 1761–1891* (Cambridge: Cambridge University Press, 2003); Barbara Weinmann, *Eine andere Bürgergesellschaft. Klassischer Republikanismus und Kommunalismus im Kanton Zürich im späten 18. und 19. Jahrhundert* (Göttingen: Vandenhoeck & Ruprecht, 2002).

14. Chapter 2 gives a more detailed account of this understanding of liberalism. See Simon Gunn and James Vernon, "Introduction: What Was Liberal Modernity and Why Was It Peculiar in Imperial Britain?," in *The Peculiarities of Liberal Modernity in Imperial Britain*, ed. Simon Gunn and James Vernon (Berkeley: University of California Press, 2011), 1–18; Patrick Joyce, *The Rule of Freedom: Liberalism and the Modern City* (London: Verso, 2003), 4.

15. On the example of British liberalism see Patrick Joyce, *The State of Freedom: A Social History of the British State since 1800* (Cambridge: Cambridge University Press, 2013).

16. On the politics and everyday practices involved in the plurality of currencies around 1800 see Rebecca Spang, *Stuff and Money in the Time of the French Revolution* (Cambridge, MA: Harvard University Press, 2015).

17. On the concept of property in liberalism see Robert Descimon, "Reading Tocqueville: Property and Aristocracy in Modern France," in *Tocqueville and Beyond: Essays on the Old Regime in Honor of David D. Bien*, ed. Robert Schneider and Robert M. Schwartz (Newark: University of Delaware Press, 2003), 111–26; Dieter Schwab, "Eigentum," in *Geschichtliche Grundbegriffe. Historisches Lexikon zur politisch-sozialen Sprache in Deutschland*, ed. Otto Brunner, Werner Conze, and Reinhart Koselleck (Stuttgart: Klett-Cotta, 1975), 2:65–115. An important study that illuminates the multiple meanings of "property" in everyday transactions is Jonathan Sperber, *Property and Civil Society in South-Western Germany 1820–1914* (Oxford: Oxford University Press, 2005).

18. Rebekka Habermas, *Thieves in Court: The Making of the German Legal System in the Nineteenth Century*, trans. Kathleen Mitchell Dell'Orto (Cambridge: Cambridge University Press, 2016), 4.

19. *Code Civil des Français: Édition originale et seule officielle* (Paris, 1804), 134, §544: "La propriété est le droit de jouir et disposer des choses de la manière la plus absolue, pourvu qu'on n'en fasse pas un usage prohibé par les lois ou par

les règlements." That despite this definition the code did not lay out a consistent conception of property is the fascinating argument of Mikhaïl Xifaras, *La propriété: étude de philosophie du droit* (Paris: Presses Universitaires de France, 2004).

20. The concept "economy of makeshifts" comes from Olwen Hufton, *The Poor of Eighteenth-Century France: 1750–1789* (Oxford: Clarendon, 1974). The concept "subaltern class," borrowed from Antonio Gramsci, is a relational, conflict-oriented concept of social power relations that emphasizes the subjective, culturally mediated side of social positions. See Antonio Gramsci, *Prison Notebooks*, ed. Joseph A. Buttigieg (New York: Columbia University Press, 2011), 2:24–5 and 2:91–2.

21. On the history of strategies of grappling with poverty used by poor people see Laurence Fontaine, *The Moral Economy: Poverty, Credit, and Trust in Early Modern Europe* (Cambridge: Cambridge University Press, 2014); Laurence Fontaine and Jürgen Schlumbohm, eds., *Household Strategies for Survival 1600–2000: Fission, Faction, and Cooperation* (Cambridge: Cambridge University Press, 2000); Katrin Marx-Jaskulski, *Armut und Fürsorge auf dem Land. Vom Ende des 19. Jahrhunderts bis 1933* (Göttingen: Wallstein, 2008), particularly part 5; Rachel G. Fuchs, *Gender and Poverty in Nineteenth-Century Europe* (Cambridge: Cambridge University Press, 2005); Robert Jütte, *Arme, Bettler, Beutelschneider. Eine Sozialgeschichte der Armut in der Frühen Neuzeit* (Weimar: Verlag Hermann Böhlaus Nachfolger, 2000); Paul Johnson, *Saving and Spending: The Working-Class Economy in Britain, 1870–1939* (Oxford: Clarendon, 1985).

22. Alexandra Binnenkade, *KontaktZonen. Jüdisch-christlicher Alltag in Lengnau* (Cologne: Böhlau, 2009), chap. 5.

23. On the history of Swiss banking see Franz Ritzmann, *Die Schweizer Banken: Geschichte—Theorie—Statistik* (Bern: Haupt, 1973); Malik Mazbouri, *L'émergence de la place financière Suisse (1890–1913)* (Lausanne: Éditions Antipodes, 2005); Béatrice Veyrassat, *Négociants et fabricants dans l'industrie cotonnière suisse, 1760–1840: aux origines financières de l'industrialisation* (Lausanne: Payot Lausanne, 1982).

24. For an anthropological perspective on law in face-to-faceless relations see Laura Nader, *The Life of the Law: Anthropological Projects* (Berkeley: University of California Press, 2002), 54–57.

25. A point demonstrated by a pioneering study that for the first time analyzed the relation between savings banks, private credit, and the end of land charges in the German-speaking countries. See Johannes Bracht, *Geldlose Zeiten und überfüllte Kassen: Sparen, Leihen und Vererben in der ländlichen Gesellschaft Westfalens (1830–1866)* (Stuttgart: Lucius & Lucius, 2013), 202–9.

26. William M. Reddy, *Money and Liberty in Modern Europe: A Critique of Historical Understanding* (Cambridge: Cambridge University Press, 1987), xi.

27. This is demonstrated by some impressive studies from the past few years, which document that the early modern period had a vigorous market society and that, conversely, personalized, culturally coded credit relations continued to hold great significance in the nineteenth century. See Clare Haru Crowston, *Credit, Fashion, Sex: Economies of Regard in Old Regime France* (Durham, NC: Duke University Press, 2013); Fontaine, *Moral Economy;* Craig Muldrew, *The Economy of Obligation: The Culture of Credit and Social Relations in Early Modern England*

(Basingstoke: Palgrave Macmillan, 1998); Margot Finn, *The Character of Credit: Personal Debt in English Culture, 1740–1914* (Cambridge: Cambridge University Press, 2003).

28. Claire Lemercier and Claire Zalc, "Pour une nouvelle approche de la relation de crédit en histoire contemporaine," *Annales HSS* 67, no. 4 (2012): 979–1009; Clare Haru Crowston, "Credit and the Metanarrative of Modernity," *French Historical Studies* 34, no. 1 (2011): 7–19; Philip T. Hoffman, Gilles Postel-Vinay, and Jean-Laurent Rosenthal, *Priceless Markets: The Political Economy of Credit in Paris, 1660–1870* (Chicago: University of Chicago Press, 2000).

29. David Graeber, *Debt: The First 5000 Years* (New York: Melville House, 2011), 121.

30. Finn, *Character of Credit*, 10.

31. In Gaston Bachelard's conception, epistemology observes historically specific forms of the "striving towards rationality and towards construction" by laying bare the "conditions of objective knowledge" and placing them within a "system of thought." Gaston Bachelard, *The Formation of the Scientific Mind: A Contribution to a Psychoanalysis of Objective Knowledge*, trans. Mary McAllester Jones (Manchester: Clinamen, 2002), 26, 238. Chapter 3 of this book goes deeper into conceptions of historical epistemology.

32. For other perspectives on the limits of finance economy from sociology and literary studies, respectively, see Urs Stäheli, *Spectacular Speculation: Thrills, the Economy, and Popular Discourse*, trans. Eric Savoth (Stanford, CA: Stanford University Press, 2013); Alex Preda, *Framing Finance: The Boundaries of Markets and Modern Capitalism* (Chicago: University of Chicago Press, 2009); Mary Poovey, *Genres of the Credit Economy: Mediating Value in Eighteenth- and Nineteenth-Century Britain* (Chicago: University of Chicago Press, 2008).

33. For critical perspectives on the theoretical and methodological issues at stake here see Gary Wilder, "From Optic to Topic: The Foreclosure Effect of Historiographic Turns," *American Historical Review* 117 (2012): 723–45; Patrick Joyce, "What Is the Social in Social History?," *Past and Present* 206 (2010): 213–48; William Sewell, *Logics of History: Social Theory and Social Transformation* (Chicago: University of Chicago Press, 2005); Manu Goswami, *Producing India: From Colonial Economy to National Space* (Chicago: University of Chicago Press, 2004); Timothy Mitchell, *Rule of Experts: Egypt, Techno-Politics, Modernity* (Berkeley: University of California Press, 2002).

34. See Joyce, "What Is the Social," 221; Mitchell, *Rule of Experts*, 2–3.

35. Sewell, *Logics of History*, 348.

36. The fragmentary third volume of *Capital* notes: "An exhaustive analysis of the credit system and of the instruments which it creates for its own use (credit money, etc.) lies beyond our plan." Karl Marx, *Capital*, vol. 3 (New York: International Publishers, 1998), 397. However, see Suzanne de Brunhoff, *Marx on Money*, trans. Duncan Foley and Maurice Goldbloom (London: Pluto, 1977) for a reconstruction of the role of money and credit in Marx's work.

37. Jonathan Sperber, *Karl Marx: A Nineteenth-Century Life* (New York: Liveright, 2013), 296–302, 482–86.

38. The entry is dated March 1865. A facsimile of the album is reproduced in Izumi Omura, Valerij Fomičev, Rolf Hecker, and Shun-ichi Kubo, eds., *Familie*

Marx privat. Die Foto- und Fragebogen-Alben von Marx' Töchtern Laura und Jenny (Berlin: Akademie, 2005), 119. I would like to thank Markus Bürgi for drawing my attention to this source.

39. Peter Stallybrass, "Marx's Coat," in *Border Fetishisms: Material Objects in Unstable Spaces*, ed. Patricia Spyer (New York: Routledge, 1998), 183–207. See also Sperber, *Karl Marx*, 253–58; Finn, *Character of Credit*, 7.

40. Karl Marx, *Capital: Volume 1*, trans. Ben Fowkes (London: Penguin, 1990), 209.

41. Karl Marx, "Comments on James Mill, *Élémens d'économie politique*," in *Marx and Engels Collected Works* (London: Lawrence & Wishart, 2010), 3:212–13.

42. Marx, "James Mill," 214.

43. Marx, "James Mill," 214.

44. Marx, "James Mill," 215.

45. Marx, "James Mill," 215.

46. Marx, "James Mill," 215.

47. Marx, "James Mill," 215.

48. For another interpretation of Marx as a theorist of debt and subjectification see Maurizio Lazzarato, *The Making of Indebted Man*, trans. Joshua David Jordan (Los Angeles: Semiotext(e), 2012).

49. Michel Foucault, "The Subject and Power," *Critical Inquiry* 8, no. 4 (1982): 777–95.

50. Foucault, "The Subject and Power," 789.

51. In the same vein but with different premises and conclusions: Louis Althusser, "Ideology and Ideological State Apparatuses," in *Lenin and Philosophy and Other Essays*, trans. Ben Brewster (New York: Monthly Review Press, 2001), 85–126; Judith Butler, *The Psychic Life of Power: Theories in Subjection* (Stanford, CA: Stanford University Press, 1997).

52. Judith Butler, "Bodies and Power Revisited," in *Feminism and the Final Foucault*, ed. Dianna Taylor and Karen Vintges (Urbana: University of Illinois Press, 2004), 193.

53. Foucault, "The Subject and Power," 789.

54. Foundational here are Pierre Bourdieu's elaborations on the role of intervals in the strategies of practical action: Pierre Bourdieu, *Outline of a Theory of Practice*, trans. Richard Nice (Cambridge: Cambridge University Press, 1977), 6–15.

55. Jane Guyer, "Prophecy and the Near Future: Thoughts on Macroeconomic, Evangelical, and Punctuated Time," *American Ethnologist* 34, no. 3 (2007): 409–21.

56. Hoffman, Postel-Vinay, and Rosenthal, *Priceless Markets*; Timothy W. Guinnane, "Cooperatives as Information Machines: German Rural Credit Cooperatives, 1883–1914," *Journal of Economic History* 63, no. 2 (2001): 366–89; Hartmut Berghoff, "Markterschließung und Risikomanagement. Die Rolle der Kreditauskunfteien und Rating-Agenturen im Industrialisierungs- und Globalisierungsprozess des 19. Jahrhunderts," *Vierteljahrschrift für Sozial- und Wirtschaftsgeschichte* 92 (2005): 141–62; Josh Lauer, "From Rumor to Written Record: Credit Reporting and the Invention of Financial Identity in Nineteenth-Century America," *Technology and Culture* 49 (2008): 301–24.

57. For a survey of the adaption of information economics in historiography see Alessandro Stanziani, "Information, institutions et temporalité. Quelques remarques critiques sur l'usage de la nouvelle économie de l'information en histoire," *Revue de synthèse* 4, nos. 1–2 (2000): 117–55.

58. Peter Burke, *A Social History of Knowledge: From Gutenberg to Diderot* (Cambridge: Polity Press, 2000), 11.

59. Markus Krajewski, "In Formation. Aufstieg und Fall der Tabelle als Paradigma der Datenverarbeitung," *Nach Feierabend. Zürcher Jahrbuch für Wissensgeschichte* 3 (2007): 37–55; Alain Desrosières, *The Politics of Large Numbers: A History of Statistical Reasoning*, trans. Camille Naish (Cambridge, MA: Harvard University Press, 2002), 248.

60. Daniel R. Headrick, *When Information Came of Age: Technologies of Knowledge in the Age of Reason and Revolution, 1700–1850* (Oxford: Oxford University Press, 2000), 4.

61. Lisa Gitelman, ed., *"Raw Data" Is an Oxymoron* (Cambridge, MA: MIT Press, 2013).

62. Clifford Geertz, an anthropologist open to the theories of information economics, describes how the search for "pure information" ("kbar" in the language of his Moroccan informants) defines strategies at the bazaar, all the while demonstrating that "pure information" can only be obtained through elaborate, culturally coded forms of communication whose distinguishing feature is the way they distort this "pure information" itself. See Clifford Geertz, "Suq: The Bazaar Economy in Sefrou," in Clifford Geertz, Hildred Geertz, and Paul Rabinow, *Meaning and Order in Moroccan Society: Three Essays in Cultural Analysis* (Cambridge: Cambridge University Press, 1979), 198–212.

63. See Ben Kafka, *The Demon of Writing: Powers and Failures of Paperwork* (New York: Zone Books, 2012). See also Cornelia Vismann, *Files: Law and Media Technology*, trans. Geoffrey Winthrop-Young (Stanford, CA: Stanford University Press, 2008 [2000]); Peter Becker and William Clark, Introduction to *Little Tools of Knowledge: Historical Essays on Academic and Bureaucratic Practices* (Ann Arbor: University of Michigan Press, 2001), 1–33.

64. Jürgen Kocka, *Capitalism: A Short History*, trans. Jeremiah Riemer (Princeton, NJ: Princeton University Press, 2016); Gunilla Budde, ed., *Kapitalismus. Historische Annäherungen* (Göttingen: Vandenhoeck & Ruprecht, 2011); Joyce Appleby, *The Relentless Revolution: A History of Capitalism* (New York: W. W. Norton, 2010); Jonathan Ira Levy, *Freaks of Fortune: The Emerging World of Capitalism and Risk in America* (Cambridge, MA: Harvard University Press, 2012).

65. On the role of organized violence, however, see Sven Beckert, *Empire of Cotton: A Global History* (New York: Knopf, 2014).

66. See the survey of extant research in Jeffrey Sklansky, "The Elusive Sovereign: New Intellectual and Social Histories of Capitalism," *Modern Intellectual History* 9 (2012): 233–48.

67. A few examples include Scott Sandage, *Born Losers: A History of Failure in America* (Cambridge, MA: Harvard University Press, 2005) and Edward J. Balleisen, *Navigating Failure: Bankruptcy and Commercial Society in Antebellum America* (Chapel Hill: University of North Carolina Press, 2001).

68. On the genesis of forms of self as they related to money and pedagogy in the

nineteenth century see Sandra Maß, "Mäßigung der Leidenschaften. Kinder und monetäre Lebensführung im 19. Jahrhundert," in *Das schöne Selbst. Zur Genealogie des modernen Subjekts zwischen Ethik und Ästhetik*, ed. Jens Elberfeld (Bielefeld: transcript, 2009), 55–81; Sandra Maß, "Formulare des Ökonomischen in der Geldpädagogik des 18. und 19. Jahrhunderts," *WerkstattGeschichte* 58 (2011): 9–28; Gary J. Kornblith and Michael Zakim, eds., *Capitalism Takes Command: The Social Transformation of Nineteenth-Century America* (Chicago: University of Chicago Press, 2012); Beverly Lemire, "Budgeting for Everyday Life. Gender Strategies, Material Practice and Institutional Innovation in Nineteenth Century Britain," *L'Homme: Zeitschrift für feministische Geschichtswissenschaft* 22 (2011): 11–27.

69. Harry Harootunian, *History's Disquiet: Modernity, Cultural Practice, and the Question of Everyday Life* (New York: Columbia University Press, 2000); Massimiliano Tomba, *Marx's Temporalities* (Leiden: Brill, 2013).

70. The concept has been used in vastly different ways by Rosa Luxemburg, Walter Benjamin, Henri Lefebvre, and Louis Althusser, just to name a few. They all share a common heritage with, yet are clearly distinct from, the view of Leo Trotsky, who coined the term "uneven and combined development." My use of the term is especially indebted to Harry Harootunian und Massimiliano Tomba, who point to the importance of colliding temporalities in the process of capitalism's expansion.

71. Clifford Geertz, *The Interpretation of Cultures: Selected Essays* (New York: Basic Books, 1973), 22.

72. George Marcus, "Ethnography in/of the World System: The Emergence of Multi-Sited Ethnography," *Annual Review of Anthropology* 24 (1995): 95–117.

73. Thomas Osborne, "The Ordinariness of the Archive," *History of the Human Sciences* 12, no. 2 (1999): 52; Andrew Zimmerman, "Africa in Imperial and Transnational History: Multi-Sited Historiography and the Necessity of Theory," *Journal of African History* 54 (2013): 331–40.

74. For an interpretation of this concept that differs from that developed here, see Malte Bachem and Ruben Hackler, "Überlegungen zu einer historischen Anthropologie des Verfahrens," *H-Soz-Kult,* June 19, 2012, https://www.hsozkult.de/debate/id/diskussionen-1801.

75. On the cultural history of law in the nineteenth century, see Habermas, *Thieves in Court*; Ann Goldberg, *Honor, Politics and the Law in Imperial Germany, 1870–1914* (Cambridge: Cambridge University Press, 2010); Sperber, *Property*; Edward Palmer Thompson, *Whigs and Hunters: The Origin of the Black Act* (New York: Pantheon, 1975).

76. Edward Palmer Thompson, *The Poverty of Theory* (London: Merlin, 1995 [1978]), 130. See also Carolyn Steedman, "At Every Bloody Level: A Magistrate, a Framework-Knitter, and the Law," *Law and History Review* 30, no. 2 (2012): 387–422.

77. Simona Cerutti, "Microhistory: Social Relations versus Cultural Models?," in *Between Sociology and History. Essays on Microhistory, Collective Action, and Nation-Building*, ed. Anna-Majia Castrén (Helsinki: SKS/Finnish Literature Society, 2004), 17–40; Simona Cerutti, "Normes et pratiques, ou de la légitimité de leur opposition," in *Les formes de l'expérience: Une autre histoire sociale*, ed. Bernard Lepetit (Paris: Albin Michel, 1995), 127–49.

78. Annelise Riles, *Collateral Knowledge: Legal Reasoning in the Global Financial Markets* (Chicago: University of Chicago Press, 2011), 20.

79. Influential for my research here is Anna Lowenhaupt Tsing, *Friction: An Ethnography of Global Connection* (Princeton, NJ: Princeton University Press, 2005), xi.

80. See Jean-Claude Passeron and Jacques Revel, "Penser par Cas. Raisonner à partir des singularités," in *Penser par cas*, ed. Jean-Claude Passeron and Jacques Revel (Paris: Éditions EHESS, 2005), 9–44.

81. See Jean-Louis Fabiani, "La généralisation dans les sciences historiques: Obstacle épistémologique ou ambition légitime?," *Annales HSS* 62, no. 1 (2007): 9–28.

Chapter 1

1. Olivier Meuwly, *Louis Ruchonnet, 1834–1893. Un homme d'Etat entre action et idéal* (Lausanne: Bibliothèque historique vaudoise, 2006), 347.

2. There are several historical nodal points in which these processes of conceptual disentanglement and reification can be observed. Timothy Mitchell's thesis of the emergence of "the economy" in the interwar period has been profoundly productive and evocative for this debate, but does, however, overstate its case. See Mitchell, *Rule of Experts*. For a more detailed discussion, see Mischa Suter, "Das Wissen der Schulden: Recht, Kulturtechnik und Alltagserfahrung im liberalen Kapitalismus," *Berichte zur Wissenschaftsgeschichte* 37, no. 2 (2014): 148–64.

3. Alfred Brüstlein (1853–1924) studied law in Basel, began working for the Swiss Federal Justiz- und Polizeidepartements in 1879, and headed the federal authority for debt collection and bankruptcy from 1891 to 1896. Meuwly, *Louis Ruchonnet*, 340–47, particularly 342, note 335; Erich Gruner, *Die Schweizerische Bundesversammlung 1848–1920* (Bern: Francke, 1966), 1:441.

4. Here and in the following: *Zur Volksabstimmung vom 17. November 1889. Ein Wort der Aufklärung an das Schweizervolk zum Bundesgesetze über Schuldbetreibung und Konkurs* (Bern, 1889), 6.

5. *Zur Volksabstimmung*, S. 2.

6. Pio Caroni, "Der 'demokratische' code unique von 1881. Eine Studie zur ideologischen Beziehung von Sonderrecht und Demokratie," in *Das Obligationenrecht 1883–1983*, ed. Pio Caroni (Bern: P. Haupt, 1984), 19–68.

7. The Verein Schweizerischer Geschäftsreisender (Association of Swiss Traveling Businessmen) filed, in 1879, a lengthy petition pleading for the speedy passage of a federal law on debt enforcement and emphasized their position in a second petition in 1882. Schweizerisches Bundesarchiv (hereafter BAR) E22#1000/134#2608*, Az. 6.7.4, Petition des Vereins der schweizerischen Geschäftsreisenden, November 20, 1879; BAR E22#1000/134#2609*, Az. 6.7.4, Petition des Vereins der schweizerischen Geschäftsreisenden, June 1, 1882.

8. Alfred Brüstlein, *Die Grundzüge des Entwurfes eines eidgenössischen Betreibungs- und Konkursgesetzes. Eine Streitschrift als Entgegnung auf die Broschüre des Herrn Nationalrath J. H. Bachmann* (Basel, 1888), 51.

9. BAR E22#1000/134#2612*, Az. 6.7.4, Bericht der nationalräthlichen

Kommission zum Gesetzesentwurfe betreffend Schuldbetreibung und Konkurs (March 28, 1887).

10. On the legal advisers see Lutz Raphael, "Rechtskultur, Verrechtlichung, Professionalisierung. Anmerkungen zum 19. Jahrhundert aus kulturanthropologischer Perspektive," in *Rechtskultur, Rechtswissenschaft, Rechtsberufe im 19. Jahrhundert: Professionalisierung und Verrechtlichung in Deutschland und Italien*, ed. Christof Dipper (Berlin: Duncker & Humblot, 2000), 44. On Jewish brokers who acquired titles of debt and negotiated settlements in the Basel region in the first half of the nineteenth century, see Susanne Bennewitz, *Basler Juden, französische Bürger. Migration und Alltag einer jüdischen Gemeinde im frühen 19. Jahrhundert* (Basel: Schwabe, 2008), 355–57. Contemporaneous regulatory authorities polemicized against the business agents as "an estate largely consisting of bankrupts and other disreputable persons." See *Siebenzehnter Rechenschaftsbericht des Obergerichts an den Großen Rath des Standes Zürich über das Jahr 1847* (Zurich, 1848), 31.

11. In 1868, a cantonal conference decided to take on the project of unifying debt enforcement procedures in Switzerland; beginning in 1874, the project was pursued with a mandate derived from the revised constitution of 1874. Pio Caroni, "Rechtseinheit in der Schweiz. Zur Geschichte einer späten Verfassungsreform," in *Rechtseinheit. Drei historische Studien zu Art. 64 BV* (Basel: Helbing & Lichtenhahn, 1986), 9–54.

12. Nevertheless, the debtor could freely choose to offer a creditor assets in order to escape bankruptcy.

13. [Andreas Heusler,] *Bundesgesez [sic] über Schuldbetreibung und Konkurs. Erster Entwurf mit Motiven* (Bern, 1874), 58.

14. Heusler, *Bundesgesez 1874*, 62.

15. This was the opinion in St. Gallen: BAR E22#1000/134#2607*, Az. 6.7.4, Mittheilungen aus den Eingaben kantonaler Behörden zu dem Entwurfe eines Bundesgesezes über Schuldbetreibung und Konkurs, Bern 1874, 31.

16. BAR E22#1000/134#2607*, Az. 6.7.4, Mittheilungen aus den Eingaben kantonaler Behörden zu dem Entwurfe eines Bundesgesezes über Schuldbetreibung und Konkurs (Bern, 1874), 52.

17. Eastern Switzerland had a system in which the first creditor to make a claim had priority of payment over other creditors. Botschaft des Bundesrathes an die Bundesversammlung zu dem vom Bundesrathe am 23. Februar 1886 festgestellten Entwurfe eines Bundesgesetzes über Schuldbetreibung und Konkurs (of April 6, 1886), *Schweizerisches Bundesblatt* vol. 2, 38, no. 20 (May 8, 1886), 16–20. BAR E22#1000/134#2609*, Az. 6.7.4, Verhandlungen des schweizerischen Juristenvereins 1881, Referat Obergerichtspräsident [Johann Jakob] Oberer, Liestal, "Welches System der Schuldbetreibung hat die größern Vorzüge?," 10; *Botschaft des Bundesrathes 1886*, 21–22

18. BAR E22#1000/134#2609*, Az. 6.7.4, Johann Jakob Oberer an Bundesrat Louis Ruchonnet, Liestal June 2, 1882. Oberer based his estimate on a statistical survey of the cantons of Zurich, Schaffhausen, and Basel-Land.

19. A comprehensive statistical study failed because of the cantons' varying practices of record keeping, which made comparison impossible. The estimate lined up precisely with the situation in the canton of Bern, where in 1879 and

1880, 63 percent, in 1881 and 1882, 65 percent of all unsecured creditors' claims were for sums less than one hundred francs. In the cantons of Lucerne, Zug, Basel-Stadt, Basel-Land, St. Gallen, Aargau, Neuchâtel, and Geneva, the proportion of small to mid-sized claims was even higher. For the order to collect data and the responses of the cantons, see BAR E22#1000/134#2609*, Az. 6.7.4, Kreisschreiben des Eidgenössischen Justiz- und Polizeidepartements an sämtliche Kantonsregierungen, October 9, 1882. The material was prepared and appended in print to: *Botschaft des Bundesrathes 1886*.

20. Alessandro Stanziani, *Rules of Exchange: French Capitalism in Comparative Perspective, Eighteenth to Early Twentieth Centuries* (Cambridge: Cambridge University Press, 2012), 44–48; Claire Lemercier, "Discipliner le commerce sans corporations. La loi, le juge, l'arbitre et le commerçant à Paris au XIXe siècle," *Le Mouvement social* 224 (2008): 61–74.

21. Here and in the following: Caroni, "Code unique."

22. Martin Lüpold, "Der Ausbau der 'Festung Schweiz': Aktienrecht und Corporate Governance in der Schweiz, 1881–1961," (PhD diss., University of Zurich, 2010), 68; Thomas Widmer, *Die Schweiz in der Wachstumskrise der 1880er Jahre* (Zurich: Chronos, 1992), 270.

23. Walther Munzinger, *Motive zu dem Entwurfe eines schweizerischen Handelsrechtes* (Bern, 1865), 15.

24. Here and in the following: Munzinger, *Motive*, 19, emphasis in the original.

25. On the connections of Zurich businesses to Paris see Hans Conrad Peyer, *Von Handel und Bank im alten Zürich* (Zurich: Berichthaus, 1968).

26. Helpful illustrations of how bills of exchange worked can be found in Francesca Trivellato, "Credit, Honor, and the Early Modern French Legend of the Jewish Invention of Bills of Exchange," *Journal of Modern History* 84, no. 2 (2012): 293–97; Markus A. Denzel, *Das System des bargeldlosen Zahlungsverkehrs europäischer Prägung vom Mittelalter bis 1914* (Stuttgart: Steiner, 2008), chap. 1.

27. Trivellato, "Credit."

28. Dorothea Riedi Hunold, *Die Einführung der allgemeinen Wechselfähigkeit in der Schweiz in der zweiten Hälfte des 19. Jahrhunderts* (Frankfurt am Main: Peter Lang, 2004) for a survey of Swiss perspectives on bills of exchange.

29. C[arl] Einert, *Das Wechselrecht nach dem Bedürfniss des Wechselgeschäfts des 19ten Jahrhunderts* (Leipzig, 1839), 49.

30. Einert, *Wechselrecht*, 35.

31. Einert, *Wechselrecht*, 117.

32. Einert, *Wechselrecht*, 90.

33. Einert, *Wechselrecht*, 17–18.

34. Riedi Hunold, *Einführung*, 82.

35. J. U. Burkhardt-Fürstenberger, *Entwurf einer Schweizerischen Wechselordnung mit Motiven* (Zurich, 1857), 44.

36. Riedi Hunold, *Einführung*, 80–84.

37. Burkhardt-Fürstenberger, *Entwurf*, 171.

38. Einert, *Wechselrecht*, 117.

39. Nicos Poulantzas, *State, Power, Socialism*, trans. Patrick Camiller (London: Verso, 1980), 103.

40. Poulantzas, *State*, 110.

41. William Sewell, "The Temporalities of Capitalism," *Socio-Economic Review* 6 (2008): 527.

42. Harry Harootunian, *Marx after Marx: History and Time in the Expansion of Capitalism* (New York: Columbia University Press, 2015), 25.

43. BAR E22#1000/134#2607*, Az. 6.7.4, Antwort des Obergerichts Bern auf den Ersten Gesetzesentwurf, September 17, 1874, 12.

44. BAR E22#1000/134#2607*, Az. 6.7.4, Mittheilungen aus den Eingaben kantonaler Behörden zu dem Entwurfe eines Bundesgesezes über Schuldbetreibung und Konkurs, Bern 1874, 15.

45. Here and in the following: BAR E22#1000/134#2607*, Az. 6.7.4, Mittheilungen aus den Eingaben kantonaler Behörden zu dem Entwurfe eines Bundesgesezes [sic] über Schuldbetreibung und Konkurs, Bern 1874, 22–23.

46. See Pierre Bourdieu, *Esquisse d'une théorie de la pratique: Précédé de trois études d'ethnologie kabyle* (Paris: Seuil, 2000), 377–85, esp. 379–80.

47. BAR E22#1000/134#2608*, Az. 6.7.4, Bundesgesez über Schuldbetreibung und Konkurs. Entwurf mit Motiven, vorgelegt durch die Kommissions-Minderheit, welche das System der Pfändung im Gegensaze zu demjenigen des Konkurses aufrecht hält, Bern 1875 [submitted January 1876], 74.

48. See also the report from Obwalden, BAR E22#1000/134#2607*, Az. 6.7.4, Mittheilungen aus den Eingaben kantonaler Behörden zu dem Entwurfe eines Bundesgesezes über Schuldbetreibung und Konkurs, Bern 1874, 15.

49. BAR E22#1000/134#2608*, Az. 6.7.4, Bundesgesez über Schuldbetreibung und Konkurs. Entwurf mit Motiven, vorgelegt durch die Kommissions-Minderheit, welche das System der Pfändung im Gegensatze zu demjenigen des Konkurses aufrecht hält, Bern 1875 [submitted January 1876], 73.

50. On the growth of grain imports spurred by sinking transport costs, see Béatrice Veyrassat, "Wirtschaft und Gesellschaft an der Wende zum 20. Jahrhundert," in *Wirtschaftsgeschichte der Schweiz im 20. Jahrhundert*, ed. Patrick Halbeisen, Margrit Müller, and Veyrassat Béatrice (Basel: Stämpfli, 2012), 38–41. I thank Roman K. Abt for pointing this reference out to me.

51. Heiner Ritzmann-Blickenstorfer, ed., *Historische Statistik der Schweiz* (Zurich: Chronos, 1996), 396, 401.

52. Widmer, *Schweiz*, 134–36.

53. An early Swiss example is Isaak Iselin, "Väterlicher Rath an meinen Sohn, der sich der Handelsschaft widmet," in *Moral für Kaufleute und väterlicher Rath für meinen Sohn, der sich der Handlungswissenschaft widmet. Neue Auflage*, ed. C. A. Büsch (Leipzig, n.d., ca. 1800), 47–90. On these sorts of advice manuals see Sven Reichardt, "Soziales Kapital 'im Zeitalter materieller Interessen'. Konzeptionelle Überlegungen zum Vertrauen in der Zivil- und Marktgesellschaft des langen 19. Jahrhunderts (1780–1914)" (WZB Discussion Paper no. SP IV 03–503, Wissenschaftszentrum Berlin für Sozialforschung, 2003).

54. Here and in the following: Heinrich Sulzer, *Vermächtniss für meinen Enkel. Lehren, Ermahnungen und Warnungen* (Winterthur, 1833), 56, 57. See also Heinrich Sulzer, *Lehren für Jünglinge, die sich der Handelschaft widmen werden, für die Lehr- und Fremde-Zeit* (N.p. [Winterthur], 1830).

55. Here and in the following: BAR E22#1000/134#2608*, Az. 6.7.4, Bundesgesetz über Schuldbetreibung und Konkurs. Entwurf mit Motiven, vorgelegt durch die Kommissions-Minderheit, welche das System der Pfändung im Gegensaze zu demjenigen des Konkurses aufrecht hält (Bern, 1875 [submitted January 1876]), 76–77.

56. For instance, J. H. Bachmann, *Die Grundzüge des Entwurfes eines eidgenössischen Betreibungs- und Konkursgesetzes. Rede, gehalten in der Sitzung des schweizerischen Nationalrates den 13. April 1887* (Frauenfeld, 1887).

57. The towns were Winterthur, Baden, Zofingen, and Lenzburg. Jörg Thalmann, "Von der Euphorie zum Kollaps: Die Geschichte der Schweizerischen Nationalbahn," in *Die Nationalbahn. Vision einer Volksbahn,* ed. Hans-Peter Bärtschi, Hans-Peter Bärtschi, Sylvia Bärtschi-Baumann, Peter Niederhauser and Peter Güller (Wetzikon: Profile, 2009), 19–44. See also BAR E22#1000/134#2610*, Az. 6.7.4, F. Meili, Rechtsgutachten und Gesetzesvorschlag betreffend die Schuldexekution und den Konkurs gegen Gemeinden, ausgearbeitet im Auftrage des schweiz. Justiz- und Polizeidepartements, Bern 1885.

58. Hans-Peter Bärtschi, *Industrialisierung, Eisenbahnschlachten und Städtebau. Die Entwicklung des Zürcher Industrie- und Arbeiterstadtteils Aussersihl: Ein vergleichender Beitrag zur Architektur- und Technikgeschichte* (Basel: Birkhäuser, 1983), 168–72.

59. BAR E22#1000/134#2611*, Az. 6.7.4, Grütliverein, Arbeitertag, Schweizerischer Gewerkschaftsbund: Petition betreffend den Entwurf eines eidg. Schuldentrieb- und Konkursgesetzes, St. Gallen January 1887, 3.

60. *Neue Zürcher Zeitung,* no. 235, August 23, 1883, morning edition, 1.

61. BAR E22#1000/134#2612*, Az. 6.7.4, Verhandlungen der ständeräthlichen Kommission betreffend den vom Bundesrathe am 23. Februar 1886 festgestellten Entwurf eines Bundesgesetzes über Schuldbetreibung und Konkurs (not paginated).

62. BAR E22#1000/134#2611*, Az. 6.7.4, P. Speiser (Basel), Gutachten über den Entwurf eines eidg. Betreibungs- und Konkursgesetzes, erstattet an das eidg. Justizdepartement am 31. December 1885, S. 4.

63. Carl Hilty, "Eidgenössische Politik, Gesetzgebung und politische Literatur," *Politisches Jahrbuch der schweizerischen Eidgenossenschaft* 1 (1886): 571.

64. Munzinger, *Motive,* 24.

65. BAR E22#1000/134#2611*, Az. 6.7.4, P. Speiser (Basel), Gutachten über den Entwurf eines eidg. Betreibungs- und Konkursgesetzes, erstattet an das eidg. Justizdepartement am 31. December 1885, 6.

66. Small business partnerships (which had their own special legal form in Switzerland), joint stock companies, limited liability companies, cooperatives, commercial associations, and "merchant" businesses were obliged to register. See Leo Weber, "Handelsregister," in *Volkswirthschafts-Lexikon der Schweiz,* ed. Alfred Furrer (Bern, 1889), 2:8.

67. BAR E22#1000/134#2611*, Az. 6.7.4, P. Speiser (Basel), Gutachten über den Entwurf eines eidg. Betreibungs- und Konkursgesetzes, erstattet an das eidg. Justizdepartement am 31. December 1885, S. 6.

68. Joyce, *The State of Freedom,* 101–20; Joyce, *The Rule of Freedom;* Chris Otter, *The Victorian Eye: A Political History of Light and Vision in Britain, 1800–1910* (Chicago: University of Chicago Press, 2008).

69. Keith Tribe, *Strategies of Economic Order: German Economic Discourse, 1750–1950* (Cambridge: Cambridge University Press, 1995), 73.

70. Harun Maye, "Was ist eine Kulturtechnik?," *Zeitschrift für Medien- und Kulturforschung* 1 (2010): 121–35; Monika Dommann, "Verbandelt im Welthandel: Spediteure und ihre Papiere seit dem 18. Jahrhundert," *WerkstattGeschichte* 58 (2011): 33–34.

71. Cornelia Vismann, "Kulturtechniken und Souveränität," *Zeitschrift für Medien- und Kulturforschung* 1 (2010): 176. On registers in general, see Cornelia Vismann, *Files*, 79–85.

72. The comparison between the title register and the commercial register was drawn in Munzinger, *Motive*, 30. On the history of the title register in Switzerland see Daniel Speich, "Das Grundbuch als Grund aller Pläne. Präzision und die Fiktion der Überschaubarkeit im Entstehungsprozess eines modernen Rechtsstaats," in *Vermessene Landschaften. Kulturgeschichte und technische Praxis im 19. und 20. Jahrhundert*, ed. David Gugerli (Zurich: Chronos, 1999), 137–48.

73. Alain Pottage, "The Originality of Registration," *Oxford Journal of Legal Studies* 15 (1995): 371–401.

74. On the key role that extraction and abstraction play for accounting see Bruce Carruthers and Wendy Nelson Espeland, "Accounting for Rationality: Double-Entry Bookkeeping and the Rhetoric of Economic Rationality," *American Journal of Sociology* 97, no. 1 (1991): 56–60.

75. Schweizerisches Wirtschaftsarchiv Basel, Vo H IV 11, Dossiersammlung Handelsregister, Revidirte Verordnung über Handelsregister und Handelsamtsblatt, December 7, 1882.

76. Stanziani, *Rules of Exchange*, 42.

77. August Rothpletz, "Handelsregister," in *Handwörterbuch der Schweizerischen Volkswirtschaft, Sozialpolitik und Verwaltung*, ed. Naum Reichersberg (Bern, n.d., ca. 1900), 2:545–47.

78. Max Rintelen, *Untersuchungen über die Entwicklung des Handelsregisters* (Stuttgart: Encke, 1914), 335–47; Ed[uard] Eichholzer, *Zur Geschichte von Handelsregister und Firmenrecht im Kanton Zürich* (Zurich: Schulthess, 1917); L. Siegmund, "Zur Geschichte der Gesetzgebung über Ragionenbuch und Wechselrecht in Basel," *Zeitschrift für schweizerisches Recht*, n.s., 1 (1882): 79–134.

79. Lüpold, "Aktienrecht," chap. 2; Peter Knuchel, "Aktienrechtliche Gesetzgebung und strukturelle Stabilität. Die Schweizer Aktiengesellschaft und ihr Recht in der zweiten Hälfte des 19. Jahrhunderts" (unpublished thesis, Universität Zürich, 2007), 26.

80. Botschaft des Bundesrathes an die hohe Bundesversammlung zu einem Gesezentwurfe [*sic*], enthaltend Schweizerisches Obligationen- und Handelsrecht (vom 27. November 1879), *Schweizerisches Bundesblatt* 32, no. 4 (January 24, 1880): 58.

81. The additional list was compiled because persons removed from the commercial register remained subject to bankruptcy for a period of six months thereafter. L. Siegmund, *Handbuch für die schweizerischen Handelsregisterführer. Im Auftrage des schweizerischen Justiz- und Polizeidepartementes* (Basel, 1892), 152.

82. Elisabeth Joris, "Kinship and Gender: Property, Enterprise, and Politics," trans. Hillary Crowe, in *Kinship in Europe: Approaches to Long-Term Development*

(1300–1900), ed. David W. Sabean, Simon Teuscher, and Jon Mathieu, (New York: Berghahn Books, 2007), 231–57.

83. Siegmund, *Handbuch*, 111–14.

84. Verhandlungen der ständeräthlichen Kommission betreffend den vom Bundesrathe am 23. Februar 1886 festgestellten Entwurf eines Bundesgesetzes über Schuldbetreibung und Konkurs, *Schweizerisches Bundesblatt*, 38, vol. 3, no. 48 (November 20, 1886): 618.

85. See BAR E22#1000/134#2308*, Az. 6.3.5 on the various positions: the first draft by Fick from July 10, 1882; explicitly against a substantive definition was the report of the Geneva chamber of commerce (n.d.). See also BAR E22#1000/134#2309*, Az. 6.3.5, Revidierte Verordnung vom 7. Dezember 1882 über Handelsregister und Handelsamtsblatt. This decree drew on a draft by Basel government adviser Paul Speiser, as ordered by a parliamentary commission of July 15, 1882. The draft dispensed with a substantive definition, which, in turn, provoked concern from the Association of Commerce and Industry (Handels- und Industrieverein). (BAR E22#1000/134#2309*, Az. 6.3.5, Handels- und Industrieverein, Präsident des Vorortes Zürich des Handels- und Industrievereins, Cramer-Frey, an Eidgenössisches Justiz- und Polizeidepartement, September 19, 1882).

86. BAR E22#1000/134#2310*, Az. 6.3.5, Kreisschreiben des Bundesrathes an sämmtliche Kantonsregierungen, betreffend Eintragungen in's Handelsregister (from March 13, 1883).

87. Archiv für Zeitgeschichte ETH Zürich (hereafter AfZ ETHZ), Vorort-Archiv, Protokoll der Ordentlichen Delegiertenversammlung des Schweizerischen Handels- und Industrievereins, April 30, 1892; Protokoll der Ordentlichen Delegiertenversammlung des Schweizerischen Handels- und Industrievereins, April 29, 1893.

88. In a vote among fifteen business associations, six opposed this recommendation. The representative of the Vaud chamber of commerce opined that ten thousand francs was too low, arguing that the many petty salesmen and craftsmen who easily earned the equivalent revenue of thirty francs a day did not belong in the register. AfZ ETHZ, Vorort-Archiv, Protokoll der Ordentlichen Delegiertenversammlung des Schweizerischen Handels- und Industrievereins, April 29, 1893, 10–11.

89. For comparison, a contemporaneous report estimated that about 800,000 legally competent men lived in Switzerland. Ritzmann-Blickenstorfer, *Historische Statistik*, 906; Alfred Brüstlein, *Die Grundzüge des Entwurfes eines eidgenössischen Betreibungs- und Konkursgesetzes*, 23.

90. Staatsarchiv Zürich, O 38.c1, Handelsregister, Direktionssekretär an Direktion des Inneren des Kantons Zürich, May 7, 1890.

91. BAR E22#1000/134#2611*, Az. 6.7.4, Bundesgesetz betreffend Schuldbetreibung und Konkurs, Bericht des Vorortes Zürich des Schweiz. Handels- und Industrievereins, Zurich 1886, 7.

92. Vismann, "Kulturtechniken," 176.

93. I'd like to thank Ute Tellmann for this insight. See Ute Tellmann, "Sozialtheorie der Schulden—über ein sozialtheoretisches Desiderat" (paper presented at the University of Lucerne, December 3, 2013).

94. On the difference between perspectives focused on technical setups divorced from time and those that focus on the contextual conditions of possibility of such setups see Knut Ebeling, "Das technische Apriori," *Archiv für Mediengeschichte* 6 (2006): 11–22. This passage draws on Goswami, *Producing India*, 78–79, which puts forward a similar argument.

95. For instance, "Obstruction und Revision," *Neue Zürcher Zeitung* no. 93, April 3, 1889, morning edition, 1.

96. Urs Altermatt, *Katholizismus und Moderne. Zur Sozial- und Mentalitätsgeschichte der Schweizer Katholiken im 19. und 20. Jahrhundert* (Zurich: Benziger, 1989).

97. Altermatt, *Katholizismus,* 144; Erich Gruner, *Die Parteien in der Schweiz,* 2nd ed. (Bern: Francke, 1977), 108.

98. Theres Maurer, *Ulrich Dürrenmatt, 1849–1908: Ein schweizerischer Oppositionspolitiker* (Bern: Stämpfli, 1975), 176–86.

99. *Vaterland,* no. 256, November 6, 1889, 1. The article quoted a past speech made by Federal Councilor Louis Ruchonnet in order to depict the federal law as inherently contradictory. It claimed that in his time as a representative in Vaud's parliament, he had made the exact opposite claims that he was now making in support of the federal law.

100. Here and in the following: *Trau! Schau! Wem? Ein freies Wort an das Schweizervolk über das neue Schulden-Betreibungsgesetz* (Bern, 1889), 25.

101. *Vaterland,* no. 257, November 7, 1889, 1.

102. *Berner Volkszeitung,* no. 88, November 2, 1889, supplement. Similarly, *Vaterland,* no. 264, November 15, 1889, 1.

103. *Vaterland,* no. 264, November 15, 1889, 1; *Berner Volkszeitung,* no. 43, May 29, 1889, 1.

104. *Berner Volkszeitung,* no. 54, July 6, 1889, 1.

105. *Berner Volkszeitung,* no. 45, June 5, 1889, 1; *Berner Volkszeitung,* no. 59, July 24, 1889, 1; *Berner Volkszeitung,* no. 65, August 14, 1889; *Vaterland,* no. 261, November 12, 1889, 1; *Vaterland,* no. 260, November 10, 1889, 2; *Vaterland,* no. 265, November 16, 1889, 1. Jakob Tanner, "Diskurse der Diskriminierung: Antisemitismus, Sozialdarwinismus und Rassismus in den schweizerischen Bildungseliten," in *Krisenwahrnehmungen im Fin de Siècle. Jüdische und katholische Bildungseliten in Deutschland und der Schweiz,* ed. Michael Graetz and Aram Mattioli (Zurich: Chronos, 1997), 323–40; Aram Mattioli, ed., *Antisemitismus in der Schweiz 1848–1960. Mit einem Vorwort von Alfred A. Häsler* (Zurich: Orell Füssli, 1998).

106. *Trau! Schau! Wem?,* 24; *Vaterland,* no. 257, November 7, 1889, 1. On the anti-Semitism of the Berner Volkspartei see Theres Maurer, "Die 'Berner Volkszeitung' von Ulrich Dürrenmatt," in Mattioli, *Antisemitismus,* 241–64.

107. *Vaterland,* no. 259, November 8, 1889, 1.

108. *Vaterland,* no. 261, November 12, 1889, 1. Similarly, *Berner Volkszeitung,* no. 55, July 10, 1889, 1–2. On antiplutocratic rhetoric in the discourse of crisis in the 1880s see Widmer, *Schweiz,* 129–42; *Vaterland,* no. 239, October 16, 1889, 1; *Vaterland,* no. 256, November 6, 1889, 1.

109. Olaf Blaschke, "Antikapitalismus und Antisemitismus: Die Wirtschaftsmentalität der Katholiken im Wilhelminischen Deutschland," in *Shylock? Zinsverbot und Geldverleih in jüdischer und christlicher Tradition,* ed. Johannes

Heil (Munich: Fink, 1997), 114–46, on usury 128–30. On finance capital see Mark Loeffler, "Das 'Finanzkapital'—Diskurse in Deutschland und England zur Jahrhundertwende," in *Kapitalismusdebatten um 1900: Über antisemitisierende Semantiken des Jüdischen,* ed. Nicolas Berg (Leipzig: Leipziger Universitätsverlag, 2011), 115–40.

110. Theodor W. Adorno and Max Horkheimer, *Dialectic of Enlightenment: Philosophical Fragments,* ed. Gunzelin Schmid Noerr, trans. Edmund Jephcott (Stanford, CA: Stanford University Press, 2002), 143.

111. Adorno and Horkheimer, *Dialectic,* 149–50.

112. Raymond Williams, *The Country and the City* (New York: Oxford University Press, 1975), chap. 16.

113. [Carl] Schröter, *Die öffentlich rechtlichen Folgen der fruchtlosen Pfändung und des Konkurses in der Schweiz* (Bern: Schmid & Francke, 1902). For a survey of the different cantonal regulations in the 1890s see Staatsarchiv des Kantons Bern (in the following STABE), BB 3.1.540 Ehrenfolgengesetz, Beilagen zum Entwurf eines Gesetzes über die öffentlich-rechtlichen Folgen des Konkurses und der fruchtlosen Pfändung, n.d., ca. 1897.

114. See Maurer, *Dürrenmatt,* 186–96. See also *Berner Volkszeitung,* no. 28, April 8, 1893, 1; *Berner Volkszeitung,* no. 30, April 15, 1893, 1; *Berner Volkszeitung,* no. 36, May 5, 1894, 1, *Berner Volkszeitung,* no. 37, May 9, 1894, 1; *Berner Volkszeitung,* no. 15, February 19, 1896, 1; *Berner Volkszeitung,* no. 17, February 26, 1896, 1; *Berner Volkszeitung,* no. 19, March 4, 1896, 1; *Berner Volkszeitung,* no. 32, April 20, 1898, 1; *Berner Volkszeitung,* no. 33, April 23, 1898, 1; *Berner Volkszeitung,* no. 34, April 27, 1898, 1; *Berner Volkszeitung,* no. 35, April 30, 1898; *Berner Volkszeitung,* no. 36, May 4, 1898.

115. Maurer, *Dürrenmatt,* 186–96.

116. In the previous system in Bern, a creditor had to explicitly request bankruptcy with "honor sanctions" after a series of deadlines had been violated and had to advance the costs of the proceedings himself. In the new law, honor sanctions were automatically imposed twenty-five days after an official determined the person to be without sufficient assets. See STABE BB 3.1.540 Ehrenfolgengesetz, Berner Betreibungsbeamte an Grossen Rat, December 1892.

117. *Berner Volkszeitung,* no. 28, April 8, 1893, 1; *Berner Volkszeitung,* no. 32, April 22, 1893.

118. *Die schweizerischen Falliten vor 1892 und nach 1892 an das Schweizervolk und seine Behörden. Ein Beitrag zur Lösung der schweiz. "Fallitenfrage" von den Gesuchstellern in der Schweizerischen Republik* (N.p., April 1893), 14.

119. *Das Ehrenfolgengesetz. Aufklärung für die Abstimmung vom 6. Mai 1894 und Aufruf zur Verwerfung. Von einem Volksfreund,* (n.p., n.d.).

120. STABE BB 3.1.540 Ehrenfolgengesetz, Petition des Grütlivereins an den Grossen Rat in Bern, February 5, 1894, emphasis in original.

121. Here and in the following: BAR E22#1000/134#2645*, Az.6.7.4, Eingaben zur Revision des Bundesgesetzes über Schuldbetreibung und Konkurs, [Alfred Brüstlein]: Vorläufige Vorschläge für eine Revision des Betreibungsgesetzes, June 18, 1893 (talk held at Bern's Handels- und Industrieverein).

122. See Gustav Peebles, "The Anthropology of Credit and Debt," *Annual Review of Anthropology* 39 (2010): 225–40, esp. 234.

123. Catherine Davies, *Transatlantic Speculations: Globalization and the Panics of 1873* (New York: Columbia University Press, 2018).

124. Beginning in the 1870s with the works of William Stanley Jevons in Great Britain, Carl Menger in Austria, and Léon Walras in Switzerland and France. See Philip Mirowski, *More Heat than Light: Economics as Social Physics, Physics as Nature's Economics* (Cambridge: Cambridge University Press, 1989), chap. 5.

125. J. L. Weibel, "Die rechtliche Behandlung des Wuchers," *Verhandlungen des schweizerischen Juristenvereins 1884* 1 (1884): 72.

126. Verein für Socialpolitik, ed. *Der Wucher auf dem Lande: Berichte und Gutachten veröffentlicht vom Verein für Socialpolitik* (Leipzig, 1887); Lorenz von Stein, *Der Wucher und sein Recht: ein Beitrag zum wirthschaftlichen und rechtlichen Leben unserer Zeit* (Vienna, 1880); Ernst Brenner, "Der Wucher und seine Bekämpfung," *Schweizerische Zeitschrift für Gemeinnützigkeit* 20 (1881): 197–213; Mischa Suter, "Usury and the Problem of Exchange under Capitalism: A Late-Nineteenth-Century Debate on Economic Rationality," trans. Adam Bresnahan, *Social History* 42, no. 4 (2017): 501–23.

127. The Creditreform association was founded in 1879 in Mainz "to protect against unsavory creditors." Berghoff, "Markterschließung und Risikomanagement," 158.

128. Verein Creditreform, *Statut der Schweizer Vereinigung gegen schädliches Creditgeben (Verein Creditreform—Union Suisse pour la sauvegarde des crédits). Nach den Beschlüssen des IV. Verbandstages zu Frankfurt a./M. am 27. und 28. Juni 1886, sowie der constituierenden Generalversammlung in Basel vom 2. Juli 1888* (Zurich, 1888); *Ein schweizerischer Creditorenverband: ein Projekt, ausgearbeitet von Delegierten der Vereine "Creditreform," "Schweiz. Manufakturisten-Verband" und "Verein schweiz. Geschäftsreisender"* (Zurich, 1897). It seems that Confidentia began publishing a paper in 1878. The earliest volume still preserved is from 1904. In October 1880, Confidentia was bought by Bern businessman Adolf Gugger. Certainly in 1904, but probably earlier, the company had three pillars: credit reports, debt collection, and a biweekly paper that in 1904 had a run of between six and ten thousand. See *Confidentia: Schweizer Handels-Auskunftsblatt. Allgemeines schweizerisches Sammelblatt für amtliche und ausseramtliche Bekanntmachungen* 26 (1904). In 1884, the Swiss Association of Commerce and Industry also discussed such credit agencies, without, however, acting on behalf of big industry in this matter of small-time merchants. AfZ ETHZ, Vorort-Archiv 1.4.2.2.1., Protokoll der 5. Sitzung der Schweizerischen Handelskammer, October 30, 1884.

129. Julia Laura Rischbieter, "Wer nicht wagt, der nicht gewinnt? Kaffeegroßhändler als Spekulanten im Kaiserreich," *Jahrbuch für Wirtschaftsgeschichte* 54 (2013): 71–94; Alexander Engel, "Buying Time: Futures Trading and Telegraphy in Nineteenth-Century Global Commodity Markets," *Journal of Global History* 10, no. 2 (2015): 284–306; Jonathan Ira Levy, "Contemplating Delivery: Futures Trading and the Problem of Commodity Exchange in the United States," *American Historical Review* 111 (2006): S. 307–35.

130. *Zur Volksabstimmung*, 6–7.

Chapter 2

1. Johann Tobler, *Gutartige Hierarchie. Armenbesorgung, und die schöne Friedensbitte* (Zurich, 1800), 12. "Archdeacon" was the name given to an originally Catholic rank of priesthood, which the Grossmünster congregation retained after the Reformation and the reorganization of the Chorherrenstift. A law from 1833 reduced the priests working at the Grossmünster to a pastor and a deacon. Johannes Tobler (1732–1808) was named archdeacon in 1777; he published many didactic writings and articles on contemporary events. See Kaspar Wirz, *Etat des Zürcher Ministeriums von der Reformation bis zur Gegenwart: aus gedruckten und ungedruckten Quellen zusammengestellt und nach Kirchgemeinden geordnet* (Zurich, 1890), 63–64, 73. I thank Werner Gysel, former pastor of the Zurich Grossmünster, for drawing my attention to this source and sending me a copy of it.

2. Tobler, *Gutartige Hierarchie*, 13.

3. An abolition of feudal dues intended to be adopted in 1798 in the Helvetic Republic that would have been favorable for the dues-paying peasants was never implemented and ultimately abandoned in the spring of 1800. Resolutions applicable to all of Switzerland foundered. The law that was ultimately adopted in the canton of Zurich in 1803 was considerably less favorable. It forced peasants to pay a fee over twenty-five years to finally be freed of their bonds and was implemented with military force in the "Bocken War" of 1804. See Rudolf Johann Böppli, "Die Zehntablösung in der Schweiz, speziell im Kanton Zurich" (doctoral diss., Universität Zürich, 1914), 75–84, 96–100.

4. Rolf Graber, *Zeit des Teilens: Volksbewegungen und Volksunruhen auf der Zürcher Landschaft 1794–1804* (Zurich: Chronos, 2003).

5. On the gradual dissolution of feudal dues in the canton of Zurich see Bruno Fritzsche and Max Lemmenmeier, "Die revolutionäre Umgestaltung von Wirtschaft, Gesellschaft und Staat 1780–1870," in *Geschichte des Kantons Zurich*, ed. Niklaus Flüeler and Marianne Flüeler-Grauwiller, vol. 3, *19. und 20. Jahrhundert*, ed. Niklaus Flüeler and Bruno Fritzsche (Zurich: Werd, 1994), 30–33; Böppli, "Zehntablösung."

6. A social history of agriculture in Zurich's lowlands has yet to be written. Interesting are Karin Beereuter, "Sozio-politischer und sozio-ökonomischer Wandel einer agrarischen Gemeinde im Zürcher Unterland vom späten 18. Jahrhundert bis 1840 (Stadel)" (unpublished thesis, Universität Zurich, 1994); Lukas Meyer, "Wirtschaft und Gesellschaft einer agrarischen Gemeinde im Zürcher Unterland des 18. Jahrhunderts (Schöfflisdorf)" (unpublished thesis, Universität Zurich, 1989); Thomas Meier, *Handwerk, Hauswerk, Heimarbeit: nichtagrarische Tätigkeiten und Erwerbsformen in einem traditionellen Ackerbaugebiet des 18. Jahrhunderts (Zürcher Unterland)* (Zurich: Chronos, 1986); Graber, *Zeit des Teilens*, 86.

7. Staatsarchiv Zurich (in the following STAZH) KIII 212.1–3, Oberamt Regensberg.

8. For a comparison of maiden names and married names see STAZH BVII 208.20 Oberwaisenamt Regensberg, Protokoll 1816–1826; STAZH BVII 208.21 Oberwaisenamt Regensberg, Protokoll Feb. 1826–Juli 1831.

9. Gottfried von Meiss, *Das Pfand-Recht und der Pfand- oder Betreibungs-Proceß in seinem ganzen Umfang: Nach den Gesetzen und der Uebung des Eidgen. Cantons Zurich / Ein civilrechtlicher Versuch* (Zurich, 1821), 30.

10. On the tense relations between family lines and marital alliances see Margareth Lanzinger, Gunda Barth-Scalmani, Ellinor Forster, and Gertrude Langer-Ostrawsky, eds., *Aushandeln von Ehe. Heiratsverträge der Neuzeit im europäischen Vergleich* (Vienna: Böhlau, 2010).

11. Here and in the following: STAZH KIII 212.1–3, Regula Meyer, Regula Markwalder, Barbara Kistler, Regula Schütz, Anna Merki, Anna Binder, Barbara Ganz, Kleofea Zöbeli an Kommission für administrative Streitigkeiten, 27. August 1829. The heirs of a deceased Anna Matthis added their names as the ninth signatory of the letter.

12. On the corporative community system made up of "full citizens," "residents," and "denizens" with lesser rights, which continued to exist after the demise of the Ancien Régime, see Graber, *Zeit des Teilens*, S. 97 f.

13. Bankruptcy was, of course, not the only occasion that could lead to a woman being placed under the gender tutelage of a legally appointed guardian; others included the death of the husband and the "prodigiality" of the husband and/or wife. Still, bankruptcies were a common cause. In 1819, a year of reference for which good sources are available, nine of thirty cases of gender tutelage administered by the Unterwaisenamt Schöfflistorf/Oberweningen were occasioned by bankruptcy. STAZH BVII 208.23 Bevogtigungs-Etat, Oberamt Regensberg.

14. STAZH BVII 208.20 Oberwaisenamt Regensberg, Protokoll für Regensberg 1816–1826, Jahresbericht November 1, 1821; Jahresbericht September 23, 1824; Jahresbericht 1822, n.d.

15. On the inspection of the so-called "Schirmladen" see STAZH BVII 208.21 Protokoll Oberwaisenamt Regensberg Feb. 1826–Juli 1831, Jahresbericht 1825 [*sic*] vom 7. Januar 1828. Allgemein zur Schirmlade STAZH BVII 208.20 Oberwaisenamt Regensberg, Protokoll für Regensberg 1816–1826, konstituierende Sitzung des Oberwaisenamts 1816.

16. Here and in the following: STAZH KIII 212.1–3, Gemeindevorsteherschaft Oberweningen an die Kommission für administrative Streitigkeiten, November 21, 1829.

17. STAZH BVII 208.22 Oberamt Regensberg. Protokoll über sämtliche Gemeinderechnungen Jan. 1817–Jan. 1834.

18. Here and in the following: STAZH BVII 208.17, Kopierbuch des Oberamts Regensberg, Nov. 1825–July 1831, Oberamt Regensberg: Kopie eines Schreibens an die Commission für administrative Streitigkeiten, December 18, 1829.

19. Conflicts over common forests have long occupied social historians. Noteworthy are Jonathan Sperber, "Angenommene, vorgetäuschte und eigentliche Normenkonflikte bei der Waldbenutzung im 19. Jahrhundert," *Historische Zeitschrift* 290 (2010): 681–702; Richard Hölzl, *Umkämpfte Wälder: Die Geschichte einer ökologischen Reform in Deutschland 1760–1860* (Frankfurt am Main: Campus, 2010); Josef Mooser, "'Furcht bewahrt das Holz'. Holzdiebstahl und sozialer Konflikt in der ländlichen Gesellschaft 1800–1850 an westfälischen Beispielen,"

in *Räuber, Volk und Obrigkeit. Studien zur Geschichte der Kriminalität in Deutschland seit dem 18. Jahrhundert*, ed. Heinz Reif (Frankfurt am Main: Suhrkamp, 1984), 43–99. On the theft of wood in the canton of Zurich see Fritzsche and Lemmenmeier, "Die revolutionäre Umgestaltung," 26. On sharing common land in the eighteenth century see Peter Rásonyi, *Promotoren und Prozesse institutionellen Wandels: Agrarreformen im Kanton Zurich im 18. Jahrhundert* (Berlin: Dunckcr & Humblot, 2000).

20. Beereuter, "Wandel," 97–99. On the agricultural crisis in eastern Switzerland in the 1820s, which came about after price increases during the hunger crisis of 1817 and was characterized by a lack of liquidity caused by falling product prices and rising property prices, see Hans Brugger, *Die schweizerische Landwirtschaft in der ersten Hälfte des 19. Jahrhunderts* (Frauenfeld: Huber, 1956), 127–32, 230.

21. Rásonyi, *Promotoren*. A statement made by the municipal council makes clear that Oberweningen did not have a system of "Gerechtigkeiten." STAZH KIII 212.1–3, Gemeindevorsteherschaft Oberweningen an die Kommission für administrative Streitigkeiten, November 21, 1829.

22. Among other factors, in 1807 and 1818 new forestry laws entered into effect, and in 1822 the superior forestry administration was established, which placed constraints on municipalities who supplemented their treasuries with earnings from lumber. Beereuter, "Wandel," 67, 73, 90–91.

23. On the rhetorical activation of "old rights" see Edward Palmer Thompson, "Custom, Law and Common Right," in *Customs in Common: Studies in Traditional Popular Culture* (New York: Penguin, 1991), 97–184.

24. Similar conclusions about the expanded freedom of action experienced by the wives of bankrupt men are reached in Albert Vogt's micro-historical study of a village in the municipality of Solothurn: Albert Vogt, *Aedermannsdorf. Bevölkerung, Wirtschaft, Gesellschaft und Kultur im 19. Jahrhundert* (Zurich: Chronos, 2003), 201–2, 694.

25. Claudia Honegger and Bettina Heintz, "Zum Strukturwandel weiblicher Widerstandsformen im 19. Jahrhundert," in *Listen der Ohnmacht. Zur Sozialgeschichte weiblicher Widerstandsformen*, ed. Claudia Honegger and Bettina Heintz (Frankfurt am Main: Europäische Verlagsanstalt, 1981), 7–68.

26. Timothy Mitchell, "Society, Economy, and the State Effect," in *State/Culture: State-Formation after the Cultural Turn*, ed. George Steinmetz (Ithaca, NY: Cornell University Press, 1999), 91; Louis Althusser, "From *Capital* to Marx's Philosophy," in Louis Althusser and Étienne Balibar, *Reading Capital*, trans. Ben Brewster (London: Verso, 2009), 70–72.

27. Clifford Geertz, "Local Knowledge: Fact and Law in Comparative Perspective," in *Local Knowledge: Further Essays in Interpretive Anthropology* (New York: Basic Books, 1983), 167–234.

28. Harald Fischer-Tiné, *Pidgin Knowledge. Wissen und Kolonialismus* (Zurich: diaphanes, 2014), 12–13, 57.

29. Here and in the following: Johann Jakob Leuthy, *Handbuch der Schweizerischen Handels-, Gewerbs- und Niederlassungs-Verhältnisse für Beamte, Rechtsanwälte, Notare, Kaufleute, Geschäftsmänner, u. a.* (Zurich, 1849), vol. 4, appendix, 2–14.

30. *Acht und zwanzigster Rechenschaftsbericht des Obergerichts an den Großen Rath des Standes Zurich über das Jahr 1858* (Zurich, 1859), 66.

31. Alexander Reichel, "Referat: Das Betreibungsamt im schweizerischen Recht," *Zeitschrift für schweizerisches Recht* 28 (1887): 570.

32. Fr. von Wyß, "Die Schuldbetreibung nach schweizerischen Rechten," *Zeitschrift für schweizerisches Recht* 7 (1858): 3.

33. *Privatrechtliches Gesetzbuch für den Kanton Zurich,* 4 vols. (Zurich, 1854–56); *Satz- und Ordnungen einer frey-loblichen Statt-Gerichts zu Zurich* (Zurich, 1715). See Johann Caspar Bluntschli, *Staats- und Rechtsgeschichte der Stadt und Landschaft Zurich,* 2 vols., 2nd ed. (Zurich, 1856).

34. On this point see Bernard Lepetit, "Le présent de l'histoire," in *Les formes de l'expérience: Une autre histoire sociale,* ed. Bernard Lepetit (Paris: Albin Michel, 1995), 273–98.

35. Lerner, *Laboratory;* Craig, *Triumph of Liberalism;* Rolf Graber, Introduction to *Wege zur direkten Demokratie in der Schweiz. Eine kommentierte Quellenauswahl von der Frühneuzeit bis 1874* (Vienna: Böhlau, 2013), 13–63.

36. Weinmann, *Eine andere Bürgergesellschaft,* 208; Lerner, *Laboratory.*

37. Regula Argast, *Staatsbürgerschaft und Nation: Ausschluss und Integration in der Schweiz 1848–1933* (Göttingen: Vandenhoeck & Ruprecht, 2007), 62, 72. On the municipality as a unit that helped integrate the central Swiss cantons—which were defeated in the Sonderbundskrieg—see Zimmer, *A Contested Nation,* 151.

38. Lerner, *Laboratory;* Elisabeth Joris, *Liberal und eigensinnig. Die Pädagogin Josephine Stadlin—die Homöopathin Emilie Paravicini-Blumer* (Zurich: Chronos, 2010).

39. Otter, *The Victorian Eye;* Joyce, *State of Freedom;* Joyce, *Rule of Freedom;* Procacci, *Gouverner;* François Ewald, *L'état providence* (Paris: Bernard Grasset, 1986).

40. Consider criminal justice in Zurich: Francisca Loetz, *A New Approach to the History of Violence: "Sexual Assault" and "Sexual Abuse" in Europe, 1500–1850,* trans. Rosemary Selle (Leiden: Brill, 2015), 15–16, 37, 48.

41. On the *Monatschronik der zürcherischen Rechtspflege* see Katharina M. Saleski, *Theorie und Praxis des Rechts im Spiegel der frühen Zürcher und Schweizer juristischen Zeitschriften* (Zurich: Schulthess, 2007), 24–83. On the restructuring of the judiciary in the 1830s see Fritzsche and Lemmenmeier, "Die revolutionäre Umgestaltung," 131–36; Thomas Weibel, *Friedrich Ludwig Keller und das Obergericht des Kantons Zurich* (Zurich: Obergericht des Kantons Zürich, 2006).

42. Gunn and Vernon, "Introduction," 9.

43. Joyce, *Rule of Freedom,* 3–4.

44. Verordnung vom 16ten May 1804, betreffend den Handelsverkehr der Juden, in: Officielle Sammlung der von dem Großen Rathe des Cantons Zurich gegebenen Gesetze und gemachten Verordnungen, und der von dem Kleinen Rath emanierten allgemeinen Landes- und Polizey-Verordnungen (Zurich, 1805), 2:94–95. Zurich's anti-Semitic rules against Jewish businesses were particularly restrictive compared to other Swiss cantons. See Annette Brunschwig, Ruth Heinrichs, and Karin Huser, *Geschichte der Juden im Kanton Zurich: Von den Anfängen bis in die heutige Zeit* (Zurich: Orell Füssli, 2005), 158–59.

45. STAZH KIII 542.3–4, Nr. 38, Gutachten der Industrie-Section an die

Kommission des Inneren betreffend den Verkehr der Juden, 3. Juni 1809. The source contains an extensive account of a Jewish creditor who sought to collect on a debt in 1825 by means of compulsory debt enforcement and was hindered by multiple local authorities.

46. David von Wyß, *Politisches Handbuch für die erwachsene Jugend der Stadt und Landschaft Zurich* (Zurich, 1796), 183.

47. *Privatrechtliches Gesetzbuch für den Kanton Zurich* (Zurich, 1856), § 879.

48. Staatsarchiv des Kantons St. Gallen (in the following STASG) KA R 77.2, Anfrage des Bezirksammannamts Neutoggenburg über die Erstellung eines einheitlichen Glücksscheinsformulars, December 6, 1845.

49. *Acht und zwanzigster Rechenschaftsbericht des Obergerichts an den Großen Rath des Standes Zurich über das Jahr 1858* (Zurich, 1859), 40.

50. Rudolf Braun, *Industrialisierung und Volksleben: Die Veränderungen der Lebensform in einem ländlichen Industriegebiet vor 1800 (Zürcher Oberland)* (Erlenbach: Eugen Rentsch, 1960), 224–25; Felix Meier, *Geschichte der Gemeinde Wetzikon* (Zurich: Lesegesellschaft Oberwetzikon, 1881), 447.

51. Staatsarchiv des Kantons Luzern (in the following: STALU) Akt 35.21 A.1, Antrag des Ratsmitglieds Hertenstein, June 12, 1848; Dekret des Präsidenten und Grossen Rats für einstweilige Aufhebung der öffentlichen Ausstellung der Failliten, June 15, 1848; Trompeter Kaspar Sigrist an Polizeikommission des Kantons Luzern, January 8, 1848. The authorities adhered to the distinction between punishments ordered by a "court of corrections" (*Korrektionsgericht*), which concerned matters like "foolishness," and punishments ordered by criminal courts for offenses like "fraud."

52. Fabian Brändle, ed., *Das lange Leben eines Toggenburger Hausierers: Gregorius Aemisegger 1815–1913* (Wattwil: Toggenburger Verlag, 2007), 62; Hermann Bendiner, *Das Wirtshausverbot. Eine schweizerische Strafe und Verwaltungsregel* (Zurich: E. Kreutler, 1917).

53. Johann Jakob Reithard, "Eine schweizerische Dorfgeschichte," in *Neue Alpenrosen. Eine Gabe schweizerischer Dichter,* ed. Johann Jakob Reithard (Zurich, 1848), 338–50. See Claudia Weilenmann, "Johann Jakob Reithard (1805–1857)," in *Sagenerzähler und Sagensammler der Schweiz. Studien zur Produktion volkstümlicher Geschichte und Geschichten vom 16. bis zum frühen 20. Jahrhundert,* ed. Rudolf Schenda (Bern: Haupt, 1988), 223–44; Uwe Baur, *Dorfgeschichte. Zur Entstehung und gesellschaftlichen Funktion einer literarischen Gattung im Vormärz* (Munich: Fink, 1978), 18–20. On the genre of "village stories," see Markus Twellmann, *Dorfgeschichten. Wie die Welt zur Literatur kommt* (Göttingen: Wallstein, 2019), esp. chap. 4: "Der Staat vor Ort: Dorfgeschichten des Liberalismus."

54. Hochobrigkeitliche Verordnung vom 16ten Julii [*sic*] 1805, betreffend die Auffallsverhandlungen, Pfandbücher und Pfandversilberungen, in *Officielle Sammlung der von dem Großen Rathe des Cantons Zurich gegebenen Gesetze und gemachten Verordnungen, und der von dem Kleinen Rath emanierten allgemeinen Landes- und Polizey-Verordnungen* (Zurich, 1808), 3:108.

55. Alain Corbin, *Village Bells: The Culture of the Senses in the Nineteenth-Century French Countryside,* trans. Martin Thom (New York: Columbia University Press, 1998), chap. 2.

56. For an analysis using Arnold van Gennep's concept of rites of passage see Corbin, *Village Bells*, 159 ff (L'état civil sonore).

57. Rudolf Schlögl, "Kommunikation und Vergesellschaftung unter Anwesenden: Formen des Sozialen und ihre Transformation in der Frühen Neuzeit," *Geschichte und Gesellschaft* 34 (2008): 155–224.

58. Gantordnung des Kantons Zürchs, erlassen vom Regierungsrat 9. März 1843, 21. Dezember 1843 in Gesetzessammlung aufgenommen, in *Officielle Sammlung der seit Annahme der Verfassung vom Jahre 1831 erlassenen Gesetze, Beschlüsse und Verordnungen des Eidgenössischen Standes Zurich* (Zurich, 1843), 7:96–104, here 98.

59. *Der Bote von Uster*, no. 23, June 6, 1845. Later renamed *Boten von Uster*, and in 1846 for a short period *Noth- und Hülfsblatt*. On the paper and its founder Johann Jakob Treichler see Rudolf Braun, *Sozialer und kultureller Wandel in einem ländlichen Industriegebiet im 19. und 20. Jahrhundert* (Zurich: Eugen Rentsch, 1999 [1965]), 121–23, footnote 41; Franz Wirth, *Johann Jakob Treichler und die soziale Bewegung im Kanton Zürich (1845/1846)* (Basel: Helbing & Lichtenhahn, 1981).

60. Meier, *Geschichte der Gemeinde Wetzikon*, 447.

61. von Meiss, *Pfand-Recht*, 127–28.

62. Alfred Messerli, *Lesen und Schreiben 1700 bis 1900. Untersuchung zur Durchsetzung der Literalität in der Schweiz* (Tübingen: Niemeyer, 2002), 392–94.

63. von Meiss, *Pfand-Recht*, 129.

64. Here and in the following STAZH P 5.2, Vorsteherschaft der Gemeinde Uhwiesen an den Grossen Rat, February 4, 1834, emphasis in original.

65. Braun, *Industrialisierung und Volksleben*, 235; Erwin Kunz, *Die lokale Selbstverwaltung in den zürcherischen Landsgemeinden im 18. Jahrhundert* (Zurich: Weiss, 1948), 29.

66. *Vierter Rechenschaftsbericht des Obergerichts an den Großen Rath des Standes Zurich über das Jahr 1834* (Zurich, 1835), 13.

67. *Elfter Rechenschaftsbericht des Obergerichts an den Großen Rath des Standes Zurich über das Jahr 1841* (Zurich, 1842), 22.

68. *Achtzehnter Rechenschaftsbericht des Obergerichts an den Großen Rath des Standes Zurich über das Jahr 1848* (Zurich, 1849), 17–18.

69. *Vier und zwanzigster Rechenschaftsbericht des Obergerichts an den Großen Rath des Standes Zurich über das Jahr 1854* (Zurich, 1855), 31–32.

70. *Fünf und zwanzigster Rechenschaftsbericht des Obergerichts an den Großen Rath des Standes Zurich über das Jahr 1855* (Zurich, 1856), 34–35.

71. *Zweiunddreißigster Rechenschaftsbericht des Obergerichts an den Großen Rath des Standes Zurich über das Jahr 1862* (Zurich, 1863), 55–60, esp. 59.

72. On communal poor relief as a factor in the exclusion of people from citizenship see Argast, *Staatsbürgerschaft und Nation*, 250–51; Helene Baltensberger, *Das Armenwesen des Kantons Zurich vom Armengesetz von 1836 bis zu den Revisionsbestrebungen der 60er Jahre* (Zurich: Lang, 1940).

73. STAZH P.5.2.2. Obergericht des Standes Zurich, Aufsicht der Gemeindeammänner durch die Schuldenschreiber, January 6, 1849.

74. *Fünfter Rechenschaftsbericht des Obergerichts an den Großen Rath des Standes Zurich über das Jahr 1835* (Zurich, 1836), 12; similarly: *Vierzehnter*

Rechenschaftsbericht des Obergerichts an den Großen Rath des Standes Zurich über das Jahr 1844 (Zurich, 1845), 20; *Drei und zwanzigster Rechenschaftsbericht des Obergerichts an den Großen Rath des Standes Zurich über das Jahr 1853* (Zurich, 1854), 25–26.

75. *Acht und zwanzigster Rechenschaftsbericht des Obergerichts an den Großen Rath des Standes Zurich über das Jahr 1858* (Zurich, 1859), 36–37.

76. Michael Bordo and Harold James, "Die Nationalbank 1907–1946: Glückliche Kindheit oder schwierige Jugend?," in *Die Schweizerische Nationalbank 1907–2007*, ed. Schweizerische Nationalbank (Zurich: Neue Zürcher Zeitung, 2007), 32.

77. David von Wyß, *Politisches Handbuch*, 172.

78. *Auszüge aus den obergerichtlichen Rechenschaftsberichten von den Jahren 1872 bis und mit 1885, hauptsächlich das Notariatswesen und die Gemeindeammänner betreffend, möglichst alphabetisch geordnet. Jedermann als Hülfs- und Nachschlagbuch dienend* (Affoltern am Albis, 1887), 16. Similar rules for the purchase of basic goods were prevalent in all of Europe. On gender tutelage and consumption on credit see Erika Rappaport, "'A Husband and His Wife's Dresses': Consumer Credit and the Debtor Family in England, 1864–1914," in *The Sex of Things: Gender and Consumption in Historical Perspective*, ed. Victoria De Grazia (Berkeley: University of California Press, 1996), 163–87.

79. Gesetz über die Polizey an Sonn- und Festtagen, über die Wirthschaften und das Spielen, 20. Weinmonat 1834, in *Offizielle Sammlung der seit 10. März 1831 erlassenen Gesetze, Beschlüsse und Verordnungen des Eidgenössischen Standes Zurich* (Zurich, 1833), 3:301–302.

80. Johann Samuel Müller, *Praktisches Handbuch zur rechtlichen Eintreibung der verschiedenen Arten von Schulden, nebst aller Arten in das Schuldbetreibungsfach einschlagenden Formulars* (Bern: Maurhofer & Dellenbach, 1811), 11–12.

81. On the various forms of real estate as a collateral asset see Markus Mattmüller, "Agrargeschichte der Schweiz im Ancien Régime," vol. 2, "Vorlesung im WS 1978/79 und SS 1979" (unpublished manuscript, Historisches Seminar Basel, 1979), 365–78; Hermann Schulin, "Zur Entwicklung des Grundpfandrechts in der Schweiz," in *Wissenschaft und Kodifikation des Privatrechts im 19. Jahrhundert*, ed. Helmut Coing and Walter Wilhelm, vol. 3 *Die rechtliche und wirtschaftliche Entwicklung des Grundeigentums und Grundkredits* (Frankfurt am Main: Vittorio Klostermann, 1976), 373–414. On agrarian regions in the canton of Zurich in particular see Meyer, "Wirtschaft und Gesellschaft," 87–96; Fr. von Wyß, "Die Gült und der Schuldbrief nach Zürcherischem Rechte," *Zeitschrift für schweizerisches Recht* 9 (1861): 2–67.

82. Mattmüller, "Agrargeschichte," 376.

83. In the Ancien Régime, debtors had to pay specified amounts with interest over a certain period of time; overpayment to complete the debt early, for instance, was not permitted. In the nineteenth century, mortgage notes could be canceled by the debtor at any time by paying the principal plus interest due. F. G. Erhardt, *Inhalt, Entstehung und Untergang des Schuldbriefes nach zürcherischem Rechte* (Zurich, 1846), 38.

84. Erhardt, *Inhalt, Entstehung und Untergang*, 27.

85. *Bericht der Finanzdirektion an den hohen Regierungsrath betreffend die*

Bankfrage (Zurich, 1868); Gottfried Farner, *Das zürcherische Bodenkreditwesen unter den Anforderungen der Gegenwart* (Zurich, 1863), 2.

86. "Gesetz über die Ablösung grundversicherter Forderungen überhaupt und über die Natur und Wiederauflösung der durch den Uebergang von Unterpfändern auf dritte Besitzer entstehenden Rechtsverhältnisse insbesondere," in *Officielle Sammlung der seit Annahme der Verfassung vom Jahre 1831 erlassenen Gesetze, Beschlüsse und Verordnungen des Eidgenössischen Standes Zurich* (Zurich, 1853), 9:280–286.

87. Ritzmann, *Die Schweizer Banken*, 91.

88. On the establishment of the Kreditanstalt see Joseph Jung, *Alfred Escher (1819–1882): Der Aufbruch zur modernen Schweiz,* vol. 3, *Schweizerische Kreditanstalt, Eidgenössisches Polytechnikum, Aussenpolitik* (Zurich: Neue Zürcher Zeitung, 2006), 733–854.

89. Ritzmann, *Die Schweizer Banken*, 32. On the savings banks' philanthropic aspect see Mischa Suter, "Ökonomischer Individualismus und moralischer Paternalismus. Sparkassen im Kanton Zurich während der Zeit des Pauperismus (um 1820–1860)," *Die Produktion von Ungleichheiten—La production des inégalités,* ed. Thomas David et al. (Zurich: Chronos, 2010), 133–44.

90. Gottfried Farner, *Der Schuldbriefverkehr und das zürcherische Notariatswesen unter der Initiative* (Zurich, 1869), 9. See also Martin Schaffner, *Die demokratische Bewegung der 1860er Jahre: Beschreibung und Erklärung der Zürcher Volksbewegung von 1867* (Basel: Helbing & Lichtenhahn, 1982), 189–91.

91. On the urban underclasses' role in the Democratic Movement see Hans-Ulrich Schiedt, *Die Welt neu erfinden: Karl Bürkli (1823–1901) und seine Schriften* (Zurich: Chronos, 2002), 228–31.

92. Beckert, *Empire of Cotton,* chaps. 9–11; Geoff Eley, *Forging Democracy: The History of the Left in Europe, 1850–2000* (Oxford: Oxford University Press, 2002), 5, 30–33.

93. Karl Bürkli, *Eine Kantonalbank, aber keine Herren-, sondern eine Volksbank, keine 5 und 6%, sondern 2, höchstens 3 Prozent Zins. Sturz der Geldaristokratie durch eine Staatsbank ohne Gold- und Silbergeld* (Zurich, 1866). On Karl Bürkli's campaigning for a cantonal bank see Schiedt, *Welt neu erfinden.*

94. STASG KA R 77.2, Schadenersatzklagen gegen Konkursbehörden, Präsident der Verwaltungskommission der St. Galler Creditanstalt an Landammann und Kleinen Rat, August 14, 1858.

95. Brigitte Tanner, "Essen—Kaufen—Sparen. Die Anfänge der Konsumvereinsbewegung im Kanton Zurich um 1850 zwischen Tradition und Innovation" (unpublished thesis, Universität Zürich, 2006). On Germany see Uwe Spiekermann, *Basis der Konsumgesellschaft. Entstehung und Entwicklung des modernen Kleinhandels in Deutschland 1850–1914* (Munich: C. H. Beck, 1999), 481–85, 566–69.

96. Lemercier and Zalc, "Pour une nouvelle approche," 1003.

97. Their power was expanded in the Zurich constitution of 1814: they now sat on the municipal council and headed the municipal poor relief and orphanage. Weinmann, *Eine andere Bürgergesellschaft,* 233.

98. Reithard, "Dorfgeschichte," 309.

99. Beschluss des Kleinen Raths vom 28sten Januar 1812, an sämmtliche

Bezirks- und Unterstatthalter und die Bezirksgerichte, betreffend die Behandlung des Rechtstriebs für laufende Schulden, in *Officielle Sammlung der von dem Großen Rathe des Cantons Zurich gegebenen Gesetze und gemachten Verordnungen, und der von dem Kleinen Rath emanierten allgemeinen Landes- und Polizey-Verordnungen* (Zurich, 1813), 5:248–252, here 5:250–51.

100. Popular court newspapers are a fruitful source for documenting these sorts of cases, but such a paper was only established in Zurich in 1890 (the *Schweizer Kriminal-Zeitung*).

101. *Schweizer Kriminal-Zeitung*, no. 44, October 29, 1892, 3.

102. STAZH P 5.2, Petition des Vorstehers der Gesellschaft der Gemeindeammänner des Bezirkes Zurich namens derselben, zum Rechtstriebgesetz, February 3, 1842.

103. A dunning letter cost six schillings, the seizure of an asset twenty-five schillings, and the liquidation of pledged assets another thirty schillings. In bankruptcy proceedings, the "Schreckzettel" cost ten schillings, a single "Ruf" thirteen schillings. If minor debt enforcement was proceded major debt enforcement, a fee of one gulden and twenty-three schillings was assessed. In the years around 1830, a small debt could be directly collected by the municipality's bailiff, so long as the debtor and creditor lived near one another. Then, the dunning letter only cost two schillings, asset seizure fifteen. But creditors could choose between the two procedures; the fees had to be paid by the debtor. See also Christine von Arb, "'Und so wird unsere Forderung als billig und gerecht anerkannt werden'. Die Eingaben der Einwohner des Bezirks Hinwil zur Revision der Zürcher Kantonsverfassung 1830/31" (unpublished paper, Historisches Seminar Universität Basel, 1991), 39–40.

104. STAZH K IV 124.1 Betreibungsgesetz 1832.

105. STAZH K IV 124.1 Betreibungsgesetz 1832; STAZH KIII 543.1, Johann Heinrich Schinz an Notariatskommission, February 17, 1827.

106. J. H. Gwalter, *Das zürcherische Schuldbetreibungsgesetz vom 1. April 1851. Mit Erläuterungen unter vorzüglicher Berücksichtigung der gerichtlichen Praxis* (Zurich, 1853), Ad §3.

107. Joyce, *Rule of Freedom*, 100.

108. Gesetz, betreffend die Form und Kosten des Rechtstriebs [of December 17, 1803], in *Officielle Sammlung der von dem Großen Rathe des Cantons Zurich gegebenen Gesetze und gemachten Verordnungen, und der von dem Kleinen Rath emanierten allgemeinen Landes- und Polizey-Verordnungen* (Zurich, 1804), 193.

109. Gesetz betreffend die Schuldbetreibung, June 29, 1832, in *Officielle Sammlung der seit Annahme der Verfassung vom Jahre 1831 erlassenen Gesetze, Beschlüsse und Verordnungen des Eidgenössischen Standes Zurich* (Zurich, 1832), 2:79–103.

110. The wave of 270 petitions sent in on the encouragement of Zurich's parliament are held in STAZH KIII 258.3 (nos. 201–270); KIII 258.3a (nos. 1–75); K III 259.1 (nos. 133–200); K III 259.1a (nos. 76–132). A thematically organized, numbered compilation is [David Ulrich], *Uebersicht der der Verfassungs-Commission gemachten Eingaben, in so fern dieselben sich nicht zunächst auf die Staatsverfassung, sondern auf die verschiedenen Zweige der Verwaltung, der Justizpflege*

und der Gesetzgebung beziehen (Zurich, 1831), 31. A detailed study of the petitions can be found in Weinmann, *Eine andere Bürgergesellschaft*, 204–67, esp. 238–52.

111. STAZH M 2.18.1, Eingabe an den Verfassungsrat Nr. 18, Neumünster, May 12, 1868, for a salient example of this line of argumentation.

112. The petitions are held in STAZH M 2.18.1; of about 160 petitions, 81 originals have been preserved. A printed compilation can be found in STAZH III Aaa 2, Systematische Uebersicht der bei dem Verfassungsrathe eingereichten und der in der ersten Berathung desselben gemachten Vorschläge betreffend die Verfassungsrevision, in Protokolle des Verfassungsrathes des eidgenössischen Standes Zurich 1868, 1869. On the petitions see Schaffner, *Demokratische Bewegung*, 45–65, esp. 55.

113. Joyce, *Rule of Freedom*.

114. On this interpretation see Martin Schaffner, "Direkte Demokratie: 'Alles für das Volk—alles durch das Volk,'" in *Eine kleine Geschichte der Schweiz. Der Bundesstaat und seine Traditionen,* ed. Manfred Hettling, Mario König, and Martin Schaffner (Frankfurt am Main: Suhrkamp, 1998), 189–226; Lerner, *Laboratory*.

115. I follow here the work of Susanne Lüdemann, who, following Cornelius Castoriadis, understands the political imaginary as a set of collective notions and attitudes that exert real effects in material relations. See Lüdemann, *Metaphern der Gesellschaft: Studien zum soziologischen und politischen Imaginären* (Munich: Fink, 2004); Cornelius Castoriadis, *The Imaginary Institution of Society*, trans. Kathleen Blamey (Cambridge, MA: MIT Press, 1987).

116. Janet Roitman, *Anti-Crisis* (Durham, NC: Duke University Press, 2014).

117. The expression can be found, for example, in the minutes of the June 15, 1804, intercantonal negotiations on the enforcement of debts across cantonal lines. In the discussions on the federal constitution in 1848, the formulation "debtor capable of paying" was used, but the representatives of the canton of Schwyz successfully petitioned for "the older popular expression: 'the upright debtor,' because an individual can, under certain circumstances, be capable of paying, without one being able to ascribe to him the predicate of economic integrity." *Auszug aus dem Abschiede der ordentlichen eidgenössischen Tagsatzung des Jahres 1847, IV. Theil: Verhandlungen, betreffend die Revision des Bundesvertrages* (Bern, n.d., ca. 1848), 271.

118. Weinmann, *Eine andere Bürgergesellschaft*, 204.

119. STAZH K III 258.3a, Petitionen des Zürcher Volkes 1830/31, no. 1–75, no. 40, Wetzikon, im Christmonat 1830.

120. Robert Beachy, "Bankruptcy and Social Death: The Influence of Credit-Based Commerce on Cultural and Political Values," *Zeitsprünge. Forschungen zur Frühen Neuzeit* 4, no. 4 (2000): 329–43.

121. Gerlind Rüve, *Scheintod. Zur kulturellen Bedeutung der Schwelle zwischen Leben und Tod um 1800* (Bielefeld: transcript, 2008).

122. Brigitta Bernet, "'Der bürgerliche Tod': Entmündigungsangst, Psychiatriekritik und die Krise des liberalen Subjektentwurfs um 1900," in *Zwang zur Ordnung. Psychiatrie im Kanton Zurich, 1870–1970,* ed. Brigitta Bernet et al. (Zurich: Chronos, 2007), 128.

123. Lukas Messmer, "Hans Conrad Finslers 'Sturz in die schmälichste Tiefe'.

Bankrott, Scheitern und die Folgen in Zurich 1829" (unpublished thesis, Universität Zurich, 2012), 114–15.

124. STAZH M2 18.1. Eingaben Verfassungsrat 1868, no. 94, n.d.

125. Friedrich Ludwig Keller, born in 1799, studied in Berlin under Friedrich Carl von Savigny and in Göttingen. In 1829, he was elected to Zurich's legislature as the leader of the liberal-radical party; after the liberal turn in 1830, he became president of Zurich's new high court, from which he resigned in 1837. During the Züriputsch he fled to Baden. In 1842, he rejected an offer to return to Zurich's legislature and in 1844 he emigrated to Halle, where he taught Roman law. In 1847, he was hired to fill the professorship that Savigny had once held at the University of Berlin. See Weibel, *Friedrich Ludwig Keller;* Saleski, *Theorie und Praxis des Rechts,* 30–31; Ferdinand Elsener, *Die Schweizer Rechtsschulen vom 16. bis zum 19. Jahrhundert unter besonderer Berücksichtigung des Privatrechts: Die kantonalen Kodifikationen bis zum schweizerischen Zivilgesetzbuch* (Zurich: Schulthess, 1975), 366–81.

126. Friedrich Ludwig Keller, "Ueber den Rechtszustand der Falliten," *Monatschronik der zürcherischen Rechtspflege* 1 (1833): 113.

127. Keller, "Ueber den Rechtszustand der Falliten," 114, 117.

128. Keller, "Ueber den Rechtszustand der Falliten," 119.

129. Keller, "Ueber den Rechtszustand der Falliten," 118.

130. STAZH KIII 212.1–3, Gemeindevorsteherschaft Oberweningen an Kommission für administrative Streitigkeiten, November 21, 1829.

131. Toby L. Ditz, "Shipwrecked; or Masculinity Imperiled: Mercantile Representations of Failure and the Gendered Self in Eighteenth Century Philadelphia," *Journal of American History* 81 (1994): 51–80.

132. STAZH P.5.2.1., Heinrich Jägli, n.p., Konrad Leimbacher von Neftenbach an den Grossen Rat, January 27 and 30, 1840.

133. STAZH KIII 212.1–3, Regula Meyer u. a. an Kommission für administrative Streitigkeiten, August 27, 1829.

134. On the social history of Zurich's bourgeoisie see Albert Tanner, *Arbeitsame Patrioten—wohlanständige Damen: Bürgertum und Bürgerlichkeit in der Schweiz 1830–1914* (Zurich: Orell Füssli, 1995), 623–46.

135. Messmer, "Hans Conrad Finslers," 33–36. For a further example of powerful Swiss merchants settling their debts out of court (in this case, the creditors fared much better with 70 percent) see Maya Zellweger, "Konkurs im Ostschweizer Textilhandel 1817–Verlust des 'symbolischen Kapitals der Ehre,'" in *Wirtschaftsrechtsgeschichte der Modernisierung in Mitteleuropa: Zur Wechselwirkung zwischen wirtschaftlichen und rechtlichen Entwicklungen im Rahmen der grossen Transformation 1750–1850,* ed. Lukas Gschwend and René Pahud de Mortanges (Zurich: Dike, 2009), 171–87.

136. STAZH P.5.2.1., Heinrich Jägli, n.p., Konrad Leimbacher von Neftenbach an den Grossen Rat, January 27 and 30, 1840.

137. The best account of the "Züriputsch" is Lerner, *Laboratory,* chap. 5.

138. STAZH P.5.2.1., Heinrich Jägli, n.p., Konrad Leimbacher von Neftenbach an den Grossen Rat, January 27 and 30, 1840.

139. STAZH P.5.2.1., Heinrich Freytag und J. Däniker an den Grossen Rat, March 28, 1848.

140. On the context of these rumors, which evoked the Uster arson of 1832 and were spread by an *agent provocateur* who had been paid by a factory owner from the Zurich highlands, see Wirth, *Johann Jakob Treichler*, 190–200. On Treichler's tumultuous political career, in the run of which he successfully became part of railway and bank magnate Alfred Escher's social group, see Braun, *Sozialer und kultureller Wandel*, 121–23, footnote 41.

141. Johann Jakob Treichler, *Politische Grundsätze* (Basel, 1846), not paginated. The manifesto was also reproduced in the *Noth- und Hülfsblatt*.

142. Albert Tanner, "Ein Staat nur für die 'Hablichen'? Demokratie und politische Elite im frühen Bundesstaat," in *Etappen des Bundesstaates. Staats- und Nationsbildung der Schweiz, 1848–1998*, ed. Brigitte Studer (Zurich: Chronos, 1998), 63–88; Albert Tanner, *Arbeitsame Patrioten*, 568–74, esp. 569.

143. Staatsarchiv Basel-Stadt, Justiz J 4, Fallitenverein an Regierung, August 4, 1848.

144. Roitman, *Anti-Crisis*.

145. Certainly, statistics on bankruptcy had existed before, but they were intended for a small group of experts. For example, in governmental discussions on intercantonal tariffs, free trade, and protective tariffs, a member of Zurich's industry commission compiled, "from the public reports" (i.e. official publications on bankruptcy), data for the years 1781–1841. Christian Beyel, *Commissionalbericht über die Schweizerischen Verkehrsverhältnisse zu Handen der zürcherischen Industriegesellschaft, (vorgetragen in dem größeren Ausschusse des Zürcherischen Industrievereins den 21. Februar 1843)* (n.p. [Zurich], 1843), 1:16–17. See also Ulrich Menzel, *Auswege aus der Abhängigkeit: Die entwicklungspolitische Aktualität Europas* (Frankfurt am Main: Suhrkamp, 1988), 54–55, 114–15.

146. STAZH P.5.2.1., Heinrich Freytag und J. Däniker an den Grossen Rat, March 28, 1848.

147. On the Democratic Movement see Schiedt, *Welt neu erfinden*; Schaffner, *Demokratische Bewegung*; on its use of media see Daniela Decurtins and Susi Grossmann, "Die Bedeutung sozialer Vernetzung bei der Gründung der Zürcher Kantonalbank 1870," in *Banken und Kredit in der Schweiz (1850–1930)*, ed. Youssef Cassis and Jakob Tanner (Zurich: Chronos, 1993), 105–28.

148. Workers rarely took on mortgage debt that could be collected through bankruptcy. Moreover, the bankruptcy law of 1857 de facto prohibited bankruptcy proceedings if the debtor's assets were not of sufficient value to cover the bankruptcy fees, because if a debtor owned no real estate, then the creditor seeking to collect had to pay forty francs as a deposit to ensure that the fees would be paid. Schaffner, *Demokratische Bewegung*, 128–29. Gesetz betreffend die Schuldbetreibung vom April 5, 1851, in *Offizielle Sammlung der seit 10. März 1831 erlassenen Gesetze, Beschlüsse und Verordnungen des eidgenössischen Standes Zürich* (Zurich, 1850), 8:241–290, § 44, S. 257.

149. Schaffner, *Demokratische Bewegung*, 133.

150. Schaffner, *Demokratische Bewegung*, 123.

151. *Schweizerisches Volksblatt vom Bachtel*, no. 85, October 24, 1867 (not paginated).

152. Here and in the following: STAZH P 5.2.2., Jakob Bänz von Wülflingen an Grossen Rat (n.d., ca. Dezember 1849).

230 Notes to Pages 67-72

153. Here and in the following: STAZH M 2.18.1, Eingaben an den Verfassungsrat, Eingabe no. 17, Caspar Meyer von Uster, May 12, 1868.

154. Muldrew, *The Economy of Obligation*, 260–62.

155. Unchanged, however, was the rule that stripped the poor of their civic rights for the duration of their dependence on poor relief and the civic rights of those convicted of certain crimes deemed dishonorable.

156. Friedrich Haab, *Ueber die Einstellung der Konkursiten ins Aktivbürgerrecht* (Zurich, 1871), 4.

157. STAZH III Aaa 2, Protokoll des Verfassungsrathes, September 8, 1868.

158. See Baltensberger, *Armenwesen*. On the moral language of poor relief see Sabine Lippuner, *Bessern und verwahren. Die Praxis der administrativen Versorgung von "Liederlichen" und "Arbeitsscheuen" in der thurgauischen Zwangsarbeitsanstalt Kalchrain* (Frauenfeld: Historischer Verein des Kantons Thurgau, 2005); Procacci, *Gouverner.*

159. Itself not an inevitable development. See Pierre-Cyrille Hautcœur, "Produire des statistiques: pour quoi faire? L'échec de la statistique de faillites en France au XIXe siècle," *Histoire et mesure* 23 (2008): 85–136. On account of them being an object of political contention, statistics had an uncertain epistemic status, a point made well by Mary Poovey, *A History of the Modern Fact: Problems of Knowledge in the Sciences of Wealth and Society* (Chicago: University of Chicago Press, 1998), chap. 7.

160. As discussed in chapter 1, the various honor sanctions that differed from canton to canton remained in effect even after the passage of the 1889 federal bankruptcy law. Schröter, *Die öffentlichrechtlichen Folgen.*

161. On the history of the concept of the social and the welfare of society see Sewell, *Logics of History*, 321–28.

162. Jacques Donzelot, *L' invention du social: essai sur le déclin des passions politiques* (Paris: Fayard, 1984).

163. Ewald, *L'état providence.* On the category of risk see Levy, *Freaks of Fortune.*

164. Christian Topalov, *Naissance du chômeur 1880–1910* (Paris: Albin Michel, 1994).

165. Ewald, *L'état providence*, 64–70.

166. Topalov, *Naissance*, 203–206, 359–62.

167. Joyce, *Rule of Freedom*, 261.

168. STALU AKT 35.21 a.15, Petition an den Grossen Rath des Kantons Luzern um Classification der Konkursiten, December 31, 1880.

Chapter 3

1. One of the subheadings of section 23 of the first book from the original 1887 German publication of Ferdinand Tönnies, *Community and Civil Society,* ed. Jose Harris, trans. Margaret Hollis (Cambridge: Cambridge University Press, 2001), 60–62.

2. Tönnies, *Community and Civil Society*, 62.

3. Marx, "James Mill," 214.

4. Marcel Mauss, *The Gift: The Form and Reason for Exchange in Archaic Societies*, trans. W. D. Halls (London: Routledge, 2002), 7, 100.

5. Mauss always wrote of "échange." Alain Guery, "L'insoutenable ambiguïté du don," *Annales HSS* 68, no. 3 (2013): 830.

6. Claude Lévi-Strauss, *Introduction to the Work of Marcel Mauss*, trans. Felicity Baker (London: Routledge, 1987), 39.

7. Lévi-Strauss, *Introduction*, 43.

8. A competitive exchange, to be sure. See Fernand Braudel, "History and the Social Sciences: The *Longue Durée*," trans. Immanuel Wallerstein, *Review* 32, no. 2 (2009): 195–97; Claude Lévi-Strauss, "History and Anthropology," in *Structural Anthropology*, trans. Claire Jacobson and Brooke Grundfest Schoepf (New York: Basic Books, 1963), 1–27.

9. Gilles Postel-Vinay, *La terre et l'argent. L'agriculture et le crédit en France du XVIIIe au début du XXe siècle* (Paris: Albin Michel, 1998), 75.

10. This passage is greatly indebted to Laurence Fontaine's etymological research in *The Moral Economy*, 8–14, esp. 10.

11. Émile Benveniste, *Indo-European Language and Society*, trans. Elizabeth Palmer (Coral Gables, FL: University of Miami Press, 1973), 149; Émile Benveniste, *Problems in General Linguistics*, trans. Mary Elizabeth Meek (Coral Gables, FL: University of Miami Press, 1971), 272.

12. *Deutsches Wörterbuch von Jacob Grimm und Wilhelm Grimm*, s.v. "borgen," http://woerterbuchnetz.de/DWB/call_wbgui_py_from_form?sigle=DWB&mod e=Volltextsuche&hitlist=&patternlist=&lemid=GB09983#XGB09983.

13. Mauss, *Gift*, 58.

14. Carlo Ginzburg, "Lectures de Mauss," *Annales HSS* 65, no. 6 (2010): 1303–20.

15. Mauss, *Gift*, 1–3, 13–14, 31–32.

16. This aspect of *The Gift* seems to have made it particularly conducive to Jacques Derrida's reading of it. Hans-Jörg Rheinberger, a historian of knowledge inspired by Derrida, claims that these operations of channeling, paraphrasing, and connecting information are constitutive for the generation of scientific knowledge. See Jacques Derrida, *Given Time: I. Counterfeit Money*, trans. Peggy Kamuf (Chicago: University of Chicago Press, 1992); Hans-Jörg Rheinberger, *Toward a History of Epistemic Things: Synthesizing Proteins in the Test Tube* (Stanford, CA: Stanford University Press, 1997), chaps. 4 and 10.

17. Mauss, *Gift*, 25, 33, 76.

18. Lévi-Strauss, *Introduction*, 47; Claude Lévi-Strauss, *The Savage Mind* (Chicago: Chicago University Press, 1966).

19. Mauss, *Gift*, 30.

20. Mauss, *Gift*, 79.

21. Mauss, *Gift*, 81, footnote 122.

22. *Deutsches Wörterbuch von Jacob Grimm und Wilhelm Grimm*, s.v. "borgen."

23. Marilyn Strathern, *The Gender of the Gift: Problems with Women and Problems with Society in Melanesia* (Berkeley: University of California Press, 1988), 120–27.

24. Marilyn Strathern, "Qualified Value: The Perspective of Gift Exchange," in *Barter, Exchange and Value: An Anthropological Approach*, ed. Caroline Humphrey

and Stephen Hugh-Jones (Cambridge: Cambridge University Press, 1992), 169–91.

25. Strathern, "Qualified Value," 186.

26. Strathern, "Qualified Value," 178–79.

27. For an anthropological critique of the distinctions between "modern" and "traditional" societies and "commodities" and "gifts" see Jonathan Parry and Maurice Bloch, Introduction to *Money and the Morality of Exchange*, ed. Jonathan Parry and Maurice Bloch (Cambridge: Cambridge University Press, 1989), 1–32.

28. Expanding on Mauss's research, Natalie Zemon Davis identified a "gift mode" in early modern France and pointed to the power-laden, ambivalent relationships it engendered. Natalie Zemon Davis, *The Gift in Sixteenth-Century France* (Madison: University of Wisconsin Press, 2000), 9.

29. Chris Gregory, *Gifts and Commodities* (London: HAU, 1982), 115.

30. James Carrier, *Gifts and Commodities: Exchange and Western Capitalism since 1700* (London: Routledge, 1995).

31. Jonathan Parry, "'The Gift,' The Indian Gift and the 'Indian Gift,'" *Man*, n.s., 21, no. 3 (1986): 453–73. This position was recently put forth again by Graeber, *Debt*.

32. Andrea Muehlebach, *The Moral Neoliberal: Welfare and Citizenship in Italy* (Chicago: University of Chicago Press, 2012).

33. Because structures and systems inhere neither in things nor in the actions of people, the opposition between gift and commodity is a fiction with which researchers tend to destabilize whichever concept they choose not to work with. On this argument, see Strathern, *Gender*, chap. 1.

34. Harry Liebersohn, *The Return of the Gift: European History of a Global Idea* (Cambridge: Cambridge University Press, 2011).

35. Louis Althusser, "The Object of Capital," in Louis Althusser and Étienne Balibar, *Reading Capital*, trans. Ben Brewster (London: Verso, 2009), 77–220.

36. Tomba, *Marx's Temporalities*, chap. 3.

37. Étienne Balibar, *The Philosophy of Marx*, trans. Chris Turner (London: Verso, 1995), 56–62.

38. Janet Roitman, *Fiscal Disobedience: An Anthropology of Economic Regulation in Central Africa* (Princeton, NJ: Princeton University Press, 2005), 73.

39. Ute Tellmann, "Die moralische Ökonomie der Schulden," *Ilinx. Berliner Beiträge zur Kulturwissenschaft* 3 (2013): 3–24.

40. Peter Burke, *History and Social Theory*, 2nd ed. (Ithaca, NY: Cornell University Press, 2005), 69.

41. Edward Palmer Thompson, "The Moral Economy of the English Crowd in the Eighteenth Century," *Past and Present* 50 (1971): 77.

42. Thompson, "Moral Economy," 79; Mauss, *Gift*, 100–101.

43. Thompson, "Moral Economy," 131.

44. This is a straw man in an argument that seeks to position "moral" and "political economy" as polar opposites. In order to support the claim that free, rational decision making guided historical actors, the criticism is made that the notion of the "moral economy" treats them as irrational, yet "overcultured," sentimental subjects. See James Scott, "The Moral Economy as an Argument and as a Fight," in *Moral Economy and Popular Protest: Crowds, Conflict and Authority*,

ed. Andrew Charlesworth and Adrian Randall (Basingstoke: Palgrave Macmillan, 2000), 188.

45. Edward Palmer Thompson, "The Moral Economy Reviewed," in *Customs in Common: Studies in Traditional Popular Culture* (New York: Penguin, 1991), 304–5, 337–38.

46. Ahlrich Meyer, "Massenarmut und Existenzrecht: Zur Geschichte der sozialen Bewegungen 1789/1848," *Autonomie. Materialien gegen die Fabrikgesellschaft,* n.s., 14 (1985): 111.

47. Here and in the following I draw on Didier Fassin, "Les économies morales revisitées," *Annales HSS* 64 (2009): 1237–66.

48. Fassin, "Economies morales revisitées," 1255.

49. Fassin, "Economies morales revisitées," 1257.

50. Fassin, "Economies morales revisitées," 1265.

51. See Lorraine Daston, "The Moral Economy of Science," *Osiris* 10 (1995): 2–24.

52. On these issues—although explicitly limited to research on protests—see Johanna Siméant, "Économie morale et protestation—détours africains," *Genèses* 81 (2010): 142–60.

53. Keller, "Ueber den Rechtszustand der Falliten," 118.

54. It is not for nothing that the title of Thompson's article refers to the moral economy of the English "crowd."

55. In relation to the present see Lazzarato, *Indebted Man.*

56. In discussing rural lending, Gilles Postel-Vinay speaks of a "moral economy without a crowd." See Postel-Vinay, *Terre,* 359.

57. Clara Han, *Life in Debt: Times of Care and Violence in Neoliberal Chile* (Berkeley: University of California Press, 2012).

58. Julia Elyachar, *Markets of Dispossession: NGOs, Economic Development, and the State in Cairo* (Durham, NC: Duke University Press, 2005).

59. Jean-Christophe Agnew, "Capitalism, Culture, and Catastrophe," in *The Cultural Turn in U.S. History: Past, Present, and Future,* ed. James W. Cook, Lawrence B. Glickman, and Michael O'Malley (Chicago: University of Chicago Press, 2008), 383–415. The literature on debt peonage and indentured is immense. Interesting studies include Marcel van der Linden, *Workers of the World: Essays toward a Global Labor History* (Leiden: Brill, 2008), chaps. 2–4; Gwyn Campbell and Alessandro Stanziani, eds., *Debt and Slavery in the Mediterranean and Atlantic Worlds* (London: Pickering and Chatto, 2013).

60. Michael Taussig, *Shamanism, Colonialism, and the Wild Man: A Study in Terror and Healing* (Chicago: University of Chicago Press, 1987), 70.

61. Ian Hacking, "Making up People," in *Historical Ontology* (Cambridge, MA: Harvard University Press, 2002), 99–114; Theresa Wobbe, "Making up People: Berufsstatistische Klassifikation, geschlechtliche Kategorisierung und wirtschaftliche Inklusion um 1900 in Deutschland," *Zeitschrift für Soziologie* 41, no. 1 (2012): 41–57; Topalov, *Naissance.*

62. Mary Poovey in analyzing generic categories, Urs Stäheli in analyzing debates over key semantic distinctions, and Alex Preda in discussing the "observational boundaries" of nineteenth-century finance. Poovey, *Genres of the Credit Economy;* Urs Stäheli, *Spectacular Speculation;* Preda, *Framing Finance.*

63. Hans-Jörg Rheinberger, *On Historicizing Epistemology: An Essay*, trans. David Fernbach (Stanford, CA: Stanford University Press, 2010), 2–3.

64. Ann Laura Stoler, *Along the Archival Grain: Epistemic Anxieties and Colonial Common Sense* (Princeton, NJ: Princeton University Press, 2009), 42; Poovey, *History of the Modern Fact*, 16. An application of this approach to the early modern financial revolution, during which English philosophers and political economists debated over different notions of trust when discussing how trust in government-issued paper money could be cultivated, is Carl Wennerlind, *Casualties of Credit: The English Financial Revolution, 1620–1720* (Cambridge, MA: Harvard University Press, 2011), chap. 3.

65. Alain Pottage and Martha Mundy, eds., *Law, Anthropology, and the Constitution of the Social: Making Persons and Things* (Cambridge: Cambridge University Press, 2004).

66. On the notion that things be grasped as concepts not because they possess a prediscursive materiality, but because the experience of things produces new concepts, see Amira Henare, Martin Holbraad, and Sari Wastell, Introduction to *Thinking through Things: Theorising Artefacts Ethnographically*, ed. Amira Henare, Martin Holbraad, and Sari Wastell (London: Routledge, 2007), 1–31.

Chapter 4

1. Poovey, *Genres of the Credit Economy*. On public rather than private credit, see Patrick Brantlinger, *Fictions of State: Culture and Credit in Britain 1694–1994* (Ithaca, NY: Cornell University Press, 1996). On anxieties about an alleged excess of imagination and fictionalization in the wake of the early modern financial revolution in Great Britain, see J. G. A. Pocock, *Virtue, Commerce, and History: Essays on Political Thought and History, Chiefly in the Eighteenth Century* (Cambridge: Cambridge University Press, 1985).

2. Maß, "Formulare des Ökonomischen"; Sandage, *Born Losers*.

3. Geneviève Fraisse, "Feministische Singularität. Kritische Historiographie der Geschichte des Feminismus in Frankreich," *Feministische Studien* 4, no. 2 (1985): 134–40.

4. Carlo Ginzburg, "Microhistory: Two or Three Things that I Know about It," trans. John Tedeschi and Anne C. Tedeschi, *Critical Inquiry* 20, no. 1 (1993): 21.

5. Poovey, *Genres of the Credit Economy*.

6. Examples of urban journalism from Germanophone Switzerland include the reports of Zurich teacher Heinrich Grunholzer on the lives of the underclasses in Berlin tenements around 1840. He treated rent, burial costs, confirmation clothes, and household goods as elements of an economy of lending and borrowing in which pawned clothes and other goods functioned as money. See Heinrich Grunholzer, "Erfahrungen eines jungen Schweizers im Vogtlande," in *Dies Buch gehört dem König* [1843], ed. Bettine von Arnim, vol. 3 in Bettine von Arnim, *Werke und Briefe*, ed. Wolfgang Bunzel et al. (Frankfurt am Main: Suhrkamp, 1995), 329–68. I would like to thank Markus Bürgi for pointing this source out to me.

335

7. Maurice Alhoy, *Physiologie du créancier et du débiteur* (Paris, 1842). Alhoy was incarcerated in the debtor's prison at Sainte Pélagie and later edited a newspaper by fellow prisoners called *Pauvre Jacques*. See Erika Vause, *In the Red and in the Black: Debt, Dishonor, and the Law in France between Revolutions* (Charlottesville: University of Virginia Press, 2018), 176, 193.

8. Beat Kümin, "Das vormoderne Wirtshaus im Spannungsfeld zwischen Arbeit und Freizeit," *Freizeit und Vergnügen vom 14. bis zum 20. Jahrhundert*, ed. Hans-Jörg Gilomen, Beatrice Schumacher, and Laurent Tissot (Zurich: Chronos, 2005), 87–98.

9. Jeremias Gotthelf, *Der Geltstag oder die Wirtschaft nach der neuen Mode*, vol. 8 of *Sämtliche Werke in 24 Bänden*, ed. Rudolf Hunziker and Hans Bloesch (Erlenbach-Zurich: E. Rentzsch, 1923 [1846]); Michael Lauener, *Jeremias Gotthelf—Prediger gegen den Rechtsstaat* (Zurich: Schulthess, 2011).

10. Sandra Maß, *Kinderstube des Kapitalismus? Monetäre Erziehung im 18. und 19. Jahrhundert* (Munich: De Gruyter Oldenbourg, 2017); Maß, "Mäßigung der Leidenschaften," 55–81; Lemire, "Budgeting for Everyday Life."

11. Muldrew, *Economy of Obligation*, 64; Daniel Vickers, "Errors Expected: The Culture of Credit in Rural New England, 1750–1800," *Economic History Review* 63, no. 4 (2010): 1032–57.

12. Muldrew, *Economy of Obligation*, 156, 329–33.

13. Finn, *Character of Credit*, 20–21, 281–83, 320.

14. Gabriele Jancke and Claudia Ulbrich, "Vom Individuum zur Person. Neue Konzepte im Spannungsfeld von Autobiographietheorie und Selbstzeugnisforschung," *Querelles. Jahrbuch für Frauen- und Geschlechterforschung* 10 (2005): 7–27.

15. Pierre Bourdieu, "The Biographical Illusion," in *Biography in Theory*, ed. Wilhelm Hemecker and Edward Saunders (Berlin: de Gruyter, 2017), 210–16.

16. Staatsarchiv Zürich (hereafter: STAZH), WI 33 a.22.29, Gustav Anton Schulthess-Rechberg, "Meine Lebensbeschreibung." On the construction of memory through (auto)biographical writing in Pietism see Erika Hebeisen, *Leidenschaftlich fromm: Die pietistische Bewegung in Basel 1750–1850* (Cologne: Böhlau, 2005).

17. On religious interpretations of economic crisis in Protestantism, and particularly on the thought of Malthus's protege Thomas Chalmers (whose work was influential in Zurich), see Boyd Hilton, *The Age of Atonement: The Influence of Evangelicalism on Social and Economic Thought, 1795–1865* (Oxford: Oxford University Press, 1988). On the spread of Chalmers's ideas in Zurich see Baltensberger, *Das Armenwesen des Kantons Zürich*, 18; Robert Barth, *Protestantismus, soziale Frage und Sozialismus im Kanton Zürich 1830–1914* (Zurich: Theologischer Verlag, 1981), 32.

18. Bernard Mandeville, *The Fable of the Bees: or, Private Vices, Publick Benefits. Containing, Several Discourses, to Demonstrate, that Human Frailties, during the Degeneracy of Mankind, May be Turn'd to the Advantage of the Civil Society, and Made to Supply the Place of Moral Virtues* (London, 1714).

19. For Jakob Stutz's family tree see Antiquarische Gesellschaft Pfäffikon ZH, ed., *Jakob Stutz 1801–1877: Zürcher Oberländer Volksdichter und Zeitzeuge. Beiträge und Würdigungen* (Pfäffikon, 2001), 100–101.

20. Zentralbibliothek Zürich (hereafter: ZBZH), Handschriftenabteilung, Ms N 626, Tagebuch Jakob Stutz, March 3, 1852, 33.

21. According to a household budget for the highlands municipality of Bauma compiled by the poor relief administration in 1854. STAZH N 58.1, Notizen über den Haushalt verschiedener Familien vom geringern Stand in der Gemeinde Bauma, im Februar 1854: household budget no. 5 for the family of silk weavers, no. 1 for that of cotton weavers. See also the discussion of household budgets in Martin Salzmann, *Die Wirtschaftskrise im Kanton Zürich 1845 bis 1848: Ihre Stellung und Wertung im Rahmen der wirtschaftlich-sozialen Entwicklung in der ersten Hälfte des 19. Jahrhunderts* (Bern: Lang, 1978), 277–80.

22. According to Jakob Stutz's diary for 1853, ZBZH Ms N 628, Tagebuch Jakob Stutz, January 18, 1854, 73–74. STAZH N 58.1, Notizen über den Haushalt verschiedener Familien vom geringern Stand in der Gemeinde Bauma, im Februar 1854, Budget no. 2.

23. For dates and context see Jakob Stutz, *Siebenmal sieben Jahre aus meinem Leben: Als Beitrag zur näheren Kenntnis des Volkes. Mit einem Nachwort und einer Bibliographie von Walter Haas und Anmerkungen von August Steiger* (Frauenfeld: Huber, 1983 [1853]) and Antiquarische Gesellschaft, *Jakob Stutz*; Balz Spörri, *Studien zur Sozialgeschichte von Literatur und Leser im Zürcher Oberland des 19. Jahrhunderts* (Bern: Lang, 1987), 141–49; Ursula Brunold-Bigler, "Jakob Stutz' (1801–1877) Autobiographie 'Sieben mal sieben Jahre aus meinem Leben' als Quelle 'populärer Lesestoffe' im 19. Jahrhundert," *Schweizerisches Archiv für Volkskunde* 75 (1979): 28–42.

24. STAZH [call number yet to be assigned], Tagebuch Heinrich Senn, 10 MS vols., 1850–1885. Helpful for reading this source is Matthias Peter, *Jakob und Heinrich Senn. Zeitbilder der Schweiz aus dem 19. Jahrhundert* (Zurich: Neue Zürcher Zeitung, 2004).

25. From the period of pauperism in the canton of Zurich: Ulrich Zehnder, *Die Noth der Verarmung oder der Pauperismus und die Mittel dagegen mit besonderer Rücksicht auf den Kanton Zürich* (Zurich, 1848); J[ohann] L[udwig] Spyri, *Der Pauperismus der Zeit mit vorzüglicher Berücksichtigung der östlichen Gegenden des Kantons Zürich* (Zurich, 1848); Eduard Sulzer, *Ein Beitrag zu Lösung einer der wichtigsten Fragen unserer Zeit* (Zurich, 1852). Early assessments of crisis in the 1830s include Ludwig Jakob Schweizer, *Ueber den zunehmenden Verdienstmangel in den östlichen Gemeinden des Cantons Zürich* (Zurich, 1831); J. R. Waser, *Der Pfarrer als Armenbesorger in seiner Gemeinde. Ein Wort über Armenunterstützungen und einige darauf bezügliche Vorschläge neuerer und neuster Zeit* (Zurich, 1836).

26. Salzmann, *Wirtschaftskrise*; Elisabeth Joris and Heidi Witzig, *Brave Frauen, aufmüpfige Weiber: Wie sich die Industrialisierung auf Alltag und Lebenszusammenhänge von Frauen auswirkte (1820–1940)* (Zurich: Chronos, 1992), 20–21. In 1848, the state encouraged emigration as a means to combat the crisis. See Zehnder, *Noth*, 73.

27. Classic texts are Hufton, *The Poor of Eighteenth-Century France*; Braun, *Sozialer und kultureller Wandel*, chap. 1.

28. Suggestions for promoting new industries and retraining workers can be found in Zehnder, *Noth*, 73; on the marginal economy of straw weaving see STAZH [call number yet to be assigned], Tagebuch Heinrich Senn, vol. 3, May 10, 1852, 174.

29. For instance, a relative of Jakob Stutz who took work weaving silk yarn in Oberwinterthur. See ZBZH Ms N 626, Tagebuch Jakob Stutz, August 1, 1852, 87.

30. Beverly Lemire, *The Business of Everyday Life: Gender, Practice, and Social Politics in England, c. 1600–1900* (Manchester: Manchester University Press, 2005), chap. 6. On educational initiatives in Switzerland see Ursula Krattiger, *Mündigkeit: Ein Fragenkomplex in der schweizerischen Diskussion im 19. Jahrhundert, vor allem zur Zeit der Armennot von 1840 bis 1860* (Bern: Lang, 1972).

31. Spyri, *Pauperismus*, 3.

32. Lemire, *Business of Everyday Life*, chap. 6.

33. ZBZH Ber 219, Die Direction der zinstragenden Ersparnißcassa für alle Stände des Cantons Zürich an das Publicum, October 1821; Sulzer, *Beitrag*, 85–86; J[ohann] L[udwig] Spyri, *Bericht über die Sparkassen des Kantons Zürich vom Jahr 1859/1860* (Zurich, 1860); Suter, "Ökonomischer Individualismus," 134–35, 139–40.

34. Laurence Américi, "Preparing the People for Capitalism: Relations with Depositors in a French Savings Bank during the 1820s," *Financial History Review* 9, no. 1 (2002): 5–19.

35. On this relation of exchange in more detail see Mischa Suter, "Die Rappenkasse des Jakob Stutz: Erziehung zur Sparsamkeit und die Ökonomie symbolischer Güter im 19. Jahrhundert," *traverse* 3 (2009): 120–33.

36. On the different aspects of the concept "Volk" (the people) in nineteenth-century Swiss political rhetoric see Schaffner, "Direkte Demokratie," 192–203.

37. Stutz attended meetings of charitable associations, where he was honored for his work with local children's savings banks and savings associations. He also received a letter of thanks from Pfäffikon municipal president and cantonal representative Henrich Gujer for his initiative. See ZB Ms N 628, Tagebuch Jakob Stutz, February 24, 1854, 130–32.

38. Here and in the following: ZBZH Ms N 620, Tagebuch Jakob Stutz, January 29, 1846, 15. In his autobiography, Stutz writes that it was founded in spring 1847. But his diary notes that at that time, the Schillingverein was already celebrating its first anniversary. Whether this was an error or whether the association only really got running after a year is unclear. See ZBZH Ms N 621, Tagebuch Jakob Stutz, January 11, 1847, 15.

39. Stutz, *Siebenmal sieben Jahre*, 434–35.

40. ZBZH Ms N 622, Tagebuch Jakob Stutz, November 13, 1848, 159–64. Johann Ulrich Furrer, *Schweizerländli 1848: Das Tagebuch eines jungen Sternenbergers* (Stäfa: Rothenhäusler, 1997), 75 (November 18, 1848).

41. Pierre Bourdieu, *Language and Symbolic Power*, ed. John B. Thompson, trans. Gino Raymond and Matthew Adamson (Cambridge: Polity Press, 1991), 117–26.

42. ZB Ms N 628, Tagebuch Jakob Stutz, January 18, 1854, 73–74; 250 letters sent, 160 received. Similarly, he noted how many guests attended his name day celebration (ZBZH Ms N 620, July 26, 1846, 84–97; ZBZH Ms N 621, July 26, 1847, 61–63) and the value of the gifts he received subtracted from the costs of organizing the event (ZBZH Ms N 624, July 25, 1850, 77–85). Though I did not conduct a systematic analysis of Stutz's entries on celebrations and honors, there are many examples: ZBZH Ms N 621, January 11, 1847, 15; ZBZH Ms N 621,

July 26, 1847, 61–63; ZBZH Ms N 622, May 10, 1848, 55–56; ZBZH Ms N 623, May 27, 1849, 119; ZBZH Ms N 623, July 27, 1849, 26; ZBZH Ms N 623, August 26, 1849, 153–59; ZBZH Ms N 624, July 25, 1850, 77–85; ZBZH Ms N 625, December 25, 1850, 8–9; ZBZH Ms N 625, October 19, 1851, 99; ZBZH Ms N 625, November 27, 1851, 103–110; ZBZH Ms N 627, May 5, 1853, 74–75; ZBZH Ms N 627, May 16, 1853, 85–86; ZBZH Ms N 627, June 19, 1853, 142; ZBZH Ms N 627, July 19, 1853, 177; ZBZH Ms N 627, August 7, 1853, 209–10; ZBZH Ms N 627, August 9, 1853, 212; ZBZH Ms N 627, September 11, 1853, 279; ZBZH Ms N 627, October 13, 1853, 321; ZBZH Ms N 627, November 13, 1853, 368–71.

43. *Ernste und heitere Bilder*, 1, no. 3 (March, 1850): 65–82.

44. ZBZH Ms N 623, Tagebuch Jakob Stutz, August 26, 1849, 153–59.

45. For a critical perspective on Stutz's attempts to distinguish himself see Jakob Senn, *Ein Kind des Volkes: Schweizerisches Lebensbild* (Zurich: Rohr, 1966 [1888]), 198–99.

46. Regina Schulte, "Gerede und Arbeit im Dorf," *Historische Anthropologie* 20, no. 1 (2012): 76–89; Tobias Kies, "Hörensagen. Gerüchtekommunikation und lokale Öffentlichkeit im frühen 19. Jahrhundert," in *Sehnsucht nach Nähe. Interpersonale Kommunikation in Deutschland seit dem 19. Jahrhundert*, ed. Moritz Föllmer (Stuttgart: Steiner, 2004), 45–64; on the politics of rumors in early modern Switzerland see Andreas Würgler, "Fama und Rumor. Gerücht, Aufruhr und Presse im Ancien Régime," *WerkstattGeschichte* 15 (1996): 20–32. On how rumors could serve as evidence in criminal cases when the accused was unable to convincingly deflate the rumor see Alexandra Ortmann, "Jenseits von Klassenjustiz: Ein Blick in die ländliche Gesellschaft des deutschen Kaiserreichs," *Geschichte und Gesellschaft* 35, no. 4 (2009): 638.

47. On "village discourse" see Regina Schulte, *Das Dorf im Verhör: Brandstifter, Kindsmörderinnen und Wilderer vor den Schranken des bürgerlichen Gerichts Oberbayern* (Reinbek bei Hamburg: Rowohlt, 1989), 281, and David W. Sabean, *Power in the Blood: Popular Culture and Village Discourse in Early-Modern Germany* (Cambridge: Cambridge University Press, 1984).

48. On the significance of besmirched honor in the nineteenth century see Goldberg, *Honor*.

49. ZBZH Ms N 620, Tagebuch Jakob Stutz, March 18, 1846, 39. On the continued negotiation over the money to travel, which came too late because Johann Jakob Kägi died in Augsburg, see ZBZH Ms N 620, March 23, 1846, 42; ZBZH Ms N 620, March 28, 1846, 45–46.

50. ZBZH Ms N 620, Tagebuch Jakob Stutz, March 18, 1846, 39.

51. ZBZH Ms N 626, Tagebuch Jakob Stutz, March 14, 1852, 34.

52. His past was well known in the town. See, for instance, STAZH [call number yet to be assigned], Tagebuch Heinrich Senn, vol. 3, April 14, 1852, 161.

53. ZBZH Ms N 626, Tagebuch Jakob Stutz, April 7, 1852, 53; April 13, 1852, 56; April 16, 1852, 61. On the trial against Stutz see Antiquarische Gesellschaft, *Jakob Stutz*, 102–7.

54. ZBZH Ms N 627, Tagebuch Jakob Stutz, May 28, 1853, 99.

55. ZBZH Ms N 627, Tagebuch Jakob Stutz, June 2, 1853, 115. The "cousin" Hans Jakob Lattmann was actually his nephew and godson. Stutz called him

"cousin" elsewhere too, such as in ZBZH Ms N 628, Tagebuch Jakob Stutz, January 25, 1854, 94.

56. On the normative concept of "Hausen" see David W. Sabean, *Property, Production and Family in Neckarhausen, 1700–1870* (Cambridge: Cambridge University Press, 1990), chap. 3.

57. ZBZH Ms N 627, Tagebuch Jakob Stutz, August 25, 1853, 251.

58. *Amtsblatt des Kantons Zürich,* 10, no. 11, February 7, 1843, 42: date of the schedule of claims: March 8, 1843. STAZH B XI Bauma 65, Grundprotokoll Gemeinde Sternenberg, 1841–1843, 303: Kollokation vom March 8, 1843.

59. See also Binnenkade, *KontaktZonen,* 253.

60. ZBZH Ms N 626, Tagebuch Jakob Stutz, January 16, 1852, 18; February 13, 1852, 13.

61. STAZH B XI Bauma 67, Grundprotokoll Gemeinde Sternenberg, Notariat Bauma, vol. 67, 350–61; ZBZH Ms N 626, Tagebuch Jakob Stutz, August 6, 1852, 88.

62. ZBZH Ms N 626, Tagebuch Jakob Stutz, August 13, 1852, 90.

63. ZBZH Ms N 628, Tagebuch Jakob Stutz, May 19, 1854, 259.

64. ZBZH Ms N 628, Tagebuch Jakob Stutz, May 13, 1854, 250–51; May 14, 1854, 253; May 16, 1854, 254–55; May 17, 1854, 256.

65. ZBZH Ms N 628, Tagebuch Jakob Stutz, May 20, 1854, 262.

66. ZBZH Ms N 628, Tagebuch Jakob Stutz, June 18, 1854, 305; June 25, 1854, 319; July 4, 1854, 329–30.

67. STAZH [call number yet to be assigned], Tagebuch Heinrich Senn, vol. 6, November 16, 1856 [?], 133.

68. STAZH [call number yet to be assigned], Tagebuch Heinrich Senn, vol. 6, November 16, 1856 [?], 134.

69. STAZH [call number yet to be assigned], Tagebuch Heinrich Senn, vol. 6, November 16, 1856 [?], 132.

70. STAZH [call number yet to be assigned], Tagebuch Heinrich Senn, vol. 5, June 27, 1856, 233–34.

71. STAZH [call number yet to be assigned], Tagebuch Heinrich Senn, vol. 6, November 16, 1856 [?], 132–33.

72. STAZH [call number yet to be assigned], Tagebuch Heinrich Senn, vol. 6, November 16, 1856 [?], letter of attorney Eduard Rüegg to Jakob Senn from August 11, 1856, 133.

73. Binnenkade, *KontaktZonen,* 254, 266–70.

74. Ulrich Pfister, "Le petit crédit rural en Suisse aux XVIe–XVIIIe siècles," *Annales HSS* 49 (1994): 1339–57; Fontaine, *Moral Economy,* 63.

75. Bracht, *Geldlose Zeiten,* 189, 208.

76. Ginzburg, "Microhistory," 21.

77. For this insight I thank Han, *Life in Debt,* 49.

78. Cerutti, "Microhistory," 29–35.

79. Jürgen Schlumbohm, ed., Introduction to *Soziale Praxis des Kredits. 16.–20. Jahrhundert,* ed. Jürgen Schlumbohm (Hannover: Verlag Hahnsche Buchhandlung, 2007), 10.

80. Bracht, *Geldlose Zeiten,* 146–47, 207.

81. STAZH [call number yet to be assigned], Tagebuch Heinrich Senn, vol. 6, letter from Jakob Stutz, September 2, 1856, 136–37.

82. Gottfried Keller, "Pankraz, der Schmoller," in *Die Leute von Seldwyla,* ed. Peter Villwock et al. (Zurich: Stroemfeld, 2000 [1856]), 26–27.

83. On the economic system of Seldwyla see Jörg Kreienbrock, "Das Kreditparadies Seldwyla. Zur Beziehung von Ökonomie und Literatur in Gottfried Kellers Die Leute von Seldwyla," in *Gottfried Keller, Die Leute von Seldwyla. Kritische Studien—Critical Essays,* ed. Hans-Joachim Hahn and Uwe Seja (Bern: Lang, 2007), 117–34.

84. Studying the bourgeoisie through the medium of literature has a long tradition. See Franco Moretti, *The Bourgeois: Between History and Literature* (London: Verso, 2013). On how novels can support research on the Swiss bourgeoisie see Manfred Hettling, *Politische Bürgerlichkeit: Der Bürger zwischen Individualität und Vergesellschaftung in Deutschland und der Schweiz von 1860 bis 1914* (Göttingen: Vandenhoeck & Ruprecht, 1999), 291–317.

85. Manfred Hettling, "Behagliches Unbehagen. Gottfried Keller im demokratischen Kleinstaat," in *Verehrung, Kult, Distanz. Vom Umgang mit dem Dichter im 19. Jahrhundert,* ed. Wolfgang Braungart (Tübingen: Niemeyer, 2004), 243–57.

86. Beachy, "Bankruptcy and Social Death"; Dorothee Guggenheimer, *Kredite, Krisen und Konkurse. Wirtschaftliches Scheitern in der Stadt St. Gallen im 17. und 18. Jahrhundert* (Zurich: Chronos, 2014).

87. Jan Goldstein, *The Post-Revolutionary Self: Politics and Psyche in France, 1750–1850* (Cambridge, MA: Harvard University Press, 2005), esp. chap. 4 on the history of the unified masculine self—the "moi" of bourgeois man—in the philosophy of Victor Cousin.

88. On Keller's persistent debts up until his forty-second year of life, which were again and again paid off by his mother, particularly during his time in Munich and Berlin, see Wilhelm Höck, "Gottfried Keller," in *Genie und Geld: Vom Auskommen deutscher Schriftsteller,* ed. Karl Corino (Nördlingen: Rowohlt, 1987), 258–69.

89. Ulrich Kittstein, *Gottfried Keller* (Stuttgart: WBG, 2008), 13–17; Walter Morgenthaler et al., eds., *Gottfried Keller: Sämtliche Werke. Historisch-kritische Ausgabe,* vol. 21, *Leute von Seldwyla: Apparat zu Band 4 und 5* (Basel: Stroemfeld, 2000), 19–25.

90. Letter to Hermann Hettner, October 21, 1854, in Morgenthaler, *Apparat,* 445–46.

91. Here and in the following: Morgenthaler, *Apparat,* 472. On the debts to Hermann Hettner see the letter to him from June 25, 1855, Morgenthaler, *Apparat,* 451.

92. Letter to Hermann Hettner, June 25, 1855, in Morgenthaler, *Apparat,* 451.

93. Letter to Eduard Vieweg, November 10, 1855, in Morgenthaler, *Apparat,* 474–75.

94. Morgenthaler, *Apparat,* 29–30.

95. Roland Barthes, "The Reality Effect," in *The Rustle of Language,* trans. Richard Howard (Berkeley: University of California Press, 1989), 148.

96. Stephen Greenblatt, *Shakespearean Negotiations: The Circulation of Social*

Energy in Renaissance England (Berkeley: University of California Press, 1998). Alongside Greenblatt, key texts for this analysis of literature as an expression of social relations are Poovey, *Genres*; Ulrike Vedder, *Das Testament als literarisches Dispositiv. Kulturelle Praktiken des Erbes in der Literatur des 19. Jahrhunderts* (Munich: Fink, 2011); Catherine Gallagher, *The Body Economic: Life, Death, and Sensation in Political Economy and the Victorian Novel* (Princeton, NJ: Princeton University Press, 2007); Brantlinger, *Fictions*.

97. This point is noted by Martin Stingelin, "Seldwyla als inszenierte semiotische Welt. Ein unvermuteter schweizerischer Schauplatz der Zeichenreflexion," *Inszenierte Welt. Theatralität als Argument literarischer Texte*, ed. Ethel Matala de Mazza and Clemens Pornschlegel (Freiburg im Breisgau: Rombach, 2003), 209–26.

98. Here and in the following: Kreienbrock, "Kreditparadies."

99. Gottfried Keller, *The People of Seldwyla* in *A Selection of His Tales*, trans. Kate Freiligrath Kroeker (London, 1891), 48.

100. Keller, *The People of Seldwyla*, 46.

101. Keller, *The People of Seldwyla*, 46.

102. Keller, *The People of Seldwyla*, 47.

103. Keller, *The People of Seldwyla*, 47.

104. Keller, *The People of Seldwyla*, 49.

105. Keller, *The People of Seldwyla*, 52–53.

106. Keller, *The People of Seldwyla*, 53.

107. Keller, *The People of Seldwyla*, 50.

108. Fritz Breithaupt, "Homo Oeconomicus (Junges Deutschland, Psychologie, Keller und Freytag)," in *1848 und das Versprechen der Moderne*, ed. Jürgen Fohrmann and Helmut J. Schneider (Würzburg: Königshausen & Neumann, 2003), 85.

109. On *Seldwyla* as a critique of epistemology see Stingelin, "Seldwyla."

110. Gottfried Keller, *Seldwyla Folks: Three Singular Tales*, trans. Wolf von Schierbrand (New York: Brentano's, 1919), 1.

111. Vedder, *Testament*, S. 315.

112. Keller, *Seldwyla Folks*, 54.

113. Keller, *Seldwyla Folks*, 54.

114. Keller, *Seldwyla Folks*, 55.

115. Keller, *Seldwyla Folks*, 21–22. This, too, was a matter of judgment. As Ulrike Vedder notes, seven hundred gulden was "not an all too grand inheritance." Vedder, *Testament*, 317.

116. Vedder, *Testament*, 317–18, esp. note 131.

117. Keller, "Regel Amrain und ihr Jüngster," in Keller, *Die Leute von Seldwyla*, 162.

118. Keller, "Regel Amrain," 214.

119. Keller, "Regel Amrain," 180.

120. Keller, "Regel Amrain," 197.

121. Keller, "Regel Amrain," 208.

122. Keller, "Regel Amrain," 208.

123. Keller, "Regel Amrain," 214.

124. Goldstein, *Post-Revolutionary Self*, 4.

125. Keller, *Seldwyla Folk,* 159. The story was inspired by a note in the September 30, 1847, edition of the Zurich Friday paper. Morgenthaler, *Apparat,* 17.

126. Keller, *Seldwyla Folk,* 112.

127. Keller, *Seldwyla Folk,* 206–7.

128. Keller, *Seldwyla Folk,* 212.

129. Keller, *Seldwyla Folk,* 233.

130. Keller, *Seldwyla Folk,* 244.

131. Gottfried Keller, *Martin Salander,* trans. Kenneth Halwas (London: John Calder, 1964), 207. The translation has been modified to more accurately reflect the original "Börsenspiel," an expression used to condemn the allegedly unfettered financial sphere.

132. On the male economy of honor see Pierre Bourdieu, "The Economy of Symbolic Goods," in *Practical Reason: On the Theory of Action* (Stanford, CA: Stanford University Press, 1998), 92–123. On the honor of businesspeople see Goldberg, *Honor,* 56–59; Erika Vause, "'He Who Rushes to Riches Will Not Be Innocent': Commercial Values and Commercial Failure in Postrevolutionary France," *French Historical Studies* 35 (2012): 321–49.

133. Schweizerisches Bundesarchiv, BAR E22#1000/134#2611*, Az. 6.7.4, Petition des thurgauischen landwirthschaftlichen Vereins, unterstützt durch die landwirthschaftliche Gesellschaft des Kantons St. Gallen, betreffend den Entwurf eines eidgen. Schuldbetreibungs- und Konkursgesetzes, St. Gallen 1887. Eduard Thurneysen, *Eine offene Wunde unsers Volkslebens: Ein Wort wider das Bürgschaftswesen in unserer Zeit* (Zurich, 1888); Gottlieb Egli, "Die Bürgschaft," *Der Gerichtssaal: Zeitschrift für schweizerische Civil- und Strafrechtspflege* 4, no. 14 (February 16, 1887): 72–73.

134. Alexander Isler, "Die Gefahren der Bürgschaft. Warnung vor ihrer Eingehung und Vorschläge zur Abhülfe," *Schweizerische Zeitschrift für Gemeinnützigkeit* 26 (1887): 339.

135. Keller, *Martin Salander,* 22.

136. Keller, *Martin Salander,* 18.

137. Keller, *Martin Salander,* 83.

138. Keller, *Martin Salander,* 89.

139. Keller, *Martin Salander,* 66–67.

140. Keller, *Martin Salander,* 178.

141. Keller, *Martin Salander,* 223–25.

142. On Swiss merchants and slaveholders in Brazil see Béatrice Ziegler, "Sklaven und Moderne—eine unerträgliche, aber nicht unverträgliche Kombination," in *Die Moderne in Lateinamerika. Zentren und Peripherien des Wandels,* ed. Stephan Scheuzger and Peter Fleer (Frankfurt am Main: Vervuert, 2009), 139–60.

143. Keller, *Martin Salander,* 56.

144. Keller, *Martin Salander,* 39.

145. Keller, *Martin Salander,* 20.

146. Keller, *Martin Salander,* 81.

147. Widmer, *Die Schweiz in der Wachstumskrise,* 136–39; Loeffler, "Finanzkapital."

148. Keller, *Martin Salander,* 230.

149. See STAZH P 37a on mutual aid associations for restoring damaged credit. The source includes two cases from 1843 in the Kyburg-Winterthur area and one from 1856 in Guntalingen in which associations were founded with the aim of reorganizing property relations and re-establishing the regions' collapsed credit systems.

150. See Hansjörg Siegenthaler, "Martin Salander in seiner Zeit" (lecture, Zentralbibliothek Zürich, November 16, 2004), www.gottfriedkeller.ch/aufsatz/salander.htm.

151. For an interpretation of the novel as an expression of "disillusionment" see Michael Böhler, "'Fettaugen über einer Wassersuppe'—frühe Moderne-Kritik beim späten Gottfried Keller. Die Diagnose einer Verselbständigung der Zeichen und der Ausdifferenzierung autonomer Kreisläufe," in *Nachmärz. Der Ursprung der ästhetischen Moderne in einer nachrevolutionären Konstellation*, ed. Thomas Koebner and Sigrid Weigel (Opladen: Springer, 1996), 295.

152. Patrick Eiden-Offe, "Die Immobilienblase von Münsterburg. Gottfried Keller unterscheidet guten von bösem Kapitalismus," *Merkur* 715 (2008): 1155–59; Leo Löwenthal, "Gottfried Keller—die bürgerliche Regression," in *Erzählkunst und Gesellschaft. Die Gesellschaftsproblematik in der deutschen Literatur des 19. Jahrhunderts* (Neuwied am Rhein: Luchterhand, 1971), 206–25.

153. On Switzerland in the world economy of the 1880s, which was sometimes referred to as "globalized," see Thomas David, "Croissance économique et mondialisation. Le cas de la Suisse, 1870–1914," in *Globalisierung—Chancen und Risiken: die Schweiz in der Weltwirtschaft, 18.–20. Jahrhundert*, ed. Hans-Jörg Gilomen, Margrit Müller, and Béatrice Veyrassat (Zurich: Chronos, 2003), 145–69; Veyrassat, "Wirtschaft und Gesellschaft."

154. Keller, *Martin Salander*, 83, translation modified.

155. Keller, *Martin Salander*, 231. Satire was the genre of bankruptcy because its essence was to point out failures. See Brantlinger, *Fictions*, 41–42.

156. Walter Benjamin, "Gottfried Keller: In Honor of a Critical Edition of His Works," in *Selected Writings* (Cambridge, MA: Belknap Press, 2005), 2:54.

157. Collectif Révoltes logiques, "Deux ou trois choses que l'historien social ne veut pas savoir," *Le mouvement social* 100 (1977): 30.

158. Wolfgang Schieder, *Anfänge der deutschen Arbeiterbewegung: Die Auslandsvereine im Jahrzehnt nach der Julirevolution von 1830* (Stuttgart: Klett, 1963), 51. Waltraud Seidel-Höppner's monumental biography was a breakthrough in research on Weitling. See Waltraud Seidel-Höppner, *Wilhelm Weitling (1808–1871). Eine politische Biografie*, 2 vols. (Frankfurt am Main: Lang, 2014). I also referred to Otto Brugger, *Geschichte der deutschen Handwerkervereine in der Schweiz 1836–1843. Die Wirksamkeit Weitlings (1841–1843)* (Bern: Haupt, 1932); Waltraud Seidel-Höppner, *Wilhelm Weitling—der erste deutsche Theoretiker und Agitator des Kommunismus* (Berlin (GDR): Dietz, 1961); Marc Vuilleumier, "Weitling, les communistes allemands et leurs adeptes en Suisse. Quelques Documents (1843–1847)," *Revue européenne des sciences sociales* 11, no. 29 (1973): 37–100; Ahlrich Meyer, *Frühsozialismus. Theorien der sozialen Bewegung 1789–1848* (Freiburg im Breisgau: Alber, 1977); Hans-Arthur Marsiske, *"Wider die Umsonstfresser": Der Handwerkerkommunist Wilhelm Weitling* (Hamburg: Ergebnisse-Verlag, 1986); Hans-Arthur Marsiske, *Eine Republik der Arbeiter ist möglich. Der*

Beitrag Wilhelm Weitlings zur Arbeiterbewegung in den Vereinigten Staaten von Amerika 1846–1856 (Hamburg: Hamburger Institut für Sozialforschung, 1990); Jürg Haefelin, *Wilhelm Weitling. Biographie und Theorie—Der Zürcher Kommunistenprozess von 1843* (Bern: Lang, 1986).

159. Though my reading of Weitling's work focuses on debts, it nevertheless draws considerably on Ahlrich Meyer's analysis of revolutionary subjectivity in the early industrial period. Meyer, "Massenarmut und Existenzrecht"; Meyer, *Frühsozialismus*, 157–222, esp. 214–22.

160. This distinguished the ideas about money substitutes and systems of accounting that he sought to institute in the United States from the bank projects of Pierre-Joseph Proudhon, though he quoted the latter in various contexts. Marsiske, *Republik der Arbeiter*, 196–99. Weitling was never a follower of Proudhon. See Seidel-Höppner, *Weitling*, 1:244, 2:1327–28.

161. On communism as a politics of the present see Meyer, *Frühsozialismus*, 209.

162. On the "utopian impulse" see Fredric Jameson, *Archaeologies of the Future: The Desire Called Utopia and Other Science Fictions* (London: Verso, 2005); see also Karl Mannheim, *Ideology and Utopia* (New York: Harcourt, Brace & Co., 1954 [1929]), chap. 4 ("The Utopian Mentality").

163. Wilhelm Weitling, *Das Evangelium des armen Sünders* (Reinbek bei Hamburg: Rowohlt, 1971 [1843/45]), 15.

164. Weitling, *Evangelium*, 15–16.

165. Olivier Chaïbi, "Entre crédit public et crédit mutuel: un aperçu des théories du crédit au XIXe siècle," *Romantisme* 151 (2011): 53–66.

166. Schiedt, *Die Welt neu erfinden*, 85–100; Wirth, *Johann Jakob Treichler*, 118–20.

167. Schieder, *Anfänge*, 97, 105.

168. Sigrid Wadauer, *Die Tour der Gesellen. Mobilität und Biographie im Handwerk vom 18. bis zum 20. Jahrhundert* (Frankfurt am Main: Campus, 2005), 127–57.

169. Founded in Geneva in 1838, the Grütli assocation was only open to Swiss journeymen and explicitly positioned itself against the associations dominated by German migrants in western Switzerland. See Felix Müller, "Zur Kultur und zum gesellschaftlichen Bewußtsein handwerklicher Arbeiter im dritten Viertel des 19. Jahrhunderts—Vereinsleben und Diskussionen im Schweizerischen Grütliverein," in *Handwerker in der Industrialisierung. Lage, Kultur und Politik vom späten 18. bis ins frühe 20. Jahrhundert*, ed. Ulf Engelhardt (Stuttgart: Klett-Cotta, 1984), 552–88.

170. Seidel-Höppner, *Weitling*, 1:207; Brugger, *Handwerkervereine*, chap. 2.

171. Seidel-Höppner, *Weitling*, 1:276–94; Schieder, *Anfänge*, 122–23; Brugger, *Handwerkervereine*, 95, 136.

172. Seidel-Höppner, *Weitling*, 1:234; Schieder, *Anfänge*, 153; Meyer, *Frühsozialismus*, 184; Brugger, *Handwerkervereine*, 88.

173. Seidel-Höppner, *Weitling*, 1:567.

174. Karin Huser, *Bildungsort, Männerhort, politischer Kampfverein: Deutsche Arbeitervereine in der Schweiz—"Eintracht Zürich" (1840–1916)* (Zurich: Chronos, 2012), 58–68; Seidel-Höppner, *Weitling*, 1:597–610.

175. Observers of the time agreed that the arrest targeted less Weitling and

more the radical Julius Fröbel, a thorn in the side of the conservative member of cantonal government Johann Caspar Bluntschli. See Seidel-Höppner, *Weitling*, 1: chap. 5; Haefelin, *Weitling*; Marc Vuilleumier, "De l'usage du communisme dans la Suisse des années 1840," in *Histoire(s) de l'anticommunisme en Suisse–Geschichte(n) des Antikommunismus in der Schweiz*, ed. Michel Caillat (Zurich: Chronos, 2009), 47–60. The insight was made earliest by Brugger, *Handwerkervereine*, 171–74.

176. Here and in the following: Wilhelm Weitling, *Gerechtigkeit. Ein Studium in 500 Tagen: Bilder der Wirklichkeit und Betrachtungen des Gefangenen—Nachwort von Ahlrich Meyer* (Berlin: Karin Kramer, 1977 [1845?]), 150–51.

177. On the journeyman's passport see Simona Cerutti, "Travail, mobilité et légitimité: suppliques au roi dans une société d'Ancien Régime (Turin, XVIIIe siècle)," *Annales HSS* 65, no. 3 (2010): 588–92; Alain Cottereau, "Droit et bon droit: un droit des ouvriers instauré, puis évincé par le droit du travail (France, XIX siècle)," *Annales HSS* 57, no. 6 (2002): 1536–40. Published in France and Switzerland around the same time as Weitling's short books was [René-Louis] Villermé, *Tableau de l'état physique et moral des ouvriers employés dans les manufactures de coton, de laine et de soie. Ouvrage entrepris par ordre et sous les auspices de l'Académie des Sciences Morales et Politiques, par V., membre de cette Académie, tome second* (Paris, 1840), chaps. 5 and 6.

178. Seidel-Höppner, *Weitling*, 1:49; Schieder, *Anfänge*, 52; Brugger, *Handwerkervereine*, 160.

179. *Die junge Generation* 11 (November 1842): 187. On Weitling's use of natural law in his arguments, which drew on François-Noël Babeuf and contained ideas from the late Enlightenment, see Meyer, *Frühsozialismus*, 160–70. In contrast to Babeuf, Weitling believed less in natural equality and more in establishing equal conditions for all different individuals. Seidel-Höppner, *Weitling*, 1:316–17.

180. Wilhelm Weitling, *Garantien der Harmonie und Freiheit*, with an introduction and annotations by Fr. Mehring (Berlin: Vorwärts, 1908 [1842]), 63, 238.

181. Weitling, *Garantien*, 54.

182. *Die junge Generation* 2, no. 5 (May 1843): 71. Despite how this text may appear, Weitling's depictions of misery were not informed by a belief that worsening material conditions would automatically lead to resistance and he thus did not welcome them. See *Die junge Generation* 12 (December 1842): 202.

183. *Die junge Generation* 2, no. 3 (March 1843): 40. For narratives about more concealed forms of poverty in Switzerland see Weitling, *Garantien*, 103.

184. Wilhelm Weitling, *Die Menschheit, wie sie ist und wie sie sein sollte* (Reinbek bei Hamburg: Rowohlt, 1971 [1839]), 145.

185. Weitling, *Garantien*, 96–97.

186. Thomas Welskopp, *Das Banner der Brüderlichkeit: Die deutsche Sozialdemokratie vom Vormärz bis zum Sozialistengesetz* (Bonn: Dietz, 2000), 622–39; Gareth Stedman Jones, "Rethinking Chartism," in *Languages of Class: Studies in English Working Class History 1832–1982* (Cambridge: Cambridge University Press, 1983), 119; Richard Biernacki, *The Fabrication of Labor: Germany and Britain, 1640–1914* (Berkeley: University of California Press, 1995), 395–99.

187. Weitling, *Garantien*, 59.

188. *Die junge Generation* 7 (July 1842): 127.

189. *Die junge Generation* 8 (August 1842): 134.
190. *Die junge Generation* 8 (August 1842): 135.
191. The author of the article is difficult to determine. Seidel-Höppner suggests it may have been August Becker, a former student of theology in Giessen and a friend of Weitling during his exile in Geneva. See Seidel-Höppner, *Weitling*, 1:241.
192. *Die junge Generation* 4 (April 1842): 62.
193. Lorenz von Stein, for instance, wrote, "Only the deplorable confusion of a Weitling and his comrades could speak of the rights of a thieving proletariat." Lorenz von Stein, *Geschichte der sozialen Bewegung in Frankreich von 1789 bis auf unsere Tage* (Munich: Drei Masken, 1921 [1842]), 1:115.
194. *Die junge Generation* 10 (October 1842). Similar: *Die junge Generation* 2, no. 4 (April 1843): 51.
195. Weitling, *Garantien*, 79.
196. Weitling, *Garantien*, 191.
197. References to Proudhon in letters to Weitling suggest that Weitling corresponded with Proudhon. Schieder, *Anfänge*, 255.
198. Weitling, *Garantien*, 191.
199. *Die junge Generation*, 2, no. 3 (March 1843): 40–48; *Die junge Generation* 2, no. 5 (May 1843): 71–73.
200. Johann Caspar Bluntschli, *Die Kommunisten in der Schweiz nach den bei Weitling vorgefundenen Papieren. Wörtlicher Abdruck des Kommissionalberichtes an die H. Regierung des Standes Zürich* (Zurich, 1843), 106–15. On the letters' context see Seidel-Höppner, *Weitling*, 1:537.
201. Weitling, *Menschheit*, 150–51.
202. On Bürkli's plans for Fourier-style credit reforms see Schiedt, *Welt neu erfinden*, 81–100.
203. *Die junge Generation* 3 (March 1842): 60. This position was also taken by some representatives of the early workers' movement in France. See Jacques Rancière, *Proletarian Nights: The Workers' Dream in Nineteenth-Century France*, trans. John Drury (London: Verso, 2012), 47–48.
204. *Bete und arbeite! Ein wohlgemeintes Wort an die Arbeiter gegeben in drei gekrönten Volksschriften über den Segen der Sparkassen: Zur Förderung des geistigen und materiellen Wohles aller Arbeiter, herausgegeben von der Seidenindustrie-Gesellschaft des Kantons Zürich*, 2nd ed. (Stäfa, 1859), 48.
205. Weitling, *Evangelium*, 89.
206. Mannheim, *Ideology and Utopia*, 191, 195.
207. Weitling, *Evangelium*, 64–66, 95–97, 101. The article "Die Kommunion und die Kommunisten" in *Hülferuf der deutschen Jugend* triggered a lengthy debate carried out both in the paper and outside it. See *Der Hülferuf der deutschen Jugend* 3 (November 1841): 33–39.
208. Weitling, *Evangelium*, 127.
209. *Die junge Generation* 12 (December 1842): 193.
210. On French workers' associations' responses to this issue see Rancière, *Nights*, chap. 5.
211. Weitling, *Evangelium*, 124.
212. Here and in the following: Weitling, *Evangelium*, 130.

213. The commerce hours had already been discussed in *Menschheit*, 163–66. Models of "work money" were common in the workers' movement and had been around in England since the 1830s. Nigel Dodd, *The Social Life of Money* (Princeton, NJ: Princeton University Press, 2014), 342–46. For a detailed analysis of Weitling's concept of "commerce hours" and its reception see Seidel-Höppner, *Weitling*, 1: chap. 4.

214. Weitling, *Garantien*, 155.

215. Seidel-Höppner, *Weitling*, 1:346–47.

216. Weitling, *Garantien*, 157.

217. Weitling, *Garantien*, 157–58.

218. Weitling, *Garantien*, 164.

219. Weitling, *Garantien*, 170–71.

220. Seidel-Höppner, *Weitling*, 2: chap. 10. See P. W. Annenkow, "Bericht über eine Sitzung des Kommunistischen Korrespondenzkomitees in Brüssel, 30. März 1846," *Der Bund der Kommunisten. Dokumente und Materialien*, vol. 1, *1836–1849*, ed. Institut für Marxismus-Leninismus beim ZK der SED (Berlin (GDR): Dietz, 1970), 301–5, and Wilhelm Weitling, "Brief aus Brüssel an Moses Hess in Verviers, 31. März 1846," in Institut für Marxismus-Leninismus beim ZK der SED, *Der Bund der Kommunisten*, 307–8.

221. "Reform-Pläne," *Der Urwähler. Organ des Befreiungsbundes: Eine Wochenschrift* 4 (October 1848), 25–27. On the paper *Der Urwähler*, which Weitling edited in autumn 1848, see Seidel-Höppner, *Weitling*, 2:1137–63.

222. "Association," *Der Urwähler. Organ des Befreiungsbundes: Eine Wochenschrift* 3 (October 1848): 18. Seidel-Höppner, *Weitling*, 2:1162.

223. Seidel-Höppner, *Weitling*, 2:1257–59, 2:1396–1403; Marsiske, *Republik*, 198–202, 203–8.

224. Marsiske, *Republik*, 62–65; Seidel-Höppner, *Weitling*, 2:1404–37.

225. Marsiske, *Republik*, 102.

226. Marsiske, *Republik*, 153–54.

227. New York Public Library (hereafter NYPL), Wilhelm Weitling Papers, Box 3, Eintrag of June 7, 1866. On Weitling's final years, which he spent on the Lower East Side, see Seidel-Höppner, *Weitling*, 2:1485–1560.

228. NYPL, Wilhelm Weitling Papers, Box 3, Eintrag of December 21, 1869.

229. NYPL, Wilhelm Weitling Papers, Box 3, Eintrag of December 22, 1869.

230. Adalbert Evers and Helga Nowotny, *Über den Umgang mit Unsicherheit: Die Entdeckung der Gestaltbarkeit von Gesellschaft* (Frankfurt am Main: Suhrkamp, 1987), 91; Ewald, *L'état*, 82.

231. Outside of law because of the charge of vagrancy, outside of rationality because of the charge of foolishness. John Seed, "'Free Labour = Latent Pauperism': Marx, Mayhew, and the 'Reserve Army of Labour' in Mid-Nineteenth-Century London," in *The Peculiarities of Liberal Modernity in Imperial Britain*, ed. Simon Gunn and James Vernon (Berkeley: University of California Press, 2011), 54–71.

232. Salomon Schinz, "Das höhere Gebirg des Kantons Zürich, und ökonomisch-moralischer Zustand der Bewohner, mit Vorschlägen der Hülfe und Auskunft für die bey mangelnder Fabrik-Arbeit brotlose Uebervölkerung, [. . .] in der Synodal-Rede 1817," *Der gemeinnützige Schweizer* 3 (1818): 184, 198.

233. Schinz, "Gebirg," 180.
234. Schinz, "Gebirg," 183.
235. Eva Sutter, *"Ein Act des Leichtsinns und der Sünde": Illegitimität im Kanton Zürich: Recht, Moral und Lebensrealität (1800–1860)* (Zurich: Chronos, 1995).
236. Meyer, "Massenarmut und Existenzrecht," 131.
237. *Die junge Generation* 11 (November 1842): 182–84.
238. Weitling, *Gerechtigkeit*, 100, 154–57; NYPL, Weitling Papers, box 3, entry of October 21, 1858, in which Weitling contemplates whether to raise his child as a Christian. See also Meyer, *Frühsozialismus*, 159.
239. Luc Boltanski, *On Critique: A Sociology of Emancipation*, trans. Gregory Elliott (Cambridge: Polity, 2011).
240. Manfred Hettling and Stefan-Ludwig Hoffmann, eds., *Der bürgerliche Wertehimmel: Innenansichten des 19. Jahrhunderts* (Göttingen: Vandenhoeck & Ruprecht, 2000); Stäheli, *Spectacular Speculation;* Ulrich Bröckling, *The Entrepreneurial Self: Fabricating a New Type of Subject*, trans. Steven Black (London: Sage, 2015).
241. Fraisse, "Feministische Singularität"; Rancière, *Nights*.

Chapter 5

1. Here and in the following: Staatsarchiv Basel-Stadt (hereafter: STABS) Justiz J6, Einzelne Rehabilitationen 1846–1856, Rehabilitationsgesuch Rudolf Hunziker, September 5, 1856, emphasis in original.

2. Regina Wecker, "1833 bis 1910: Die Entwicklung zur Grossstadt," in *Basel—Geschichte einer städtischen Gesellschaft*, ed. Georg Kreis and Beat von Wartburg (Basel: Merian, 2000), 199.

3. STABS Justiz J6, Einzelne Rehabilitationen 1846–1856, Gutachten Rehabilitationsgesuch Rudolf Hunziker, October 10, 1854.

4. Marx, "James Mill," 214.

5. STABS Justiz J7, Einzelne Concurssachen 1853–1862, Verhör mit Rudolf Vest, December 2, 1857, emphasis in original.

6. STABS Justiz J7, Einzelne Concurssachen 1853–1862, Polizeidirektion, December 2, 1857.

7. The reports of the civil court administration researched here are not entirely comprehensive. I transcribed the reports from the years 1841 to 1851 and then a considerably lesser sample of reports from 1862 to 1863 to enable diachronic comparison. The 151 police interrogations conducted between 1841 and 1869 make up all protocols contained in the archives I consulted, but it is assumed that not all protocols have been preserved.

8. STABS GA REG 2d, 3–1. 2. 13, Handakten Zivilgerichtspräsident, Staatsanwalt J. J. Burckhardt an Gerichtsämter, November 11, 1868.

9. STABS Justiz J 8, Collocationen 1860–1880, C. F. Burckhardt für die Amtsgerichte an den Kleinen Rat, December 19, 1867.

10. Desrosières, *The Politics of Large Numbers*, 277.

11. Boltanski, *On Critique*, 69–70.

12. Poovey, *Genres of the Credit Economy*. On budgeting as a source of legiti-

macy in the nineteenth century see Carruthers and Espeland, "Accounting for Rationality"; Eve Chiapello, "Die Geburt des Kapitalismus aus der Idee der doppelten Buchführung," *WestEnd. Neue Zeitschrift für Sozialforschung* 4 (2007): 64–95.

13. Stoler, *Archival Grain.*

14. *Bevölkerungs-Aufnahme von Basel-Stadttheil am 3. Februar 1847. Bericht an den E. E. Kleinen Rath* (Basel, 1848), table I; *Bevölkerungs-Aufnahme von Basel-Stadttheil am 10. December 1860. Bericht an den E. E. Kleinen Rath* (Basel, 1861), table I; Hermann Kinkelin, *Die Bevölkerung des Kantons Basel-Stadt am 1. Dezember 1870. Bericht an den E. E. Kleinen Rath* (Basel, 1872), table I; see also Philipp Sarasin, *Stadt der Bürger. Struktureller Wandel und bürgerliche Lebenswelt—Basel 1870–1900,* 1st ed. (Basel: Helbing & Lichtenhahn, 1990), 433; Argast, *Staatsbürgerschaft und Nation,* 228.

15. Martin Schaffner, *Die Basler Arbeiterbevölkerung im 19. Jahrhundert. Beiträge zur Geschichte ihrer Lebensformen* (Basel: Helbing & Lichtenhahn, 1972), 2, and the statistics in the previous endnote.

16. Beginning in 1866, people born in Basel became citizens without fee; for others, though, the fees were still quite high. See Argast, *Staatsbürgerschaft and Nation,* 238–40.

17. Philipp Sarasin, *Stadt der Bürger. Bürgerliche Macht und städtische Gesellschaft. Basel 1846–1914,* 2nd ed. (Göttingen: Vandenhoeck & Ruprecht, 1997), 35.

18. Sarasin, *Stadt der Bürger,* 2nd ed., 49.

19. Martin Schaffner, "Geschichte des politischen Systems von 1833 bis 1905," *Das politische System Basel-Stadt. Geschichte, Strukturen, Institutionen, Politikbereiche,* ed. Lukas Burckhardt (Basel: Helbing & Lichtenhahn, 1984), 43–45; Barbara Keller, *Von Speziererinnen, Wegglibuben und Metzgern. Lebensmittelhandwerk und -handel in Basel 1850–1914* (Zurich: Chronos, 2001), 43–51.

20. Here and in the following: Sarasin, *Stadt der Bürger,* 2nd ed., 51–52; Schaffner, *Arbeiterbevölkerung,* 2.

21. On consumer staples see Keller, *Speziererinnen;* Martin Leschhorn, "Mikrohistorische Studie des Basler Metzgergewerbes in der ersten Hälfte des 19. Jahrhunderts" (unpublished thesis, Historisches Seminar Universität Basel, 1998).

22. Sarasin, *Stadt der Bürger,* 2nd ed., 74–75.

23. Sarasin, *Stadt der Bürger,* 2nd ed., 52.

24. Peter Stolz, *Basler Wirtschaft in vor- und frühindustrieller Zeit. Ökonomische Theorie und Wirtschaftsgeschichte im Dialog* (Zurich: Schulthess, 1977), 80–81.

25. On the basis of the census counts from 1837, 1847, and 1870, I assume that the number of households increased in the city (excluding the three rural municipalities). The census counts defined a household as having its own oven or means of cooking (which poses the problem that a boarder was counted in it and not for themself). I am aware that this is not an ideal unit of measure, but I find that it says more than the mere count of individuals in the population. The count of bankruptcies before 1847 was conducted on the basis of schedules of claims in the city (excluding the three rural municipalities) contained in the administrative reports, and after 1847 on the basis of the "completed bankruptcies" (many negotiations over bankruptcies overlapped two years), under

which waivers of inheritance are also counted. Here, too, the two sources are not equivalent and should only be compared with caution. *Bevölkerungs-Aufnahme 1837 von Basel-Stadttheil am 25. Jenner 1837. Bericht an den E. E. Kleinen Rath* (Basel, 1838); *Bevölkerungs-Aufnahme 1847*; Hermann Kinkelin, *Bevölkerung; Verwaltungsbericht[e] des Kleinen Raths an E. Großen Rath des Kantons Basel-Stadt vom Jahr* . . . [1840 ff.]; *Berichte des Appellations-Gerichts des Kantons Basel-Stadt über die Justizverwaltung vom Jahr [1847–1870], an den Großen Rath.*

26. I compiled a sample of about 40 percent of the bankruptcies listed in the bankruptcy register along with their concrete occupations. The purpose was to balance out the reports of the court administration and look beyond the classes of occupations used in their statistics. I elected not to come up with my own classes of occupations. The sample consists of 708 entries between 1840 and 1869 for people with last names between A and D and S and V; thus, it is not random in the strict sense. I do not view it as anything more than an illustrative supplement.

27. Stanziani, *Rules of Exchange*, 42.

28. Here and in the following: *Berichte des Appellations-Gerichts des Kantons Basel-Stadt über die Justizverwaltung vom Jahr [1847–1870], an den Großen Rath.* See Keller, *Speziererinnen*; STABS Gerichtsarchiv G hoch 2, 1, Fallitenregister 1806–1891; *Bevölkerungs-Aufnahme 1847*, xvii–xxvii; *Bevölkerungs-Aufnahme 1860*, xix–xxv.

29. That it was difficult to get footing without one's own means was expressed by both citizens and residents in police interrogations, such as in STABS Justiz J 7, Einzelne Concurssachen 1836–1845, Verhör mit Andreas Imhof, April 28, 1841; Verhör mit Georg Strub, February 17, 1845; Verhör mit Rudolf Kübler, February 17, 1845; STABS Justiz J 7, Einzelne Concurssachen, 1846–1852, Verhör mit Friedrich Hodel, Schuhmacher, April 20, 1846; Verhör mit Rudolf Karli, July 10, 1846; Verhör mit Mathias Rimensperger, October 15, 1847; Verhör Valentin Rimmensperger, October 16, 1847; Verhör mit Christoph Kehlstadt, January 22, 1849; Verhör mit Johann Heinrich Gaß-Sixt, October 10, 1849; Verhör mit Christoph Grey, December 11, 1849; STABS Justiz J 8, Collocationen 1852–1859, Verhör mit Heinrich Thurneißen, April 15, 1854; Verhör mit Sebastian Huber, October 18, 1854; Verhör mit Christoph Lehr, April 15, 1859; STABS Justiz J 7, Einzelne Concurssachen, 1863–68, Verhör mit Andreas Steiger, April 24, 1864; Verhör mit Heinrich Lacher, May 9, 1865; Verhör mit Rudolf Buchmann-Faesch, Oktober 3, 1866. There are many more examples.

30. Keller, *Speziererinnen*, 226–29. For comparisons with other parts of Europe see Heinz-Gerhard Haupt and Geoffrey Crossick, *Die Kleinbürger. Eine europäische Sozialgeschichte* (Munich: C. H. Beck, 1998), 240–48; Spiekermann, *Basis der Konsumgesellschaft*, 481–85, 566–69; Ira Spieker, *Ein Dorf und sein Laden: Warenangebot, Konsumgewohnheiten und soziale Beziehungen um die Jahrhundertwende* (Münster: Waxmann, 2000).

31. STABS Justiz J 6, Einzelne Rehabilitationen, Rehabilitationsgesuch Jakob Henz, August 9, 1847.

32. The source material analyzed here confirms the conclusion drawn by Fontaine, *Moral Economy*, 282–83.

33. STABS Justiz J 7, Einzelne Konkurssachen 1836–1845, Verhör mit Rudolf Vest, May 8, 1845.

34. STABS Justiz J 8, Collocationen der Stadt 1840–1851, Bericht January 13, 1848.

35. See for instance the southern German discussion during the Napoleonic Wars: Ute Planert, *Der Mythos vom Befreiungskrieg. Frankreichs Kriege und der deutsche Süden: Alltag—Wahrnehmung—Deutung 1792–1841* (Stuttgart: Ferdinand Schöningh, 2007), 240.

36. For instance, in the 1840s: STABS Justiz J 7, Einzelne Concurssachen 1836–1845, Verhör mit Christoph Gysin, May 8, 1845; Verhör mit Rudolf Kübler, February 17, 1845; STABS Justiz J 7, Einzelne Concurssachen 1846–1852, Verhör mit Friedrich Klingelfuß, February 4, 1846; Verhör mit Otto Landerer, February 6, 1846; Verhör mit Friedrich Otto, February 6, 1846; Verhör mit Johann Georg Oppermann, October 18, 1847; Verhör mit Johann Jacob Reischacher-Hirt, January 26, 1848; Verhör mit Johann Jakob Schlueb, April 11, 1848; Verhör mit Johann Carl Peschel, April 30, 1849.

37. STABS Justiz J 8, Collocationen 1840–1851, Bericht January 26, 1847.

38. STABS Justiz J 8, Collocationen 1840–1851, Bericht January 26, 1847, Bericht April 19, 1847.

39. STABS Justiz J 8, Collocationen 1840–1851, Bericht July 13, 1847.

40. STABS Justiz J 8, Collocationen 1840–1851, Bericht July 10, 1848.

41. STABS Justiz J 8, Collocationen 1840–1851, Bericht January 13, 1848.

42. STABS Justiz J 8, Collocationen 1840–1851, Bericht January 19, 1849.

43. STABS Justiz J 8, Collocationen 1840–1851, Bericht July 2, 1849.

44. STABS Justiz J 8, Collocationen 1840–1851, Bericht July 2, 1849.

45. STABS Justiz J 8, Collocationen 1840–1851, Bericht July 1, 1851.

46. STABS Justiz J 8, Collocationen 1840–1851, Bericht May 5, 1845.

47. STABS Justiz J 8, Collocationen 1840–1851, Bericht May 5, 1845.

48. STABS Justiz J 8, Collocationen 1840–1851, Bericht January 7, 1850.

49. STABS Justiz J 8, Collocationen 1840–1851, Bericht January 13, 1848.

50. STABS Justiz J 7, Einzelne Concurssachen 1846–1852, Polizeirapport von Wachtmeister Thommen über Abraham Sixt, April 23, 1846.

51. STABS Justiz J 8, Collocationen 1840–1851, Bericht January 13, 1848. During the interrogation, however, Samuel Barth said that he needed the horses in question for business trips, had not owned a full team for a long time, and had no intention of acting "fraudulently." STABS Justiz J 7, Einzelne Concurssachen, 1846–1852, Verhör mit Samuel Barth, January 22, 1848.

52. STABS Gerichtsarchiv G hoch 1–3: Zivilgericht, Album der Falliten, Mai 1861–Juni 1866, S. 116, Eintrag vom February 21, 1862.

53. STABS Justiz J 8, Collocationen 1840–1851, Bericht July 16, 1845 zu J. J. Sandreuter, Schuhmacher.

54. See Leonore Davidoff, "'Alte Hüte'. Öffentlichkeit und Privatheit in der feministischen Geschichtsschreibung," *L'Homme: Zeitschrift für feministische Geschichtswissenschaft* 4, no. 2 (1993): 7–36; see also, from a different theoretical perspective, Bourdieu, *Theory of Practice*, chap. 2.

55. Beispielsweise STABS Justiz J 8, Collocationen 1840–1851, July 16, 1845,

Bericht über Johann Georg David; October 26, 1846, Bericht über Heinrich Plattner.

56. For the 1840s see: STABS Justiz J 8, Collocationen 1840–1851, Bericht über Friedrich Weber-Lichtenhan, August 17, 1842; Bericht über Heinrich Märklin, October 27, 1845; Bericht über Otto Landmann, January 31, 1846; Bericht über Jacob Märklin, July 6, 1846; Bericht über Heinrich Plattner, October 26, 1846; Bericht über Niklaus Feßler, January 26, 1847; Bericht über Johann Rudolf Fäß-Bachmann, April 19, 1847; Bericht über Johannes Krattiger, April 19, 1847; Bericht über Friedrich Plattner, January 19, 1849; Bericht über Heinrich Rublin, January 19, 1849; Bericht über Niklaus Schimpf, October 6, 1849. Numerous examples from the 1850s and 1860s could be listed.

57. In a study on a later period, Christoph Guggenbühl traces the boom of newly opened inns to the economic crisis around 1880. According to him, precarious independence was an individual attempt at managing the crisis. See Christoph Guggenbühl, "Heaven or Hell? The Public House and its Social Perception in Nineteenth- and Early Twentieth-Century Switzerland," in *Eating Out in Europe. Picnics, Gourmet Dining and Snacks since the Late Eighteenth Century*, ed. Marc Jacobs and Peter Scholliers (Oxford: Berg, 2003), 100–101.

58. STABS Justiz J 8, Collocationen 1840–1851, Bericht October 20, 1841.

59. STABS Justiz J 8, Collocationen 1840–1851, Bericht über Adam Scherb, January 22, 1844.

60. STABS Justiz J 8, Collocationen 1840–1851, Bericht über Martin Rapp, October 27, 1845.

61. STABS Justiz J 8, Collocationen 1840–1851, Bericht über den Hafner Richard Landerer, July 17, 1843.

62. Bernhard Kleeberg, "Schlechte Angewohnheiten. Einleitung," in *Schlechte Angewohnheiten. Eine Anthologie 1750–1900*, ed. Bernhard Kleeberg (Frankfurt am Main: Suhrkamp, 2012), 9–66.

63. STABS Justiz J 8, Collocationen der Stadt, 1840–1851, Bericht October 5, 1848.

64. An intact moral reputation, especially as concerns sexuality, was significant for others' estimations of one's discipline and trustworthiness in both the early modern period and the nineteenth century. See Fontaine, *Moral Economy*, 275–77; Berghoff, "Markterschließung und Risikomanagement."

65. On the importance of words like "scheming," "treacherously," "rascal," and other metaphors of "deception" in this context, see Ditz, "Shipwrecked," 59.

66. STABS Justiz J 8, Collocationen 1840–1851, Bericht July 16, 1845.

67. STABS Justiz J 8, Collocationen 1840–1851, Bericht über Christoph Heckendorn, August 17, 1842.

68. Sarasin, *Stadt der Bürger*, 2nd ed., 265.

69. STABS Justiz J 8, Collocationen 1840–1851, Bericht July 13, 1847.

70. STABS Justiz J 7, Einzelne Concurssachen 1853–1862, Verhör mit Alexander Hill, August 23, 1855.

71. STABS Justiz J 7, Einzelne Concurssachen 1853–1862, Polizeidirektor Bischoff an Kleinen Rat, August 23, 1855. A copy is also contained in STABS Justiz J 1 Allgemeine Betreibungs- und Konkurssachen, Liquidationen 1828–1936.

72. STABS Justiz J 8, Collocationen 1852–1859, Justizkollegium an Bürgermeister und Kleinen Rat, January 9, 1855.

73. STABS Justiz J 1 Allgemeine Betreibungs- und Konkurssachen, Liquidationen 1828–1936, Zivilgerichtspräsident Schnell an Kleinen Rat, September 10, 1855.

74. STABS Justiz J 8, Collocationen 1852–1859, Justizkollegium an Kleinen Rat, September 25, 1855.

75. This time it wasn't the police making the complaint, but the prosecutor. See STABS GA-REG 2d 3–1, 2. 13, Handakten von Zivilgerichtspräsident NN, Staatsanwalt JJ Burckhardt an die Gerichtsämter, November 26, 1868.

76. Though these files were not an innovation of the 1860s. Called the "album of the bankrupt," sources exist from the 1830s and then again for the 1860s. Sources are lacking for the 1840s and 1850s, but it seems probable that such comprehensive files were compiled on bankrupts for the entire period. Nevertheless, a comparison between the files and the reports sent to the government for the 1860s suggest that, in contrast to the 1840s, more weight was given to the bankrupts' versions of events. See STABS Gerichtsarchiv G hoch 1, Stadtgericht, Zivilgericht: Fallimentsfälle.

77. STABS Justiz J 8, Collocationen 1860–1880, Bericht über Adolf Spiller, April 12, 1862. Further references to slipshod accounting: Bericht über den Schneider Hieronymus Bischoff, January 2, 1862; Bericht über die Spezereihändlerin Anna Maria Meyer geb. Müller, January 2, 1862; Bericht über den Orchestermusiker und Zigarrenhändler Bernhard Loebe, July 30, 1862; Bericht über den Schneider Johann Friedrich Ungerer, April 12, 1862; Bericht über den Holzhändler und Kostgeber Peter Madörin, April 12, 1862. As early as the 1850s, the sources discuss lapidary accounting; for instance, STABS Justiz J 8, Collocationen 1852–1859, Verhör mit David Wilhelm Goetz, November 27, 1856, and STABS Justiz J 8, Collocationen 1852–1859, Bericht über Franz Brändlin, March 2, 1858: both state: "As usual, there's no accounting at all."

78. On the first see STABS Justiz J 8, Collocationen 1860–1880, Bericht über Bernhard Loebe, July 30, 1862. The entry in the "album of bankrupts" spoke of "stories with a shopgirl": STABS Gerichtsarchiv G hoch 1, Stadtgericht, Zivilgericht, Fallimentsfälle 3, 121. On the second point see STABS Justiz J 8, Collocationen 1860–1880, Bericht über Hieronymus Bischoff, January 2, 1862.

79. STABS Gerichtsarchiv G hoch 1, Stadtgericht, Zivilgericht: Fallimentsfälle, Album der Falliten May 1861–July 2 1866, 137.

80. STABS Justiz J 8, Collocationen 1860–1880, C. F. Burckhardt für die Amtsgerichte an Kleinen Rat, December 19, 1867.

81. STABS Justiz J 8, Collocationen 1860–1880, Bericht July 7, 1876.

82. STABS Justiz J 8, Collocationen 1852–1859, Präsident des Justizkollegs Christ an Bürgermeister und Kleinen Rat, May 16, 1854.

83. Carolyn Steedman, "Enforced Narratives: Stories of Another Self," in *Feminism and Autobiography: Texts, Theories, Methods*, ed. Tess Cosslett, Celia Lury, and Penny Summerfield (London: Routledge, 2000), 28.

84. STABS Justiz J 7, Einzelne Concurssachen, 1846–1852, Verhör mit Rudolf Hunziker, January 11, 1850.

85. For instance, STABS Justiz J 7, Einzelne Concurssachen 1836–1845,

Verhör mit Christoph Gysin, May 8, 1845; Verhör mit Rudolf Kübler, February 17, 1845; STABS Justiz J 7, Einzelne Concurssachen 1846–1852, Verhör mit Friedrich Klingelfuß, February 4, 1846; Verhör mit Otto Landerer, February 6, 1846; Verhör mit Friedrich Otto, February 6, 1846; Verhör mit Johann Georg Oppermann, October 18, 1847; Verhör mit Johann Jacob Reischacher-Hirt, January 26, 1848; Verhör mit Johann Jacob Schlueb, April 11, 1848; Verhör mit Johannes Löliger, November 28, 1848; Verhör mit Johann Carl Peschel, April 30, 1849; STABS Justiz J 7, Einzelne Concurssachen 1853–1862, Verhör mit Leon Gyger, February 20, 1860 (with a reference to the Panic of 1857); STABS Justiz J 8, Collocationen 1852–1859, Verhör mit David Wilhelm Goetz, November 27, 1856 (with reference to rising prices in the 1850s); STABS Justiz J 7, Einzelne Concurssachen 1863–1868, Verhör mit Carl Schmidt-Stengelen, September 22, 1863 (with reference to the American Civil War); Verhör mit Theophil Emanuel Falkner-Mösch, December 7, 1865; Verhör mit Carl Haas-Honold, September 18, 1866; Verhör mit Krescentia Grübler-Meier, November 25, 1868.

86. Here and in the following: STABS Justiz J 7, Einzelne Concurssachen 1846–1852, Verhör mit Friedrich Hodel, April 20, 1846.

87. On the attitudes, aspirations, and (politicized) distastes of cobblers in the nineteenth century see the classic article Eric Hobsbawm and Joan W. Scott, "Political Shoemakers," *Past and Present* 89 (1980): 86–114.

88. See STABS Justiz J 7, Einzelne Concurssachen 1836–1845, Verhör mit Christoph Holzach, July 22, 1845; STABS Justiz J 7, Einzelne Concurssachen 1846–1852, Verhör mit Jacob Meyer, October 16, 1847, who stated that he had ventured too far in his "false trust."

89. STABS Justiz J 8, Collocationen 1852–1859, Verhör mit Christoph Lehr, April 15, 1859. Similar is STABS Justiz J 7, Einzelne Concurssachen 1863–1868, Verhör mit dem Bäcker Simon Bertschmann, November 30, 1863; Verhör mit dem Bäcker Emil Höpfner, November 30, 1863.

90. STABS Justiz J 7, Concurssachen 1846–1852, Verhör mit Valentin Rimmensperger, October 16, 1847. Similar is Verhör mit Heinrich Bruckner, July 14, 1848.

91. STABS Justiz J 8, Collocationen 1852–1859, Verhör mit Heinrich Thurneißen, April 15, 1854.

92. STABS Justiz J 7, Einzelne Konkurssachen 1836–1845, Verhör mit Christoph Holzach, July 22, 1845; STABS Justiz J 7, Einzelne Concurssachen 1846–1852, Verhör mit Johann Jacob Reischacher-Hirt, January 26, 1848; Verhör mit Anton Emdtinger, October 11, 1850 (one of the few cases in which claims made by a bank are mentioned); STABS Justiz J 8, Collocationen 1852–1859, Verhör mit Rudolf Jeremias Christ, November 10, 1854; STABS Justiz J 7, Einzelne Concurssachen 1863–1868, Verhör mit Georg Enderle, September 28, 1868.

93. STABS Justiz J 7, Einzelne Concurssachen 1846–1852, Verhör mit Friedrich Löliger, November 28, 1848.

94. STABS Justiz J 7, Einzelne Concurssachen 1846–1852, Verhör mit Johann Heinrich Gaß-Sixt, October 10, 1849.

95. STABS Justiz J 7, Einzelne Concurssachen 1836–1845, Verhör mit Christoph Gysin Rosenburger, May 8, 1845. Similar is the interrogation with Ludwig Schwörer, November 4, 1845.

96. STABS Justiz J 6, Einzelne Rehabilitationen 1846–1856, Gesuch von Franz Schaub, June 7, 1851; Gesuch von Johann Ludwig Hagmann, June 27, 1851. STABS Justiz J 7, Konkurssachen 1853–1862, Verhör mit Simon Eger, September 24, 1855; Verhör mit Andreas Weiss, November 30, 1857.

97. STABS Justiz J 7, Einzelne Concurssachen 1863–1868, Verhör mit Caspar Debrunner, December 27, 1864.

98. On the inns as an institution in Switzerland see Kümin, "Das vormoderne Wirtshaus"; Guggenbühl, "Heaven."

99. On multiple occasions, bankrupts defended themselves against accusations of alcoholism by claiming that they were forced to go to inns to maintain contact with customers and suppliers. For instance, STABS Justiz J 7, Einzelne Concurssachen 1836–1845, Verhör mit Andreas Imhof, April 28, 1841; Verhör mit Johann Jacob Müller, August 26, 1842; Verhör mit Johann Georg David, undated [1845]; STABS Justiz J 8, Collocationen 1852–1859, Verhör mit Samuel Rebsamen, December 15, 1856.

100. Philipp Sarasin, "Sittlichkeit, Nationalgefühl und frühe Ängste vor dem Proletariat. Untersuchungen zu Politik, Weltanschauung und Ideologie des Basler Bürgertums in der Verfassungskrise von 1846/47," *Basler Zeitschrift für Geschichte und Altertumskunde* 84 (1984): 51–127.

101. Here and in the following: STABS Justiz J 7 Einzelne Concurssachen 1846–1852, Verhör mit Jakob Christoph Grey, May 28, 1849.

102. The following passages, as well as the approach throughout the entire chapter, is heavily indebted to David Sabean's work on the household as a site of exchange where "claims and obligations, demands and prestations, rights and performances" found their place. Sabean, *Property*, 123.

103. Amanda Vickery, "His and Hers: Gender, Consumption and Household Accounting in Eighteenth-Century England," *Past and Present* Supplement 1 (2006): 13–14; Lemire, *Business of Everyday Life*, 17; Honegger and Heintz, "Zum Strukturwandel," 16–17; Michelle Perrot, "Rebellische Weiber. Die Frau in der französischen Stadt des 19. Jahrhunderts" [1979], in Honegger and Heintz, *Listen der Ohnmacht*, 75–77.

104. STABS Justiz J 7, Einzelne Concurssachen 1836–1845, Verhör mit Johannes Haering, November 3, 1845.

105. On the gendered roles that position women as subjects with knowledge of economic facts while men claim ignorance of them see Bourdieu, "Economy of Symbolic Goods," 169.

106. STABS Justiz J 7, Einzelne Concurssachen 1846–1852, Verhör mit Johann Lucas Kappeler, February 3, 1847; Verhör mit Isaac Thommen, February 11, 1848; Verhör mit Johannes Löliger, whose wife filed for divorce because of domestic violence, November 28, 1848; Verhör mit Jacob Mangold, January 24, 1849; Verhör mit Johann Heinrich Gaß-Sixt, October 10, 1849; STABS Justiz J 8, Collocationen 1852–1859, Verhör mit Rudolf Jeremias Christ, November 10, 1854.

107. For instance, STABS Justiz J 7, Einzelne Concurssachen 1846–1852, Verhör mit Niklaus Riedtmann, July 5, 1849; STABS Justiz J 8, Collocationen 1852–1859, Verhör mit Abraham Salathe, July 8, 1853; STABS Justiz J 7, Einzelne Konkurssachen 1863–1868, Verhör mit Heinrich Lacher, May 9, 1865.

108. STABS Justiz J 8, Collocationen 1840–1851, Verhör mit Benedikt Rebsamen, January 16, 1851.

109. STABS Justiz J 7 Einzelne Concurssachen 1846–1852, Verhör mit Urs Joseph Kuhn, July 14, 1846. Similarly, STABS Justiz J 8, Collocationen 1852–1859, Verhör mit Jakob Jenny, July 7, 1853. The argument of male cluelessness is expressed in exaggerated fashion in the interrogation of Alois Stocker, whose wife was responsible for the accounts, and, as he discovered, funneled off money and burned through it all in the canton of Ticino. STABS Justiz J 8, Collocationen 1840–1851, Verhör mit Alois Stocker, July 2, 1851.

110. STABS Justiz J 8, Collocationen 1840–1851, Bericht über Rudolf Carly, July 6, 1846.

111. STABS Justiz J 7, Einzelne Concurssachen 1846–1852, Verhör mit Rudolf Karli, July 10, 1846.

112. Karin Hausen, "Die Polarisierung der 'Geschlechtscharaktere'—eine Spiegelung der Dissoziation von Erwerbs- und Familienleben," in *Sozialgeschichte der Familie in der Neuzeit Europas: Neue Forschungen*, ed. Werner Conze (Stuttgart: Klett, 1976), 363–93.

113. Karin Hausen, "Wirtschaften mit der Geschlechterordnung. Ein Essay," in *Geschlechterhierarchie und Arbeitsteilung: zur Geschichte ungleicher Erwerbschancen von Männern und Frauen*, ed. Karin Hausen (Göttingen: Vandenhoeck & Ruprecht, 1993), 40–67.

114. Highlighting the ideological function of the "home" is not to imply that this was the only type of household around at the time, nor is it an affirmation of Otto Brunner's model of an "old European economics." On the contrary, it signifies a normative fiction prevalent in the mid-nineteenth century that writers drew on for argumentative effect. See Otto Brunner, "Das 'ganze Haus' und die alteuropäische 'Ökonomik,'" in *Neue Wege der Verfassungs- und Sozialgeschichte*, (Göttingen: Vandenhoeck & Ruprecht, 1968 [1956]), 103–27. For criticism of Brunner see Claudia Opitz, "Neue Wege der Sozialgeschichte? Ein kritischer Blick auf Otto Brunners Konzept des 'ganzen Hauses,'" *Geschichte und Gesellschaft* 20 (1994): 88–98; Valentin Groebner, "Außer Haus: Otto Brunner und die alteuropäische Ökonomik," *Geschichte in Wissenschaft und Unterricht* 46, no. 2 (1995): 69–80. For a sociological analysis of the rhetoric of the "domestic world" see Luc Boltanski and Laurent Thévenot, *On Justification: The Economies of Worth.* trans. Catherine Porter (Princeton, NJ: Princeton University Press, 2006 [1991], 164–78.

115. STABS Justiz J 8, Collocationen 1852–1859, Verhör mit Gottlieb Burckhardt, July 26, 1851.

116. STABS Justiz J 7, Einzelne Concurssachen 1836–1845, Verhör mit Andreas Imhof, April 28, 1841.

117. Expectations of the bankrupts themselves, which, however, were often not met: "I had a large family and my earlier hopes that my stepchildren would support me in my work were dashed and they cost me much money and turned out bad." STABS Justiz J 7, Einzelne Concurssachen 1836–1845, Verhör mit Andreas Imhof, April 28, 1841.

118. STABS Justiz J 8, Collocationen 1852–1859, Verhör mit Franz Brändlin, March 9, 1858 (first quote); STABS Justiz J 7, Einzelne Konkurssachen 1863–

1868, Verhör mit Carl Goetz, April 29, 1867; Verhör mit Johann Leonhard Jordan, May 9, 1865 (second quote); Verhör mit Rudolf Buchmann-Faesch, October 3, 1866.

119. STABS Justiz J 6, Einzelne Rehabilitationen 1846–1856, Rehabilitationsgesuch Johann Jakob Basler, December 25, 1849.

120. STABS Justiz J 6, Einzelne Rehabilitationen 1846–1856, Gutachten Rehabilitationsgesuch Rudolf Hunziker, October 10, 1854.

121. Andreas Heusler, "Das Weibergutsprivileg und das schweizerische Concursgesetz," *Zeitschrift für schweizerisches Recht,* n.s., 23 (1882): 17–53. Heusler was primarily thinking of Basel's laws.

122. Peter Münch, *Aus der Geschichte des Basler Privatrechts im 19. Jahrhundert. Traditionsbewusstsein und Fortschrittsdenken im Widerstreit* (Basel: Helbing & Lichtenhahn, 1991), 138.

123. Regina Wecker, "Geschlechtsvormundschaft im Kanton Basel-Stadt. Zum Rechtsalltag von Frauen—nicht nur im 19. Jahrhundert," in *Weiblich—männlich, feminine—masculin. Geschlechterverhältnisse in der Schweiz: Rechtsprechung, Diskurs, Praktiken,* ed. Rudolf Jaun and Brigitte Studer (Zurich: Chronos, 1995), 90.

124. Annamarie Ryter, *Als Weibsbild bevogtet. Zum Alltag von Frauen im 19. Jahrhundert—Geschlechtsvormundschaft und Ehebeschränkungen im Kanton Basel-Landschaft* (Liestal: Verlag des Kantons Basel-Landschaft, 1994), 120.

125. Regina Wecker calculated that the thirty-seven million Swiss francs administered by the guilds in 1876 is equivalent to about 1.5 billion francs today. See Wecker, "Geschlechtsvormundschaft," 90.

126. Wecker, "Geschlechtsvormundschaft," 93.

127. Margareth Lanzinger, "Variationen des Themas: Mitgiftsysteme," in Lanzinger et al., *Aushandeln von Ehe,* 469–92; Angiolina Arru, "Die nicht bezahlte Mitgift. Ambivalenzen und Vorteile des Dotalsystems im ausgehenden 19. und beginnenden 20. Jahrhundert," *L'Homme: Zeitschrift für feministische Geschichtswissenschaft* 22 (2011): 55–69; Angiolina Arru, "'Schenken heißt nicht verlieren': Kredite, Schenkungen und die Vorteile der Gegenseitigkeit in Rom im 18. und 19. Jahrhundert," *L'Homme: Zeitschrift für feministische Geschichtswissenschaft* 9 (1998): 232–51.

128. *Der Statt Basel Statuta und Gerichtsordnung . . . ,* Basel 1849, §279.

129. STABS Justiz J 6, Einzelne Rehabilitationen 1764–1845, Gutachten zur Rehabilitation von Joseph Dollinger, September 13, 1827, emphasis in original.

130. Rathschlag und Gesetzesentwurf über die rechtlichen Folgen von Fallimenten, dem E. Großen Rath vorgelegt am 3. Dezember 1866 (= Rathschlag 357), 13.

131. Münch, *Geschichte,* 144.

132. Münch, *Geschichte,* 143.

133. Wecker, "Geschlechtsvormundschaft."

134. STABS Justiz J 6, Einzelne Rehabilitationen 1846–1856; the first attempt at rehabilitation is mentioned in Johannes Braun, Zunftmeister zur Safran, an Justizkollegium, January 23, 1849; Abraham Wertenberg an Justizkollegium, February 24, 1849.

135. STABS Justiz J 6, Einzelne Rehabilitationen 1846–1856, Rehabilitationsgesuch Abraham Wertenberg, December 29, 1848.

136. STABS Justiz J 6, Einzelne Rehabilitationen 1846–1856, Gutachten des Justizkollegiums, January 25, 1849. See also the settling of accounts with his creditors, January 13, 1849.

137. STABS Justiz J 6, Einzelne Rehabilitationen 1846–1856, Johannes Braun, Zunftmeister zur Safran, an Justizkollegium, January 23, 1849.

138. Here and in the following: STABS Justiz J 6, Einzelne Rehabilitationen 1846–1856, Gutachten des Justizkollegiums, January 25, 1849.

139. Here and in the following: STABS Justiz J 6, Einzelne Rehabilitationen 1846–1856, Abraham Wertenberg an Justizkollegium, February 14, 1849.

140. STABS Justiz J 6, Einzelne Rehabilitationen 1846–1856, Justizkollegium an den Vormund der Frau, Apotheker Kellermann, undated.

141. STABS Justiz J 6, Einzelne Rehabilitationen 1846–1856, Vormund Kellermann an Justizkollegium, May 11, 1849.

142. STABS Justiz J 6, Einzelne Rehabilitationen 1846–1856, Gerichtsschreiber an Ratsherr, May 10, 1849.

143. On this point in nineteenth-century Switzerland, see Krattiger, *Mündigkeit.*

144. David W. Sabean and Simon Teuscher, "Kinship in Europe: A New Approach to Long-Term Development," in *Kinship in Europe. Approaches to Long-Term Development (1300–1900)*, ed. David W. Sabean, Simon Teuscher, and Jon Mathieu (New York: Berghahn, 2007), 1–32; David W. Sabean, "Kinship and Class Dynamics in Nineteenth-Century Europe," in *Kinship in Europe. Approaches to Long-Term Development (1300–1900)*, ed. David W. Sabean, Simon Teuscher, and Jon Mathieu (New York: Berghahn, 2007), 301–13.

145. Writing about the expansion of capitalism, David Sabean attributes considerable significance to the abolition in Württemberg of the "Kriegsvögte," official gender guardians for women, because now women were compelled to guarantee the debts of their husbands. Sabean, *Property*, 19–20, 211–214, 430.

146. Joris, "Kinship and Gender, 231–57.

147. Zimmer, *A Contested Nation*; Tanner, "Ein Staat nur für die Hablichen?"; Schaffner, "Direkte Demokratie."

148. *Verwaltungsberichte.*

149. STABS Justiz J 6, Einzelne Rehabilitationen 1846–1856, Rehabilitationsgesuch Rudolf Hunziker, September 5, 1854.

150. STABS Justiz J 6, Einzelne Rehabilitationen 1846–1856, Rehabilitationsgesuch Jakob Lüdin, December 14, 1849.

151. STABS Justiz J 6, Einzelne Rehabilitationen 1846–1856, Rehabilitationsgesuch Benedikt Cyprian, February 29, 1856.

152. STABS Justiz J 6, Einzelne Rehabilitationen 1846–1856, Rehabilitationsgesuch Johann Ludwig Hagemann, June 27, 1851.

153. STABS Justiz J 6, Einzelne Rehabilitationen 1846–1856, Gutachten zu Heinrich Thommen, June 15, 1850; Gutachten zu Heinrich Thommen, 14. Januar 1851. Similar: STABS Justiz J 6, Einzelne Rehabilitationen 1846–1856, first rejected (January 17, 1855), then accepted (September 22, 1855) opinion on Friedrich Gerster.

154. STABS Justiz J 6, Einzelne Rehabilitationen 1846–1856, Gutachten zu J. J. Grieder, December 8, 1856. On the significance of municipal poor relief for naturalization in Basel in the nineteenth century Argast, *Staatsbürgerschaft*, 250–53.

155. STABS Justiz J 6, Einzelne Rehabilitationen 1846–1856, ablehnendes Gutachten zu Hermann Wetzel, October 25, 1851.

156. On "unsocial sociability" (Immanuel Kant) in bourgeois self-identity in nineteenth-century Switzerland see Manfred Hettling, "Bürgerlichkeit. Eine ungesellige Geselligkeit," in *Eine kleine Geschichte der Schweiz: Der Bundesstaat und seine Traditionen*, ed. Manfred Hettling et al. (Frankfurt am Main: Suhrkamp, 1998), 227–64.

157. See, for example, STABS Justiz J 6, Einzelne Rehabilitationen 1846–1856, Gutachten zu Eucharius Holzach, June 10, 1846; Martin Schneiter (undated, unclear if rehabilitation was granted); Johann Deck, January 17, 1849 (petition turned down); Abraham Wertenberg, February 21, 1849; Daniel Hülfsegger, June 25, 1851; Jakob Henz Jr., June 28, 1851; Heinrich Stohler, November 1, 1851; Heinrich Schwarz, February 25, 1852; Jakob Konrad Ungerer, June 26, 1852; Heinrich Leuber, January 12, 1856; Rudolf Stauber, June 14, 1856. The list could be expanded.

158. STABS Justiz J 6, Einzelne Rehabilitationen 1846–1856, Gutachten zu Rudolf Stauber, June 10, 1856; Gutachten zu Ludwig Kehlstadt, January 31, 1854.

159. The "Justizkollegium," which reported to the ruling Small Council, was the governing body responsible for legal issues until the introduction of departments in the Basel administration in 1875. See Stefan Nellen, "Schreibakte: Eine Mediengeschichte der Verwaltung, Basel 1803–1960" (PhD diss., University of Basel, 2012), 86, 102.

160. STABS Justiz J 6, Einzelne Rehabilitationen 1846–1856, Gutachten zu Jakob Konrad Ungerer, June 22, 1852. Similar considerations in the decision on the case of Johann Deck, January 6, 1849.

161. For instance, STABS Justiz J 6, Einzelne Rehabilitationen 1846–1856, Gutachten zu Johannes Bader, January 22, 1846; Gutachten zu Eucharius Holzach, June 10, 1846; Gutachten zu Johann Friedrich Hurst, October 22, 1846; Rehabilitationsgesuch Niklaus Stockmeier, September 18, 1852.

162. STABS Justiz J 6, Einzelne Rehabilitationen 1846–1856, Gutachten zu Franz Schaub, June 10, 1851.

163. STABS Justiz J 6, Einzelne Rehabilitationen 1846–1856, Rehabilitationsbeschluss Franz Schaub, June 14, 1851.

164. STABS Justiz J 6, Einzelne Rehabilitationen 1846–1856, Gutachten zu J. Meyerhofer-Glatt, September 23, 1856.

165. STABS Justiz J 6, Einzelne Rehabilitationen 1846–1856, Rehabilitationsgesuch Jakob Lüdin, December 14, 1849.

166. STABS Justiz J 6, Einzelne Rehabilitationen 1846–1856, Rehabilitationsgesuch Friedrich Ungerer, June 5, 1855. Silk weaver Johann Jacob Stohler, too, took about nine months to hand in the required documentation. STABS Justiz J 6, Einzelne Rehabilitationen 1846–1856, Gutachten zu Johann Jacob Stohler, December 30, 1856.

167. Rathschlag 357, 10, 4.

168. Rathschlag 357, 10.

169. I draw here on the analogous observation on liberal poor relief in Topalov, *Naissance du chômeur*, 203–209.

170. Rathschlag 357, 11.

171. As discussed in chapter 4, the metaphor was applied to divergent objects over a lengthy period of time: Beachy, "Bankruptcy and Social Death"; Bernet, "'Der bürgerliche Tod.'"

172. As evidenced by a review of cases conducted by the government in the 1880s. Ratschlag und Entwurf eines Großratsbeschlusses betreffend die bürgerliche Stellung der Falliten. Dem Großen Rate vorgelegt den 4. Dezember 1893 (= Ratschlag 968), 4.

173. Boltanski, *On Critique*, 78–81.

174. Marx, "James Mill," 214.

Chapter 6

1. Schweizerisches Bundesarchiv (hereafter BAR) BAR E22#1000/134#2645*, Az. 6.7.4, Alfred Brüstlein, lecture "Vorläufige Vorschläge für die Revision des Betreibungsgesetzes," held on June 18, 1893 at Bern's Handels- und Industrieverein.

2. BAR E22#1000/134#2609*, Az. 6.7.4, Johann Jakob Oberer to Bundesrat Louis Ruchonnet, Liestal, June 2, 1882.

3. In 1885, a sample year that I will continue to work with below, 97,097 dunning letters for debts not guaranteed by real estate were issued in the canton of Zurich and 14,740 for debts guaranteed by real estate. The canton's population was 332,605. *Fünfundfünfzigster Rechenschaftsbericht des Obergerichtes und des Kassationsgerichtes an den h. Kantonsrath des Kantons Zürich über das Jahr 1885* (Winterthur, 1886), 25, 28; *Statistische Mittheilungen betreffend den Kanton Zürich. Beilage zum Rechenschaftsbericht des Regierungsrathes für das Jahr 1885* (Winterthur, 1886), 165.

4. On bourgeois opinions on underclass fashion in the nineteenth century see Sabina Brändli, *"Der herrlich biedere Mann": Vom Siegeszug des bürgerlichen Herrenanzuges im 19. Jahrhundert* (Zurich: Chronos, 1998), 222–31; on the underclasses' symbolic and objective transactions see Hans Medick, "Plebejische Kultur, plebejische Öffentlichkeit, plebejische Ökonomie: Über Erfahrungen und Verhaltensweisen Besitzarmer und Besitzloser in der Übergangsphase zum Kapitalismus," in *Klassen und Kultur: Sozialanthropologische Perspektiven in der Geschichtsschreibung*, ed. Robert Berdahl and David W. Sabean (Frankfurt am Main: Syndikat, 1982), 157–204; Braun, *Industrialisierung*, 101–17.

5. Laurence Fontaine and Jürgen Schlumbohm, "Household Strategies for Survival: An Introduction," in Fontaine and Schlumbohm, *Household Strategies for Survival*, 14; Andrea Hauser, *Dinge des Alltags. Studien zur historischen Sachkultur eines schwäbischen Dorfes* (Tübingen: Tübinger Vereinigung für Volkskunde, 1994), 262.

6. Crowston, *Credit, Fashion, Sex*; Hans Medick, "Eine Kultur des Ansehens. Kleider und ihre Farben in Laichingen 1750–1820," *Historische Anthropologie* 2, no. 2 (1994): 193–212.

7. Albert Vogt, ed., *Unstet. Lebenslauf des Ärbeeribuebs, Chirsi- und Geschirrhausierers Peter Binz von ihm selbst erzählt* (Zurich: Chronos, 1995 [1895?]),

252–53. Peter Binz (1846–1906) was from Welschenrohr in the canton of Solothurn; he wandered through Francophone Switzerland, Germanophone Switzerland, and southern Germany all the way to Marseille.

8. Laurence Fontaine, ed., *Alternative Exchanges: Second-Hand Circulations from the Sixteenth Century to the Present* (New York: Berghahn, 2008), 127–51; Jon Stobart and Ilja Van Damme, "Introduction: Modernity and the Second-Hand Trade: Themes, Topics and Debates," in *Modernity and the Second-Hand Trade: European Consumption Cultures and Practices, 1700–1900*, ed. Jon Stobart and Ilja Van Damme (Houndsmill: Palgrave Macmillan, 2010), 1–15.

9. Hauser, *Dinge des Alltags*, 379–83.

10. Hauser, *Dinge des Alltags*, 262; Andrea Hauser, "Prekäre Subsistenz: Eine historische Rückschau auf dörfliche Bewältigungsstrategien im Umbruch zur Industrialisierung," in *Prekär arbeiten, prekär leben. Kulturwissenschaftliche Perspektiven auf ein gesellschaftliches Phänomen*, ed. Irene Götz and Barbara Lemberger (Frankfurt am Main: Campus, 2009), 263–85.

11. Henare, Holbraad, and Wastell, Introduction to *Thinking through Things*, 1–31.

12. Marx, *Capital, Vol. 1*, 125.

13. Georg Lukács, *History and Class Consciousness: Studies in Marxist Dialectics*, trans. Rodney Livingston (Cambridge, MA: MIT Press, 1971 [1923/1967]).

14. Sigfried Giedion, *Mechanization Takes Command: A Contribution to Anonymous History* (Oxford: Oxford University Press, 1948); Christoph Asendorf, *Batteries of Life: On the History of Things and Their Perception in Modernity*, trans. Don Reneau (Berkeley: University of California Press, 1993).

15. On this point with a focus on the history of things see Frank Trentmann, "Materiality in the Future of History: Things, Practices, and Politics," *Journal of British Studies* 48, no. 2 (2009): 283–307; Leora Auslander, "Beyond Words," *American Historical Review* 110 (2005): 1015–45. On credit and consumption in particular see Finn, *The Character of Credit*; Jan Logemann, "Introduction: Toward a Global History of Credit in Modern Consumer Societies," in *The Development of Consumer Credit in Global Perspective: Business, Regulation, and Culture*, ed. Jan Logemann (New York: Palgrave Macmillan, 2012), 1–20.

16. Chris Otter, "Making Liberalism Durable: Vision and Civility in the Late Victorian City," *Social History* 27 (2002): 4–5; Mauss, *Gift*, 61.

17. Xifaras, *La propriété*, 254.

18. On the history of this notion and its expansion in the liberal tradition see Margaret Jane Radin, *Reinterpreting Property* (Chicago: University of Chicago Press, 1993), 35–71.

19. Habermas, *Thieves in Court*, 41.

20. Hauser, *Dinge des Alltags*, 247, 391.

21. *Zur Volksabstimmung vom 17. November 1889. Ein Wort der Aufklärung an das Schweizervolk zum Bundesgesetze über Schuldbetreibung und Konkurs* (Bern, 1889), 6.

22. Here and in the following: *Zur Volksabstimmung*, 8.

23. Friedrich Schlatter, *Schuldbetreibung und Konkurs nach schweizerischem Recht: Ein Wegweiser* (Zurich, 1893), 20.

24. von Meiss, *Das Pfand-Recht*, 16.

25. Annelise Riles, "Collateral Expertise: Legal Knowledge in the Global

Financial Markets," *Current Anthropology* 51, no. 6 (2010): 797; Riles, *Collateral Knowledge*, 91–92, 165, 224.

26. Mauss, *Gift*.

27. Mauss, *Gift*, 61–64.

28. Friedrich Nietzsche, *On the Genealogy of Morality*, ed. Keith Ansell-Pearson, trans. Carol Diethe (Cambridge: Cambridge University Press, 2006), 40 (2nd essay, §4); Friedrich Locher, *Die Mängel des zürcherischen Konkursprozesses und deren Abhülfe* (Zurich, 1856), 9.

29. Nietzsche, *Genealogy*, 45 (2nd essay, §8).

30. Nietzsche, *Genealogy*, 35 (2nd essay, §1).

31. On references to Rome in nineteenth-century jurisprudence and historiography see Vismann, *Files*, xiii–xiv and chap. 2.

32. Marilyn Strathern, *Property, Substance, and Effect: Anthropological Essays on Persons and Things*, (London 1999), 95–105, 154–155, 155 (quote).

33. The collateral mode can thus be thought of in analogy to Arjun Appadurai's concept of the commodity as the moment in the life of things when their exchangeability becomes its primary attribute. The exchangeability of the collateral objects, however, had its own peculiarities, as the following will show. In a parallel discussion on sociological theory, Ute Tellmann writes that collateral is a distinct economic object that cannot be equated with the commodity form. Arjun Appadurai, "Introduction: Commodities and the Politics of Value," in *The Social Life of Things: Commodities in Cultural Perspective*, ed. Arjun Appadurai (Cambridge: Cambridge University Press, 1986), 13. Ute Tellmann, "Schulden—eine Kultursoziologie ökonomischer Dinge," in *Kultursoziologie im 21. Jahrhundert*, ed. Joachim Fischer and Stephan Moebius (Wiesbaden: Springer, 2014), 159–70.

34. Riles, *Collateral Knowledge*, 54–57.

35. Fontaine, *The Moral Economy*, 100–101 on early modern pawning.

36. Adam Reed, "Documents Unfolding," in *Documents: Artifacts of Modern Knowledge*, ed. Annelise Riles (Ann Arbor: University of Michigan Press, 2006), 158–77; Lisa Gitelman, *Paper Knowledge: Toward a Media History of Documents* (Durham, NC: Duke University Press, 2014), chap. 1.

37. Stadtarchiv Zürich (hereafter StadtAZH) VI.AS.C.120. Pfandbuch der gerichtlichen Pfandrechte der Gemeinde Aussersihl, 1852–1857.

38. Reed, "Documents Unfolding." The admission forms of the Burghölzli psychiatric ward from the early twentieth century have also been analyzed as "media of cases unfolding." See Brigitta Bernet, *Schizophrenie. Entstehung und Entwicklung eines psychiatrischen Krankheitsbildes um 1900* (Zurich: Chronos, 2013), 239–41.

39. Here and in the following: STAZH B XI Notariat Zürich-Aussersihl 10.27.

40. On collateral as a legal fiction see Riles, *Collateral Knowledge*, chap. 4.

41. Uniform title registers based on land value assessments were decades-long, and sometimes centuries-long projects of the nation state. Switzerland never implemented such a comprehensive, standardized register. On the history of title registers in Switzerland see Speich, "Das Grundbuch."

42. See, for example, *Wohlmeinender Rath und freundliche Erinnerung an die Landleute des Kantons Zürich; in Bezug auf eine kanzleiische Schuldenbereinigung*

und eine neue Geld-Anleihungs-Einrichtung (n.p., 1818); Farner, *Das zürcherische Bodenkreditwesen*; Arthur Wolf, *Ueber den Zinsfuss ländlicher Grundpfanddarlehen mit besonderer Berücksichtigung der zürcherischen Verhältnisse* (Bern: Scheitlin & Co., 1912) (Schweizerische Blätter für Wirtschafts- und Sozialpolitik).

43. *Schweizerisches Volksblatt vom Bachtel*, no. 92, November 17, 1867, emphasis in original.

44. Schaffner, *Die demokratische Bewegung*, chap. 3. For contemporaneous accounts of the credit crisis in agriculture in the 1860s see H. Schoffer, *Die landwirtschaftliche Kreditkrisis unserer Tage. Eine populäre Darstellung der betreffenden Verhältnisse und Beleuchtung der Hülfsmittel. Im Auftrag des Vereins für Landwirthschaft und Gartenbau im Kanton Zürich*, 2nd ed. (Zurich, 1867 [1866?]); Farner, *Der Schuldbriefverkehr.* In the late 1880s, one writer sought the cause of the poverty of Zurich's rural Aussersihl municipality in the property speculation of the 1850s, which burst a decade later with many bankruptcies in its wake: E. Wiesendanger, *Geschichte der Gemeinde Aussersihl. Vortrag, gehalten vor der "Gemeinnützigen Gesellschaft Aussersihl"* (Aussersihl, 1888).

45. See Riles, *Collateral Knowledge*, 164–65; Riles, "Collateral Expertise," 802.

46. STAZH Y 27.C.: Obergericht, Schuldbetreibung, Varia 1864–1865, Anna Jäggli an das Obergericht Zürich, September 5, 1864.

47. Schuldbetreibungsgesetz 1851, §91; Gwalter, *Schuldbetreibungsgesetz*, 196.

48. Schuldbetreibungsgesetz 1851, §86 on the chance of debtors to "explain" themselves, §84 on the judge's discretion.

49. STAZH Y 27.C.: Obergericht, Schuldbetreibung, Varia 1864–1865, Heinrich Maier an Obergericht, September 14, 1864.

50. Gwalter, *Schuldbetreibungsgesetz*, 189–90.

51. This follows out of Heinrich Maier's letter and the receipts that Anna Jäggli enclosed with her complaint.

52. STAZH Y 27.C.: Obergericht, Schuldbetreibung, Varia 1864–1865, Anna Jäggli an das Obergericht Zürich, September 5, 1864.

53. STAZH Y 27.C.: Obergericht, Schuldbetreibung, Varia 1864–1865, Heinrich Maier an Obergericht, September 14, 1864, emphasis in original.

54. A draft ordinance for Zurich's district prisons calculated ninety cents per day for normal alimentation, sixty cents for reduced alimentation. Care for prisoners seems to have included other costs. The annual reports of the Meilen district prison are the only ones that listed them. The thirteen debt prisoners held there in 1866 cost 96.25 francs to keep for a total of ninety days. In 1867, thirteen debt prisoners spent eighty-three days there, costing 91.15 francs. The six debt prisoners of 1868 spent fifty days there, costing 50.85 francs. STAZH P 296 Bezirksgefängnisse, Entwurf einer Verordnung betreffend die Bezirksgefängnisse, June 13, 1857; Jahresberichte des Statthalteramts des Bezirks Meilen, 1866–1868.

55. Gwalter, *Schuldbetreibungsgesetz*, 189.

56. Gesetz betreffend die Schuldbetreibung vom 5. April 1851, in *Offizielle Sammlung der seit 10. März 1831 erlassenen Gesetze, Beschlüsse und Verordnungen des eidgenössischen Standes Zürich* (Zurich, 1850 [*sic*]), 8:241–90, §92, 279. Release from jail, however, did not invalidate the debt warrant, and the imprisonment did not resolve the debt. Release simply suspended the measure.

57. Alphonse Rivier, "De la contrainte par corps en Suisse," *Revue de droit international et de législation comparée* 2 (1870): 52.

58. Bundesverfassung von 1874, §50, section 3: "Debt imprisonment is abolished." Quoted in Erich Appenzeller, "Der Schuldverhaft und seine Abschaffung nach den Gesetzgebungen der schweizerischen Kantone und des Bundes" (law diss., Zurich, 1923), 59–60.

59. In the 1850s, the annual average was 656 and the median was 676. To give these numbers and those that follow some context: the canton of Zurich's population as counted by the 1850 census was 250,698; in 1860, 266,265; and in 1870, 284,047.

60. *Vierunddreißigster Rechenschaftsbericht des Obergerichts an den Großen Rath des Standes Zürich über das Jahr 1864* (Zurich, 1865), 33.

61. Miranda Joseph, *Debt to Society: Accounting for Life under Capitalism* (Minneapolis: University of Minnesota Press, 2014), chaps. 1 and 2.

62. The definite book on nineteenth-century debtors' prisons is Vause, *In the Red and in the Black*. See also Finn, *Character of Credit*, Sergei Antonov, *Bankrupts and Usurers of Imperial Russia: Debt, Property, and the Law in the Age of Dostoevsky and Tolstoy* (Cambridge, MA: Harvard University Press, 2016), chap. 7, and Christoph Bergfeld, "Über die Aufhebung der Schuldhaft in Frankreich und in Deutschland," in *Wechselseitige Beeinflussungen und Rezeptionen von Recht und Philosophie in Deutschland und Frankreich*, ed. Jean-François Kervégan and Heinz Mohnhaupt (Frankfurt am Main: Vittorio Klostermann, 2001), 329–78; Michael Spann, *Der Haftungszugriff auf den Schuldner zwischen Personal- und Vermögensvollstreckung. Eine exemplarische Untersuchung der geschichtlichen Rechtsquellen ausgehend vom römischen Recht bis ins 21. Jahrhundert unter besonderer Berücksichtigung bayerischer Quellen* (Münster: LIT, 2004); Steffen Breßler, *Schuldknechtschaft und Schuldturm. Zur Personalexekution im sächsischen Recht des 13.–16. Jahrhunderts* (Berlin: Duncker & Humblot, 2004); Eduard Berdecki, "Die Einflüsse der Aufklärung auf die Schuldhaft in den deutschen Staaten und in der Schweiz" (law diss., Basel, 1959).

63. A survey of Europe is Jérôme Sgard, "Do Legal Origins Matter? The Case of Bankruptcy Laws in Europe 1808–1914," *European Review of Economic History* 10 (2006): 389–419.

64. Bruce Mann identified a similar discontinuous shift from the language of morally inept economic failure to the more sober assessment of flight risks and the like, thereby underscording the shifting significance of normative concepts like "character" and "honor." See Bruce Mann, *Republic of Debtors. Bankruptcy in the Age of American Independence* (Cambridge, MA: Harvard University Press, 2003).

65. Vause, *In the Red and in the Black*; Erika Vause, "Disciplining the Market: Debt Imprisonment, Public Credit, and the Construction of Commercial Personhood in Revolutionary France," *Law and History Review* 32, no. 3 (2014): 647–82.

66. Finn, *Character of Credit*, chaps. 3 and 4; a survey of the campaigns to transform debt imprisonment is found on pages 154–55.

67. Finn, *Character of Credit*, 152–53.

68. Finn, *Character of Credit*, 186; G. R. Rubin, "Law, Poverty and Imprisonment

for Debt, 1869–1914," in *Law, Economy and Society, 1750–1914: Essays in the History of English Law*, ed. G. R. Rubin and David Sugarman (Abingdon: Professional Books, 1984), 241–99.

69. Finn, *Character of Credit*, 154–55.

70. A similar observation is found in Gustav Peebles, "Washing Away the Sins of Debt: The Nineteenth-Century Eradication of the Debtors' Prison," *Comparative Studies in Society and History* 55, no. 3 (2013): 701–24.

71. Hermann Heinrich, *Aus der Schuldhaft! Ein Nothschrei an unsere Gesetzgeber* (Leipzig 1865).

72. Heinrich, *Aus der Schuldhaft!*, 29.

73. Already in the eighteenth century, debtors' prisons concerned classic prison reformers. In his important work on prisons, Cesare Beccaria (1738–1794) discussed them at length. An influential pamphlet that was translated into German and printed multiple times was composed by Amidei Cosimo (1725–1783), a jurist from Pisa who corresponded with Beccaria. Cesare Beccaria, *An Essay on Crimes and Punishments*, trans. Edward D. Ingraham (Philadelphia, 1819), chap. 32; Amidei Cosimo, *Discorso filosofico-politico sopra la carcere de'debitorio* (Harlem, 1771).

74. Finn, *Character of Credit*.

75. "Execution against the person" "only continued" to exist in a few cantons, wrote a jurist in 1858. His list, however, was long: Zurich, Bern, Basel-Stadt, Vaud, Genf, Neuchâtel, and Valais, among which were a few of Switzerland's industrial centers. Von Wyß, "Die Schuldbetreibung," 113.

76. P. F. Bellot, M. Schaub, M. P. Odier, M. E. Mallet, *Loi sur la procédure civile du Canton de Genève, suivie de l'Exposé des motifs*, 2nd ed. (Paris: Librairie D'Abraham Cherbulizez, 1837), 655–56.

77. [Carl Joseph Anton] Mittermaier, "Ueber den persönlichen Verhaft wegen Schulden (mit Rücksicht auf die Erfahrungen und Gesetze von Frankreich, Belgien, Genf u.A.)," *Kritische Zeitschrift für Rechtswissenschaft und Gesetzgebung des Auslandes* 10 (1838): 279.

78. Mittermaier discussed Geneva's system in a long review of Jean-Baptiste Bayle-Mouillard's 1836 study *De l'emprisonnement pour dettes*, a massive statistical work that caused a furor in France and was repeatedly referenced in later debates on debt imprisonment. Mittermaier considered France and Geneva as positive examples, though he found the Swiss city-canton more commendable in some points (and approvingly added that Baden followed Geneva), such as in allowing judges discretion and in the mentioned distinction between imprisonment as punishment and as guarantee. Because Mittermaier thought it was important to arrest merchants to conduct an investigation of their assets and believed that the normally short duration of imprisonment was bearable, he disagreed with Bayle-Mouillard's vehement repudiation of debt imprisonment. Mittermaier, "Ueber den persönlichen Verhaft"; J. B. Bayle-Mouillard, *De l'emprisonnement pour dettes; considérations sur son origine, ses rapports avec la morale publique et les intérêts du commerce, des familles, de la société, suivie de la statistique de la contrainte par corps* (Paris, 1836). On Bayle-Mouillard see Vause, *In the Red and in the Black*, chap. 4; Hautcœur, "Produire des statistiques."

79. "Loi constitutionelle rendue dans le canton de Genève sur la liberté indi-

viduelle et l'abolition de la contrainte par corps. Note explicative de la discussion, par un membre du Grand-Conseil," *Revue de droit français et étranger* 6, no. 2 (1849): 495.

80. "Loi constitutionelle," 496.

81. For instance, in the provenance archives of the canton in the Ancien Régime, the so-called "Blaues Register" in the Staatsarchiv Zürich, vol. 194, vol. 218.

82. *Satz- und Ordnungen eines frey-loblichen Statt-Gerichts zu Zürich,* part 3, p. 27, §19: "How to look for the debtor and what power should the court have?"

83. Meiss, *Pfand-Recht,* 120.

84. Appenzeller, "Schuldverhaft," 15; Berdecki, "Einflüsse," 58.

85. Beschluss des Kleinen Raths vom 28sten Januar 1812, an sämmtliche Bezirks- und Unerstatthalter und die Bezirksgerichte, betreffend die Behandlung des Rechtstriebs für laufende Schulden, vorzüglich der Pfändung, und die Ertheilung und Anwendung des Wortzeichens, in *Officielle Sammlung der von dem Großen Rathe des Cantons Zürich gegebenen Gesetze und gemachten Verordnungen, und der von dem Kleinen Rath emanierten allgemeinen Landes- und Polizey-Verordnungen* (Zurich, 1813), 5:248–252.

86. Wyß, "Schuldbetreibung," 113; Appenzeller, "Schuldverhaft," 16.

87. *Fünf und zwanzigster Rechenschaftsbericht des Obergerichts an den Großen Rath des Standes Zürich über das Jahr 1855* (Zurich, 1856), 79. Similar statements on installment payments in *Sechs und zwanzigster Rechenschaftsbericht des Obergerichts an den Großen Rath des Standes Zürich über das Jahr 1856* (Zurich, 1857), 79–80.

88. *Sieben und zwanzigster Rechenschaftsbericht des Obergerichts an den Großen Rath des Standes Zürich über das Jahr 1857* (Zurich, 1858), 55–56.

89. On the expansion, ordered by a law passed on January 26, 1852, see STAZH P 296, Allgemeine Vorschriften für den Bau der Gefangenschaften in den Bezirkshauptorten vom 23. März 1852; C. Widmer, *Zur Reform der Strafanstalt in Zürich. Ein Beitrag* (Zurich, 1855), esp. 24–26; Franz Gut, *Die Gefängnisse von Winterthur (Separatdruck aus dem Winterthurer Jahrbuch),* (Winterthur 1981–1982), 106–12.

90. Gesetz über die Schuldbetreibung, 7. April 1842, in *Offizielle Sammlung der seit 10. März 1831 erlassenen Gesetze, Beschlüsse und Verordnungen des eidgenössischen Standes Zürich* (Zurich, 1840 [*sic*]), 6:389–429, §81, 419–20.

91. The construction of workhouses was another step in this process of classifying, separating, and subjecting to different treatment different inmates, but it had not, at this point, been implemented in Zurich. See Lippuner, *Bessern und verwahren.*

92. Swiss proponents of separating prisons included Widmer, *Reform;* Balthasar Estermann, *Wechselhaft im neuen Strafvollzugswesen* (Lucerne, 1867).

93. C[onrad] M[elchior] Hirzel, *Ueber Zuchthäuser und ihre Verwandlung in Besserungshäuser* (Zurich, 1826), 59.

94. Vause, *In the Red and in the Black;* Antonov, *Bankrupts and Usurers.* For Prussia I rely on a source text from the period: Heinrich, *Aus der Schuldhaft!,* 9.

95. Abschied 89 (January 28, 1550, Baden), in *Amtliche Sammlung der ältern eidgenössischen Abschiede,* published upon decree of the federal authority under the direction of the federal archivist Jacob Kaiser, vol. 4:1e (Lucerne, 1886), 205.

96. STAZH P 296 Bezirksgefängnisse, Direktor des Gefängniswesens an Regierungsrat, April 1, 1862.

97. *Fünfzehnter Rechenschaftsbericht des Obergerichts an den Großen Rath des Standes Zürich über das Jahr 1845* (Zurich, 1846), 34.

98. Eberhard Brecht, "Wohlversorgt im 'Berg': Zürichs altes Gefängnis für Missetäter, Vagabunden und Bedürftige," *Tages-Anzeiger,* June 12, 1981, 51. STAZH P 296 Bezirksgefängnisse, Statthalteramt Zürich, Jahresbericht 1866.

99. The district president explained the dramatic rise in the number of arrests in the 1850s as a factor of increased arrests for begging. STAZH P 300.1.2, Gefängniswesen, Bezirksgerichte, Statthalter des Bezirks Zürich an die Polizeidirektion, February 13, 1855.

100. Zurich had no workhouses at this point. STAZH P 300.1.2, Gefängniswesen, Bezirksgerichte, Jahresbericht Statthalteramt Zürich 1864.

101. *Vierunddreißigster Rechenschaftsbericht des Obergerichts an den Großen Rath des Standes Zürich über das Jahr 1864* (Zurich, 1865), 33. The 331 warrants contrast with 49 actual arrests. STAZH P 300.1.2, Gefängniswesen, Bezirksgerichte, Jahresbericht Statthalteramt Zürich 1864.

102. *Statistik der Rechtspflege des Kantons Zürich 1867* (Zurich, 1868), 63.

103. STAZH P 296 Bezirksgefängnisse, Jahresbericht Statthalteramt des Bezirkes Pfäffikon 1868.

104. STAZH P 296 Bezirksgefängnisse, Jahresbericht Statthalteramt des Bezirkes Horgen 1868.

105. Added to the forty-nine persons in pretrial detention were the groups of those jailed for convictions and for fines and those recently arrested by the police.

106. Added to the forty-eight debt prisoners in Berg was one person locked up in Selnau for debts. STAZH P 300.1.2 Gefängniswesen, Bezirksgerichte: Zürich 1837–1904, Jahresbericht Statthalteramt Zürich 1864. On the 66 bankruptcies in the district of Zurich (210 in the canton as a whole) see *Vierunddreißigster Rechenschaftsbericht des Obergerichts an den Großen Rath des Standes Zürich über das Jahr 1864* (Zurich, 1865), 37, 73.

107. Xifaras, *Propriété,* 254.

108. STAZH P 37, [Conrad Melchior] Hirzel, Bürgermeister, "Dissertation über das Wortzeichen" (unpublished manuscript, n.d., before 1842). The manuscript has two parts. The pagination of the second part begins with 1. See *Gesetz über die Schuldbetreibung, 7. April 1842,* in Offizielle Sammlung der seit 10. März 1831 erlassenen Gesetze, Beschlüsse und Verordnungen des eidgenössischen Standes Zürich (Zurich, 1840 [*sic*]), 6:389–429.

109. STAZH P 37, "Dissertation über das Wortzeichen," part 1: "Über den gesezlichen Charakter, die Anwendbarkeit und die Dauer des angewandten Wortzeichens" (On the legal character, applicability and duration of the executed debt warrant), 6, 12.

110. STAZH P 37, "Dissertation über das Wortzeichen," part 1, 11.

111. STAZH P 37, "Dissertation über das Wortzeichen," part 1, 9.

112. STAZH P 37, "Dissertation über das Wortzeichen," part 1, 7.

113. There were, however, differing levels of priority for different classes of creditors based on the type of debt they held.

114. STAZH P 37, "Dissertation über das Wortzeichen," part 1, 23.

115. STAZH P 37, "Dissertation über das Wortzeichen," part 1, 23.

116. STAZH P 37, "Dissertation über das Wortzeichen," part 1, 24–25.

117. STAZH P 37, "Dissertation über das Wortzeichen," part 2: "Über die Zwekmäßigkeit der Anwendung des Wortzeichens auf Failliten, als Verhütungs und Abschrekungs Mittel von Fallimenten" (On the purposefulness of using the debt warrant against bankrupts as a means to secure and as a means to deter them).

118. STAZH P 37, "Dissertation über das Wortzeichen," part 2, 11–12.

119. STAZH P 37, "Dissertation über das Wortzeichen," part 2, 7, 8.

120. STAZH P 37, "Dissertation über das Wortzeichen," part 2, 10.

121. STAZH P 37, "Dissertation über das Wortzeichen," part 2, 11.

122. STAZH P 37, "Dissertation über das Wortzeichen," part 2, 1.

123. Of the plethora of examples, see "Beschluss der Justiz-Commission," in *Monatschronik der zürcherischen Rechtspflege* 3 (1834): 141–42. Similar is "Beschluss des Obergerichts vom 14. Christmonat [Dezember] 1833," in *Monatschronik der zürcherischen Rechtspflege* 2 (1833): 494–95; Urtheil des Bezirksgerichts Winterthur vom 9. Jenner und des Obergerichts vom 17. Hornung [February] 1835, in *Monatschronik der zürcherischen Rechtspflege* 5 (1835): 75–80.

124. *Auszüge aus den obergerichtlichen Rechenschaftsberichten von den Jahren 1872 bis und mit 1885, hauptsächlich das Notariatswesen und die Gemeindeammänner betreffend, möglichst alphabetisch geordnet. Jedermann als Hülfs- und Nachschlagbuch dienend* (Affoltern am Albis, 1887); Reglement für die Mobiliarleihkasse der Zürcher Kantonalbank (vom 30. Weinmonat 1871), in *Offizielle Sammlung der seit 10. März 1831 erlassenen Gesetze, Beschlüsse und Verordnungen des Eidgenössischen Standes Zürich* (Zurich 1873), 15:550–55.

125. Urtheil des Obergerichts vom 26. Jenner 1833, in *Monatschronik der zürcherischen Rechtspflege* 1 (1833): 68–70.

126. STAZH P 5.2.1, Petition des Vorstehers der Gesellschaft der Gemeindeammänner des Bezirkes Zürich namens derselben, zum Rechtstriebgesetz, February 3, 1842.

127. See Appadurai, Introduction to *The Social Life of Things*, 24.

128. STAZH P 5.2.1, Petition des Vorstehers der Gesellschaft der Gemeindeammänner des Bezirkes Zürich namens derselben, zum Rechtstriebgesetz, February 3, 1842.

129. According to the Stadt- und Landrecht of 1715, a building comprised "everything that touches notch and nail." In 1844, the high cantonal court admitted that "the opinions are very different" on this matter, and in 1852 it determined, "Very often, conflicts arise over whether objects [like machines—MS] should be seized as moveable assets by the municipal bailiff or as immoveable assets by the cantonal authorities." See STAZH P 5.2. Anfrage des Justizdepartements des Kantons Thurgau, August 21, 1852, and the undated draft response from the cantonal law enforcement. See also the controversy—which was answered in the positive—over whether a blacksmith's anvil bolted to the ground was to be considered as part of his real estate: *Monatschronik der zürcherischen Rechtspflege* 2 (1833): 449–55 (high court judgment from December 24, 1833).

130. "Inwieweit kann der Arbeitslohn eines Fabrikarbeiters gepfändet werden,"

Zeitschrift für Kunde und Fortbildung der Zürcherischen Rechtspflege 2 (1855): 247–50 (Rekursentscheid vom November 29, 1855).

131. *Auszüge aus den obergerichtlichen Rechenschaftsberichten von den Jahren 1872 bis und mit 1885*, 78.

132. Admittedly, the sources drawn on here do not offer much information on this point. But the case discussed above is bolstered by arguments made fifty years later in Zurich to place more restrictions on lenders: proponents stated that indebted train workers in Zurich-Aussersihl reluctantly gave in to lenders' high interest rates because they feared losing their jobs if they allowed their wages to be garnished. STAZH III JC 4 (6): Feilträger, Pfandleiher, Gelddarleiher: Initiativbegehren Advokat Dr. J. Springer an den Kantonsrat, May 6, 1908, 6–7.

133. Gesetz betreffend die Schuldbetreibung, 29. Juni 1832, in *Offizielle Sammlung der seit 10. März 1831 erlassenen Gesetze, Beschlüsse und Verordnungen des Eidgenössischen Standes Zürich* (Zurich, 1832), 2:79–103, §14, 2:83–84.

134. Gesetz über die Schuldbetreibung, 7. April 1842, in *Offizielle Sammlung der seit 10. März 1831 erlassenen Gesetze, Beschlüsse und Verordnungen des eidgenössischen Standes Zürich* (Zurich, 1840 [*sic*]), 6:389–429, § 21, 6:397.

135. On the increasing significance of godparenthood as a mode of societalization in the nineteenth century see Joris, "Kinship and Gender." Detailed studies on Württemberg and Westphalia: David W. Sabean, *Kinship in Neckarhausen, 1700–1870* (Cambridge: Cambridge University Press, 1998), 374–78; Christine Fertig, *Familie, verwandtschaftliche Netzwerke und Klassenbildung im ländlichen Westfalen (1750–1874)* (Stuttgart: Lucius & Lucius, 2012), chap. 5.

136. Here and in the following: Rechtstriebgesetz 1851, §21; Eugen Meier, *Die Beschränkungen der Zwangsvollstreckung (Lehre von den Kompetenzstücken) nach schweizerischem Recht. Mit einer allgemein-geschichtlichen Einleitung* (Zurich: Schulthess, 1907), 37–38.

137. "Zur Erläuterung des § 21 lit. b. des Schuldbetreibungsgesetzes," *Beiträge zur Kunde und Fortbildung der zürcherischen Rechtspflege* 9 (1848): 444–48, 445.

138. The law of 1871 more precisely defined indispensable clothes as one set of work clothes and one set of Sunday clothes and added "indispensable cooking utensils" to the list of protected items. See Gesetz betreffend die Schuldbetreibung vom 29. Weinmonat 1871, in *Offizielle Sammlung der seit 10. März 1831 erlassenen Gesetze, Beschlüsse und Verordnungen des eidgenössischen Standes Zürich* (Zurich, 1873), 16:181–237, §53, 193.

139. J. H. Weber, *Schweizerischer Rechtsgeschäftsfreund. Vollständige Sammlung der Schuldbetreibungs-, Konkurs- und Sportelngesetze aller Kantone der Schweiz; mit einem Anhang über allgemeines Wechselrecht* (Zurich, 1869); Meier, *Beschränkung der Zwangsvollstreckung*, 42–54.

140. "Ein Gesetz von eminenter Tragweite," in *Der Gerichtssaal: Zeitschrift für schweizerische Civil- und Strafrechtspflege* 3, no. 3 (January 8, 1887): 9–10, here 9.

141. *Bundesgesetz über Schuldbetreibung und Konkurs: Textausgabe mit Gebühren und Tarifen*, ed. H. Hafner (Zurich, 1892), §92.

142. BAR E22#1000/134#2608*, Az. 6.7.4, *Bundesgesez über Schuldbetreibung und Konkurs. Entwurf mit Motiven: Vorgelegt durch die Kommissions-Minderheit, welche das System der Pfändung im Gegensaze zu demjenigen des Konkurses aufrecht hält, September 1875* (Bern, 1875), 88–89.

143. Here and in the following: Weber/Brüstlein, *Bundesgesetz erläutert*, S. 92.
144. Here and in the following: BAR E22#1000/134#2611*, Az. 6.7.4, P. Speiser (Basel), Gutachten über den Entwurf eines eidg. Betreibungs- und Konkursgesetzes, erstattet an das eidg. Justizdepartement am 31. December 1885. On the position of the Handels- und Industrievereins, which supported setting the limit at one hundred francs, see BAR E22#1000/134#2611*, Az. 6.7.4, Bundesgesetz betreffend Schuldbetreibung und Konkurs. Bericht des Vorortes Zürich des Schweiz. Handels- und Industrie-Vereins (Zurich, 1886), 13.
145. Determining the minimum level of subsistence revealed itself to be difficult in political debates. In 1887, the Grütliverein and the unions petitioned that "everything necessary for the humane existence of the debtor and his family" be protected, without, however, defining what exactly those things were. See BAR E22#1000/134#2611*, Az. 6.7.4, Grütliverein, Aktionskomitee, Schweizerischer Gewerkschaftsbund, Petition betreffend den Entwurf eines eidg. Schuldentrieb- und Konkursgesetzes (St. Gallen, 1887), 5–6.
146. "Die Humanität im Betreibungsgesetz," *Neue Zürcher Zeitung*, no. 306, November 2, 1889, 1.
147. G. Wolf, *Verhältniß der Wohnungs-Vermiether & -Miether zum neuen Konkurs- und Betreibungsgesetz, mit einem Vorwort betreffend die übrigen Neuerungen im Betreibungsverfahren* (Zurich, n.d. [1889]), 9. The speaker, a Zurich high court judge, nevertheless tried to dispel the audience's fears.
148. "Agitation für das eidg. Betreibungs- und Konkursgesetz. Schaffhausen (4.11.1889)," *Neue Zürcher Zeitung*, no. 310, November 6, 1889, morning edition, 2.
149. On the politics of the minimum see Dana Simmons, *Vital Minimum: Need, Science, and Politics in Modern France* (Chicago: University of Chicago Press, 2015), 91.
150. Peter Wagner, "'An Entirely New Object of Consciousness, of Volition, of Thought': The Coming into Being and (almost) Passing Away of 'Society' as a Scientific Object," in *Biographies of Scientific Objects*, ed. Lorraine Daston (Chicago: University of Chicago Press, 2000), 155.
151. These new actors were organized in associations. In 1870, the Handels- und Industrieverein was organized; in 1880, the Gewerbeverband. In 1880, the Swiss umbrella organization of labor unions—the Schweizerische Gewerkschaftsbund—was formed; in 1888, the Social Democratic Party and the Swiss Charitable Women's Association (Schweizerische Gemeinnützige Frauenverein); in 1890, the Coalition of Swiss Workers' Associations.
152. The first *Statistische Jahrbuch der Schweiz* was published in 1891. State-run and philanthropic statistical projects compiled data on factories, housing, international trade, alcohol consumption, and prisons. Jakob Tanner, "Der Tatsachenblick auf die 'reale Wirklichkeit': zur Entwicklung der Sozial- und Konsumstatistik in der Schweiz," *Schweizerische Zeitschrift für Geschichte* 45 (1995): 98; Barbara Koller, *"Gesundes Wohnen". Ein Konstrukt zur Vermittlung bürgerlicher Werte und Verhaltensnormen und seine praktische Umsetzung in der Deutschschweiz 1880–1940* (Zurich: Chronos, 1994), 33–34.
153. The Federal Office of Statistics (Eidgenössische Statistische Bureau) was overrun with work in the 1880s and 1890s. Hans-Ulrich Jost, *Von Zahlen*

und Macht. Statistiker, Statistik und politische Autoritäten in der Schweiz, 18. bis 20. Jahrhundert (Bern: Bundesamt für Statistik, 1995), 70.

154. Quantitatively speaking, the numbers of labor struggles in the 1880s were modest compared to later developments. Though strikes increased exponentially in the last third of the nineteenth century, the number of strikes in the 1880s (137 in all of Switzerland) was much lower than the peak between 1900 and 1914 (more than 1,800 strikes). But the 1880s saw the formation of key labor organizations. Christian Koller, *Streikkultur. Performanzen und Diskurse des Arbeitskampfes im schweizerisch-österreichischen Vergleich (1860–1950)* (Münster: LIT, 2009), 46–50, 179–92; Hans Hirter, "Die Streiks in der Schweiz in den Jahren 1880–1914: Quantitative Streikanalyse," in *Arbeiterschaft und Wirtschaft in der Schweiz 1880–1914: Soziale Lage, Organisation und Kämpfe von Arbeitern und Unternehmern, politische Organisation und Sozialpolitik*, ed. Erich Gruner (Zurich: Chronos, 1988), 2:846–55.

155. This passage is influenced by Simmons, *Vital Minimum*, 95–115.

156. Widmer, *Die Schweiz in der Wachstumskrise*, 139.

157. On Hilty as a key thinker for liberal governments see Bernet, *Schizophrenie*, 283–88.

158. Widmer, *Schweiz in der Wachstumskrise*, 748–53; Tanner, "Diskurse der Diskriminierung."

159. "Die Humanität im Betreibungsgesetz," *Neue Zürcher Zeitung*, no. 306, November 2, 1889, 1.

160. Widmer, *Schweiz in der Wachstumskrise*, 569, notes a social-political turn in legislation in the mid-1880s. A similar point is made about the 1907 civil law codex by Pio Caroni, *Privatrecht: Eine sozialhistorische Einführung* (Basel: Helbing & Lichtenhahn, 1988), 90–96.

161. Leo Weber and Alfred Brüstlein, *Das Bundesgesetz über Schuldbetreibung und Konkurs für den praktischen Gebrauch erläutert* (Zurich, 1890), 128.

162. A German encyclopedia thus called the Swiss laws backwards. Flesch, "Zwangsvollstreckung," in *Handwörterbuch der Staatswissenschaften*, 2nd ed., ed. Johannes Conrad (Jena: Fischer, 1901), 1095.

163. Meier, *Beschränkungen der Zwangsvollstreckung*, 78.

164. Meier, *Beschränkungen der Zwangsvollstreckung*, 90–94. However, if a debtor sold a protected asset, the creditor could take the earnings. See *Archiv für Schuldbetreibung und Konkurs* 1 (1892): 74–78.

165. Meier, *Beschränkungen der Zwangsvollstreckung*, 103, 99.

166. Meier, *Beschränkungen der Zwangsvollstreckung*, 102.

167. Meier, *Beschränkungen der Zwangsvollstreckung*, 78, 104, 116.

168. Meier, *Beschränkungen der Zwangsvollstreckung*, 78, 103. Jakob Messerli, *Gleichmässig—pünktlich—schnell: Zeiteinteilung und Zeitgebrauch im 19. Jahrhundert in der Schweiz* (Zurich: Chronos, 1993), 147–48 quotes an 1893 Federal Council resolution on indispensable assets in bankruptcy proceedings that gave special significance to industrial workers' watches.

169. Meier, *Beschränkungen der Zwangsvollstreckung*, 104.

170. "Woher kommt das Mißtrauen gegen die moderne Rechtspflege [Teil] III," *Schweizer Kriminal-Zeitung: Organ für Kriminal-, Polizei- und Civil-Gerichtspflege, Unterhaltung und Humor* 25, June 24, 1893, 1–2; "Um das Konkursgesetz herum,"

Schweizer Kriminal-Zeitung: Organ für Kriminal-, Polizei- und Civil-Gerichtspflege, Unterhaltung und Humor 32, August 12, 1893, 4.

171. *Vierundvierzigster Rechenschaftsbericht des Obergerichtes an den h. Kantonsrath des Kantons Zürich über das Jahr 1874* (Zurich, 1875), 20.

172. *Bundesgesetz über Schuldbetreibung und Konkurs: Textausgabe mit Gebühren und Tarifen,* ed. H. Hafner, §93.

173. "Richterliches Ermessen und Willkür," *Schweizer Kriminal-Zeitung: Organ für Kriminal-, Polizei- und Civil-Gerichtspflege, Unterhaltung und Humor* 26, June 25, 1892, 2.

174. *Archiv für Schuldbetreibung und Konkurs* 2 (1893), 50–51.

175. The authorities' judgments on this point adhere to the general rhetoric of "false" needs that became more prominent with the rise of workers' movement and its demands. See the discussion of the debate in France in Simmons, *Vital Minimum,* 104–5.

176. Here and in the following: "Die Pfändung des Lohnes," *Schweizer Kriminal-Zeitung: Organ für Kriminal-, Polizei- und Civil-Gerichtspflege, Unterhaltung und Humor* 32, August 12, 1893, 1. See also *Archiv für Schuldbetreibung und Konkurs* 2 (1893): 10; *Archiv für Schuldbetreibung und Konkurs* 1 (1892), 107–8.

177. Simmons, *Vital Minimum,* 1.

178. On the economy as "a macroscopic phenomenon outside the control of individuals" in early modern poverty see Fontaine, *The Moral Economy,* 21. On the mobility of the Zurich underclasses at the end of the nineteenth century see Daniel Künzle, "Stadtwachstum, Quartierbildung und soziale Konflikte am Beispiel von Zürich-Aussersihl 1850–1914," in *Schweiz im Wandel. Studien zur neueren Gesellschaftsgeschichte: Festschrift für Rudolf Braun zum 60. Geburtstag,* ed. Sebastian Brändli et al. (Basel: Helbing & Lichtenhahn, 1990), 43–58. Moving and skipping town were double-edged swords, however, because they meant leaving the social networks of the economy of makeshifts. See Gabriela Suter, "Die transparenten Armen. Generierung von Wissen über Bedürftige am Beispiel der Freiwilligen und Einwohnerarmenpflege der Stadt Zürich 1895–1928" (unpublished thesis, Historisches Seminar Universität Zürich, 2004), 93–94.

179. On these organizations, discussed in chapter 1, see *Ein schweizerischer Creditorenverband;* F. Meili, *Der gesetzgeberische Kampf gegen Schädigungen im Bauhandwerk, in der illoyalen Konkurrenz und im Kreditwesen: Drei Gesetzgebungsfragen* (Zurich: Orell Füssli, 1901) (Schweizer Zeitfragen 32).

180. This is one of the key insights of Simmons, *Vital Minimum,* 104–15.

181. Carl Landolt, "Zehn Basler Arbeiterhaushaltungen," *Zeitschrift für Schweizerische Statistik* 27 (1891): 281–372. Landolt's study was not the only one of its kind. Other studies on household budgets from the 1890s include E. Hofmann, "Vier thurgauische Haushaltsbudgets," *Zeitschrift für schweizerische Statistik* 29 (1893): 499–531. But Hofmann did not compile an inventory of the families' moveable assets and did not discuss the types of payment the households used and the types of transactions they engaged in to get what they needed.

182. Landolt, "Arbeiterhaushaltungen," 341. On Landolt's study see Regina Wecker, *Zwischen Ökonomie und Ideologie: Arbeit im Lebenszusammenhang von Frauen im Kanton Basel-Stadt 1870–1910* (Zurich: Chronos, 1997), 159–70; on the shortcomings of his method see Jakob Tanner, *Fabrikmahlzeit: Ernährungswissenschaft,*

Industriearbeit und Volksernährung in der Schweiz 1890–1950 (Zurich: Chronos, 1999), 143–50.

183. Landolt, "Arbeiterhaushaltungen," 284.

184. Landolt, "Arbeiterhaushaltungen," 365.

185. Landolt, "Arbeiterhaushaltungen," 360.

186. Here and in the following: Landolt, "Arbeiterhaushaltungen," 313.

187. See Norbert Schindler's analysis of early modern labor as necessitating a combination of varying sources of income, which was also true for many urban workers at the end of the nineteenth century. This is obscured by the domesticizing representations of the workers' movement, which, in pursuing the goal of gaining dominance over labor power as a commodity, emphasized single sources of income. Norbert Schindler, "Jenseits des Zwangs? Zur Ökonomie des Kulturellen inner- und ausserhalb der bürgerlichen Gesellschaft," in *Widerspenstige Leute. Studien zur Volkskultur in der frühen Neuzeit* (Frankfurt am Main: Fischer, 1992), 20–46.

188. *Die Ausbeutung der Arbeiter und die Ursachen ihrer Verarmung: Ein Beitrag zur socialen Frage. Preisgekrönt mit der Goldenen Medaille auf dem Internationalen Wettstreit zur Verbesserung der Lage der Arbeiter zu Köln a. Rh. 1890,* 2nd ed. (Kiel/Leipzig, 1892). The pamphlet's points on debt enforcement were discussed at the twenty-second German Jurists' Conference, which was then discussed by Swiss jurists. Falkmann, "Gutachten [. . .] über die Frage: Empfiehlt sich eine grundsätzliche Vermehrung der bestehenden Beschränkungen der Zwangsvollstreckung, etwa in Richtung einer allgemeinen Competenzwohlthat?," *Verhandlungen des 22. deutschen Juristentages* (Berlin, 1892), 1:240–64; Meier, *Beschränkungen der Zwangsvollstreckung,* 4.

189. *Ausbeutung,* 3.

190. *Ausbeutung,* 28.

191. *Ausbeutung,* 32.

192. J. L. Spyri, "Ueber Pfand- und Leihhäuser," *Schweizerische Zeitschrift für Gemeinnützigkeit* 3 (1864): 235–53.

193. Johann Ludwig Spyri (1822–1895), a brother-in-law of author Johanna Spyri and father of the first female jurist in Switzerland, Emilie Kempin Spyri, became a member of Schweizerischen Gemeinnützigen Gesellschaft in 1853 and was its president from 1875 until his death. He also worked as the head statistician of the Nordostbahn started by Zurich bank magnate Alfred Escher from 1875 until his death. His political positions were informed by the "perspective of the so-called Manchester men" (as an obituary put it). After helping put the finances of the deindustrialized Zurich municipality Fischenthal in order and participating in an informal group of liberal thinkers in the late 1840s, he became a proponent of savings banks as a way to solve social issues. Fritz Hunziker, "J. L. Spyri," *Schweizerische Zeitschrift für Gemeinnützigkeit* 36 (1896): 90. On the history of medieval mounts of piety—charitable lending houses run by the church— see Fontaine, *The Moral Economy,* chap. 6; on the significance of pawning in the material cultural of the early modern everyday economy see Anne McCants, "Goods at Pawn: The Overlapping Worlds of Material Possessions and Family Finance in Early Modern Amsterdam," *Social Science History* 31 (2007): 213–38. Works on the history of pawning in the nineteenth century that were helpful

for my analysis in this section include Wendy A. Woloson, *In Hock: Pawning in America from Independence through the Great Depression* (Chicago: University of Chicago Press, 2009); Karl Christian Führer, "Pawning in German Working-Class Life before the First World War," *International Review of Social History* 46 (2001): 29–44; Melanie Tebutt, *Making Ends Meet: Pawnbroking and Working-Class Credit* (Leicester: Methuen, 1983); Johnson, *Saving and Spending*, 165–88.

194. Spyri, "Ueber Pfand- und Leihhäuser," 235.

195. Spyri, "Ueber Pfand- und Leihhäuser," 245.

196. Spyri, "Ueber Pfand- und Leihhäuser," 247.

197. For instance, it passed over the Caisse publique de prêts sur gage, founded in 1872 in Geneva, and the one run by the Creditanstalt St. Gallen. The directory only includes entries from twelve cantons. Twenty-eight of the seventy-one were in Geneva, fifteen in the canton of St. Gallen, seven in Basel-Stadt. In 1885, Basel had 69,922 residents and, in 1888, 15,880 households, so that there was one pawnshop for every 2,269 households. *Gewerbe- und Handels-Adressbuch der Schweiz / Annuaire du commerce et de l'industrie Suisse* (Basel, 1885), 571–72; Ritzmann-Blickenstorfer, *Historische Statistik der Schweiz*, 94, 98.

198. Thus an encyclopedia relying on the directory speaks of "at least 70 private pawnshops." Hans Balmer, "Pfandleihgewerbe," in *Volkswirthschafts-Lexikon der Schweiz* (Bern, 1889), 568.

199. Demonstrated by a pamphlet published in Bern that discusses attaching pawnshops to the existing credit institutes and then rejects the idea on moral and practical grounds (such as the fear that investors in the savings bank could take out their money if they decided to enter the pawning business themselves). See Andreas Matthys, *Ansichtsäußerung über die Frage: Ob die Spar- und Leihkasse in der Stadt Bern für ihre Rechnung und Gefahr eine Pfandleih-Anstalt errichten soll?* (Bern, 1862).

200. Martin Isler, *Die Vorgeschichte der städtischen Mobiliar-Leihkasse 1843–1884* (St. Gallen: K. Weiss, 1943).

201. Basel's Craftsmen's Bank opened its doors on July 1, 1860. It was started by the Handwerker- und Gewerbeverein (Craftsmen and Commerce Association); in 1861, it partnered with the Society for the Good and the Common Welfare. STABS PA 146, H 17.2, Handwerkerbank 1862–1872.

202. Isler, *Vorgeschichte*, 22.

203. Schweizerisches Wirtschaftsarchiv (hereafter SWA) J X 1, Gesetz über das Hausirwesen, die Wanderlager, den zeitweiligen Gewerbstrieb, die öffentlichen Aufführungen und Schauvorstellungen, das Trödel- und Pfandleihgewerbe vom 13. November 1882.

204. SWA H + I D 601, Bericht der Basler Pfandleih-Anstalt über die erste Geschäftsperiode vom 15. Januar 1884 bis 30. Juni 1885, genehmigt durch die Actionärsversammlung am 11. November 1885 (Basel, 1885), 3–4.

205. Führer, "Pawning."

206. *Rechenschaftsberichte über die Verwaltung der Zürcher Kantonalbank, 1872–1902.*

207. Reglement für die Mobiliarleihkasse der Zürcher Kantonalbank (vom 30. Weinmonat 1871), in *Offizielle Sammlung der seit 10. März 1831 erlassenen Gesetze,*

Beschlüsse und Verordnungen des Eidgenössischen Standes Zürich (Zurich, 1873), 15:550–55, here 552, §10; SWA H + I D 601 Bericht der Basler Pfandleih-Anstalt über die erste Geschäftsperiode vom 15. Januar 1884 bis 30. Juni 1885, genehmigt durch die Actionärsversammlung am 11. November 1885 (Basel, 1885), 6.

208. Here and in the following: SWA H + I D 601, Bericht der Basler Pfandleih-Anstalt über die zwölfte Geschäftsperiode vom 1. Juli 1895 bis 30. Juni 1896 (Basel, 1896), 8. In July 1890, the fee was reduced from twenty to ten centimes. Bericht der Basler Pfandleih-Anstalt über die siebente Geschäftsperiode vom 1. Juli 1890 bis 31. Juni 1891 (Basel, 1891), 8.

209. *Rechenschaftsbericht über die Verwaltung der Zürcher Kantonalbank umfassend das Jahr 1879, dem h. Kantonsrath erstattet vom Bankrathe* (Zurich, 1880), 47; SWA H + I D 601, Bericht der Basler Pfandleih-Anstalt über die neunte Geschäftsperiode vom 1. Juli 1892 bis 30. Juni 1893 (Basel, 1893), 9; L. Maisch, *Der Kampf gegen den Wucher und die gesetzliche Ordnung des Gelddarleih- und Pfandleih-Gewerbes* (N.p. [Bern?], 1887), 30. The St. Galler pawnshop seems to have not asked the names of borrowers well into the 1870s. See Isler, *Vorgeschichte*, 8–10.

210. Here and in the following: SWA H + I D 601, Berichte der Basler Pfandleih-Anstalt 1884/85–1904/05.

211. Chris Otter, "Making Liberal Objects: British Techno-Social Relations 1800–1900," *Cultural Studies* 21 (2007): 577. Wendy Woloson sees the increase in pawned pocket watches as emblematic of the relation between industrial capitalism and pawning. Comparing the records of various American pawnshops, she shows that pocket watches made up 14 percent of all pawned objects in 1838, 25 percent in 1863, and 44 percent in 1897. Woloson, *In Hock*, 105.

212. Here and in the following: Messerli, *Gleichmässig*, 149–51.

213. During the first decade of its existence, the St. Gallen pawnshop was searched multiple times by the police. Isler, *Vorgeschichte*.

214. *Ueber die Gründung einer Mobiliar-Leihkasse in Basel, in Verbindung mit einer Handwerker-Bank* (Basel, 1864), 17.

215. This is the interpretation of lower sums borrowed in Führer, *Pawning*, 36, and Tebutt, *Making Ends Meet*, 131.

216. *Ueber die Gründung einer Mobiliar-Leihkasse*, 8.

217. Carl Landolt, for instance, wrote, "A shirt that can be used for 5 years will hardly still have its retail value even after one use; but for its owner, it still has a value of 4 francs after being used for one year, 3 francs after 2 years." Landolt, "Basler Arbeiterhaushaltungen," 283.

218. Spyri, "Ueber Pfand- und Leihhäuser," 248–49.

219. Herbert Conrad, *Die Pfändungsbeschränkungen zum Schutze des schwachen Schuldners: eine juristische und sozialpolitische Studie* (Jena: G. Fischer, 1906), 71. The author quotes an article by an economist of the Austrian school of marginalism, Eugen von Böhm-Bawerk, "Wert," in *Handwörterbuch der Staatswissenschaften* Bd. 6, ed. Johannes Conrad (Jena: G. Fischer, 1895), 6:682.

220. On the rhetoric of "false" needs in the late nineteenth century and the distinction between subjective needs and objective claims, see Simmons, *Vital Minimum*, 104–5.

221. W. Schmidlin, "Ueber Pfand- und Leihhäuser (monts de Piété): Referat

in der Versammlung der Schweizerischen gemeinnützigen Gesellschaft zu Basel den 22. September 1864 von Dr. W. Schmidlin, Director der schweizerischen Centralbahn," *Schweizerische Zeitschrift für Gemeinnützigkeit* 4 (1865): 67.

222. "Diskussion über die Pfand- und Leihhäuser," *Schweizerische Zeitschrift für Gemeinnützigkeit* 4 (1865): 68.

223. Johnson, *Saving and Spending,* 176.

224. Schmidlin's formulation contained in "Diskussion," 73.

225. Schmidlin, "Ueber Pfand- und Leihhäuser," 56.

226. Schmidlin, "Ueber Pfand- und Leihhäuser," 53.

227. Here and in the following: Schmidlin, "Ueber Pfand- und Leihhäuser," 54. See the very similar position in Spyri, "Ueber Pfand- und Leihhäuser," 246.

228. Spyri, "Ueber Pfand- und Leihhäuser," 247.

229. *Der Mont de Piété in Basel* (Basel, 1865), 5.

230. "Diskussion," 70.

231. *Mont de Piété in Basel,* 18.

232. *Mont de Piété in Basel,* 20.

233. *Mont de Piété in Basel,* 15.

234. Woloson, *In Hock,* 112–17.

235. Stallybrass, "Marx' Coat," 196.

236. Georg Simmel, *Philosophy of Money,* trans. Tom Bottomore and David Frisby (London: Routledge & Kegan Paul, 1978 [1900]), 508.

237. Simmel, *Money,* 443.

238. Simmel, *Money,* 444.

239. Simmel, *Money,* 478.

240. Simmel, *Money,* 476.

241. Simmel, *Money,* 479.

242. Simmel, *Money,* 483.

243. Simmel, *Money,* 495.

244. Simmel, *Money,* 500.

245. Simmel, *Money,* 508.

246. Marilyn Strathern, "Cutting the Network," *Journal of the Royal Anthropological Institute,* n.s., 2 (1996): 517–35.

Conclusion

1. See chapter 2. Tobler, *Gutartige Hierarchie,* 12.

2. See chapter 6. Schweizerisches Bundesarchiv BAR E22#1000/134#2645*, Az. 6.7.4, Alfred Brüstlein, Referat "Vorläufige Vorschläge für die Revision des Betreibungsgesetzes."

3. On the development of an autonomous world economy see, for instance, Quinn Slobodian, "How to See the World Economy: Statistics, Maps, and Schumpeter's Camera in the First Age of Globalization," *Journal of Global History* 10 (2015): 307–32.

4. Wagner, "An Entirely New Object."

5. Harootunian, *History's Disquiet.*

6. For a superb survey see Jeffrey Sklansky, "Labor, Money, and the Financial

Turn in the History of Capitalism," *Labor: Studies in Working-Class History of the Americas* 11 (2014): 23–46.

7. Fr. von Wyß, "Schuldbetreibung," in *Deutsches Staats-Wörterbuch,* ed. Johann Caspar Bluntschli and Karl L. Th. Brater (Stuttgart/Leipzig, 1865), note on page 264.

8. Wyß, "Schuldbetreibung," 263.

9. On Franklin and on maneuvering the bonds of debt see Muldrew, *The Economy of Obligation,* 1–2.

10. Foundational on this point is Giovanni Levi, *Inheriting Power: The Story of an Exorcist,* trans. Lydia G. Cochrane (Chicago: University of Chicago Press, 1988).

11. *Zur Volksabstimmung vom 17. November 1889.*

Bibliography

Archival Sources

Archiv für Zeitgeschichte ETH Zürich (AfZ ETHZ)

AfZ ETHZ, Vorort-Archiv, Protokolle der Ordentlichen Delegiertenversammlung des Schweizerischen Handels- und Industrievereins 1880ff.
AfZ ETHZ, Vorort-Archiv, Protokolle der Schweizerischen Handelskammer 1880ff.

Schweizerisches Bundesarchiv, Bern (BAR)

BAR E22#1000/134#2308*, Az. 6.3.5—E22#1000/134#2310*, Az. 6.3.5, Handelsrecht und Handelsregister
BAR E22#1000/134#2607*, Az. 6.7.4—E22#1000/134#2645*, Az. 6.7.4, Bundesgesetz über Schuldbetreibung und Konkurs

New York Public Library (NYPL)

Wilhelm Weitling Papers

Staatsarchiv des Kantons Basel-Stadt (STABS)

STABS Gerichtsarchiv G hoch 1, Stadtgericht, Zivilgericht: Fallimentsfälle
STABS Gerichtsarchiv G hoch 1–3, Zivilgericht, Album der Falliten
STABS Gerichtsarchiv G hoch 2, 1, Fallitenregister 1806–1891
STABS Neueres Gerichtsarchiv, GA-REG 2d, 3–1 (13), Handakten Zivilgerichtspräsident
STABS Justiz J 1, allgemeine Betreibungs- und Konkurssachen
STABS Justiz J 4, Rechtliche Folgen des Falliments
STABS Justiz J 6, Einzelne Rehabilitationen
STABS Justiz J 7, Einzelne Konkurssachen
STABS Justiz J 8, Collocationen der Stadt
STABS PA 146, H 17.2, Handwerkerbank

Staatsarchiv des Kantons Bern (STABE)

STABE BB 3.1.540, Materialien zum Gesetz über die öffentlich-rechtlichen Folgen (Ehrenfolgen) des Konkurses und der fruchtlosen Pfändung (1893)

Staatsarchiv des Kantons Luzern (STALU)

STALU AKT 35/21–22, Schuldbetreibung und Konkurs

Staatsarchiv des Kantons St. Gallen (STASG)

KA VIII Justiz R 77, Akten Konkurswesen

Staatsarchiv des Kantons Zürich (STAZH)

STAZH III Aaa 2 Protokolle des Verfassungsrathes des eidgenössischen Standes Zürich 1868, 1869
STAZH III JC 4 (6), Feilträger, Pfandleiher, Gelddarleiher
STAZH B VII 208.17 Kopierbuch des Oberamts Regensberg, Nov. 1825–July 1831
STAZH B VII 208.20 Oberwaisenamt Regensberg, Protokoll 1816–1826
STAZH B VII 208.21 Oberwaisenamt Regensberg, Protokoll Feb. 1826–July 1831
STAZH BVII 208.22 Oberamt Regensberg. Protokoll über sämtliche Gemeinderechnungen Jan. 1817–Jan. 1834.
STAZH BVII 208.23 Bevogtigungs-Etat, Oberamt Regensberg
STAZH B XI Bauma 65, Grundprotokoll Gemeinde Sternenberg
STAZH B XI Bauma 67, Grundprotokoll Gemeinde Sternenberg
STAZH B XI Notariat Zürich-Aussersihl 10.27
STAZH B XI 10.27 Notariat Zürich-Aussersihl, Konkursprotokolle 1884–1885
STAZH K III 212.1–3, Oberamt Regensberg
STAZH K III 258.3 (Nr. 201–270), Petitionen 1830/31
STAZH K III 258.3a (Nr. 1–75), Petitionen 1830/31
STAZH K III 259.1 (Nr. 133–200), Petitionen 1830/31
STAZH K III 259.1a (Nr. 76–132), Petitionen 1830/31
STAZH K III 542, Notariatswesen, Landschreibereisachen, Rechtsbetrieb (1822–1826)
STAZH KIII 543, Notariatswesen, Landschreibereisachen, Rechtsbetrieb (1827–1835)
STAZH K IV 124.1, Justizkommission, Justizwesen überhaupt (1831–1832)
STAZH M 2.18. Petitionen an den Verfassungsrat 1869
STAZH N 58.1 Armen- und Unterstützungswesen Bezirk Pfäffikon (1841–1902)
STAZH O 38.c1, Handelsregister (1882–1899)
STAZH P 5.2, Gesetze zur Schuldbetreibung (1832–1895)
STAZH P 37, Schuldforderungen, auch aus Konkurs (1836–1921)
STAZH P 37a, Hilfsvereine zur Herstellung des gefährdeten Kredites
STAZH P 296–300, Bezirksgefängnisse (1805–1925)
STAZH WI 33 a.22.29, Gustav Anton Schulthess-Rechberg: "Meine Lebensbeschreibung"

STAZH X 347 (6), Schmähschrift gegen Altschuldenschreiber Schinz
STAZH Y 25–27, Obergericht, Schuldbetreibungen (1832–1889)
STAZH [noch ohne Signatur], Tagebuch Heinrich Senn, 10 Ms. vols., 1850–1885

Stadtarchiv Zürich (StadtAZH)

VI.AS.C.120. Pfandbuch der gerichtlichen Pfandrechte der Gemeinde Aussersihl

Schweizerisches Wirtschaftsarchiv Basel (SWA)

SWA H + I D 601, Berichte der Basler Pfandleih-Anstalt 1885ff.
SWA Vo H IV 11, Dossiersammlung Handelsregister
SWA J X 1, Gesetz über das Hausirwesen, die Wanderlager, den zeitweiligen Gewerbstrieb, die öffentlichen Aufführungen und Schauvorstellungen, das Trödel- und Pfandleihgewerbe vom 13. November 1882

Zentralbibliothek Zürich (ZBZH)

Ber 219, Die Direction der zinstragenden Ersparnißcassa für alle Stände des Cantons Zürich an das Publicum, October 1821
Handschriftenabteilung, Ms N 620–630, Tagebuch Jakob Stutz 1846–1856

Printed Sources

Official Documents

Abschied 89 (January 28, 1550, Baden). In *Amtliche Sammlung der ältern eidgenössischen Abschiede.* Published upon decree of the federal authority under the direction of the federal archivist Jacob Kaiser, 203–23. Vol. 4, bk. 1e. Lucerne, 1886.
Auszug aus dem Abschiede der ordentlichen eidgenössischen Tagsatzung des Jahres 1847. Part 4: Verhandlungen, betreffend die Revision des Bundesvertrages. Bern, n.d. [1848].
Auszüge aus den obergerichtlichen Rechenschaftsberichten von den Jahren 1872 bis und mit 1885, hauptsächlich das Notariatswesen und die Gemeindeammänner betreffend, möglichst alphabetisch geordnet. Jedermann als Hülfs- und Nachschlagbuch dienend. Affoltern am Albis, 1887.
Bericht der Finanzdirektion an den hohen Regierungsrath betreffend die Bankfrage. Zurich, 1868.
Berichte des Appellations-Gerichts des Kantons Basel-Stadt über die Justizverwaltung vom Jahr . . . an den Großen Rath [1847–1870].
Berti, Stephen V. *Swiss Debt Enforcement and Bankruptcy Law: English Translation of the Amended Federal Statute on Debt Enforcement and Bankruptcy (SchKG).* Zurich: Schulthess, 1997.
Beschluss des Kleinen Raths vom 28sten Januar 1812, an sämmtliche Bezirks- und Unterstatthalter und die Bezirksgerichte, betreffend die Behandlung des

Rechtstriebs für laufende Schulden. In *Officielle Sammlung der von dem Großen Rathe des Cantons Zürich gegebenen Gesetze und gemachten Verordnungen, und der von dem Kleinen Rath emanierten allgemeinen Landes- und Polizey-Verordnungen,* 248–52. Vol. 5. Zurich, 1813.

Bevölkerungs-Aufnahme von Basel-Stadttheil am 25. Jenner 1837. Bericht an den E. E. Kleinen Rath. Basel, 1838.

Bevölkerungs-Aufnahme von Basel-Stadt am 3. Februar 1847. Bericht an E. E. Kleinen Rath. Basel, 1848.

Bevölkerungs-Aufnahme von Basel-Stadt am 10. Dezember 1860. Bericht an E. E. Kleinen Rath. Basel, 1861.

Botschaft des Bundesrathes an die hohe Bundesversammlung zu einem Gesezentwurfe [*sic*], enthaltend Schweizerisches Obligationen- und Handelsrecht (of November 27, 1879). *Schweizerisches Bundesblatt* 32, no. 4 (January 24, 1880): 58.

Botschaft des Bundesrathes an die Bundesversammlung zu dem vom Bundesrathe am 23. Februar 1886 festgestellten Entwurfe eines Bundesgesetzes über Schuldbetreibung und Konkurs (of April 6, 1886). *Schweizerisches Bundesblatt,* vol. 2, 38, no. 20 (May 8, 1886).

Bundesgesetz über Schuldbetreibung und Konkurs: Textausgabe mit Gebühren und Tarifen. Edited by H. Hafner. Zurich, 1892.

Code Civil des Français. Version seule et officielle. Paris, 1804.

Fünfundfünfzigster Rechenschaftsbericht des Obergerichtes und des Kassationsgerichtes an den h. Kantonsrath des Kantons Zürich über das Jahr 1885. Winterthur, 1886.

Gesetz, betreffend die Form und Kosten des Rechtstriebs [of December 17, 1803]. In *Officielle Sammlung der von dem Großen Rathe des Cantons Zürich gegebenen Gesetze und gemachten Verordnungen, und der von dem Kleinen Rath emanierten allgemeinen Landes- und Polizey-Verordnungen,* 193–203. Vol. 1. Zurich, 1804.

Gesetz betreffend die Schuldbetreibung, 29. Juni, 1832. In *Officielle Sammlung der seit Annahme der Verfassung vom Jahre 1831 erlassenen Gesetze, Beschlüsse und Verordnungen des Eidgenössischen Standes Zürich,* 79–103. Vol. 2. Zurich, 1832.

Gesetz über die Polizey an Sonn- und Festtagen, über die Wirthschaften und das Spielen, 20. Weinmonat 1834. In *Offizielle Sammlung der seit 10. März 1831 erlassenen Gesetze, Beschlüsse und Verordnungen des Eidgenössischen Standes Zürich,* 301–302. Vol. 3. Zurich, 1833.

Gesetz über die Schuldbetreibung, 7. April, 1842. In *Offizielle Sammlung der seit 10. März 1831 erlassenen Gesetze, Beschlüsse und Verordnungen des eidgenössischen Standes Zürich,* 389–429. Vol. 6. Zurich, 1840 [*sic*].

Gesetz betreffend die Schuldbetreibung vom 5. April 1851. In *Offizielle Sammlung der seit 10. März 1831 erlassenen Gesetze, Beschlüsse und Verordnungen des eidgenössischen Standes Zürich,* 241–90. Vol. 8. Zurich, 1850 [*sic*].

Gesetz betreffend die Schuldbetreibung vom 29. Weinmonat 1871. In *Offizielle Sammlung der seit 10. März 1831 erlassenen Gesetze, Beschlüsse und Verordnungen des eidgenössischen Standes Zürich,* 181–237. Vol. 16. Zurich, 1873.

Gesetz über die Ablösung grundversicherter Forderungen überhaupt und über die Natur und Wiederauflösung der durch den Uebergang von Unterpfändern auf dritte Besitzer entstehenden Rechtsverhältnisse insbesondere. In

Officielle Sammlung der seit Annahme der Verfassung vom Jahre 1831 erlassenen Gesetze, Beschlüsse und Verordnungen des Eidgenössischen Standes Zürich, 280–86. Vol. 9. Zurich, 1853.

[Heusler, Andreas]. *Bundesgesez [sic] über Schuldbetreibung und Konkurs. Erster Entwurf mit Motiven.* Bern, 1874.

Hochobrigkeitliche Verordnung vom 16ten Julii [sic] 1805, betreffend die Auffallsverhandlungen, Pfandbücher und Pfandversilberungen. In *Officielle Sammlung der von dem Großen Rathe des Cantons Zürich gegebenen Gesetze und gemachten Verordnungen, und der von dem Kleinen Rath emanierten allgemeinen Landes- und Polizey-Verordnungen*, 108–113. Vol. 3. Zurich, 1808.

Kinkelin, Hermann. *Die Bevölkerung des Kantons Basel-Stadt am 1. Dezember 1870. Bericht an den E. E. Kleinen Rath.* Basel, 1872.

Officielle Sammlung der von dem Großen Rathe des Cantons Zürich gegebenen Gesetze und gemachten Verordnungen, und der von dem Kleinen Rath emanierten allgemeinen Landes- und Polizey-Verordnungen [1803–1830].

Offizielle Sammlung der seit 10. März 1831 erlassenen Gesetze, Beschlüsse und Verordnungen des Eidgenössischen Standes Zürich [1831–1885].

Privatrechtliches Gesetzbuch für den Kanton Zürich. 4 vols. Zurich, 1854–56.

Ratschlag und Entwurf eines Grossratsbeschlusses betreffend die bürgerliche Stellung der Falliten. Dem Grossen Rate vorgelegt den 4. Dezember 1893 (= Ratschlag 968). Basel, 1893.

Rathschlag und Gesetzesentwurf über die rechtlichen Folgen von Fallimenten, dem E. Großen Rath vorgelegt am 3. Dezember 1866 (= Rathschlag 357). Basel, 1866.

Rechenschaftsbericht des Obergerichts an den Großen Rath des Standes Zürich über das Jahr . . . [1831–1869].

Rechenschaftsbericht über die Verwaltung der Zürcher Kantonalbank umfassend das Jahr . . . , dem h. Kantonsrath erstattet vom Bankrathe. Zurich, 1871–1890.

Reglement für die Mobiliarleihkasse der Zürcher Kantonalbank (vom 30. Weinmonat 1871). In *Offizielle Sammlung der seit 10. März 1831 erlassenen Gesetze, Beschlüsse und Verordnungen des Eidgenössischen Standes Zürich*, 108–13. Vol. 15. Zurich, 1873.

Satz- und Ordnungen eines frey-loblichen Statt-Gerichts zu Zürich. Zurich, 1715.

Statistik der Rechtspflege des Kantons Zürich 1867. Zurich, 1868.

Statistische Mittheilungen betreffend den Kanton Zürich. Beilage zum Rechenschaftsbericht des Regierungsrathes für das Jahr 1885. Winterthur, 1886.

Der Statt Basel Statuta und Gerichtsordnung . . . . Basel, 1849.

Verhandlungen der ständeräthlichen Kommission betreffend den vom Bundesrathe am 23. Februar 1886 festgestellten Entwurf eines Bundesgesetzes über Schuldbetreibung und Konkurs. *Schweizerisches Bundesblatt*, vol. 3, 38, no. 48 (November 20, 1886).

Verordnung vom 16ten May 1804, betreffend den Handelsverkehr der Juden. In *Officielle Sammlung der von dem Großen Rathe des Cantons Zürich gegebenen Gesetze und gemachten Verordnungen, und der von dem Kleinen Rath emanierten allgemeinen Landes- und Polizey-Verordnungen*, 94–95. Vol. 2. Zurich, 1805.

Verwaltungsbericht[e] des Kleinen Raths an E. Großen Rath des Kantons Basel-Stadt vom Jahr . . . [1840–1869].

Periodicals

Allgemeines Noth- und Hülfsblatt (1846)
Amtsblatt des Kantons Zürich (February 7, 1843)
Archiv für Schuldbetreibung und Konkurs (1892–1906)
Beiträge zur Kunde und Fortbildung der zürcherischen Rechtspflege (1841–1854)
Berner Volkszeitung (1889, 1893–1898)
Der Bote von Uster (1845)
*Confidentia: Schweizer Handels-Auskunftsblatt. Allgemeines schweizerisches Sammelblatt
    für amtliche und ausseramtliche Bekanntmachungen* (1904)
Ernste und heitere Bilder aus dem Leben unseres Volkes (1850–1855)
Der Gerichtssaal: Zeitschrift für schweizerische Civil- und Strafrechtspflege (1887–1890)
Der Hülferuf der deutschen Jugend (September–December 1841; reprint Leipzig
    1972)
Die junge Generation (January 1842–May 1843; reprint Leizpig 1972)
Monatschronik der zürcherischen Rechtspflege (1833–1838)
Neue Zürcher Zeitung (1889, 1892)
Politisches Jahrbuch der schweizerischen Eidgenossenschaft (1886–1892)
Schweizerisches Bundesblatt
Schweizerisches Volksblatt vom Bachtel (1867)
Schweizerische Zeitschrift für Gemeinnützigkeit (1862–1890)
*Schweizer Kriminal-Zeitung: Organ für Kriminal-, Polizei- und Civil-Gerichtspflege,
    Unterhaltung und Humor* (1892–1895)
Der Urwähler. Organ des Befreiungsbundes: Eine Wochenschrift (1848)
Das Vaterland. Konservatives Zentralorgan für die deutsche Schweiz (1889)
Zeitschrift für Kunde und Fortbildung der zürcherischen Rechtspflege (1854–1870)
Zeitschrift für schweizerisches Recht (1852–1892)

Articles, Reports, Studies, Fiction

Alhoy, Maurice. *Physiologie du créancier et du débiteur.* Paris, 1842.
Annenkow, P. W. "Bericht über eine Sitzung des Kommunistischen Korrespon-
    denzkomitees in Brüssel, 30. März 1846." In *Der Bund der Kommunisten. Doku-
    mente und Materialien,* edited by Institut für Marxismus-Leninismus beim ZK
    der SED. Vol. 1, *1836–1849,* 301–305. Berlin (GDR): Dietz, 1970.
*Die Ausbeutung der Arbeiter und die Ursachen ihrer Verarmung: Ein Beitrag zur socialen
    Frage. Preisgekrönt mit der Goldenen Medaille auf dem Internationalen Wettstreit
    zur Verbesserung der Lage der Arbeiter zu Köln a. Rh. 1890.* 2nd ed. Kiel/Leipzig,
    1892.
Bachmann, J. H. *Die Grundzüge des Entwurfes eines eidgenösssischen Betreibungs- und
    Konkursgesetzes. Rede, gehalten in der Sitzung des schweizerischen Nationalrates den
    13. April 1887.* Frauenfeld, 1887.
Balmer, Hans. "Pfandleihgewerbe." In *Volkswirthschafts-Lexikon der Schweiz,* edited
    by Alfred Furrer, 568–71. Vol. 2. Bern, 1889.
Bayle-Mouillard, J. B. *De l'emprisonnement pour dettes; considérations sur son origine,
    ses rapports avec la morale publique et les intérêts du commerce, des familles, de la
    société, suivie de la statistique de la contrainte par corps.* Paris, 1836.

Beccaria, Cesare. *An Essay on Crimes and Punishments*. Translated by Edward D. Ingraham. Philadelphia, 1819 [1764].

P. F. Bellot, M. Schaub, M. P. Odier, M. E. Mallet. *Loi sur la procédure civile du Canton de Genève, suivie de l'Exposé des motifs*. 2nd ed. Paris: Librairie D'Abraham Cherbuliez, 1837.

Bendiner, Hermann. *Das Wirtshausverbot. Eine schweizerische Strafe und Verwaltungsregel*. Zurich: E. Kreutler, 1917.

Bete und arbeite! Ein wohlgemeintes Wort an die Arbeiter gegeben in drei gekrönten Volksschriften über den Segen der Sparkassen: Zur Förderung des geistigen und materiellen Wohles aller Arbeiter, herausgegeben von der Seidenindustrie-Gesellschaft des Kantons Zürich. 2nd ed. Stäfa, 1859.

Beyel, Christian. *Commissionalbericht über die Schweizerischen Verkehrsverhältnisse zu Handen der zürcherischen Industriegesellschaft, (vorgetragen in dem größeren Ausschusse des Zürcherischen Industrievereins den 21. Februar 1843)*. Vol. 1. N.p. [Zurich], 1843.

Blumenbach, Johann Friedrich. *Über den Bildungstrieb und das Zeugungsgeschäfte*. Göttingen, 1781.

Bluntschli, Johann Caspar. *Die Kommunisten in der Schweiz nach den bei Weitling vorgefundenen Papieren. Wörtlicher Abdruck des Kommissionalberichtes an die H. Regierung des Standes Zürich*. Zurich, 1843.

Bluntschli, Johann Caspar. *Staats- und Rechtsgeschichte der Stadt und Landschaft Zürich*. 2 vols., 2nd ed. Zurich, 1856.

Böhm-Bawerk, Eugen von. "Wert." In Vol. 6 of *Handwörterbuch der Staatswissenschaften*, 2nd ed., edited by Johannes Conrad, 681–698. Jena: G. Fischer, 1895.

Böppli, Rudolf Johann. "Die Zehntablösung in der Schweiz, speziell im Kanton Zürich." Doctoral dissertation, Universität Zürich, 1914.

Brändle, Fabian, ed. *Das lange Leben eines Toggenburger Hausierers: Gregorius Aemisegger 1815–1913*. Wattwil: Toggenburger Verlag, 2007.

Brenner, Ernst. "Der Wucher und seine Bekämpfung." *Schweizerische Zeitschrift für Gemeinnützigkeit* 20 (1881): 197–213.

Brüstlein, Alfred. *Die Grundzüge des Entwurfes eines eidgenössischen Betreibungs- und Konkursgesetzes. Eine Streitschrift als Entgegnung auf die Broschüre des Herrn Nationalrath J. H. Bachmann*. Basel, 1888.

[Brüstlein, Alfred]. *Zur Volksabstimmung vom 17. November 1889. Ein Wort der Aufklärung an das Schweizervolk zum Bundesgesetze über Schuldbetreibung und Konkurs*. Bern, 1889.

Bürkli, Karl. *Eine Kantonalbank, aber keine Herren-, sondern eine Volksbank, keine 5 und 6%, sondern 2, höchstens 3 Prozent Zins. Sturz der Geldaristokratie durch eine Staatsbank ohne Gold- und Silbergeld*. Zurich, 1866.

Burkhardt-Fürstenberger, J. U. *Entwurf einer Schweizerischen Wechselordnung mit Motiven*. Zurich, 1857.

Conrad, Herbert. *Die Pfändungsbeschränkungen zum Schutze des schwachen Schuldners: eine juristische und sozialpolitische Studie*. Jena: G. Fischer, 1906.

Cosimo, Amidei. *Discorso filosofico-politico sopra la carcere de'debitorio*. Harlem, 1771.

"Diskussion über die Pfand- und Leihhäuser." *Schweizerische Zeitschrift für Gemeinnützigkeit* 4 (1865): 68–74.

Egli, Gottlieb. "Die Bürgschaft." *Der Gerichtssaal: Zeitschrift für schweizerische Civil- und Strafrechtspflege* 4, no. 14 (February 16, 1887): 72–73.

Das Ehrenfolgengesetz. Aufklärung für die Abstimmung vom 6. Mai 1894 und Aufruf zur Verwerfung. Von einem Volksfreund. N.p., n.d.

Eichholzer, Ed[uard]. *Zur Geschichte von Handelsregister und Firmenrecht im Kanton Zürich.* Zurich: Schulthess, 1917.

Einert, C[arl]. *Das Wechselrecht nach dem Bedürfniss des Wechselgeschäfts des 19ten Jahrhunderts.* Leipzig, 1839.

Ein schweizerischer Creditorenverband: ein Projekt, ausgearbeitet von Delegierten der Vereine "Creditreform," "Schweiz. Manufakturisten-Verband" und "Verein schweiz. Geschäftsreisender". Zurich, 1897.

Erhardt, F. G. *Inhalt, Entstehung und Untergang des Schuldbriefes nach zürcherischem Rechte.* Zurich, 1846.

Die schweizerischen Falliten vor 1892 und nach 1892 an das Schweizervolk und seine Behörden. Ein Beitrag zur Lösung der schweiz. "Fallitenfrage" von den Gesuchstellern in der Schweizerischen Republik." N.p., April 1893.

Estermann, Balthasar. *Wechselhaft im neuen Strafvollzugswesen.* Lucerne, 1867.

Falkmann. "Gutachten [. . .] über die Frage: Empfiehlt sich eine grundsätzliche Vermehrung der bestehenden Beschränkungen der Zwangsvollstreckung, etwa in Richtung einer allgemeinen Competenzwohlthat?" *Verhandlungen des 22. deutschen Juristentages,* 240–64. Vol. 1. Berlin, 1892.

Farner, Gottfried. *Das zürcherische Bodenkreditwesen unter den Anforderungen der Gegenwart.* Zurich, 1863.

Farner, Gottfried. *Der Schuldbriefverkehr und das zürcherische Notariatswesen unter der Initiative.* Zurich, 1869.

Flesch. "Zwangsvollstreckung." In *Handwörterbuch der Staatswissenschaften,* edited by Johannes Conrad, 1088–95. 2nd ed. Vol. 7. Jena: G. Fischer, 1901.

Furrer, Johann Ulrich. *Schweizerländli 1848: Das Tagebuch eines jungen Sternenbergers.* Stäfa: Rothenhäusler, 1997.

Gewerbe- und Handels-Adressbuch der Schweiz / Annuaire du commerce et de l'industrie Suisse. Basel, 1885.

Gotthelf, Jeremias. *Der Geltstag oder die Wirtschaft nach der neuen Mode.* Vol. 8 of *Sämtliche Werke in 24 Bänden,* edited by Rudolf Hunziker and Hans Bloesch. Erlenbach-Zurich: E. Rentzsch, 1923 [1846].

Grunholzer, Heinrich. "Erfahrungen eines jungen Schweizers im Vogtlande." In *Dies Buch gehört dem König* [1843], edited by Bettine von Arnim. Vol. 3 of Bettine von Arnim, *Werke und Briefe,* edited by Wolfgang Bunzel, Ulrike Landfester, Walter Schmitz, and Sibylle von Steinsdorff, 329–68. Frankfurt am Main: Suhrkamp, 1995.

Gwalter, J. H. *Das zürcherische Schuldbetreibungsgesetz vom 1. April 1851. Mit Erläuterungen unter vorzüglicher Berücksichtigung der gerichtlichen Praxis.* Zurich, 1853.

Haab, Friedrich. *Ueber die Einstellung der Konkursiten ins Aktivbürgerrecht.* Zurich, 1871.

Heinrich, Hermann. *Aus der Schuldhaft! Ein Nothschrei an unsere Gesetzgeber.* Leipzig, 1865.

Heusler, Andreas. "Das Weibergutsprivileg und das schweizerische Concursgesetz." *Zeitschrift für schweizerisches Recht,* n.s., 23 (1882): 17–53.

Hilty, Carl. "Eidgenössische Politik, Gesetzgebung und politische Literatur." *Politisches Jahrbuch der Schweizerischen Eidgenossenschaft* 1 (1886): 491–612.

Hirzel, C[onrad] M[elchior]. *Ueber Zuchthäuser und ihre Verwandlung in Besserungshäuser.* Zurich, 1826.

Hofmann, E. "Vier thurgauische Haushaltsbudgets." *Zeitschrift für schweizerische Statistik* 29 (1893): 499–531.

Hunziker, Fritz. "J. L. Spyri." *Schweizerische Zeitschrift für Gemeinnützigkeit* 36 (1896): 85–91.

Iselin, Isaak. "Väterlicher Rath an meinen Sohn, der sich der Handelsschaft widmet." In *Moral für Kaufleute und väterlicher Rath für meinen Sohn, der sich der Handlungswissenschaft widmet. Neue Auflage,* edited by C. A. Büsch, 47–90. Leipzig, n.d. [ca. 1800].

Isler, Alexander. "Die Gefahren der Bürgschaft. Warnung vor ihrer Eingehung und Vorschläge zur Abhülfe." *Schweizerische Zeitschrift für Gemeinnützigkeit* 26 (1887): 339–89.

Keller, Friedrich Ludwig. "Ueber den Rechtszustand der Falliten." *Monatschronik der zürcherischen Rechtspflege* 1 (1833): 113–21.

Keller, Gottfried. *Die Leute von Seldwyla.* Edited by Peter Villwock, Walter Morgenthaler, Peter Stocker, and Thomas Binder. Vol. 5 of *Sämtliche Werke. Historisch-Kritische Ausgabe.* Basel: Stroemfeld, 2000 [1856].

Keller, Gottfried. *Martin Salander.* Translated by Kenneth Halwas. London: John Calder, 1964.

Keller, Gottfried. *Martin Salander.* Edited by Thomas Binder, Karl Grob, Peter Stocker, and Walter Morgenthaler. Vol. 8 of *Sämtliche Werke. Historisch-Kritische Ausgabe.* Basel: Stroemfeld, 2004 [1886].

Keller, Gottfried. *The People of Seldwyla.* In *A Selection of His Tales,* translated by Kate Freiligrath Kroeker. London, 1891.

Keller, Gottfried. *Seldwyla Folks: Three Singular Tales.* Translated by Wolf von Schierbran. New York: Brentano's, 1919.

Landolt, Carl. "Zehn Basler Arbeiterhaushaltungen." *Zeitschrift für Schweizerische Statistik* 27 (1891): 281–372.

Leuthy, Johann Jakob. *Handbuch der Schweizerischen Handels-, Gewerbs- und Niederlassungs-Verhältnisse für Beamte, Rechtsanwälte, Notare, Kaufleute, Geschäftsmänner, u.a.* Vol. 4. Zurich, 1849.

Locher, Friedrich. *Die Mängel des zürcherischen Konkursprozesses und deren Abhülfe.* Zurich, 1856.

"Loi constitutionelle rendue dans le canton de Genève sur la liberté individuelle et l'abolition de la contrainte par corps. Note explicative de la discussion, par un membre du Grand-Conseil." *Revue de droit français et étranger* 6, no. 2 (1849): 493–99.

Maisch, L. *Der Kampf gegen den Wucher und die gesetzliche Ordnung des Gelddarleih- und Pfandleih-Gewerbes.* N.p. [Bern?], 1887.

Mandeville, Bernard. *The Fable of the Bees: or, Private Vices, Publick Benefits. Containing, Several Discourses, to Demonstrate, that Human Frailties, during the Degeneracy of Mankind, May be Turn'd to the Advantage of the Civil Society, and Made to Supply the Place of Moral Virtues.* London, 1714.

Marx, Karl. *Capital: Volume 1.* Translated by Ben Fowkes. London: Penguin, 1990 [1867].

Marx, Karl. *Capital: Volume 3.* Vol. 37 of *Collected Works.* New York: International Publishers, 1998 [1894].

Marx, Karl. "Comments on James Mill, *Élémens d'économie politique.*" In *Marx and Engels Collected Works.* Vol. 7, *Karl Marx, March 1843–August 1844,* 211–28. London: Lawrence & Wishart, 2010.

Matthys, Andreas. *Ansichtsäußerung über die Frage: Ob die Spar- und Leihkasse in der Stadt Bern für ihre Rechnung und Gefahr eine Pfandleih-Anstalt errichten soll?* Bern, 1862.

Meier, Eugen. *Die Beschränkungen der Zwangsvollstreckung (Lehre von den Kompetenzstücken) nach schweizerischem Recht. Mit einer allgemein-geschichtlichen Einleitung.* Zurich: Schulthess, 1907.

Meier, Felix. *Geschichte der Gemeinde Wetzikon.* Zurich: Lesegesellschaft Oberwetzikon, 1881.

Meili, F. *Der gesetzgeberische Kampf gegen Schädigungen im Bauhandwerk, in der illoyalen Konkurrenz und im Kreditwesen: Drei Gesetzgebungsfragen.* Zurich: Orell Füssli, 1901.

Meiss, Gottfried von. *Das Pfand-Recht und der Pfand- oder Betreibungs-Proceß in seinem ganzen Umfang: Nach den Gesetzen und der Uebung des Eidgen. Cantons Zürich/Ein civilrechtlicher Versuch.* Zurich, 1821.

Mittermaier, [Carl Joseph Anton]. "Ueber den persönlichen Verhaft wegen Schulden (mit Rücksicht auf die Erfahrungen und Gesetze von Frankreich, Belgien, Genf u. A.)." *Kritische Zeitschrift für Rechtswissenschaft und Gesetzgebung des Auslandes* 10 (1838): 272–99.

Der Mont de Piété in Basel. Basel, 1865.

Morgenthaler, Walter, Peter Villwock, Peter Stocker, and Thomas Binder, eds. *Gottfried Keller: Sämtliche Werke. Historisch-kritische Ausgabe.* Vol. 21, *Leute von Seldwyla: Apparat zu Band 4 und 5.* Basel: Stroemfeld, 2000.

Müller, Johann Samuel. *Praktisches Handbuch zur rechtlichen Eintreibung der verschiedenen Arten von Schulden, nebst aller Arten in das Schuldbetreibungsfach einschlagenden Formulars.* Bern: Maurhofer & Dellenbach, 1811.

Munzinger, Walther. *Motive zu dem Entwurfe eines schweizerischen Handelsrechtes.* Bern, 1865.

"Natur-Triebe", *Grosses vollständiges Universal-Lexicon aller Wissenschaften und Künste,* vol. 23, (Leipzig, 1740), 1225–26.

Nietzsche, Friedrich. *On the Genealogy of Morality.* Edited by Keith Ansell-Pearson. Translated by Carol Diethe. Cambridge: Cambridge University Press, 2006 [1887].

Omura, Izumi, Valerij Fomičev, Rolf Hecker, and Shun-ichi Kubo, eds. *Familie Marx privat. Die Foto- und Fragebogen-Alben von Marx' Töchtern Laura und Jenny.* Berlin: Akademie, 2005.

Reichel, Alexander. "Referat: Das Betreibungsamt im schweizerischen Recht." *Zeitschrift für schweizerisches Recht* 28 (1887): 567–607.

Reithard, Johann Jakob. "Eine schweizerische Dorfgeschichte." In *Neue Alpenrosen. Eine Gabe schweizerischer Dichter,* edited by Johann Jakob Reithard, 249–350. Zurich, 1848.

Rintelen, Max. *Untersuchungen über die Entwicklung des Handelsregisters.* Stuttgart: Encke, 1914.

Ritzmann-Blickenstorfer, Heiner, ed. *Historische Statistik der Schweiz*. Zurich: Chronos, 1996.

Rivier, Alphonse. "De la contrainte par corps en Suisse." *Revue de droit international et de législation comparée* 2 (1870): 42–52.

Rothpletz, August. "Handelsregister." In *Handwörterbuch der Schweizerischen Volkswirtschaft, Sozialpolitik und Verwaltung*, edited by Naum Reichersberg, 545–47. Vol. 2. Bern, n.d. [ca. 1900].

Schinz, Salomon. "Das höhere Gebirg des Kantons Zürich, und ökonomisch-moralischer Zustand der Bewohner, mit Vorschlägen der Hülfe und Auskunft für die bey mangelnder Fabrik-Arbeit brotlose Uebervölkerung, [. . .] in der Synodal-Rede 1817." *Der gemeinnützige Schweizer* 3 (1818): 174–206.

Schlatter, Friedrich. *Schuldbetreibung und Konkurs nach schweizerischem Recht: Ein Wegweiser*. Zurich, 1893.

Schmidlin, W. "Ueber Pfand- und Leihhäuser (monts de Piété): Referat in der Versammlung der Schweizerischen gemeinnützigen Gesellschaft zu Basel den 22. September 1864 von Dr. W. Schmidlin, Director der schweizerischen Centralbahn." *Schweizerische Zeitschrift für Gemeinnützigkeit* 4 (1865): 41–67.

Schoffer, H. *Die landwirtschaftliche Kreditkrisis unserer Tage. Eine populäre Darstellung der betreffenden Verhältnisse und Beleuchtung der Hülfsmittel. Im Auftrag des Vereins für Landwirthschaft und Gartenbau im Kanton Zürich*. 2nd ed. Zurich, 1867 [1866?].

Schröter, [Carl]. *Die öffentlichrechtlichen Folgen der fruchtlosen Pfändung und des Konkurses in der Schweiz*. Bern: Schmid & Francke, 1902.

Schweizer, Ludwig Jakob. *Ueber den zunehmenden Verdienstmangel in den östlichen Gemeinden des Cantons Zürich*. Zurich, 1831.

Senn, Jakob. *Ein Kind des Volkes: Schweizerisches Lebensbild*. Zurich: Rohr, 1966 [1888].

Siegmund, L. "Zur Geschichte der Gesetzgebung über Ragionenbuch und Wechselrecht in Basel." *Zeitschrift für schweizerisches Recht*, n.s., 1 (1882): 79–134.

Siegmund, L. *Handbuch für die schweizerischen Handelsregisterführer. Im Auftrage des schweizerischen Justiz- und Polizeidepartementes*. Basel, 1892.

Simmel, Georg. *The Philosophy of Money*. Translated by Tom Bottomore and David Frisby. London: Routledge & Kegan Paul, 1978 [1900].

Spyri, J[ohann] L[udwig]. *Der Pauperismus der Zeit mit vorzüglicher Berücksichtigung der östlichen Gegenden des Kantons Zürich*. Zurich, 1848.

Spyri, J[ohann] L[udwig]. *Bericht über die Sparkassen des Kantons Zürich vom Jahr 1859/1860*. Zürich 1860.

Spyri, J[ohann] L[udwig]. "Ueber Pfand- und Leihhäuser." *Schweizerische Zeitschrift für Gemeinnützigkeit* 3 (1864): 235–53.

Stein, Lorenz von. *Geschichte der sozialen Bewegung in Frankreich von 1789 bis auf unsere Tage*. 3 vols. Munich: Drei Masken, 1921 [1842].

Stein, Lorenz von. *Der Wucher und sein Recht: ein Beitrag zum wirthschaftlichen und rechtlichen Leben unserer Zeit*. Vienna, 1880.

Stutz, Jakob. *Siebenmal sieben Jahre aus meinem Leben: Als Beitrag zur näheren Kenntnis des Volkes. Mit einem Nachwort und einer Bibliographie von Walter Haas und Anmerkungen von August Steiger*. Frauenfeld: Huber, 1983 [1853].

Sulzer, Eduard. *Ein Beitrag zu Lösung einer der wichtigsten Fragen unserer Zeit*. Zurich, 1852.

Sulzer, Heinrich. *Lehren für Jübanglinge, die sich der Handelschaft widmen werden, für die Lehr- und Fremde-Zeit.* N.p. [Winterthur], 1830.

Sulzer, Heinrich. *Vermächtniss für meinen Enkel. Lehren, Ermahnungen und Warnungen.* Winterthur, 1833.

Thurneysen, Eduard. *Eine offene Wunde unsers Volkslebens: Ein Wort wider das Bürgschaftswesen in unserer Zeit.* Zurich, 1888.

Tobler, Johann. *Gutartige Hierarchie. Armenbesorgung, und die schöne Friedensbitte. Von Archidiakon Tobler, nicht eben für jezt und kaum für hier.* Zurich, 1800.

Tönnies, Ferdinand. *Community and Civil Society.* Edited by Jose Harris and translated by Margaret Hollis. Cambridge: Cambridge University Press, 2001.

Trau! Schau! Wem? Ein freies Wort an das Schweizervolk über das neue Schulden-Betreibungsgesetz. Bern, 1889.

Treichler, Johann Jakob. *Politische Grundsätze.* Basel, 1846.

"Trib," *Schweizerisches Idiotikon. Wörterbuch der schweizerdeutschen Sprache,* vol. 14, (Frauenfeld: Verlag Huber & Co., 1987), 64–166.

Ueber die Gründung einer Mobiliar-Leihkasse in Basel, in Verbindung mit einer Handwerker-Bank. Basel, 1864.

[Ulrich, David]. *Uebersicht der der Verfassungs-Commission gemachten Eingaben, in so fern dieselben sich nicht zunächst auf die Staatsverfassung, sondern auf die verschiedenen Zweige der Verwaltung, der Justizpflege und der Gesetzgebung beziehen.* Zurich, 1831.

Verein Creditreform. *Statut der Schweizer Vereinigung gegen schädliches Creditgeben (Verein Creditreform—Union Suisse pour la sauvegarde des crédits). Nach den Beschlüssen des IV. Verbandstages zu Frankfurt a. M. am 27. und 28. Juni 1886, sowie der constituierenden Generalversammlung in Basel vom 2. Juli 1888.* Zurich, 1888.

Verein für Socialpolitik, ed. *Der Wucher auf dem Lande: Berichte und Gutachten veröffentlicht vom Verein für Socialpolitik.* Leipzig, 1887.

Villermé, [René-Louis]. *Tableau de l'état physique et moral des ouvriers employés dans les manufactures de coton, de laine et de soie. Ouvrage entrepris par ordre et sous les auspices de l'Académie des Sciences Morales et Politiques, par V., membre de cette Académie, tome second.* Paris, 1840.

Vogt, Albert, ed. *Unstet. Lebenslauf des Ärbeeribuebs, Chirsi- und Geschirrhausierers Peter Binz von ihm selbst erzählt.* Zurich: Chronos, 1995 [1895?].

Waser, J. R. *Der Pfarrer als Armenbesorger in seiner Gemeinde. Ein Wort über Armenunterstützungen und einige darauf bezügliche Vorschläge neuerer und neuster Zeit.* Zurich, 1836.

Weber, J. H. *Schweizerischer Rechtsgeschäftsfreund. Vollständige Sammlung der Schuldbetreibungs-, Konkurs- und Sportelngesetze aller Kantone der Schweiz; mit einem Anhang über allgemeines Wechselrecht.* Zurich, 1869.

Weber, Leo. "Handelsregister." In *Volkswirthschafts-Lexikon der Schweiz,* edited by Alfred Furrer, 8–12. Vol. 2. Bern, 1889.

Weber, Leo, and Alfred Brüstlein. *Das Bundesgesetz über Schuldbetreibung und Konkurs für den praktischen Gebrauch erläutert.* Zurich, 1890.

Weibel, J. L. "Die rechtliche Behandlung des Wuchers." *Verhandlungen des schweizerischen Juristenvereins 1884* 1 (1884): 53–87.

Weitling, Wilhelm. *Die Menschheit, wie sie ist und wie sie sein sollte.* Reinbek bei Hamburg: Rowohlt, 1971 [1839].

Weitling, Wilhelm. *Garantien der Harmonie und Freiheit.* With an introduction and annotations by Fr. Mehring. Berlin: Vorwärts, 1908 [1842].

Weitling, Wilhelm. *Das Evangelium des armen Sünders.* Reinbek bei Hamburg: Rowohlt, 1971 [1843/45].

Weitling, Wilhelm. *Gerechtigkeit. Ein Studium in 500 Tagen: Bilder der Wirklichkeit und Betrachtungen des Gefangenen—Nachwort von Ahlrich Meyer.* Berlin: Karin Kramer, 1977 [1845?].

Weitling, Wilhelm. "Brief aus Brüssel an Moses Hess in Verviers, 31. März 1846." In *Der Bund der Kommunisten. Dokumente und Materialien,* edited by Institut für Marxismus-Leninismus beim ZK der SED. Vol. 1, *1836–1849,* 307–308. Berlin (GDR): Dietz, 1970.

Widmer, C. *Zur Reform der Strafanstalt in Zürich. Ein Beitrag.* Zurich, 1855.

Wiesendanger, E. *Geschichte der Gemeinde Aussersihl. Vortrag, gehalten vor der "Gemeinnützigen Gesellschaft Aussersihl".* Aussersihl, 1888.

Wirz, Kaspar. *Etat des Zürcher Ministeriums von der Reformation bis zur Gegenwart: aus gedruckten und ungedruckten Quellen zusammengestellt und nach Kirchgemeinden geordnet.* Zurich, 1890.

Wohlmeinender Rath und freundliche Erinnerung an die Landleute des Kantons Zürich; in Bezug auf eine kanzleiische Schuldenbereinigung und eine neue Geld-Anleihungs-Einrichtung. N.p., 1818.

Wolf, Arthur. *Ueber den Zinsfuss ländlicher Grundpfanddarlehen mit besonderer Berücksichtigung der zürcherischen Verhältnisse.* Bern: Scheitlin & Co., 1912.

Wolf, G. *Verhältniß der Wohnungs-Vermiether & -Miether zum neuen Konkurs- und Betreibungsgesetz, mit einem Vorwort betreffend die übrigen Neuerungen im Betreibungsverfahren.* Zurich, n.d. [1889].

Wyß, David von. *Politisches Handbuch für die erwachsene Jugend der Stadt und Landschaft Zürich.* Zurich, 1796.

Wyß, Fr. von. "Die Schuldbetreibung nach schweizerischen Rechten." *Zeitschrift für schweizerisches Recht* 7 (1858): 3–114.

Wyß, Fr. von. "Die Gült und der Schuldbrief nach Zürcherischem Rechte." *Zeitschrift für schweizerisches Recht* 9 (1861): 2–67.

Wyß, Fr. von. "Schuldbetreibung." In vol. 9 of *Deutsches Staats-Wörterbuch,* edited by Johann Caspar Bluntschli and Karl L. Th. Brater, 258–64. Stuttgart/Leipzig, 1865.

Zehnder, Ulrich. *Die Noth der Verarmung oder der Pauperismus und die Mittel dagegen mit besonderer Rücksicht auf den Kanton Zürich.* Zurich, 1848.

Secondary Literature

Adorno, Theodor W., and Max Horkheimer. *Dialectic of Enlightenment: Philosophical Fragments.* Edited by Gunzelin Schmid Noerr, translated by Edmund Jephcott. Stanford, CA: Stanford University Press, 2002.

Agnew, Jean-Christophe. "Capitalism, Culture, and Catastrophe." In *The Cultural Turn in U.S. History: Past, Present, and Future,* edited by James W. Cook, Lawrence B. Glickman, and Michael O'Malley, 383–415. Chicago: University of Chicago Press, 2008.

Altermatt, Urs. *Katholizismus und Moderne. Zur Sozial- und Mentalitätsgeschichte der Schweizer Katholiken im 19. und 20. Jahrhundert.* Zurich: Benziger, 1989.

Althusser, Louis. "Ideology and Ideological State Apparatuses." In *Lenin and Philosophy and Other Essays,* translated by Ben Brewster, 85–126. New York: Monthly Review Press, 2001 [1969].

Althusser, Louis, and Étienne Balibar. *Reading Capital.* Translated by Ben Brewster. London: Verso, 2009 [1965].

Américi, Laurence. "Preparing the People for Capitalism: Relations with Depositors in a French Savings Bank during the 1820s." *Financial History Review* 9, no. 1 (2002): 5–19.

Antiquarische Gesellschaft Pfäffikon ZH, ed. *Jakob Stutz 1801–1877: Zürcher Oberländer Volksdichter und Zeitzeuge. Beiträge und Würdigungen.* Pfäffikon, 2001.

Antonov, Sergei. *Bankrupts and Usurers of Imperial Russia: Debt, Property, and the Law in the Age of Dostoevsky and Tolstoy.* Cambridge, MA: Harvard University Press, 2016.

Appadurai, Arjun. *The Social Life of Things: Commodities in Cultural Perspective.* Cambridge: Cambridge University Press, 1986.

Appenzeller, Erich. "Der Schuldverhaft und seine Abschaffung nach den Gesetzgebungen der schweizerischen Kantone und des Bundes." Law dissertation, Zurich, 1923.

Appleby, Joyce. *The Relentless Revolution: A History of Capitalism.* New York: W. W. Norton, 2010.

Arb, Christine von. "'Und so wird unsere Forderung als billig und gerecht anerkannt werden'. Die Eingaben der Einwohner des Bezirks Hinwil zur Revision der Zürcher Kantonsverfassung 1830/31." Unpublished paper, Historisches Seminar Universität Basel, 1991.

Argast, Regula. *Staatsbürgerschaft und Nation: Ausschluss und Integration in der Schweiz 1848–1933.* Göttingen: Vandenhoeck & Ruprecht, 2007.

Arru, Angiolina. "Die nicht bezahlte Mitgift. Ambivalenzen und Vorteile des Dotalsystems im ausgehenden 19. und beginnenden 20. Jahrhundert." *L'Homme: Zeitschrift für feministische Geschichtswissenschaft* 22 (2011): 55–69.

Arru, Angiolina. "'Schenken heißt nicht verlieren': Kredite, Schenkungen und die Vorteile der Gegenseitigkeit in Rom im 18. und 19. Jahrhundert." *L'Homme: Zeitschrift für feministische Geschichtswissenschaft* 9 (1998): 232–51.

Asendorf, Christoph. *Batteries of Life: On the History of Things and Their Perception in Modernity.* Translated by Don Reneau. Berkeley: University of California Press, 1993.

Auslander, Leora. "Beyond Words." *American Historical Review* 110 (2005): 1015–45.

Bachelard, Gaston. *The Formation of the Scientific Mind.* Translated by Mary McAllester Jones. Manchester: Clinamen Press, 2002 [1938].

Bachem, Malte, and Ruben Hackler. "Überlegungen zu einer historischen Anthropologie des Verfahrens." *H-Soz-Kult,* June 19, 2012. http://hsozkult.geschichte.hu-berlin.de/forum/type=diskussionen&id=1801.

Bärtschi, Hans-Peter. *Industrialisierung, Eisenbahnschlachten und Städtebau. Die Entwicklung des Zürcher Industrie- und Arbeiterstadtteils Aussersihl: Ein vergleichender Beitrag zur Architektur- und Technikgeschichte.* Basel: Birkhäuser, 1983.

Balibar, Étienne. *The Philosophy of Marx.* Translated by Chris Turner. London: Verso, 1995.

Balleisen, Edward J. *Navigating Failure: Bankruptcy and Commercial Society in Antebellum America.* Chapel Hill: University of North Carolina Press, 2001.

Ballenegger, Cédric. *Le droit vaudois des poursuites, 1803–1891.* Lausanne: Bibliothèque historique vaudoise, 2013.

Baltensberger, Helene. *Das Armenwesen des Kantons Zürich vom Armengesetz von 1836 bis zu den Revisionsbestrebungen der 60er Jahre.* Zurich: Lang, 1940.

Barth, Robert. *Protestantismus, soziale Frage und Sozialismus im Kanton Zürich 1830–1914.* Zurich: Theologischer Verlag, 1981.

Barthes, Roland. "The Reality Effect." In *The Rustle of Language,* translated by Richard Howard, 141–48. Berkeley: University of California Press, 1989 [1968].

Baur, Uwe. *Dorfgeschichte. Zur Entstehung und gesellschaftlichen Funktion einer literarischen Gattung im Vormärz.* Munich: Fink, 1978.

Beachy, Robert. "Bankruptcy and Social Death: The Influence of Credit-Based Commerce on Cultural and Political Values." *Zeitsprünge. Forschungen zur Frühen Neuzeit* 4, no. 4 (2000): 329–43.

Becker, Peter, and William Clark, eds. *Little Tools of Knowledge. Historical Essays on Academic and Bureaucratic Practices.* Ann Arbor: University of Michigan Press, 2001.

Beckert, Sven. *Empire of Cotton: A Global History.* New York: Knopf, 2014.

Beereuter, Karin. "Sozio-politischer und sozio-ökonomischer Wandel einer agrarischen Gemeinde im Zürcher Unterland vom späten 18. Jahrhundert bis 1840 (Stadel)." Unpublished thesis, Universität Zürich, 1994.

Benjamin, Walter. "Gottfried Keller: In Honor of a Critical Edition of His Works." In *Selected Writings,* vol. 2, bk. 1, 51–62. Cambridge, MA: Belknap Press, 2005 [1927].

Bennewitz, Susanne. *Basler Juden, französische Bürger. Migration und Alltag einer jüdischen Gemeinde im frühen 19. Jahrhundert.* Basel: Schwabe, 2008.

Benveniste, Émile. *Indo-European Language and Society.* Translated by Elizabeth Palmer. Coral Gables, FL: University of Miami Press, 1973 [1969].

Benveniste, Émile. *Problems in General Linguistics.* Translated by Mary Elizabeth Meek. Coral Gables, FL: University of Miami Press, 1971.

Berdecki, Eduard. "Die Einflüsse der Aufklärung auf die Schuldhaft in den deutschen Staaten und in der Schweiz." Law dissertation, Basel, 1959.

Bergfeld, Christoph. "Über die Aufhebung der Schuldhaft in Frankreich und in Deutschland." In *Wechselseitige Beeinflussungen und Rezeptionen von Recht und Philosophie in Deutschland und Frankreich,* edited by Jean-François Kervégan and Heinz Mohnhaupt, 329–78. Frankfurt am Main: Vittorio Klostermann, 2001.

Berghoff, Hartmut. "Markterschließung und Risikomanagement: Die Rolle der Kreditauskunfteien und Rating-Agenturen im Industrialisierungs- und Globalisierungsprozess des 19. Jahrhunderts." *Vierteljahrschrift für Sozial- und Wirtschaftsgeschichte* 92 (2005): 141–62.

Bernet, Brigitta. "'Der bürgerliche Tod': Entmündigungsangst, Psychiatriekritik und die Krise des liberalen Subjektentwurfs um 1900." In *Zwang zur Ordnung.*

Psychiatrie im Kanton Zürich, 1870–1970, edited by Brigitta Bernet, Roswitha Dubach, Urs Germann, and Marietta Meier, 117–53. Zurich: Chronos, 2007.

Bernet, Brigitta. *Schizophrenie. Entstehung und Entwicklung eines psychiatrischen Krankheitsbildes um 1900.* Zurich: Chronos, 2013.

Biernacki, Richard. *The Fabrication of Labor: Germany and Britain, 1640–1914.* Berkeley: University of California Press, 1995.

Binnenkade, Alexandra. *KontaktZonen. Jüdisch-christlicher Alltag in Lengnau.* Cologne: Böhlau, 2009.

Blaschke, Olaf. "Antikapitalismus und Antisemitismus: Die Wirtschaftsmentalität der Katholiken im Wilhelminischen Deutschland." In *Shylock? Zinsverbot und Geldverleih in jüdischer und christlicher Tradition,* edited by Johannes Heil, 114–46. Munich: Fink, 1997.

Böhler, Michael. "'Fettaugen über einer Wassersuppe'—frühe Moderne-Kritik beim späten Gottfried Keller. Die Diagnose einer Verselbständigung der Zeichen und der Ausdifferenzierung autonomer Kreisläufe." In *Nachmärz. Der Ursprung der ästhetischen Moderne in einer nachrevolutionären Konstellation,* edited by Thomas Koebner and Sigrid Weigel, 292–305. Opladen: Springer, 1996.

Boltanski, Luc. *On Critique: A Sociology of Emancipation.* Translated by Gregory Elliott. Cambridge: Polity Press, 2011.

Boltanski, Luc, and Laurent Thévenot. *On Justification: The Economies of Worth.* Translated by Catherine Porter. Princeton, NJ: Princeton University Press, 2006 [1991].

Bordo, Michael, and Harold James. "Die Nationalbank 1907–1946: Glückliche Kindheit oder schwierige Jugend?" In *Die Schweizerische Nationalbank 1907–2007,* edited by the Schweizerische Nationalbank, 29–118. Zurich: Neue Zürcher Zeitung, 2007.

Bourdieu, Pierre. "The Biographical Illusion." In *Biography in Theory,* edited by Wilhelm Hemecker and Edward Saunders, 210–16. Berlin: de Gruyter, 2017 [1986].

Bourdieu, Pierre. "The Economy of Symbolic Goods." In *Practical Reason: On the Theory of Action,* 92–123. Stanford, CA: Stanford University Press, 1998 [1986].

Bourdieu, Pierre. *Esquisse d'une théorie de la pratique: Précédé de trois études d'ethnologie kabyle.* Paris: Seuil, 2000 [1972].

Bourdieu, Pierre. *Language and Symbolic Power.* Edited by John B. Thompson, translated by Gino Raymond and Matthew Adamson. Cambridge: Polity Press, 1991.

Bourdieu, Pierre. *Outline of a Theory of Practice.* Translated by Richard Nice. Cambridge: Cambridge University Press, 1977 [1972].

Bracht, Johannes. *Geldlose Zeiten und überfüllte Kassen: Sparen, Leihen und Vererben in der ländlichen Gesellschaft Westfalens (1830–1866).* Stuttgart: Lucius & Lucius, 2013.

Brändli, Sabina. *"Der herrlich biedere Mann": Vom Siegeszug des bürgerlichen Herrenanzuges im 19. Jahrhundert.* Zurich: Chronos, 1998.

Brantlinger, Patrick. *Fictions of State: Culture and Credit in Britain 1694–1994.* Ithaca, NY: Cornell University Press, 1996.

Braudel, Fernand. "History and the Social Sciences: The *Longue Durée*." Translated by Immanuel Wallerstein. *Review* 32, no. 2 (2009) [1958]: 171–203.

Braun, Rudolf. *Industrialisierung und Volksleben: Die Veränderungen der Lebensformen in einem ländlichen Industriegebiet vor 1800 (Zürcher Oberland).* Erlenbach: Eugen Rentsch, 1960.

Braun, Rudolf. *Sozialer und kultureller Wandel in einem ländlichen Industriegebiet im 19. und 20. Jahrhundert.* Zurich: Eugen Rentsch, 1999 [1965].

Brecht, Eberhard. "Wohlversorgt im 'Berg': Zürichs altes Gefängnis für Missetäter, Vagabunden und Bedürftige." *Tages-Anzeiger,* June 12, 1981, 51.

Breithaupt, Fritz. "Homo Oeconomicus (Junges Deutschland, Psychologie, Keller und Freytag)." In *1848 und das Versprechen der Moderne,* edited by Jürgen Fohrmann and Helmut J. Schneider, 85–112. Würzburg: Königshausen & Neumann, 2003.

Breßler, Steffen. *Schuldknechtschaft und Schuldturm. Zur Personalexekution im sächsischen Recht des 13.–16. Jahrhunderts.* Berlin: Duncker & Humblot, 2004.

Bröckling, Ulrich. *The Entrepreneurial Self: Fabricating a New Type of Subject.* Translated by Steven Black. London: Sage, 2015.

Brugger, Hans. *Die schweizerische Landwirtschaft in der ersten Hälfte des 19. Jahrhunderts.* Frauenfeld: Huber, 1956.

Brugger, Otto. *Geschichte der deutschen Handwerkervereine in der Schweiz 1836–1843. Die Wirksamkeit Weitlings (1841–1843).* Bern: Haupt, 1932.

de Brunhoff, Suzanne. *Marx on Money.* Translated by Duncan Foley and Maurice Goldbloom. London: Pluto, 1977.

Brunner, Otto. "Das 'ganze Haus' und die alteuropäische 'Ökonomik.'" In *Neue Wege der Verfassungs- und Sozialgeschichte,* 103–27. Göttingen: Vandenhoeck & Ruprecht, 1968 [1956].

Brunold-Bigler, Ursula. "Jakob Stutz' (1801–1877) Autobiographie 'Sieben mal sieben Jahre aus meinem Leben' als Quelle 'populärer Lesestoffe' im 19. Jahrhundert." *Schweizerisches Archiv für Volkskunde* 75 (1979): 28–42.

Brunschwig, Annette, Ruth Heinrichs, and Karin Huser. *Geschichte der Juden im Kanton Zürich: Von den Anfängen bis in die heutige Zeit.* Zurich: Orell Füssli, 2005.

Budde, Gunilla, ed. *Kapitalismus. Historische Annäherungen.* Göttingen: Vandenhoeck & Ruprecht, 2011.

Burke, Peter. *History and Social Theory.* 2nd ed. Ithaca, NY: Cornell University Press, 2005.

Burke, Peter. *A Social History of Knowledge: From Gutenberg to Diderot.* Cambridge: Polity Press, 2000.

Butler, Judith. "Bodies and Power Revisited." In *Feminism and the Final Foucault,* edited by Dianna Taylor and Karen Vintges, 183–94. Urbana: University of Illinois Press, 2004.

Butler, Judith. *The Psychic Life of Power: Theories in Subjection.* Stanford, CA: Stanford University Press, 1997.

Campbell, Gwyn, and Alessandro Stanziani, eds. *Debt and Slavery in the Mediterranean and Atlantic Worlds.* London: Pickering and Chatto, 2013.

Caroni, Pio. "Der 'demokratische' code unique von 1881. Eine Studie zur ideologischen Beziehung von Sonderrecht und Demokratie." In *Das Obligationen-recht 1883–1983*, edited by Pio Caroni, 19–68. Bern: P. Haupt, 1984.

Caroni, Pio. *Privatrecht: Eine sozialhistorische Einführung*. Basel: Helbing & Lichtenhahn, 1988.

Caroni, Pio. "Rechtseinheit in der Schweiz. Zur Geschichte einer späten Verfassungsreform." In *Rechtseinheit. Drei historische Studien zu Art. 64 BV*, 9–54. Basel: Helbing & Lichtenhahn, 1986.

Carrier, James. *Gifts and Commodities: Exchange and Western Capitalism since 1700*. London: Routledge, 1995.

Carruthers, Bruce, and Wendy Nelson Espeland. "Accounting for Rationality: Double-Entry Bookkeeping and the Rhetoric of Economic Rationality." *American Journal of Sociology* 97, no. 1 (1991): 31–69.

Castel, Robert. *From Manual Workers to Wage Laborers: Transformation of the Social Question*. Translated and edited by Richard Boyd. London: Routledge, 2017 [1995].

Castoriadis, Cornelius. *The Imaginary Institution of Society*. Translated by Kathleen Blamey. Cambridge, MA: MIT Press, 1987 [1975].

Cerutti, Simona. "Microhistory: Social Relations versus Cultural Models?" In *Between Sociology and History: Essays on Microhistory, Collective Action, and Nation-Building*, edited by Anna-Majia Castrén, 17–40. Helsinki SKS/Finnish Literature Society, 2004.

Cerutti, Simona. "Normes et pratiques, ou de la légitimité de leur opposition." In *Les formes de l'expérience: Une autre histoire sociale*, edited by Bernard Lepetit, 127–49. Paris: Albin Michel, 1995.

Cerutti, Simona. "Travail, mobilité et légitimité: suppliques au roi dans une société d'Ancien Régime (Turin, XVIIIe siècle)." *Annales HSS* 65, no. 3 (2010): 571–611.

Chaïbi, Olivier. "Entre crédit public et crédit mutuel: un aperçu des théories du crédit au XIXe siècle." *Romantisme* 151 (2011): 53–66.

Chiapello, Eve. "Die Geburt des Kapitalismus aus der Idee der doppelten Buchführung." *WestEnd. Neue Zeitschrift für Sozialforschung* 4 (2007): 64–95.

Collectif Révoltes logiques. "Deux ou trois choses que l'historien social ne veut pas savoir." *Le mouvement social* 100 (1977): 21–30.

Cottereau, Alain. "Droit et bon droit: un droit des ouvriers instauré, puis évincé par le droit du travail (France, XIX siècle)." *Annales HSS* 57, no. 6 (2002): 1521–57.

Corbin, Alain. *Les cloches de la terre: paysage sonore et culture sensible dans les campagnes au XIXe siècle*. Paris: Albin Michel, 1994.

Craig, Gordon A. *The Triumph of Liberalism: Zurich in the Golden Age, 1830–1869*. New York: Scribner, 1988.

Crowston, Clare Haru. "Credit and the Metanarrative of Modernity." *French Historical Studies* 34, no. 1 (2011): 7–19.

Crowston, Clare Haru. *Credit, Fashion, Sex: Economies of Regard in Old Regime France*. Durham, NC: Duke University Press, 2013.

Daston, Lorraine. "The Moral Economy of Science." *Osiris* 10 (1995): 2–24.

David, Thomas. "Croissance économique et mondialisation. Le cas de la Suisse, 1870–1914." In *Globalisierung—Chancen und Risiken: die Schweiz in der*

Weltwirtschaft, 18.–20. Jahrhundert, edited by Hans-Jörg Gilomen, Margrit Müller, and Béatrice Veyrassat, 145–69. Zurich: Chronos, 2003.

Davidoff, Leonore. "'Alte Hüte'. Öffentlichkeit und Privatheit in der feministischen Geschichtsschreibung." *L'Homme: Zeitschrift für feministische Geschichtswissenschaft* 4, no. 2 (1993): 7–36.

Davies, Catherine. *Transatlantic Speculations: Globalization and the Panics of 1873.* New York: Columbia University Press, 2018.

Davis, Natalie Zemon. *The Gift in Sixteenth-Century France.* Madison: University of Wisconsin Press, 2000.

Decurtins, Daniela, and Susi Grossmann. "Die Bedeutung sozialer Vernetzung bei der Gründung der Zürcher Kantonalbank 1870." In *Banken und Kredit in der Schweiz (1850–1930)*, edited by Youssef Cassis and Jakob Tanner, 105–28. Zurich: Chronos, 1993.

Denzel, Markus A. *Das System des bargeldlosen Zahlungsverkehrs europäischer Prägung vom Mittelalter bis 1914.* Stuttgart: Steiner, 2008.

Derrida, Jacques. *Given Time: I. Counterfeit Money.* Translated by Peggy Kamuf. Chicago: University of Chicago Press, 1992 [1991].

Descimon, Robert. "Reading Tocqueville: Property and Aristocracy in Modern France." In *Tocqueville and Beyond: Essays on the Old Regime in Honor of David D. Bien*, edited by Robert Schneider and Robert M. Schwartz, 111–26. Newark: University of Delaware Press, 2003.

Desrosières, Alain. *The Politics of Large Numbers: A History of Statistical Reasoning.* Translated by Camille Nash. Cambridge, MA: Harvard University Press, 2002 [1993].

Dienst, Richard. *The Bonds of Debt: Borrowing Against the Common Good.* London: Verso, 2011.

Ditz, Toby L. "Shipwrecked; or Masculinity Imperiled: Mercantile Representations of Failure and the Gendered Self in Eighteenth Century Philadelphia." *Journal of American History* 81 (1994): 51–80.

Dodd, Nigel. *The Social Life of Money.* Princeton, NJ: Princeton University Press, 2014.

Dommann, Monika. "Verbandelt im Welthandel: Spediteure und ihre Papiere seit dem 18. Jahrhundert." *WerkstattGeschichte* 58 (2011): 29–48.

Donzelot, Jacques. *L' invention du social: essai sur le déclin des passions politiques.* Paris: Fayard, 1984.

Ebeling, Knut. "Das technische Apriori." *Archiv für Mediengeschichte* 6 (2006): 11–22.

Eiden-Offe, Patrick. "Die Immobilienblase von Münsterburg. Gottfried Keller unterscheidet guten von bösem Kapitalismus." *Merkur* 715 (2008): 1155–59.

Eley, Geoff. *Forging Democracy: The History of the Left in Europe, 1850–2000.* Oxford: Oxford University Press, 2002.

Elsener, Ferdinand. *Die Schweizer Rechtsschulen vom 16. bis zum 19. Jahrhundert unter besonderer Berücksichtigung des Privatrechts: Die kantonalen Kodifikationen bis zum schweizerischen Zivilgesetzbuch.* Zurich: Schulthess, 1975.

Elyachar, Julia. *Markets of Dispossession: NGOs, Economic Development, and the State in Cairo.* Durham, NC: Duke University Press, 2005.

Engel, Alexander. "Buying Time: Futures Trading and Telegraphy in Nineteenth-

Century Global Commodity Markets." *Journal of Global History* 10, no. 2 (2015): 284–306.

Evers, Adalbert, and Helga Nowotny. *Über den Umgang mit Unsicherheit: Die Entdeckung der Gestaltbarkeit von Gesellschaft.* Frankfurt am Main: Suhrkamp, 1987.

Ewald, François. *L'état providence.* Paris: Bernard Grasset, 1986.

Fabiani, Jean-Louis. "La généralisation dans les sciences historiques: Obstacle épistémologique ou ambition légitime?" *Annales HSS* 62, no. 1 (2007): 9–28.

Fassin, Didier. "Les économies morales revisitées." *Annales HSS* 64 (2009): 1237–66.

Fertig, Christine. *Familie, verwandtschaftliche Netzwerke und Klassenbildung im ländlichen Westfalen (1750–1874).* Stuttgart: Lucius & Lucius, 2012.

Finn, Margot. *The Character of Credit: Personal Debt in English Culture, 1740–1914.* Cambridge: Cambridge University Press, 2003.

Fischer-Tiné, Harald. *Pidgin Knowledge. Wissen und Kolonialismus.* Zurich: diaphanes, 2014.

Fontaine, Laurence, ed. *Alternative Exchanges: Second-Hand Circulations from the Sixteenth Century to the Present.* New York: Berghahn, 2008.

Fontaine, Laurence. *The Moral Economy: Poverty, Credit, and Trust in Early Modern Europe.* Cambridge: Cambridge University Press, 2014.

Fontaine, Laurence, and Jürgen Schlumbohm, "Household Strategies for Survival: An Introduction," in Fontaine, Laurence, and Jürgen Schlumbohm, eds. Household Strategies for Survival 1600–2000: Fission, Faction, and Cooperation. Cambridge: Cambridge University Press, 2000, 1–18.

Foucault, Michel. "The Subject and Power." *Critical Inquiry* 8, no. 4 (1982): 777–95.

Fraisse, Geneviève. "Feministische Singularität. Kritische Historiographie der Geschichte des Feminismus in Frankreich." *Feministische Studien* 4, no. 2 (1985): 134–40.

Fritzsche, Bruno, and Max Lemmenmeier. "Die revolutionäre Umgestaltung von Wirtschaft, Gesellschaft und Staat 1780–1870." In *Geschichte des Kantons Zurich,* edited by Niklaus Flüeler and Marianne Flüeler-Grauwiller. Vol. 3, *19. und 20. Jahrhundert,* edited by Niklaus Flüeler and Bruno Fritzsche, 20–157. Zurich: Werd, 1994.

Fuchs, Rachel G. *Gender and Poverty in Nineteenth-Century Europe.* Cambridge: Cambridge University Press, 2005.

Führer, Karl Christian. "Pawning in German Working-Class Life before the First World War." *International Review of Social History* 46 (2001): 29–44.

Gallagher, Catherine. *The Body Economic: Life, Death, and Sensation in Political Economy and the Victorian Novel.* Princeton, NJ: Princeton University Press, 2007.

Geertz, Clifford. *The Interpretation of Cultures.* New York: Basic Books, 1973.

Geertz, Clifford. "Local Knowledge: Fact and Law in Comparative Perspective." In *Local Knowledge: Further Essays in Interpretive Anthropology,* 167–234. New York: Basic Books, 1983.

Geertz, Clifford. "Suq: The Bazaar Economy in Sefrou." In Clifford Geertz, Hildred Geertz, and Paul Rabinow, *Meaning and Order in Moroccan Society: Three Essays in Cultural Analysis,* 123–244. Cambridge: Cambridge University Press, 1979.

Giedion, Sigfried. *Mechanization Takes Command: A Contribution to Anonymous History.* Oxford: Oxford University Press, 1948.

Ginzburg, Carlo. "Lectures de Mauss." *Annales HSS* 65, no. 6 (2010): 1303–20.

Ginzburg, Carlo. "Microhistory: Two or Three Things that I Know about It." Translated by John Tedeschi and Anne C. Tedeschi. *Critical Inquiry* 20, no. 1 (1993): 10–35.

Gitelman, Lisa. *Paper Knowledge: Toward a Media History of Documents.* Durham, NC: Duke University Press, 2014.

Gitelman, Lisa, ed. *"Raw Data" Is an Oxymoron.* Cambridge, MA: MIT Press, 2013.

Goldberg, Ann. *Honor, Politics and the Law in Imperial Germany, 1870–1914.* Cambridge: Cambridge University Press, 2010.

Goldstein, Jan. *The Post-Revolutionary Self: Politics and Psyche in France, 1750–1850.* Cambridge, MA: Harvard University Press, 2005.

Goswami, Manu. *Producing India: From Colonial Economy to National Space.* Chicago: University of Chicago Press, 2004.

Graber, Rolf. *Wege zur direkten Demokratie in der Schweiz. Eine kommentierte Quellenauswahl von der Frühneuzeit bis 1874.* Vienna: Böhlau, 2013.

Graber, Rolf. *Zeit des Teilens: Volksbewegungen und Volksunruhen auf der Zürcher Landschaft 1794–1804.* Zurich: Chronos, 2003.

Graeber, David. *Debt: The First 5000 Years.* New York: Melville House, 2011.

Gramsci, Antonio. *Prison Notebooks.* Edited by Joseph A. Buttigieg. New York: Columbia University Press, 2011.

Greenblatt, Stephen. *Shakespearean Negotiations: The Circulation of Social Energy in Renaissance England.* Berkeley: University of California Press, 1998 [1988].

Gregory, Chris. *Gifts and Commodities.* London: HAU, 1982.

Gregory, Chris. "On Money Debt and Morality: Some Reflections on the Contribution of Economic Anthropology." *Social Anthropology* 20, no. 4 (2012): 380–96.

Groebner, Valentin. "Außer Haus: Otto Brunner und die alteuropäische 'Ökonomik.'" *Geschichte in Wissenschaft und Unterricht* 46, no. 2 (1995): 69–80.

Gruner, Erich. *Die Parteien in der Schweiz.* 2nd ed. Bern: Francke, 1977.

Gruner, Erich. *Die Schweizerische Bundesversammlung 1848–1920.* Vol. 1, *Biographien.* Bern: Francke, 1966.

Guery, Alain. "L'insoutenable ambiguïté du don." *Annales HSS* 68, no. 3 (2013): 821–37.

Guggenbühl, Christoph. "Heaven or Hell? The Public House and its Social Perception in Nineteenth- and Early Twentieth-Century Switzerland." In *Eating Out in Europe. Picnics, Gourmet Dining and Snacks since the Late Eighteenth Century,* edited by Marc Jacobs and Peter Scholliers, 89–104. Oxford: Berg, 2003.

Guggenheimer, Dorothee. *Kredite, Krisen und Konkurse. Wirtschaftliches Scheitern in der Stadt St. Gallen im 17. und 18. Jahrhundert.* Zurich: Chronos, 2014.

Guinnane, Timothy W. "Cooperatives as Information Machines: German Rural Credit Cooperatives, 1883–1914." *Journal of Economic History* 63, no. 2 (2001): 366–89.

Gunn, Simon, and James Vernon. "Introduction: What Was Liberal Modernity and Why Was It Peculiar in Imperial Britain?" In *The Peculiarities of Liberal Modernity in Imperial Britain,* edited by Simon Gunn and James Vernon, 1–18. Berkeley: University of California Press, 2011.

Gut, Franz. *Die Gefängnisse von Winterthur (Separatdruck aus dem Winterthurer Jahrbuch)*. Winterthur, 1981–1982.

Guyer, Jane. "Prophecy and the Near Future: Thoughts on Macroeconomic, Evangelical, and Punctuated Time." *American Ethnologist* 34, no. 3 (2007): 409–21.

Habermas, Rebekka. *Thieves in Court: The Making of the German Legal System in the Nineteenth Century*. Translated by Kathleen Mitchell Dell'Orto. Cambridge: Cambridge University Press, 2016.

Hacking, Ian. *Historical Ontology*. Cambridge, MA: Harvard University Press, 2002.

Haefelin, Jürg. *Wilhelm Weitling. Biographie und Theorie—Der Zürcher Kommunistenprozess von 1843*. Bern: Lang, 1986.

Han, Clara. *Life in Debt: Times of Care and Violence in Neoliberal Chile*. Berkeley: University of California Press, 2012.

Harootunian, Harry. *History's Disquiet: Modernity, Cultural Practice, and the Question of Everyday Life*. New York: Columbia University Press, 2000.

Harootunian, Harry. *Marx after Marx: History and Time in the Expansion of Capitalism*. New York: Columbia University Press, 2015.

Haupt, Heinz-Gerhard, and Geoffrey Crossick. *Die Kleinbürger. Eine europäische Sozialgeschichte*. Munich: C. H. Beck, 1998.

Hausen, Karin. "Die Polarisierung der 'Geschlechtscharaktere'—eine Spiegelung der Dissoziation von Erwerbs- und Familienleben." In *Sozialgeschichte der Familie in der Neuzeit Europas: Neue Forschungen*, edited by Werner Conze, 363–93. Stuttgart: Klett, 1976.

Hausen, Karin. "Wirtschaften mit der Geschlechterordnung. Ein Essay." In *Geschlechterhierarchie und Arbeitsteilung: Zur Geschichte ungleicher Erwerbschancen von Männern und Frauen*, edited by Karin Hausen, 40–67. Göttingen: Vandenhoeck & Ruprecht, 1993.

Hauser, Andrea. *Dinge des Alltags. Studien zur historischen Sachkultur eines schwäbischen Dorfes*. Tübingen: Tübinger Vereinigung für Volkskunde, 1994.

Hauser, Andrea. "Prekäre Subsistenz: Eine historische Rückschau auf dörfliche Bewältigungsstrategien im Umbruch zur Industrialisierung." In *Prekär arbeiten, prekär leben. Kulturwissenschaftliche Perspektiven auf ein gesellschaftliches Phänomen*, edited by Irene Götz and Barbara Lemberger, 263–85. Frankfurt am Main: Campus, 2009.

Hautcœur, Pierre-Cyrille. "Produire des statistiques: pour quoi faire? L'échec de la statistique de faillites en France au XIXe siècle." *Histoire et mesure* 23 (2008): 85–136.

Headrick, Daniel R. *When Information Came of Age: Technologies of Knowledge in the Age of Reason and Revolution, 1700–1850*. Oxford: Oxford University Press, 2000.

Hebeisen, Erika. *Leidenschaftlich fromm: Die pietistische Bewegung in Basel 1750–1850*. Cologne: Böhlau, 2005.

Henare, Amiria, Martin Holbraad, and Sari Wastell. *Thinking through Things: Theorising Artefacts Ethnographically*. London: Routledge, 2007.

Hettling, Manfred. "Behagliches Unbehagen. Gottfried Keller im demokratischen Kleinstaat." In *Verehrung, Kult, Distanz. Vom Umgang mit dem Dichter im 19. Jah-*

rhundert, edited by Wolfgang Braungart, 243–57. Tübingen: Niemeyer, 2004.

Hettling, Manfred. "Bürgerlichkeit. Eine ungesellige Geselligkeit." In *Eine kleine Geschichte der Schweiz: Der Bundesstaat und seine Traditionen*, edited by Manfred Hettling, Mario König, Martin Schaffner, Andreas Suter, and Jakob Tanner, 227–64. Frankfurt am Main: Suhrkamp, 1998.

Hettling, Manfred. *Politische Bürgerlichkeit: Der Bürger zwischen Individualität und Vergesellschaftung in Deutschland und der Schweiz von 1860 bis 1914.* Göttingen: Vandenhoeck & Ruprecht, 1999.

Hettling, Manfred, and Stefan-Ludwig Hoffmann, eds. *Der bürgerliche Wertehimmel: Innenansichten des 19. Jahrhunderts.* Göttingen: Vandenhoeck & Ruprecht, 2000.

Hilton, Boyd. *The Age of Atonement: The Influence of Evangelicanism on Social and Economic Thought, 1795–1865.* Oxford: Oxford University Press, 1988.

Hirter, Hans. "Die Streiks in der Schweiz in den Jahren 1880–1914: Quantitative Streikanalyse." In *Arbeiterschaft und Wirtschaft in der Schweiz 1880–1914: Soziale Lage, Organisation und Kämpfe von Arbeitern und Unternehmern, politische Organisation und Sozialpolitik*, edited by Erich Gruner. Vol. 2: *Gewerkschaften und Arbeitgeber auf dem Arbeitsmarkt. Streiks, Kampf ums Recht und Verhältnis zu andern Interessengruppen*, 846–55. Zurich: Chronos, 1988.

Hobsbawm, Eric, and Joan W. Scott. "Political Shoemakers." *Past and Present* 89 (1980): 86–114.

Höck, Wilhelm. "Gottfried Keller." In *Genie und Geld: vom Auskommen deutscher Schriftsteller*, edited by Karl Corino, 258–69. Nördlingen: Rowohlt, 1987.

Hoffman, Philip T., Gilles Postel-Vinay, and Jean-Laurent Rosenthal. *Priceless Markets: The Political Economy of Credit in Paris, 1660–1870.* Chicago: University of Chicago Press, 2000.

Hölzl, Richard. *Umkämpfte Wälder: Die Geschichte einer ökologischen Reform in Deutschland 1760–1860.* Frankfurt am Main: Campus, 2010.

Honegger, Claudia, and Bettina Heintz. "Zum Strukturwandel weiblicher Widerstandsformen im 19. Jahrhundert." In *Listen der Ohnmacht. Zur Sozialgeschichte weiblicher Widerstandsformen*, edited by Claudia Honegger and Bettina Heintz, 7–68. Frankfurt am Main: Europäische Verlagsanstalt, 1981.

Hufton, Olwen. *The Poor of Eighteenth-Century France: 1750–1789.* Oxford: Clarendon, 1974.

Huser, Karin. *Bildungsort, Männerhort, politischer Kampfverein: Deutsche Arbeitervereine in der Schweiz—"Eintracht Zürich" (1840–1916).* Zurich: Chronos, 2012.

Isler, Martin. *Die Vorgeschichte der städtischen Mobiliar-Leihkasse 1843–1884.* St. Gallen: K. Weiss, 1943.

Jameson, Fredric. *Archaeologies of the Future: The Desire Called Utopia and Other Science Fictions.* London: Verso, 2005.

Jancke, Gabriele, and Claudia Ulbrich. "Vom Individuum zur Person. Neue Konzepte im Spannungsfeld von Autobiographietheorie und Selbstzeugnisforschung." *Querelles. Jahrbuch für Frauen- und Geschlechterforschung* 10 (2005): 7–27.

Johnson, Paul. *Saving and Spending: The Working-Class Economy in Britain, 1870–1939.* Oxford: Clarendon, 1985.

Joris, Elisabeth. "Kinship and Gender: Property, Enterprise, and Politics." Translated by Hillary Crowe. In *Kinship in Europe: Approaches to Long-Term Development (1300–1900)*, edited by David W. Sabean, Simon Teuscher, and Jon Mathieu, 231–57. New York: Berghahn Books, 2007.

Joris, Elisabeth. *Liberal und eigensinnig. Die Pädagogin Josephine Stadlin—die Homöopathin Emilie Paravicini-Blumer*. Zurich: Chronos, 2010.

Joris, Elisabeth, and Heidi Witzig. *Brave Frauen, aufmüpfige Weiber: Wie sich die Industrialisierung auf Alltag und Lebenszusammenhänge von Frauen auswirkte (1820–1940)*. Zurich: Chronos, 1992.

Joseph, Miranda. *Debt to Society: Accounting for Life under Capitalism*. Minneapolis: University of Minnesota Press, 2014.

Jost, Hans-Ulrich. *Von Zahlen und Macht. Statistiker, Statistik und politische Autoritäten in der Schweiz, 18. bis 20. Jahrhundert*. Bern: Bundesamt für Statistik, 1995.

Joyce, Patrick. *The Rule of Freedom: Liberalism and the Modern City*. London: Verso, 2003.

Joyce, Patrick. *The State of Freedom: A Social History of the British State Since 1800*. Cambridge: Cambridge University Press, 2013.

Joyce, Patrick. "What Is the Social in Social History?" *Past and Present* 206 (2010): 213–48.

Jütte, Robert. *Arme, Bettler, Beutelschneider. Eine Sozialgeschichte der Armut in der Frühen Neuzeit*. Weimar: Verlag Hermann Böhlaus Nachfolger, 2000.

Jung, Joseph. *Alfred Escher (1819–1882): Der Aufbruch zur modernen Schweiz*. Vol. 3, *Schweizerische Kreditanstalt, Eidgenössisches Polytechnikum, Aussenpolitik*. Zurich: Neue Zürcher Zeitung, 2006.

Kafka, Ben. *The Demon of Writing: Powers and Failures of Paperwork*. New York: Zone Books, 2012.

Keller, Barbara. *Von Speziererinnen, Wegglibuben und Metzgern. Lebensmittelhandwerk und -handel in Basel 1850–1914*. Zurich: Chronos, 2001.

Kies, Tobias. "Hörensagen. Gerüchtekommunikation und lokale Öffentlichkeit im frühen 19. Jahrhundert." In *Sehnsucht nach Nähe. Interpersonale Kommunikation in Deutschland seit dem 19. Jahrhundert*, edited by Moritz Föllmer, 45–64. Stuttgart: Steiner, 2004.

Kittstein, Ulrich. *Gottfried Keller*. Stuttgart: WBG, 2008.

Kleeberg, Bernhard, "Schlechte Angewohnheiten. Einleitung," in *Schlechte Angewohnheiten. Eine Anthologie 1750–1900*, ed. Bernhard Kleeberg (Frankfurt am Main: Suhrkamp, 2012), 9–66.

Knuchel, Peter. "Aktienrechtliche Gesetzgebung und strukturelle Stabilität. Die Schweizer Aktiengesellschaft und ihr Recht in der zweiten Hälfte des 19. Jahrhunderts." Unpublished thesis, Department of History, Universität Zürich, 2007.

Kocka, Jürgen. *Capitalism: A Short History*. Translated by Jeremiah Riemer. Princeton, NJ: Princeton University Press, 2016.

Koller, Barbara. *"Gesundes Wohnen". Ein Konstrukt zur Vermittlung bürgerlicher Werte und Verhaltensnormen und seine praktische Umsetzung in der Deutschschweiz 1880–1940*. Zurich: Chronos, 1994.

Koller, Christian. *Streikkultur. Performanzen und Diskurse des Arbeitskampfes im schweizerisch-österreichischen Vergleich (1860–1950)*. Münster: LIT, 2009.

Kornblith, Gary J., and Michael Zakim, eds. *Capitalism Takes Command: The Social Transformation of Nineteenth-Century America.* Chicago: University of Chicago Press, 2012.

Krajewski, Markus. "In Formation. Aufstieg und Fall der Tabelle als Paradigma der Datenverarbeitung." *Nach Feierabend. Zürcher Jahrbuch für Wissensgeschichte* 3 (2007): 37–55.

Krattiger, Ursula. *Mündigkeit: Ein Fragenkomplex in der schweizerischen Diskussion im 19. Jahrhundert, vor allem zur Zeit der Armennot von 1840 bis 1860.* Bern: Lang, 1972.

Kreienbrock, Jörg. "Das Kreditparadies Seldwyla. Zur Beziehung von Ökonomie und Literatur in Gottfried Kellers Die Leute von Seldwyla." In *Gottfried Keller, Die Leute von Seldwyla. Kritische Studien—Critical Essays,* edited by Hans-Joachim Hahn and Uwe Seja, 117–34. Bern: Lang, 2007.

Kümin, Beat. "Das vormoderne Wirtshaus im Spannungsfeld zwischen Arbeit und Freizeit." In *Freizeit und Vergnügen vom 14. bis zum 20. Jahrhundert,* edited by Hans-Jörg Gilomen, Beatrice Schumacher, and Laurent Tissot, 87–98. Zurich: Chronos, 2005.

Künzle, Daniel. "Stadtwachstum, Quartierbildung und soziale Konflikte am Beispiel von Zürich-Aussersihl 1850–1914." In *Schweiz im Wandel. Studien zur neueren Gesellschaftsgeschichte: Festschrift für Rudolf Braun zum 60. Geburtstag,* edited by Sebastian Brändli, David Gugerli, Rudolf Jaun, and Ulrich Pfister, 43–58. Basel: Helbing & Lichtenhahn, 1990.

Kunz, Erwin. *Die lokale Selbstverwaltung in den zürcherischen Landsgemeinden im 18. Jahrhundert.* Zurich: Weiss, 1948.

Lanzinger, Margareth. "Variationen des Themas: Mitgiftsysteme." In *Aushandeln von Ehe. Heiratsverträge der Neuzeit im europäischen Vergleich,* edited by Margareth Lanzinger, Margareth, Gunda Barth-Scalmani, Ellinor Forster, and Gertrude Langer-Ostrawsky, 469–92. Vienna: Böhlau, 2010.

Lanzinger, Margareth, Gunda Barth-Scalmani, Ellinor Forster, and Gertrude Langer-Ostrawsky, eds. *Aushandeln von Ehe. Heiratsverträge der Neuzeit im europäischen Vergleich.* Vienna: Böhlau, 2010.

Lauener, Michael. *Jeremias Gotthelf—Prediger gegen den Rechtsstaat.* Zurich: Schulthess, 2011.

Lauer, Josh. "From Rumor to Written Record: Credit Reporting and the Invention of Financial Identity in Nineteenth-Century America." *Technology and Culture* 49 (2008): 301–24.

Lazzarato, Maurizio. *The Making of Indebted Man.* Translated by Joshua David Jordan. Los Angeles: Semiotext(e), 2012.

Lemercier, Claire. "Discipliner le commerce sans corporations. La loi, le juge, l'arbitre et le commerçant à Paris au XIXe siècle." *Le Mouvement social* 224 (2008): 61–74.

Lemercier, Claire, and Claire Zalc. "Pour une nouvelle approche de la relation de crédit en histoire contemporaine." *Annales HSS* 67, no. 4 (2012): 979–1009.

Lemire, Beverly. "Budgeting for Everyday Life: Gender Strategies, Material Practice and Institutional Innovation in Nineteenth-Century Britain." *L'Homme: Zeitschrift für feministische Geschichtswissenschaft* 22 (2011): 11–27.

Lemire, Beverly. *The Business of Everyday Life: Gender, Practice, and Social Politics in England, c. 1600–1900*. Manchester: Manchester University Press, 2005.

Lepetit, Bernard. "Le présent de l'histoire." In *Les formes de l'expérience: Une autre histoire sociale*, edited by Bernard Lepetit, 273–98. Paris: Albin Michel, 1995.

Lerner, Marc H. *A Laboratory of Liberty. The Transformation of Political Culture in Republican Switzerland, 1750–1848*. Leiden: Brill, 2012.

Le Roy, Yves. "Le choix des voies de poursuites à la fin du XIXe siècle, en particulier dans le projet de loi fédérale sur la poursuite pour dettes et la faillite du 23 février 1886." In *Le Droit commercial dans la société suisse du XIXe siècle*, edited by Pio Caroni, 259–303. Fribourg: Éditions Universitaires Fribourg Suisse, 1997.

Leschhorn, Martin. "Mikrohistorische Studie des Basler Metzgergewerbes in der ersten Hälfte des 19. Jahrhunderts." Unpublished thesis, Historisches Seminar Universität Basel, 1998.

Levi, Giovanni. *Inheriting Power: The Story of an Exorcist*. Translated by Lydia G. Cochrane. Chicago: University of Chicago Press, 1988.

Lévi-Strauss, Claude. "History and Anthropology." In *Structural Anthropology*, translated by Claire Jacobson and Brooke Grundfest Schoepf, 1–27. New York: Basic Books, 1963.

Lévi-Strauss, Claude. *Introduction to the Work of Marcel Mauss*. Translated by Felicity Baker. London: Routledge, 1987 [1950].

Lévi-Strauss, Claude. *The Savage Mind*. Chicago: Chicago University Press, 1966 [1962].

Levy, Jonathan Ira. "Contemplating Delivery: Futures Trading and the Problem of Commodity Exchange in the United States." *American Historical Review* 111 (2006): 307–35.

Levy, Jonathan Ira. *Freaks of Fortune: The Emerging World of Capitalism and Risk in America*. Cambridge, MA: Harvard University Press, 2012.

Liebersohn, Harry. *The Return of the Gift: European History of a Global Idea*. Cambridge: Cambridge University Press, 2011.

Lippuner, Sabine. *Bessern und verwahren. Die Praxis der administrativen Versorgung von "Liederlichen" und "Arbeitsscheuen" in der thurgauischen Zwangsarbeitsanstalt Kalchrain*. Frauenfeld: Historischer Verein des Kantons Thurgau, 2005.

Loeffler, Mark. "Das 'Finanzkapital'—Diskurse in Deutschland und England zur Jahrhundertwende." In *Kapitalismusdebatten um 1900: Über antisemitisierende Semantiken des Jüdischen*, edited by Nicolas Berg, 115–40. Leipzig: Leipziger Universitätsverlag, 2011.

Loetz, Francisca. *A New Approach to the History of Violence: "Sexual Assault" and "Sexual Abuse" in Europe, 1500–1850*. Translated by Rosemary Selle. Leiden: Brill, 2015.

Löwenthal, Leo. "Gottfried Keller—die bürgerliche Regression." In *Erzählkunst und Gesellschaft. Die Gesellschaftsproblematik in der deutschen Literatur des 19. Jahrhunderts*, 206–25. Neuwied am Rhein: Luchterhand, 1971.

Logemann, Jan, ed. *The Development of Consumer Credit in Global Perspective: Business, Regulation, and Culture*. New York: Palgrave Macmillan, 2012.

Lüdemann, Susanne. *Metaphern der Gesellschaft. Studien zum soziologischen und politischen Imaginären*. Munich: Fink, 2004.

Lüpold, Martin. "Der Ausbau der 'Festung Schweiz': Aktienrecht und Corporate Governance in der Schweiz, 1881–1961." PhD dissertation, University of Zurich, 2010.

Lukács, Georg. *History and Class Consciousness: Studies in Marxist Dialectics.* Translated by Rodney Livingston. Cambridge, MA: MIT Press, 1971 [1923/1967].

Mann, Bruce H. *Republic of Debtors: Bankruptcy in the Age of American Independence.* Cambridge, MA: Harvard University Press, 2003.

Mannheim, Karl. *Ideology and Utopia.* New York: Harcourt, Brace & Co., 1954 [1929].

Marcus, George. "Ethnography in/of the World System: The Emergence of Multi-Sited Ethnography." *Annual Review of Anthropology* 24 (1995): 95–117.

Marsiske, Hans-Arthur. *"Wider die Umsonstfresser": Der Handwerkerkommunist Wilhelm Weitling.* Hamburg: Ergebnisse-Verlag, 1986.

Marsiske, Hans-Arthur. *Eine Republik der Arbeiter ist möglich. Der Beitrag Wilhelm Weitlings zur Arbeiterbewegung in den Vereinigten Staaten von Amerika 1846–1856.* Hamburg: Hamburger Institut für Sozialforschung, 1990.

Marx-Jaskulski, Katrin. *Armut und Fürsorge auf dem Land. Vom Ende des 19. Jahrhunderts bis 1933.* Göttingen: Wallstein, 2008.

Maß, Sandra. "Mäßigung der Leidenschaften. Kinder und monetäre Lebensführung im 19. Jahrhundert." In *Das schöne Selbst. Zur Genealogie des modernen Subjekts zwischen Ethik und Ästhetik,* edited by Jens Elberfeld, 55–81. Bielefeld: transcript, 2009.

Maß, Sandra. "Formulare des Ökonomischen in der Geldpädagogik des 18. und 19. Jahrhunderts." *WerkstattGeschichte* 58 (2011): 9–28.

Maß, Sandra. *Kinderstube des Kapitalismus? Monetäre Erziehung im 18. und 19. Jahrhundert.* Munich: De Gruyter Oldenbourg, 2017.

Mattioli, Aram, ed. *Antisemitismus in der Schweiz 1848–1960. Mit einem Vorwort von Alfred A. Häsler.* Zurich: Orell Füssli, 1998.

Mattmüller, Markus. "Agrargeschichte der Schweiz im Ancien Régime." Vol. 2, "Vorlesung im WS 1978/79 und SS 1979." Unpublished manuscript, Historisches Seminar Basel, 1979.

Maurer, Theres. *Ulrich Dürrenmatt, 1849–1908: Ein schweizerischer Oppositionspolitiker.* Bern: Stämpfli, 1975.

Maurer, Theres. "Die 'Berner Volkszeitung' von Ulrich Dürrenmatt." In *Antisemitismus in der Schweiz 1848–1960. Mit einem Vorwort von Alfred A. Häsler,* edited by Aram Mattioli, 241–64. Zurich: Orell Füssli, 1998.

Mauss, Marcel. *The Gift: The Form and Reason for Exchange in Archaic Societies.* Translated by W. D. Halls. London: Routledge, 2002 [1925].

Maye, Harun. "Was ist eine Kulturtechnik?" *Zeitschrift für Medien- und Kulturforschung* 1 (2010): 121–35.

Mazbouri, Malik. *L'émergence de la place financière suisse (1890–1913).* Lausanne: Éditions Antipodes, 2005.

McCants, Anne. "Goods at Pawn: The Overlapping Worlds of Material Possessions and Family Finance in Early Modern Amsterdam." *Social Science History* 31 (2007): 213–38.

Medick, Hans. "Plebejische Kultur, plebejische Öffentlichkeit, plebejische Ökonomie: Über Erfahrungen und Verhaltensweisen Besitzarmer und Besitzloser in der Übergangsphase zum Kapitalismus." In *Klassen und Kultur: Sozialanthropologische Perspektiven in der Geschichtsschreibung*, edited by Robert Berdahl and David W. Sabean, 157–204. Frankfurt am Main: Syndikat, 1982.

Medick, Hans. "Eine Kultur des Ansehens. Kleider und ihre Farben in Laichingen 1750–1820." *Historische Anthropologie* 2, no. 2 (1994): 193–212.

Meier, Thomas. *Handwerk, Hauswerk, Heimarbeit: nicht-agrarische Tätigkeiten und Erwerbsformen in einem traditionellen Ackerbaugebiet des 18. Jahrhunderts (Zürcher Unterland)*. Zurich: Chronos, 1986.

Menzel, Ulrich. *Auswege aus der Abhängigkeit: Die entwicklungspolitische Aktualität Europas*. Frankfurt am Main: Suhrkamp, 1988.

Messerli, Alfred. *Lesen und Schreiben 1700 bis 1900. Untersuchung zur Durchsetzung der Literalität in der Schweiz*. Tübingen: Niemeyer, 2002.

Messerli, Jakob. *Gleichmässig—pünktlich—schnell: Zeiteinteilung und Zeitgebrauch im 19. Jahrhundert in der Schweiz*. Zurich: Chronos, 1993.

Messmer, Lukas. "Hans Conrad Finslers 'Sturz in die schmälichste Tiefe'. Bankrott, Scheitern und die Folgen in Zürich 1829." Unpublished thesis, Universität Zürich, 2012.

Meuwly, Olivier. *Louis Ruchonnet, 1834–1893. Un homme d'Etat entre action et ideal*. Lausanne: Bibliothèque historique vaudoise, 2006.

Meyer, Ahlrich. *Frühsozialismus. Theorien der sozialen Bewegung 1798–1848*. Freiburg im Breisgau: Alber, 1977.

Meyer, Ahlrich. "Massenarmut und Existenzrecht: Zur Geschichte der sozialen Bewegungen 1789/1848." *Autonomie. Materialien gegen die Fabrikgesellschaft*, n.s, 14 (1985): 15–145.

Meyer, Lukas. "Wirtschaft und Gesellschaft einer agrarischen Gemeinde im Zürcher Unterland des 18. Jahrhunderts (Schöfflisdorf)." Unpublished thesis, Universität Zürich, 1989.

Mirowski, Philip. *More Heat than Light: Economics as Social Physics, Physics as Nature's Economics*. Cambridge: Cambridge University Press, 1989.

Mitchell, Timothy. *Rule of Experts: Egypt, Techno-Politics, Modernity*. Berkeley: University of California Press, 2002.

Mitchell, Timothy. "Society, Economy, and the State Effect." In *State/Culture: State-Formation after the Cultural Turn*, edited by George Steinmetz, 76–97. Ithaca, NY: Cornell University Press, 1999.

Mooser, Josef. "'Furcht bewahrt das Holz'. Holzdiebstahl und sozialer Konflikt in der ländlichen Gesellschaft 1800–1850 an westfälischen Beispielen." In *Räuber, Volk und Obrigkeit. Studien zur Geschichte der Kriminalität in Deutschland seit dem 18. Jahrhundert*, edited by Heinz Reif, 43–99. Frankfurt am Main: Suhrkamp, 1984.

Moretti, Franco. *The Bourgeois: Between History and Literature*. London: Verso, 2013.

Muehlebach, Andrea. *The Moral Neoliberal: Welfare and Citizenship in Italy*. Chicago: University of Chicago Press, 2012.

Müller, Felix. "Zur Kultur und zum gesellschaftlichen Bewußtsein handwerklicher Arbeiter im dritten Viertel des 19. Jahrhunderts—Vereinsleben und Diskussionen im Schweizerischen Grütliverein." In *Handwerker in der Industrialisierung. Lage, Kultur und Politik vom späten 18. bis ins frühe 20. Jahrhundert*, edited by Ulf Engelhardt, 552–588. Stuttgart: Klett-Cotta, 1984.

Münch, Peter. *Aus der Geschichte des Basler Privatrechts im 19. Jahrhundert. Traditionsbewusstsein und Fortschrittsdenken im Widerstreit.* Basel: Helbing & Lichtenhahn, 1991.

Muldrew, Craig. *The Economy of Obligation: The Culture of Credit and Social Relations in Early Modern England.* Basingstoke: Palgrave Macmillan, 1998.

Nader, Laura. *The Life of the Law: Anthropological Projects.* Berkeley: University of California Press, 2002.

Nellen, Stefan. "Schreibakte: Eine Mediengeschichte der Verwaltung, Basel 1803–1960." PhD dissertation, University of Basel, 2012.

Opitz, Claudia. "Neue Wege der Sozialgeschichte? Ein kritischer Blick auf Otto Brunners Konzept des 'ganzen Hauses.'" *Geschichte und Gesellschaft* 20 (1994): 88–98.

Ortmann, Alexandra. "Jenseits von Klassenjustiz: Ein Blick in die ländliche Gesellschaft des deutschen Kaiserreichs." *Geschichte und Gesellschaft* 35, no. 4 (2009): 629–58.

Osborne, Thomas. "The Ordinariness of the Archive." *History of the Human Sciences* 12, no. 2 (1999): 51–64.

Otter, Chris. "Making Liberal Objects: British Techno-Social Relations 1800–1900." *Cultural Studies* 21 (2007): 570–90.

Otter, Chris. "Making Liberalism Durable: Vision and Civility in the Late Victorian City." *Social History* 27 (2002): 1–15.

Otter, Chris. *The Victorian Eye: A Political History of Light and Vision in Britain, 1800–1910.* Chicago: University of Chicago Press, 2008.

Parry, Jonathan. "*The Gift*, The Indian Gift and the 'Indian Gift.'" *Man*, n.s., 21, no. 3 (1986): 453–73.

Parry, Jonathan, and Maurice Bloch, eds. *Money and the Morality of Exchange.* Cambridge: Cambridge University Press, 1989.

Passeron, Jean-Claude, and Jacques Revel. "Penser par Cas. Raisonner à partir des singularités." In *Penser par cas*, edited by Jean-Claude Passeron and Jacques Revel, 9–44. Paris: Éditions EHESS, 2005.

Peebles, Gustav. "The Anthropology of Credit and Debt." *Annual Review of Anthropology* 39 (2010): 225–40.

Peebles, Gustav. "Washing Away the Sins of Debt: The Nineteenth-Century Eradication of the Debtors' Prison." *Comparative Studies in Society and History* 55, no. 3 (2013): 701–24.

Perrot, Michelle. "Rebellische Weiber. Die Frau in der französischen Stadt des 19. Jahrhunderts" [1979]. In *Listen der Ohnmacht: zur Sozialgeschichte weiblicher Widerstandsformen*, edited by Bettina Heintz and Claudia Honegger, 71–97. Frankfurt am Main: Europäische Verlagsanstalt, 1981.

Peter, Matthias. *Jakob und Heinrich Senn. Zeitbilder der Schweiz aus dem 19. Jahrhundert.* Zurich: Neue Zürcher Zeitung, 2004.

Peyer, Hans Conrad. *Von Handel und Bank im alten Zürich.* Zurich: Berichthaus, 1968.

Pfister, Ulrich. "Le petit crédit rural en Suisse aux XVIe-XVIIIe siècles." *Annales HSS* 49 (1994): 1339–57.

Planert, Ute. *Der Mythos vom Befreiungskrieg. Frankreichs Kriege und der deutsche Süden: Alltag—Wahrnehmung—Deutung 1792–1841.* Stuttgart: Ferdinand Schöningh, 2007.

Pocock, J. G. A. *Virtue, Commerce, and History: Essays on Political Thought and History, Chiefly in the Eighteenth Century.* Cambridge: Cambridge University Press, 1985.

Poovey, Mary. *Genres of the Credit Economy: Mediating Value in Eighteenth- and Nineteenth-Century Britain.* Chicago: University of Chicago Press, 2008.

Poovey, Mary. *A History of the Modern Fact: Problems of Knowledge in the Sciences of Wealth and Society.* Chicago: University of Chicago Press, 1998.

Postel-Vinay, Gilles. *La terre et l'argent. L'agriculture et le crédit en France du XVIIIe au début du XXe siècle.* Paris: Albin Michel, 1998.

Pottage, Alain. "The Originality of Registration." *Oxford Journal of Legal Studies* 15 (1995): 371–401.

Pottage, Alain, and Martha Mundy, eds. *Law, Anthropology, and the Constitution of the Social: Making Persons and Things.* Cambridge: Cambridge University Press, 2004.

Poulantzas, Nicos. *State, Power, Socialism.* Translated by Patrick Camiller. London: Verso, 1980.

Preda, Alex. *Framing Finance: The Boundaries of Markets and Modern Capitalism.* Chicago: University of Chicago Press, 2009.

Procacci, Giovanna. *Gouverner la misère: La question sociale en France 1789–1848.* Paris: Éditions du Seuil, 1993.

Radin, Margaret Jane. *Reinterpreting Property.* Chicago: University of Chicago Press, 1993.

Rancière, Jacques. *Proletarian Nights: The Workers' Dream in Nineteenth-Century France.* Translated by John Drury. London: Verso, 2012.

Raphael, Lutz. "Rechtskultur, Verrechtlichung, Professionalisierung. Anmerkungen zum 19. Jahrhundert aus kulturanthropologischer Perspektive." In *Rechtskultur, Rechtswissenschaft, Rechtsberufe im 19. Jahrhundert: Professionalisierung und Verrechtlichung in Deutschland und Italien,* edited by Christof Dipper, 29–48. Berlin: Duncker & Humblot, 2000.

Rappaport, Erika. "'A Husband and His Wife's Dresses': Consumer Credit and the Debtor Family in England, 1864–1914." In *The Sex of Things: Gender and Consumption in Historical Perspective,* edited by Victoria De Grazia, 163–87. Berkeley: University of California Press, 1996.

Rásonyi, Peter. *Promotoren und Prozesse institutionellen Wandels: Agrarreformen im Kanton Zürich im 18. Jahrhundert.* Berlin: Duncker & Humblot, 2000.

Reddy, William M. *Money and Liberty in Modern Europe: A Critique of Historical Understanding.* Cambridge: Cambridge University Press, 1987.

Reed, Adam. "Documents Unfolding." In *Documents: Artifacts of Modern Knowledge,* edited by Annelise Riles, 158–77. Ann Arbor: University of Michigan Press, 2006.

Reichardt, Sven. "Soziales Kapital 'im Zeitalter materieller Interessen'. Konzeptionelle Überlegungen zum Vertrauen in der Zivil- und Marktgesellschaft des langen 19. Jahrhunderts (1780–1914)." WZB Discussion Paper Nr. SP IV 03-503, Wissenschaftszentrum Berlin für Sozialforschung, 2003.

Rheinberger, Hans-Jörg. *On Historicizing Epistemology: An Essay.* Translated by David Fernbach. Stanford, CA: Standford University Press, 2010.

Rheinberger, Hans-Jörg. *Toward a History of Epistemic Things: Synthesizing Proteins in the Test Tube.* Stanford, CA: Stanford University Press, 1997.

Riedi Hunold, Dorothea. *Die Einführung der allgemeinen Wechselfähigkeit in der Schweiz in der zweiten Hälfte des 19. Jahrhunderts.* Frankfurt am Main: Peter Lang, 2004.

Riles, Annelise. "Collateral Expertise: Legal Knowledge in the Global Financial Markets." *Current Anthropology* 51, no. 6 (2010): 795–818.

Riles, Annelise. *Collateral Knowledge: Legal Reasoning in the Global Financial Markets.* Chicago: University of Chicago Press, 2011.

Rischbieter, Julia Laura. "Wer nicht wagt, der nicht gewinnt? Kaffeegroßhändler als Spekulanten im Kaiserreich." *Jahrbuch für Wirtschaftsgeschichte* 54 (2013): 71–94.

Ritzmann, Franz. *Die Schweizer Banken: Geschichte—Theorie—Statistik.* Bern: Haupt, 1973.

Roitman, Janet. *Anti-Crisis.* Durham, NC: Duke University Press, 2014.

Roitman, Janet. *Fiscal Disobedience: An Anthropology of Economic Regulation in Central Africa.* Princeton, NJ: Princeton University Press, 2005.

Rubin, G. R. "Law, Poverty and Imprisonment for Debt, 1869–1914." In *Law, Economy and Society, 1750–1914: Essays in the History of English Law,* edited by G. R. Rubin and David Sugarman, 241–99. Abingdon: Professional Books, 1984.

Rüve, Gerlind. *Scheintod. Zur kulturellen Bedeutung der Schwelle zwischen Leben und Tod um 1800.* Bielefeld: transcript, 2008.

Ryter, Annamarie. *Als Weibsbild bevogtet. Zum Alltag von Frauen im 19. Jahrhundert— Geschlechtsvormundschaft und Ehebeschränkungen im Kanton Basel-Landschaft.* Liestal: Verlag des Kantons Basel-Landschaft, 1994.

Sabean, David W. "Kinship and Class Dynamics in Nineteenth-Century Europe." In *Kinship in Europe. Approaches to Long-Term Development (1300–1900),* edited by David W. Sabean, Simon Teuscher, and Jon Mathieu, 301–13. New York: Berghahn, 2007.

Sabean, David W. *Kinship in Neckarhausen, 1700–1870.* Cambridge: Cambridge University Press, 1998.

Sabean, David W. *Power in the Blood: Popular Culture and Village Discourse in Early-Modern Germany.* Cambridge: Cambridge University Press, 1984.

Sabean, David W. *Property, Production and Family in Neckarhausen, 1700–1870.* Cambridge: Cambridge University Press, 1990.

Sabean, David W., and Simon Teuscher. "Kinship in Europe: A New Approach to Long-Term Development." In *Kinship in Europe. Approaches to Long-Term Development (1300–1900),* edited by David W. Sabean, Simon Teuscher, and Jon Mathieu, 1–32. New York: Berghahn, 2007.

Saleski, Katharina M. *Theorie und Praxis des Rechts im Spiegel der frühen Zürcher und Schweizer juristischen Zeitschriften.* Zurich: Schulthess, 2007.

Salzmann, Martin. *Die Wirtschaftskrise im Kanton Zürich 1845 bis 1848: Ihre Stellung und Wertung im Rahmen der wirtschaftlich-sozialen Entwicklung in der ersten Hälfte des 19. Jahrhunderts.* Bern: Lang, 1978.

Sandage, Scott. *Born Losers: A History of Failure in America.* Cambridge, MA: Harvard University Press, 2005.

Sarasin, Philipp. "Sittlichkeit, Nationalgefühl und frühe Ängste vor dem Proletariat. Untersuchungen zu Politik, Weltanschauung und Ideologie des Basler Bürgertums in der Verfassungskrise von 1846/47." *Basler Zeitschrift für Geschichte und Altertumskunde* 84 (1984): 51–127.

Sarasin, Philipp. *Stadt der Bürger: Bürgerliche Macht und städtische Gesellschaft. Basel 1846–1914.* 2nd ed. Göttingen: Vandenhoeck & Ruprecht, 1997.

Sarasin, Philipp. *Stadt der Bürger. Struktureller Wandel und bürgerliche Lebenswelt— Basel 1870–1900,* 1st ed. Basel: Helbing & Lichtenhahn, 1990.

Schaffner, Martin. *Die Basler Arbeiterbevölkerung im 19. Jahrhundert. Beiträge zur Geschichte ihrer Lebensformen.* Basel: Helbing & Lichtenhahn, 1972.

Schaffner, Martin. *Die demokratische Bewegung der 1860er Jahre: Beschreibung und Erklärung der Zürcher Volksbewegung von 1867.* Basel: Helbing & Lichtenhahn 1982.

Schaffner, Martin. "Direkte Demokratie: 'Alles für das Volk—alles durch das Volk.'" In *Eine kleine Geschichte der Schweiz. Der Bundesstaat und seine Traditionen,* edited by Manfred Hettling, Mario König, and Martin Schaffner, 189–226. Frankfurt am Main: Suhrkamp, 1998.

Schaffner, Martin. "Geschichte des politischen Systems von 1833 bis 1905." In *Das politische System Basel-Stadt. Geschichte, Strukturen, Institutionen, Politikbereiche,* edited by Lukas Burckhardt, 37–53. Basel: Helbing & Lichtenhahn, 1984.

Schieder, Wolfgang. *Anfänge der deutschen Arbeiterbewegung. Die Auslandsvereine im Jahrzehnt nach der Julirevolution von 1830.* Stuttgart: Klett, 1963.

Schiedt, Hans-Ulrich. *Die Welt neu erfinden: Karl Bürkli (1823–1901) und seine Schriften.* Zurich: Chronos, 2002.

Schindler, Norbert. "Jenseits des Zwangs? Zur Ökonomie des Kulturellen inner- und ausserhalb der bürgerlichen Gesellschaft." In *Widerspenstige Leute. Studien zur Volkskultur in der frühen Neuzeit,* 20–46. Frankfurt am Main: Fischer, 1992.

Schlögl, Rudolf. "Kommunikation und Vergesellschaftung unter Anwesenden: Formen des Sozialen und ihre Transformation in der Frühen Neuzeit." *Geschichte und Gesellschaft* 34 (2008): 155–224.

Schlumbohm, Jürgen, ed. *Soziale Praxis des Kredits. 16.–20. Jahrhundert.* Hannover: Verlag Hahnsche Buchhandlung, 2007.

Schulin, Hermann. "Zur Entwicklung des Grundpfandrechts in der Schweiz." In *Wissenschaft und Kodifikation des Privatrechts im 19. Jahrhundert,* edited by Helmut Coing and Walter Wilhelm. Vol. 3, *Die rechtliche und wirtschaftliche Entwicklung des Grundeigentums und Grundkredits,* 373–414. Frankfurt am Main: Vittorio Klostermann, 1979.

Schulte, Regina. *Das Dorf im Verhör: Brandstifter, Kindsmörderinnen und Wilderer vor den Schranken des bürgerlichen Gerichts Oberbayern, 1848–1910.* Reinbek bei Hamburg: Rowohlt, 1989.

Schulte, Regina. "Gerede und Arbeit im Dorf." *Historische Anthropologie* 20, no. 1 (2012): 76–89.

Schwab, Dieter. "Eigentum." In Vol. 2 of *Geschichtliche Grundbegriffe. Historisches Lexikon zur politisch-sozialen Sprache in Deutschland,* edited by Otto Brunner, Werner Conze, and Reinhart Koselleck, 65–115. Stuttgart: Klett-Cotta, 1975.

Scott, James. "The Moral Economy as an Argument and as a Fight." In *Moral Economy and Popular Protest: Crowds, Conflict and Authority,* edited by Andrew Charlesworth and Adrian Randall, 187–208. Basingstoke: Palgrave Macmillan, 2000.

Seed, John. "'Free Labour = Latent Pauperism': Marx, Mayhew, and the 'Reserve

Army of Labour' in Mid-Nineteenth-Century London." In *The Peculiarities of Liberal Modernity in Imperial Britain*, edited by Simon Gunn and James Vernon, 54–71. Berkeley: University of California Press, 2011.

Seidel-Höppner, Waltraud. *Wilhelm Weitling (1808–1871). Eine politische Biografie.* 2 vols. Frankfurt am Main: Lang, 2014.

Seidel-Höppner, Waltraud. *Wilhelm Weitling—der erste deutsche Theoretiker und Agitator des Kommunismus.* Berlin (GDR): Dietz, 1961.

Sewell, William. *Logics of History: Social Theory and Social Transformation.* Chicago: University of Chicago Press, 2005.

Sewell, William. "The Temporalities of Capitalism." *Socio-Economic Review* 6 (2008): 517–37.

Sgard, Jérôme. "Do Legal Origins Matter? The Case of Bankruptcy Laws in Europe 1808–1914." *European Review of Economic History* 10 (2006): 389–419.

Siegenthaler, Hansjörg. "Martin Salander in seiner Zeit." Lecture presented at the Zentralbibliothek Zürich, November 2004, www.gottfriedkeller.ch/aufsatz/salander.htm.

Siméant, Johanna. "Économie morale et protestation—détours africains." *Genèses* 81 (2010): 142–60.

Simmons, Dana. *Vital Minimum: Need, Science, and Politics in Modern France.* Chicago: University of Chicago Press, 2015.

Sklansky, Jeffrey. "The Elusive Sovereign: New Intellectual and Social Histories of Capitalism." *Modern Intellectual History* 9 (2012): 233–48.

Sklansky, Jeffrey. "Labor, Money, and the Financial Turn in the History of Capitalism." *Labor: Studies in Working-Class History of the Americas* 11 (2014): 23–46.

Slobodian, Quinn. "How to See the World Economy: Statistics, Maps, and Schumpeter's Camera in the First Age of Globalization." *Journal of Global History* 10 (2015): 307–32.

Spang, Rebecca. *Stuff and Money in the Time of the French Revolution.* Cambridge, MA: Harvard University Press, 2015.

Spann, Michael. *Der Haftungszugriff auf den Schuldner zwischen Personal- und Vermögensvollstreckung. Eine exemplarische Untersuchung der geschichtlichen Rechtsquellen ausgehend vom römischen Recht bis ins 21. Jahrhundert unter besonderer Berücksichtigung bayerischer Quellen.* Münster: LIT, 2004.

Speich, Daniel. "Das Grundbuch als Grund aller Pläne. Präzision und die Fiktion der Überschaubarkeit im Entstehungsprozess eines modernen Rechtsstaats." In *Vermessene Landschaften. Kulturgeschichte und technische Praxis im 19. und 20. Jahrhundert*, edited by David Gugerli, 137–48. Zurich: Chronos, 1999.

Sperber, Jonathan. "Angenommene, vorgetäuschte und eigentliche Normenkonflikte bei der Waldbenutzung im 19. Jahrhundert." *Historische Zeitschrift* 290 (2010): 681–702.

Sperber, Jonathan. *Karl Marx: A Nineteenth-Century Life.* New York: Liveright, 2013.

Sperber, Jonathan. *Property and Civil Society in South-Western Germany 1820–1914.* Oxford: Oxford University Press, 2005.

Spieker, Ira. *Ein Dorf und sein Laden: Warenangebot, Konsumgewohnheiten und soziale Beziehungen.* Münster: Waxmann, 2000.

Spiekermann, Uwe. *Basis der Konsumgesellschaft. Entstehung und Entwicklung des modernen Kleinhandels in Deutschland 1850–1914.* Munich: C. H. Beck, 1999.

Spörri, Balz. *Studien zur Sozialgeschichte von Literatur und Leser im Zürcher Oberland des 19. Jahrhunderts.* Bern: Lang, 1987.

Stäheli, Urs. *Spectacular Speculation: Thrills, the Economy, and Popular Discourse.* Translated by Eric Savoth. Stanford, CA: Stanford University Press, 2013.

Stallybrass, Peter. "Marx's Coat." In *Border Fetishisms: Material Objects in Unstable Spaces,* edited by Patricia Spyer, 183–207. New York: Routledge, 1998.

Stanziani, Alessandro. "Information, institutions et temporalité. Quelques remarques critiques sur l'usage de la nouvelle économie de l'information en histoire." *Revue de synthèse* 4, nos. 1–2 (2000): 117–55.

Stanziani, Alessandro. *Rules of Exchange: French Capitalism in Comparative Perspective, Eighteenth to Early Twentieth Centuries.* Cambridge: Cambridge University Press, 2012.

Stedman Jones, Gareth. "Rethinking Chartism." In *Languages of Class: Studies in English Working Class History 1832–1982,* 90–178. Cambridge: Cambridge University Press, 1983.

Steedman, Carolyn. "At Every Bloody Level: A Magistrate, a Framework-Knitter, and the Law." *Law and History Review* 30, no. 2 (2012): 387–422.

Steedman, Carolyn. "Enforced Narratives. Stories of Another Self." In *Feminism and Autobiography: Texts, Theories, Methods,* edited by Tess Cosslett, Celia Lury, and Penny Summerfield, 25–39. London: Routledge, 2000.

Stingelin, Martin. "Seldwyla als inszenierte semiotische Welt. Ein unvermuteter schweizerischer Schauplatz der Zeichenreflexion." In *Inszenierte Welt. Theatralität als Argument literarischer Texte,* edited by Ethel Matala de Mazza and Clemens Pornschlegel, 209–26. Freiburg im Breisgau: Rombach, 2003.

Stobart, Jon, and Ilja Van Damme, eds. *Modernity and the Second-Hand Trade: European Consumption Cultures and Practices, 1700–1900.* Houndsmill: Palgrave Macmillan, 2010.

Stoler, Ann Laura. *Along the Archival Grain: Epistemic Anxieties and Colonial Common Sense.* Princeton, NJ: Princeton University Press, 2009.

Stolz, Peter. *Basler Wirtschaft in vor- und frühindustrieller Zeit. Ökonomische Theorie und Wirtschaftsgeschichte im Dialog.* Zurich: Schulthess, 1977.

Strathern, Marilyn. "Cutting the Network." *Journal of the Royal Anthropological Institute,* n.s., 2 (1996): 517–35.

Strathern, Marilyn. *The Gender of the Gift. Problems with Women and Problems with Society in Melanesia.* Berkeley: University of California Press, 1988.

Strathern, Marilyn. *Property, Substance, and Effect: Anthropological Essays on Persons and Things.* London, 1999.

Strathern, Marilyn. "Qualified Value: The Perspective of Gift Exchange." In *Barter, Exchange and Value. An Anthropological Approach,* edited by Caroline Humphrey and Stephen Hugh-Jones, 169–91. Cambridge: Cambridge University Press, 1992.

Suter, Gabriela. "Die transparenten Armen. Generierung von Wissen über Bedürftige am Beispiel der Freiwilligen und Einwohnerarmenpflege der Stadt Zürich 1895–1928." Unpublished thesis, Historisches Seminar Universität Zürich, 2004.

Suter, Mischa. "Die Rappenkasse des Jakob Stutz: Erziehung zur Sparsamkeit und die Ökonomie symbolischer Güter im 19. Jahrhundert." *traverse* 3 (2009): 120–33.

Suter, Mischa. "Ökonomischer Individualismus und moralischer Paternalismus. Sparkassen im Kanton Zürich während der Zeit des Pauperismus (um 1820–1860)." In *Die Produktion von Ungleichheiten—La production des inégalités*, edited by Thomas David, Valentin Groebner, Janick Marina Schaufelbuehl, and Brigitte Studer, 133–44. Zurich: Chronos, 2010.

Suter, Mischa. "Schuld und Schulden. Zürich 1842." *L'Homme: Zeitschrift für feministische Geschichtswissenschaft* 22, no. 2 (2011): 113–20.

Suter, Mischa. "Das Wissen der Schulden: Recht, Kulturtechnik und Alltagserfahrung im liberalen Kapitalismus." *Berichte zur Wissenschaftsgeschichte* 37, no. 2 (2014): 148–64.

Suter, Mischa. "Usury and the Problem of Exchange under Capitalism: A Late-Nineteenth-Century Debate on Economic Rationality." Translated by Adam Bresnahan. *Social History* 42, no. 4 (2017): 501–23.

Sutter, Eva. *"Ein Act des Leichtsinns und der Sünde": Illegitimität im Kanton Zürich: Recht, Moral und Lebensrealität (1800–1860)*. Zurich: Chronos, 1995.

Tanner, Albert. *Arbeitsame Patrioten—wohlanständige Damen: Bürgertum und Bürgerlichkeit in der Schweiz 1830–1914*. Zurich: Orell Füssli, 1995.

Tanner, Albert. "Ein Staat nur für die 'Hablichen'? Demokratie und politische Elite im frühen Bundesstaat." In *Etappen des Bundesstaates. Staats- und Nationsbildung der Schweiz, 1848–1998*, edited by Brigitte Studer, 63–88. Zurich: Chronos, 1998.

Tanner, Brigitte. "Essen—Kaufen—Sparen. Die Anfänge der Konsumvereinsbewegung im Kanton Zürich um 1850 zwischen Tradition und Innovation." Unpublished thesis, Universität Zürich, 2006.

Tanner, Jakob. "Der Tatsachenblick auf die 'reale Wirklichkeit': zur Entwicklung der Sozial- und Konsumstatistik in der Schweiz." *Schweizerische Zeitschrift für Geschichte* 45 (1995): 94–108.

Tanner, Jakob. "Diskurse der Diskriminierung: Antisemitismus, Sozialdarwinismus und Rassismus in den schweizerischen Bildungseliten." In *Krisenwahrnehmungen im Fin de Siècle. Jüdische und katholische Bildungseliten in Deutschland und der Schweiz*, edited by Michael Graetz and Aram Mattioli, 323–40. Zurich: Chronos, 1997.

Tanner, Jakob. *Fabrikmahlzeit: Ernährungswissenschaft, Industriearbeit und Volksernährung in der Schweiz 1890–1950*. Zurich: Chronos, 1999.

Taussig, Michael. *Shamanism, Colonialism, and the Wild Man: A Study in Terror and Healing*. Chicago: University of Chicago Press, 1987.

Tebutt, Melanie. *Making Ends Meet: Pawnbroking and Working-Class Credit*. Leicester: Methuen, 1983.

Tellmann, Ute. "Die moralische Ökonomie der Schulden." *Ilinx. Berliner Beiträge zur Kulturwissenschaft* 3 (2013): 3–24.

Tellmann, Ute. "Schulden—eine Kultursoziologie ökonomischer Dinge." In *Kultursoziologie im 21. Jahrhundert*, edited by Joachim Fischer and Stephan Moebius, 159–70. Wiesbaden: Springer, 2014.

Thalmann, Jörg. "Von der Euphorie zum Kollaps: Die Geschichte der Schweizerischen Nationalbahn." In *Die Nationalbahn. Vision einer Volksbahn*, edited by Hans-Peter Bärtschi, Sylvia Bärtschi-Baumann, Peter Niederhauser and Peter Güller, 19–44. Wetzikon: Profile, 2009.

Thompson, Edward Palmer. "Custom, Law and Common Right." In *Customs in*

Common: Studies in Traditional Popular Culture, 97–184. New York: Penguin, 1991.

Thompson, Edward Palmer. "The Moral Economy of the English Crowd in the Eighteenth Century." *Past and Present* 50 (1971): 76–136.

Thompson, Edward Palmer. "The Moral Economy Reviewed." In *Customs in Common: Studies in Traditional Popular Culture*, 259–351. New York: Penguin, 1991.

Thompson, Edward Palmer. *The Poverty of Theory*. London: Merlin, 1995 [1978].

Thompson, Edward Palmer. *Whigs and Hunters: The Origin of the Black Act.* New York: Pantheon, 1975.

Tomba, Massimiliano. *Marx's Temporalities*. Leiden: Brill, 2013.

Topalov, Christian. *Naissance du chômeur 1880–1910*. Paris: Albin Michel, 1994.

Trentmann, Frank. "Materiality in the Future of History: Things, Practices, and Politics." *Journal of British Studies* 48, no. 2 (2009): 283–307.

Tribe, Keith. *Strategies of Economic Order. German Economic Discourse, 1750–1950*. Cambridge: Cambridge University Press, 1995.

Trivellato, Francesca. "Credit, Honor, and the Early Modern French Legend of the Jewish Invention of Bills of Exchange." *Journal of Modern History* 84, no. 2 (2012): 289–334.

Tsing, Anna Lowenhaupt. *Friction: An Ethnography of Global Connection*. Princeton, NJ: Princeton University Press, 2005.

Twellmann, Markus. *Dorfgeschichten. Wie die Welt zur Literatur kommt*. Göttingen: Wallstein, 2019.

Van der Linden, Marcel. *Workers of the World: Essays toward a Global Labor History*. Leiden: Brill, 2008.

Vause, Erika. "Disciplining the Market: Debt Imprisonment, Public Credit, and the Construction of Commercial Personhood in Revolutionary France." *Law and History Review* 32, no. 3 (2014): 647–82.

Vause, Erika. "'He Who Rushes to Riches Will Not Be Innocent': Commercial Values and Commercial Failure in Postrevolutionary France." *French Historical Studies* 35 (2012): 321–49.

Vause, Erika. *In the Red and in the Black: Debt, Dishonor, and the Law in France between Revolutions*. Charlottesville: University of Virginia Press, 2018.

Vedder, Ulrike. *Das Testament als literarisches Dispositiv. Kulturelle Praktiken des Erbes in der Literatur des 19. Jahrhunderts*. Munich: Fink, 2011.

Veyrassat, Béatrice. *Négociants et fabricants dans l'industrie cotonnière suisse, 1760–1840: aux origines financières de l'industrialisation*. Lausanne: Payot Lausanne, 1982.

Veyrassat, Béatrice. "Wirtschaft und Gesellschaft an der Wende zum 20. Jahrhundert." In *Wirtschaftsgeschichte der Schweiz im 20. Jahrhundert*, edited by Patrick Halbeisen, Margrit Müller, and Veyrassat Béatrice, 33–81. Basel: Stämpfli, 2012.

Vickers, Daniel. "Errors Expected: The Culture of Credit in Rural New England, 1750–1800." *Economic History Review* 63, no. 4 (2010): 1032–57.

Vickery, Amanda. "His and Hers: Gender, Consumption and Household Accounting in Eighteenth-Century England." *Past and Present* Supplement 1 (2006): 12–38.

Vismann, Cornelia. *Files: Law and Media Technology*. Translated by Geoffrey Winthrop-Young. Stanford, CA: Stanford University Press, 2008 [2000].

Vismann, Cornelia. "Kulturtechniken und Souveränität." *Zeitschrift für Medien- und Kulturforschung* 1 (2010): 171–81.

Vogt, Albert. *Aedermannsdorf. Bevölkerung, Wirtschaft, Gesellschaft und Kultur im 19. Jahrhundert.* Zurich: Chronos, 2003.

Vuilleumier, Marc. "Weitling, les communistes allemands et leurs adeptes en Suisse. Quelques Documents (1843–1847)." *Revue européenne des sciences sociales* 11, no. 29 (1973): 37–100.

Vuilleumier, Marc. "De l'usage du communisme dans la Suisse des années 1840." In *Histoire(s) de l'anticommunisme en Suisse—Geschichte(n) des Antikommunismus in der Schweiz,* edited by Michel Caillat, 47–60. Zurich: Chronos, 2009.

Wadauer, Sigrid. *Die Tour der Gesellen. Mobilität und Biographie im Handwerk vom 18. bis zum 20. Jahrhundert.* Frankfurt am Main: Campus, 2005.

Wagner, Peter. "'An Entirely New Object of Consciousness, of Volition, of Thought': The Coming into Being and (almost) Passing Away of 'Society' as a Scientific Object." In *Biographies of Scientific Objects,* edited by Lorraine Daston, 132–57. Chicago: University of Chicago Press, 2000.

Wecker, Regina. "Geschlechtsvormundschaft im Kanton Basel-Stadt. Zum Rechtsalltag von Frauen—nicht nur im 19. Jahrhundert." In *Weiblich—männlich, feminine—masculin. Geschlechterverhältnisse in der Schweiz: Rechtsprechung, Diskurs, Praktiken,* edited by Rudolf Jaun and Brigitte Studer, 87–101. Zurich: Chronos, 1995.

Wecker, Regina. *Zwischen Ökonomie und Ideologie: Arbeit im Lebenszusammenhang von Frauen im Kanton Basel-Stadt 1870–1910.* Zurich: Chronos, 1997.

Wecker, Regina. "1833 bis 1910: Die Entwicklung zur Grossstadt." In *Basel— Geschichte einer städtischen Gesellschaft,* edited by Georg Kreis and Beat von Wartburg, 196–224. Basel: Merian, 2000.

Weibel, Thomas. *Friedrich Ludwig Keller und das Obergericht des Kantons Zürich.* Zurich: Obergericht des Kantons Zürich, 2006.

Weilenmann, Claudia. "Johann Jakob Reithard (1805–1857)." In *Sagenerzähler und Sagensammler der Schweiz. Studien zur Produktion volkstümlicher Geschichte und Geschichten vom 16. bis zum frühen 20. Jahrhundert,* edited by Rudolf Schenda, 223–44. Bern: Haupt, 1988.

Weinmann, Barbara. *Eine andere Bürgergesellschaft. Klassischer Republikanismus und Kommunalismus im Kanton Zürich im späten 18. und 19. Jahrhundert.* Göttingen: Vandenhoeck & Ruprecht, 2002.

Welskopp, Thomas. *Das Banner der Brüderlichkeit: Die deutsche Sozialdemokratie vom Vormärz bis zum Sozialistengesetz.* Bonn: Dietz, 2000.

Wennerlind, Carl. *Casualties of Credit: The English Financial Revolution, 1620–1720.* Cambridge, MA: Harvard University Press, 2011.

Widmer, Thomas. *Die Schweiz in der Wachstumskrise der 1880er Jahre.* Zurich: Chronos, 1992.

Wilder, Gary. "From Optic to Topic: The Foreclosure Effect of Historiographic Turns." *American Historical Review* 117 (2012): 723–45.

Williams, Raymond. *The Country and the City.* New York: Oxford University Press, 1975.

Wirth, Franz. *Johann Jakob Treichler und die soziale Bewegung im Kanton Zürich (1845/1846).* Basel: Helbing & Lichtenhahn, 1981.

Wobbe, Theresa. "Making up People: Berufsstatistische Klassifikation, geschlechtliche Kategorisierung und wirtschaftliche Inklusion um 1900 in Deutschland." *Zeitschrift für Soziologie* 41, no. 1 (2012): 41–57.

Woloson, Wendy A. *In Hock: Pawning in America from Independence through the Great Depression.* Chicago: University of Chicago Press, 2009.

Würgler, Andreas. "Fama und Rumor. Gerücht, Aufruhr und Presse im Ancien Régime." *WerkstattGeschichte* 15 (1996): 20–32.

Xifaras, Mikhail. *La propriété: étude de philosophie du droit.* Paris: Presses Universitaires de France, 2004.

Zellweger, Maya. "Konkurs im Ostschweizer Textilhandel 1817—Verlust des 'symbolischen Kapitals der Ehre.'" In *Wirtschaftsrechtsgeschichte der Modernisierung in Mitteleuropa: Zur Wechselwirkung zwischen wirtschaftlichen und rechtlichen Entwicklungen im Rahmen der grossen Transformation 1750–1850*, edited by Lukas Gschwend and René Pahud de Mortanges, 171–87. Zurich: Dike, 2009.

Ziegler, Béatrice. "Sklaven und Moderne—eine unerträgliche, aber nicht unverträgliche Kombination." In *Die Moderne in Lateinamerika. Zentren und Peripherien des Wandels*, edited by Stephan Scheuzger and Peter Fleer, 139–60. Frankfurt am Main: Vervuert, 2009.

Zimmer, Oliver. *A Contested Nation: History, Memory and Nationalism in Switzerland, 1761–1891.* Cambridge: Cambridge University Press, 2003.

Zimmerman, Andrew. "Africa in Imperial and Transnational History: Multi-Sited Historiography and the Necessity of Theory." *Journal of African History* 54 (2013): 331–40.

Index

Aargau, 51, 52, 108, 210n19
accountability of state in liberalism, 6,
  48, 193
accounting. *See* bookkeeping
agriculture and debt, 26–27, 37, 46,
  53, 178, 193
alcohol, 92, 130, 137, 138, 168, 176,
  255n99. *See also* inns
Alhoy, Maurice, 84
Alltagsgeschichte. See everyday life
Althusser, Louis, 11, 207n70
America, United States of, 62, 72, 101,
  114–15, 127–28; Civil War, 57, 169
Andelfingen, 55
animal, 5, 26, 27, 155, 173–74, 176;
  Friedrich Nietzsche on man as, 157
anti-Semitism, 37–38, 40–41, 90, 115,
  117, 178, 215n106, 221n44. *See also*
  Jews
appellate high court of Basel, 126, 140
asset seizure (attachment, *Pfand-
  nahme*), 152, 157; wages and, 174–75;
  see also clothes; collateral; indispensable goods; things; watches
auctions, 56, 135; of seized goods, 48,
  153, 154–56, 158, 185, 187; of real
  estate, 92, 101, 135, 178
Aufkündigungsgesetz (law on termina-
  tion of mortgage notes) of Zurich
  (1853), 57
Aussersihl, 160
autobiography, 85, 237n38. *See also*
  diaries; fiction; narrative

Bachelard, Gaston, 204n31
Baden (Germany), 128
Baden (Switzerland), 212n57
bakers, 106, 124, 126
bankruptcy, 4, 49; and social classification, 17, 67, chap. 5.; and homogenization in law, 20–23; of municipalities, 28–29; *see also* bankrupt
  person; Federal Statute on Debt
  Enforcement and Bankruptcy; civic
  rights; classification
bankrupt person (*Fallit*), as agent in
  the everyday economy, 7, 99, 134; as
  social-imaginary character, 60–66,
  95–102, 196
Bank Finsler, 61, 63
Bank in Zürich, 57
Bank Leu, 57, 160
banks, 56, 57, 58, 61, 85, 103, 124–
  25, 160, 184; cantonal, 8, 173, 184;
  savings, 8, 57, 88-89, 95, 111. *See
  also* Bank Bank Finsler; Bank Leu;
  Bank in Zürich; Handwerkerbank;
  Schweizerische Kreditanstalt; Swiss
  National Bank
Basel, 16, 21, 30, 31, 32, 64–65, chap. 5,
  119, 122, 123, 124, 131, 137, 140, 142,
  145, 148, 176, 180, 181, 184–86, 188,
  194, 196, 198
Basel-Land, 22, 140–41, 209n18,
  210n19
begging, 107, 116, 168-169, 267n99. *See
  also* precarity; poor relief

Benjamin, Walter, 95, 105
Benveniste, Émile, 73
Berner Volkszeitung, 37. *See also* Dürren-
    matt, Ulrich; conservatives
Berlin, 96
Bern, 16, 22, 26, 35, 37, 38, 39, 51, 56,
    185
Bettingen, 124
Bildungsroman, 146
bills of exchange, 23-25, 96–97, 98. *See
    also* credit instruments, mortgages
Bourdieu, Pierre, 205n54
Bluntschli, Johann Caspar, 107, 111, 195
Boltanski, Luc, 123
bookkeeping, 8, 21, 27, 34, 36, 45, 62,
    85, 113, 122, 123, 133, 138, 139, 158,
    171, 173, 176, 182. *See also* budgeting;
    finances
Bourgeoisie, bourgeois values, 16, 18,
    37, 50, 60, 84, 88, 96, 101, 104, 111,
    113, 117, 139, 141, 145, 146, 148–49,
    154, 155, 184, 187, 188, 191, 195
Brazil, 103
Breslau, 164
Brüstlein, Alfred, 20, 40, 152, 155, 156,
    192, 208n3
budgeting, 85, 88, 91, 129, 135, 138–39,
    150, 178, 181, 185, 188, 206–207n68
Bürkli, Karl, 111
*Bundesgesetz über Schuldbetreibung und
    Konkurs, see* Federal Statute on Debt
    Enforcement and Bankruptcy
butchers, 124, 126, 128, 131–32, 133,
    160
Butler, Judith, 12

cadaster, 159, 213n72, 262n41. *See also*
    commercial register; register
cantonal high court of Zurich, 50, 56,
    65–66, 160, 161, 163, 168, 174
capitalism, 3–4, 5, 8, 25–27, 38, 76–77,
    102, 104, 109–10, 124, 144, 184, 194–
    95; contradictions of, 9, 16, 195–96;
    historiography on, 13–14, 194–95;
    unevenness of, 14, 78, 194–95,
    207n70. *See also* debts; liberalism;
    temporalities

children (and money), 85, 88, 89,
    120, 128, 131, 133, 139, 140, 175,
    206–207n68, 237n37. *See also* family,
    masculinity, women
churches, 43, 51–53. *See also* church
    announcement
church announcement (*Kirchenruf*),
    51–52, 80, 193. *See also* churches;
    media
conservatives (political movement),
    19–20, 22, 52; and referendum
    against Federal Statute on Debt En-
    forcement and Bankruptcy, 35–40;
    and Jeremias Gotthelf, 84
cosigning on loans (*bürgen, Bürg-
    schaft*), 102, 137, 139, 145, 187, 197
citizenship (federal, cantonal, and
    municipal), 44–45, 50, 62, 64,
    107, 119, 122, 124, 126, 145–46, 149,
    196, *see also* civic rights; residence
    permits
civic rights, loss of, 5, 20, 25, 60–66,
    193, 196; conception of as "civic
    death", 60–61, 67, 96, 99, 102, 104,
    120, 149
civil courts administration of Basel,
    119, 121, 122, 127, 129, 131, 132, 133–
    34, 141, 149
classes of creditors' claims in bank-
    ruptcy (*Konkursklassen*), 141–42, 171
classification, 18, 62, 64, 67, 69, 70, 72,
    79, 81, 108, 118, 119, chap. 5, 121, 122,
    123, 126, 145, 148, 149, 168, 198
class struggle, 78, 80, 196, 271n154
clothes, 85, 103, 129, 153, 154, 155, 175,
    179, 181, 185–86, 269n138; second
    hand, 153–54. *See also* collateral;
    indispensable goods; pawn shops;
    things
Code of Obligations (*Obligationen-
    recht*), 20, 22, 29, 32
collateral, 48, 152, 172, 173, 186–87,
    262n33; body as, 153, 155, 170; as
    legal category, 156, 262n40; as an
    object of knowledge, 155–60, 190–
    91; wages as, 174. *See also* things,
    commodification

Collectif révoltes logiques, 105
colonialism, 76
commercialization, 195
commercial register, 19, 22, 159, 165;
as a cultural technique, 29–35,
192
commodification, 14, 76, 154, 262n33.
See also capitalism, collateral, things
commons, 44–47, 101, 112. *See also*
property
communism, 105, 111–12. *See also*
Weitling, Wilhelm
Confidentia (Credit reporting
agency), 41, 217n128
cotton, 57, 87, 98, 154, 236n21
credit, 3, 8, 11, 20, 37, 55, 56, 71, 90,
91, 98, 126, 129, 131, 137, 149, 153,
159, 165, 172, 187, 188, 189, 195; and
merchants, 23, 24, 28, 33–34; and
consumption, 56, 58, 76, 89, 103,
106, 179, 181; socialist visions of, 11,
106, 111, 113-114; loss of, 134–37; in
personal (face-to-face) relations,
8, 94
credit instruments, 56–57, 71, 184, see
also *Aufkündigungsgesetz*, bills of
exchange, mortgages
credit reporting agencies, 41
crisis, 3, 4, 28, 43, 46, 54, 55, 60, 63,
65, 88, 95, 102, 103, 114, 125, 127,
131, 137, 160, 177–78, 220n20; as an
object of knowledge, 60, 65, 193–94
cultural techniques, 30–32, 196. *See
also* commercial register; register
cultural turn, 9
customs and customary practices, 19,
44–47, 102, 155, 196, 199; *see also*
law, liberalism, particular history of
sysmteic regulation

Daston, Lorraine, 123
Davis, Natalie Zemon, 232n28
debt collector, bailiff (*Schuldenschreiber, Gemeindeammann*, respectively), 1–2, 5, 37, 48, 54-55, 84,
174, 179–80, 181, 198; assaults on,
58; position and income of, 58–59,

226n103; protraction of collection
procedures by, 54–55
debts: historicity of, 2, 195; as relations of forces, 2–3, 43, 58, 72–73,
90, 92-93, 95, 109–10, 140–41, 192;
semantics of, 3, 73–75, 104, 127–34;
materiality of, 9, 179, 184; as positivity, 75–76, 109; debates on during
political turning points, 193. *See also*
temporalities, credit.
Democratic Movement (*Demokratische
Bewegung*, canton of Zurich), 57, 59,
60, 65, 67–68
district administration of Zurich, 46,
55,
district courts of Zurich, 48, 160–62,
167, 175, 267n99
district jails of Zurich, 168–69. *See also*
imprisonment for debt
diaries, 85; of Jakob Stutz, 86–95
divorce, 131, 133, 135, 138. *See also* family; marriage
domestic servants, 65, 87, 88, 153
Donzelot, Jacques, 68
dowries, 100, 103, 140–44
Dürrenmatt, Ulrich, 36–37

Eastern Europe, 160, 168
economy as an autonomous sphere of
action, 19, 29, 40–42, 44, 65, 67, 71,
76, 192
economy of makeshifts, 7, 10, 80, 106,
114, 116–17, 181–83, 191, 203n20. *See
also* precarity; Hufton, Olwen
education, 88–89
emotions, 1–2, 10–11, 39–40, 54, 51,
60, 64–65, 66, 119, 130, 137, 164,
170–71
England, 10, 78, 164
epistemic anxieties, 123–24, 129, 134,
148–51, 160, 171–72, 188-183. *See also*
historical epistemology; Daston,
Lorraine; Galison, Peter; Stoler,
Ann Laura
epistemology (historical), 12-13, 60,
68-69, 77–79, 81, 122–23, 153, 157,
190–91, 204n31

epistemology of collateral, 155–60. *See also* epistemic anxieties, historical epistemology

Ernste und heitere Bilder aus dem Leben unseres Volkes (journal), 89

Escher, Alfred, 29, 68

estate (*Stand*, as in social hierarchy), 171; of merchants, 21, 24–25; of bankrupts, 119, 124–27

everyday life, 7, 21, 83, 194–95

Ewald, François, 68–69

factories, 63, 64, 65, 77, 88, 116, 125, 131, 146, 154, 174, 176, 180, 186; *see also* workers

Falliment (bankruptcy proceedings), *see* bankruptcy

Fallit. See bankrupt person

family, 86–87, 90, 126, 133, 137–40, 146, 161. *See also* children, gender, household, masculinity, women

Fassin, Didier, 79

Federal Assembly, 176

Federal Council, 33, 35, 176, 180

Federal Diet (*Tagsatzung*), 168

Federal High Court, 26, 180

Federal Statute on Debt Enforcement and Bankruptcy (*Bundesgesetz über Schuldbetreibung und Konkurs*), 4, 16, 17, 18, 19, 23, 26, 29, 32, 33, 36, 38, 40, 41, 47, 59, 70, 142, 152, 165, 174, 175–77, 191, 192, 193, chap. 1, 79, 198; referendum on, 19, 35, 155

feudal dues, 43; abolition of, 6, 46, 218n3

fiction, 7, 16, 76, 96, 98–99, 101, 104, 116–18; legal, 158, 262n40

finance, 8, 21, 29, 37, 41, 57, 97-98, 102, 103, 104, 109, 124, 138, 143, 184, 194, 204n32

finances of a person or business, 28, 44, 45, 62, 70, 96–97, 101, 138, 143, 154. *See also* bookkeeping; budgeting

Finn, Margot C., 9

Fontaine, Laurence, 231n10

Foucault, Michel, 11

Fourier, Charles, 111

France, 6, 20, 21, 43, 106, 111, 164–65, 168, 176, 180

Francophone Switzerland, 21, 22, 27, 107

Franklin, Benjamin, 197

fraud, 52, 68, 93, 103-4, 128, 131, 143, 166, 169

freedom, 7, 12, 50, 63, 80-81, 107, 113, 166–67, 172, 190

Fröbel, Julius, 107, 244–245n175

Fribourg, 26

Galison, Peter, 123

gambling, 56

Geertz, Clifford, 15, 43, 46–47, 206n62

Gemeinnützige Gesellschaft (Society for Common Welfare), 184, 187

gender, 5, 7, 44–45, 50, 62, 75, 85, 130, 138, 140–44, 150, 182, 196. *See also* family; gender hierarchy; household; masculinity; property; women

gender hierarchy, 140, 150, 196. See also family; household; masculinity; property; women

Geneva, 21, 29, 31, 165–66, 210n19

Gesellschaft für das Gute und Gemeinnützige (Society for the Good and Common Welfare), 184

Gewerkschaftsbund, 212n59, 270n145, 270n151

Germany, 20, 40, 96, 108, 114, 168, 178, 175, 176

gifts, 9, 52, 72–77, 81, 88, 91, 107, 112, 120, 140, 153, 175

Ginzburg, Carlo, 84, 94

Goswami, Manu, 215n94

Gotthelf, Jeremias (Albert Bitzius), 84, 107

Graeber, David, 8

Greenblatt, Stephen, 97

Grimm brothers, 73, 75

Grütliverein, 212n59, 216n120, 244n169, 270n145

guilds, 22, 108, 124-25, 140-141, 143

guilt (and debt), 2, 39, 40, 43, 106

Habsburg Empire, 40

Hacking, Ian, 81
Handels- und Industrieverein, 34–35, 176
Handwerkerbank (Craftmen's Bank, Basel), 184, 186, 188. *See also* banks
Hausen, Karin, 139
Heidelberg, 165
Heusler, Andreas, 21, 142
Hilty, Carl, 178
Hirzel, Conrad Melchior, 170–72
homosexuality, 1–2, 87, 91, 93, 94
honor, 20, 25, 35–40, 54, 64, 68, 74, 102, 119, 138, 139, 145, 152, 166, 193, 216n116; *see also* civic rights; masculinity
household, 33, 44, 48, 86, 87, 89, 91, 102, 103, 125, 128, 137–40, 142, 144, 178, 180–81, 188; as a normative concept, 124, 129–30, 139, 150. *See also* bookkeeping; budgeting; family
Hufton, Olwen, 203n20. *See also* economy of makeshifts

identity, and dis-identification, 83
idleness (laziness, carelessness, negligence), 51–52, 61, 68, 101, 110, 122, 129, 130, 136–37, 140, 148, 162
imprisonment for debt, 81, 153, 155–56, 160–72; and "undue hardship", 161–62; and warrant for arrest, 161, 163, 165, 167; as a way of negotiating settlement, 161, 169; numbers in canton Zurich, 163 (warrants issued), 168–69 (actual); numbers in Geneva, 165
industrialization, 195
indispensable goods (exempted from seizure), 155, 172–83, 269n138; in the Federal Statute on Debt Enforcement and Bankruptcy, 174; in the 1832 Zurich law, 175; and bankruptcy procedures, 175; fears of a too extended definition of, 177; *see also* asset seizure; collateral; subsistence level
infrastructure, 30
inheritance, 51, 61, 92, 99, 101, 142, 146

inns, 52, 56, 84, 103, 130, 137, 255n99
insurance, 69, 70, 73, 165, 176, 184
Iowa, 115
Italy, 92, 183

Jews, 50–51, 61–62, 97. *See also* anti-Semitism
journeyman's book, 113; *see also* journeymen, paperwork
journeymen, 65, 99, 107-108, 136, 153, 244n169; *see also* journeyman's book

Keller, Friedrich Ludwig, 61, 228n125
Keller, Gottfried, 7, 84, 95–105; see also *Seldwyla*; *Martin Salander*
Kleinhüningen, 124
knowledge, 10–13, 47–48, 99, 101, 105, 113, 138; and legal procedures, 9, 47–48, 68, 122, 127, 155–60, 170–72; and information, 12–13, 28–29, 31, 206n62; and morality, 150–51; *see also* rumors; epistemology (historical)

labor money, 113, 247n213
labor movement, 27, 29, 109, 114–15, 177, 186, 273n187
La Chaux-de-Fonds, 186
Landolt, Carl, 181–82
Lausanne, 84–85
law and legal procedure as an object of inquiry, 5, 8, 6, 15, 17, 47–48, 75, 80, 157, 171, 158, 194, 197; *see also* particular history of systemic regulation
Law of the Twelve Tables, 157, 171
Lenzburg, 212n57
Lévi-Strauss, Claude, 73–74
liberalism, 3–4, 6, 49–50, 59, 60, 64, 68, 88, 102, 104, 144, 165, 174, 183, 188, 191; and received practices, 5, 44, 48–53, 102, 175, 195–96; and notions of personhood, 7, 50, 60, 85, 96, 101, 152, 155, 188, 190; and governmentality, 12, 30, 47, 50, 60, 68–69, 159, 167, 172, 193; and property ownership, 188; and coercion, 196

London, 10, 107, 108
lottery, 52, 182
Lucerne, 36, 51, 70, 156, 210n19
Luddites, 63

machines, 115, 125, 145, 174, 179, 180, 186
Mandeville, Bernard, 86
Mannheim, Karl, 111–12
marriage, 52, 62, 102, 116, 128, 138,
    142, 144. *See also* divorce; dowries;
    family
Martin Salander (novel), 97, 102–5. *See
    also* Keller, Gottfried; Seldwyla
Marx, Karl, 10–11, 72, 76–77, 115, 120,
    151, 154; and notion of capital, 77
masculinity, 25, 62, 67, 96, 102, 150,
    196, 198; and role of family bread-
    winner, 139, 182
Mauss, Marcel, and *The Gift*, 72–77,
    80–81, 156, 190; and Marx, 76–77;
    see also gifts; debts
media, 19, 29–35, 51–53, 65, 198; *see
    also* cultural techniques; paperwork;
    register
merchant (*Kaufmann*), as a legal cat-
    egory, 6, 22, 25, 29–30, chap. 1; and
    bankruptcy, 6, 18; as distinguished
    from "nonmerchants" as guiding
    principle of debt enforcement and
    bankruptcy, 6, 18, 29–30, 192; *see also*
    estate
Meyer, Ahlrich, 78
microhistory, 84
Mitchell, Timothy, 208n2
Mittermaier, Carl Joseph, 165
mobility of people, 31, 87, 88, 92, 107,
    115, 128, 146, 147, 181, 272n178
*Monatschronik der zürcherischen Rechtsp-
    flege* (law journal), 50
money, 6, 20, 24, 36, 43, 56, 71, 85, 88,
    91, 93, 95, 100, 105, 106, 120, 128,
    141, 143, 146, 153, 158, 167, 170, 172,
    178, 179, 181, 183, 186, 187, 195; Marx
    on debts and, 10–11, 151, Wilhelm
    Weitling on, 109–10, 117, 197; Georg
    Simmel on things and, 189. *See also*
    bookkeeping; budgeting; children

(and money); finance; finances;
    gifts; labor money
moral economy (concept), 77–79
moral judgment, 10, 39–40, 47, 66–70,
    76, 81, 87, 91, 99-100, 104, 116–17,
    127–34, 150, 184, 193, 198
mortgages, 27, 49, 51, 56–57, 92,
    100, 102, 103, 127, 159–60, 224n83,
    229n148. *See also* credit instruments;
    property; real estate
Munzinger, Walther, 22, 23, 33

narrative, 17, 85, 95–96, 127–34. *See
    also* autobiography; diaries; fiction;
    Stutz, Jakob; Keller, Gottfried; sub-
    jectification
Nationalbahn, 29
nation-state, 5, 18, 23, 25, 66, 88, 108,
    145, 155, 177, 193
New York City, 115
Nordostbahn, 28–29
neoliberalism, 3–4
Neuchâtel, 210n19, 265n75
Neue Zürcher Zeitung (newspaper), 29,
    177, 178
Nietzsche, Friedrich, 157
Noth- und Hülfsblatt (Bote von Uster)
    (newspaper), 52–53, 64

Obwalden, 26, 27

paperwork, 13, 19, 48, 98, 103–4, 158,
    194; *see also* cultural techniques,
    media, register
Paris, 84, 135, 147, 183; Wilhelm
    Weitling in, 105–7
particular history of systemic regula-
    tion, 15, 77, 194–95, see also law,
    capitalism
pauperism, paupers, 4, 46, 64, 87, 88,
    116, 127; Wilhelm Weitling's theory
    of, 105–15; *see also* precarity, poor
    relief
pawning, 2, 7, 105, 154, 155, 181, 183–
    89, 191
pawn shops, 10, 173, 183-189; items
    pawned in, 184

peddlers, 182
people (*das Volk*) 39, 84, 88–89, 114
petitions, 16, 29, 39, 44–47, 54, 58–59, 60–63, 65, 66–67, 70, 114, 119, 122, 161, 193, 208n7; for rehabilitation, 140–50; by local bailiffs, 173
poor relief (communal), 44-45, 50, 54–55, 64, 87, 143, 176
philanthropy, 57, 88, 111, 112, 113
Philosophy of Money, 189; see also Simmel, Georg
physiologie (literary genre), 84
pietism, 85
police, 16, 58, 119, 127, 128, 132, 134, 137, 168, 196, 198, 248n7
Poulantzas, Nicos, 25-26
precarity (economic), 2, 3, 88, 105–12, 116, 130, 137–38, 161–62, 181–82, 197
property, as legal concept, 5–8, 22, 27, 32, 40, 44, 49, 61, 64, 81, 96, 116, 140–44, 152, 154-155, 156, 186, 160, 172, 190; seizure of, 5, 6–7; subaltern notions of, 7, 181, 185–88; Karl Marx on, 10–13; family and, 44–47; Wilhelm Weitling on, 106–10
Proudhon, Pierre-Joseph, 110, 244n160, 246n197
protoindustry, 16, 58, 64, 84, 87–88, 126, 173, 186. *See also* cotton; silk

qualification, 123

real estate, 28, 48, 49, 51, 54, 56–57, 61, 92, 104, 114, 127, 135, 141, 153, 159, 160, 189, 224n81. *See also* mortgages; property
realism (literary genre), 96–97
Rechtstrieb (literally: "law drive", legal term for debt collection), 1–2, 4, 54, 86; etymology of, 5
register, 31, 48, 51, 62, 104, 125–26, 192, 213n72. *See also* commercial register; cultural technique; media
reputation, 28, 40, 62, 85, 90–91, 103, 126, 130–31, 135, 136, 137, 138, 149-150, 152, 166, 171, 252n64. *See also* credit, loss of

residence permits, 113, 145; *see also* citizenship; civic rights; poor relief
responsibility, 39, 54, 65, 66–70, 113, 129, 131, 135, 146, 148, 193
revenge, 67, 101–2, 171
revolution, 22, 43, 63, 68, 78, 106–07, 114, 180
Riehen, 124
Riles, Annelise, 157
Roitman, Janet, 77
Romandie. *See* Francophone Switzerland
rumors, 90, 91, 138, 238n46
Russia, 168

Sabean, David, 144, 255n102
Sachenrecht (property law, law of things), 156
Sankt Gallen, 21, 25, 31, 58
satire, 84, 105, 179, 243n155
Schaffner, Marin, 65, 225n65
Schinz, Hans Heinrich, 1-2
Schinz, Salomon, 116
Schulthess von Rechberg, Gustav Anton, 85–86
Schulze-Delitzsch Associations, 187
Schweizerische Kreditanstalt, 57
Schweizerisches Volksblatt vom Bachtel (newspaper), 159–60; *see also* Democratic Movement
Seldwyla (novella collection), 95–102. *See also* Keller, Gottfried, *Martin Salander*
Senn, Heinrich, 87
Senn, Jakob, 87
Sewell, William Jr., 26
Shakespeare, William, 101
sickness, 29, 121, 127, 131, 133, 139, 143, 145, 161, 188
silk, 21, 87, 88, 98, 124, 125, 126, 133, 146, 173, 186, 236n21
Simmel, Georg, 189–91, 194
Simmons, Dana, 180
slavery, 57, 61, 80, 103, 177
social reformers, 182, 191. *See also* philanthropy, welfare state
speculation, 98, 102, 109, 113, 160

Speiser, Paul, 30, 176
Spyri, Johann Ludwig, 88, 183, 186, 187, 273n193
Stallybrass, Peter, 10
standardization, 6, 20, 158, 195
statistics, 55, 65–66, 80, 125–26, 168–69, 177, 181, 193, 229n145
Steedman, Carolyn, 134, 207n76
Sternenberg, 87–88
Stoler, Ann Laura, 81
Strathern, Marilyn, 75, 109
Stutz, Jakob, 84, 86–95, 117, 197
subjectification, 10–12, 62, 64-66, chap. 4, 144, 146, 185–86, 197; as a moment of surprise, 12, 80–81, 83, 95, 116–17, 147–48, 197–98; and legal status, 12, 64, 101, 163; through narratives, 83, 95–96, chap. 4
subaltern classes, 7, 63, 78–29, 88, 105, 106, 110, 117, 141, 153, 154, 155, 164, 176–78, 180, 181, 182, 186, 188, 191; Antonio Gramsci's notion of, 203n20
subsistence level (legal), 174, 177; contradistinction to definition in Germany, 178
suicide, 61, 101, 128
summary judgments, 48, 121; *see also* customs and customary practices
Swiss Confederation, founding of, in 1848, 60, 63–64, 66, 145, 193
Swiss National Bank, 55
Switzerland, and economic and political liberalism, 4, 6
synchronization, 14, 16, 192

temporalities, of debt, 3, 8, 12, 18, 48, 51–52, 53–59, 106, 112, 127, 158, 179-180, 184, 187, 192–93, 205n54; of capitalism, 14, 16, 25–27, 189–90, 192
Tellmann, Ute, 77, 214n93
Teuscher, Simon, 144
things, 9, 17, 48, 71, 74, 81, 100, 128–29, 151, 179; movable/immovable, 58, 75-76, 141, 153-154, 173-74, 178, 181, 184–85, 188; people and, 152,

155, 157, 183, 198; Georg Simmel on money and, 189; *see also* asset seizure; commodification; collateral
Thompson, Edward Palmer, 15, 78-79
Thurgau, 91
Ticino, 256n109
Tobler, Johannes, 43
Topalov, Christian, 69-70, 259n169
Tönnies, Ferdinand, 71–72, 82
Treichler, Johann Jakob, 64
trust, 36, 92–94, 119, 128, 135–36, 180

Uhwiesen, 53
Uster factory arson (*Maschinensturm*), 63
usury, 40, 108, 110-111, 184
utopia, 106; Karl Mannheim's notion of, 111–12

Valais, 29
value, 9, 23–24, 34, 77, 79, 84, 98–100, 105, 109, 139, 142, 144, 153, 157–59, 163, 170, 185, 189, 191, 198; exchange, 10–11, 154, 156, 159, 172, 182, 186, 188; use, 155; subjective vs. objective, 187
value judgments, 76, 77, 87, 104, 139, 140, 148, 149–50, 196
Vaterland (newspaper), 36
Vaud, 214n88, 215n99, 265n75
Verein Schweizerischer Geschäftsreisender (Association of Swiss Traveling Businessmen), 208n7
Vevey, 107
Vieweg, Eduard, 96–97
Vismann, Cornelia, 30

watches, 154, 179, 182, 185–86, 271n168, *see also* asset seizure; collateral; things; pawn shops
weaving. *See* protoindustry
Weber, Max, 197
Weitling, Wilhelm, 7, 84, 105–17
welfare state, 69, 177. *See also* poor relief, philanthropy, insurance
Winterthur, 212n57
Wiedikon, 160

women; and limited legal rights, 5, 56, 141–42, 194; in economic relations, 5, 56, 196–97, 32–33, 44–47, 88, 126, 139, 141, 161–62, 182; and gender tutelage, 7, 44–47, 62, 67, 124–25; and property, 32, 44, 100, 140–44, 194. *See also* dowries, gender, gender hierarchy, masculinity property

women's movement, 177

workers, 63, 64, 65, 77, 78, 85, 88, 87, 108, 110, 111, 116, 126, 131, 146, 153, 174, 176, 179-180, 182, 186. *See also* subaltern classes, labor movement

Wyß, Friedrich von, 49

Zofingen, 212n57

Zurich, 16, 34, chap. 2, 43, 48, 50, 55–57, 68, 84, 85, 86, 88, 97, 107, 108, 116, 158, 160, 163, 166, 167, 169, 172, 175, 180, 185, 190, 193, 197

Zurich Private Law Codex of 1854/56, 175

Zurich Code of 1715 (*Stadt- und Landrecht*), 166, 268n129

Printed and bound by CPI Group (UK) Ltd, Croydon, CR0 4YY

23/04/2025
14660940-0003